Basic Skills in English

Purple Level

Yellow Level

Blue Level

Orange Level

Green Level

Red Level

Basic Skills in English

Purple Level

Joy Littell, EDITORIAL DIRECTOR

McDougal, Littell & Company

Evanston, Illinois

New York   Dallas   Sacramento

AUTHORS

Joy Littell, Editorial Director, McDougal, Littell & Company

The Editorial Staff of McDougal, Littell & Company

Kraft and Kraft, Developers of Educational Materials, Stow, Massachusetts

CONSULTANTS

Carole B. Bencich, Coordinator of Secondary Language Arts, Brevard County School Board, Rockledge, Florida

Dr. Sheila F. S. Ford, Coordinator for Secondary Language Arts, Spring Branch Independent School District, Houston, Texas

Marietta H. Hickman, English Department Chairman, Wake Forest-Rolesville High School, Wake Forest, North Carolina

Mary Evans Roberts, Supervisor of English and Language Arts, Savannah-Chatham Public Schools, Savannah, Georgia

ISBN: 0-86609-509-8   TE ISBN: 0-86609-510-1

Acknowledgments

Simon & Schuster: for entries on pages 29, 31, 32, 34, 35, 42, and 456 from *Webster's New World Dictionary*, Students Edition; copyright © 1981 by Simon & Schuster, Inc. Open Court Publishing Co.: For "Kate Shelley and the Midnight Limited" by Jon Waters, from *Cricket*, 5, No. 12 (1978), pp. 27–28; copyright © 1978 by Open Court Publishing Co.

Composition

Handbook

Developing an Effective Vocabulary

Close Encounters

Learning Word Meaning from Context

Here's the Idea English is used by 400 million people all over the world. It is a continually changing language with a vocabulary that includes about 600,000 words. In view of its variety, English can be called a living and lively language.

The process of developing an effective personal vocabulary is lifelong. One important way to build vocabulary is to examine words in context. **Context** means the words and sentences around a given word. Several kinds of context clues help you to figure out the meanings of unfamiliar words.

When a **definition** is given in context, the meaning of an unfamiliar word is stated directly. Read this example.

> Many Americans are becoming interested in *ecology. Ecology* is the science that investigates the relations between living things and their environment.

When **restatement** is used, the meaning of a word is rephrased. Look for such key words as *or, which is,* or *in other words.*

> One review included many *caustic,* or sarcastic, comments expressing the critic's opinion of the new movie.

Sometimes you may be able to understand the meaning of a word through **examples** given. Look for the key words *especially, like, other, this, these, for example, for instance,* and *such as.*

> The punishments for murder, arson, and other *felonies* are more severe than those for minor crimes.

When **comparison** is used, a new word is compared with a similar word that is known to you. Look for the key words *as, like, in the same way,* and *similar to.*

> Korean *cuisine* is similar to the Chinese style of cooking.

When **contrast** is used, a word is compared with an opposite word that is known to you. Look for the key words *although, but, unlike, while, on the contrary,* and *on the other hand.*

> Pamela Klein is *taciturn,* unlike her twin sister Paula, who is talkative.

Check It Out   Read the following sentences.

1. My ten-year-old brother enjoys *puns.* A pun is a humorous play on words that have the same sound but different meanings.

2. *Insomnia,* which is a difficulty in falling asleep, is a fairly common condition.

3. A *percussion instrument,* such as a drum, is as important to an orchestra as a string, brass, or woodwind instrument.

4. The *luge* is similar to a sled, and it is raced in the winter Olympics.

- What is the meaning of each italicized word? What context clue is used in each sentence?

Try Your Skill   Choose four of these words: *drill, hammer, pliers, saw, screwdriver, wrench.* Write a sentence that explains each word. Use key words as context clues.

Keep This in Mind

- Develop your vocabulary by examining words in context. Useful context clues are definition, re-statement, examples, comparison, and contrast.

Now Write   Choose four of the following words: *biography, drama, essay, novel, poem, short story.* Write a sentence for each, using a context clue to explain the word. Use key words to signal each context clue. Use a dictionary if necessary. Label your paper **Close Encounters.** Keep your paper in your folder.

A Hint of an Idea

Inferring Word Meaning from Context

Here's the Idea You may not always be able to figure out the meaning of an unfamiliar word by relying on direct context clues. Sometimes you may have to examine the surrounding sentences, put clues together, and make a good guess at the meaning of the word. This process of reading between the lines in order to draw a conclusion about the meaning of a word is called **inference.**

The main idea of a short passage or of an entire paragraph may be related to the meaning of an unfamiliar word. In the following paragraph, for instance, try to infer the meaning of the word *lethargic.*

> I did not sleep well last night, and I awoke feeling drowsy. It seemed to take all of my energy just to get up and get dressed. I found myself dozing during the long bus ride to work. Even the thought of my first paycheck failed to excite me. I couldn't shake off my *lethargic* mood.

From this paragraph, you can infer that *lethargic* means "affected by a condition of abnormal drowsiness or inactivity."

Check It Out Read the following paragraph.

> On Tuesday a *referendum* on the proposed school tax law will be held. Many residents have expressed strong feelings on this issue, and local officials are urging them to vote. This is an important civic event. Taxpayers have an opportunity to express their opinions in a way that can be effective.

> • What can you infer about the meaning of *referendum?*

Try Your Skill As you read these passages, try to infer the meanings of the italicized words. Write definitions for them.

1. The reporter was struck by the *irony* of the news story. There had been a minor fire at the fire station. In fact, the fire had been caused by a firefighter who had been smoking in bed. Fortunately, the firefighter suffered no serious injury.

2. Mike is considering a career in *drafting*. He is a talented artist who has had a great deal of instruction in drawing. Moreover, he has always been interested in mechanical structures, especially in their design. The chance to combine his ability to draw and his interest in designing machinery appeals to him.

3. Rita's *credentials* for the job in the firm of architects were excellent. She had earned a degree from a leading university and a first-place award in a major national competition. In addition, she presented letters of recommendation from two well-known and respected architects.

4. Unfortunately, there was a feeling of *apathy* about this year's class elections. There were no heated arguments about issues, little enthusiasm for any of the candidates, and no talk of victory parties. In fact, only a small number of students even bothered to vote.

Keep This in Mind

- Inference is the process of using clues to draw a conclusion. Inferences about unfamiliar words can be drawn from the main ideas of paragraphs.

Now Write Suppose that you are telling a story about a *joyous* event. Write four or five sentences that suggest this quality without specifically defining it. Label your paper **A Hint of an Idea** and put it into your folder.

Kernels

Base Words

Here's the Idea Many of the longer words in English seem complicated and impossible to understand at first. However, these words are often made of smaller parts. When you know how to recognize the parts, you can separate one part from another. From the meanings of the word parts, you can often piece together a meaning for the whole word.

Base words, prefixes, and suffixes are word parts that it is essential for you to know. A **base word** is a short English word that lies at the heart of a longer word. A **prefix** is a word part added at the beginning of a base word, and a **suffix** is a word part added at the end. Notice that the spelling of the base word may change when an ending is added.

Following is a list of words that have come from the base word *direct*. Study the words and their meanings.

indirect	"wandering; not direct"
misdirect	"direct in the wrong or improper way"
redirect	"change the course of"
direct**ness**	"the quality of speaking frankly, directly"
direct**ion**	"the act of directing; an order or command; the way one is facing or going"
direct**ionless**	"moving or acting in a wandering way, without a plan or course"

How is the meaning of *direct* included in the meaning of each longer word?

Check It Out Examine these words and their definitions.

> distaste—"revulsion; strong opposition to"
> tasteful—"reflecting good taste or decorum"

tasty—"having a full and flavorful taste"
tasteless—"characterized by bad taste or lack of decorum"
tastelessness—"the quality of being tasteless"

- What is the base word in each longer word?
- What parts have been added in each word?
- How does the meaning of the longer word include the meaning of the base word?

Try Your Skill   The words in each of the following groups have the same base word. For each group, write the base word.

1. easy   uneasy   uneasiness
2. react   action   transaction
3. statement   restate   misstatement
4. disconnect   reconnect   connection
5. readmit   admissible   inadmissible
6. literacy   illiterate   literature
7. manager   management   mismanagement
8. glorious   inglorious   ingloriousness
9. qualified   unqualified   disqualified
10. corruption   corruptible   incorruptible

Keep This in Mind

- A base word is a shorter word from which longer words can be made by adding new parts.
- The new parts may be added at the beginning of the base word, at the end, or in both places.

Now Write   Review the groups of words in **Try Your Skill**. Choose any two groups of words to use in sentences. Write a sentence for each of the words. Label your paper **Kernels** and keep it in your folder.

Up Front

Recognizing Prefixes

Here's the Idea Many English words are made up of parts that work together. If you can recognize some common word parts, you will be able to understand many unfamilar words.

A **prefix** is a word part with its own meaning added at the beginning of a base word. The prefix *un-*, for example, means "not" or "opposite of." If you recognize this prefix and its meaning, you know that *unsteady* means "not firm or stable; changeable." You also know that *unpack* means "to open and remove the packed contents of." You can see how the addition of prefixes affects the meanings of the base words *steady* and *pack*.

Study this list of common prefixes.

Prefix	Meaning	Example
in- (also **il-**, **im-**, and **ir-**)	"not"	inactive, illogical, imbalance, irreligious
non-	"not"	nonfattening
pre-	"before"	prearrange
mis-	"wrong, bad"	mismanage
trans-	"across, through," or "changed"	transatlantic, transform
re-	"again" or "back"	reapply, replace
dis-	"opposite of" or "away"	disrespect, dislodge

Not all words contain prefixes, however. To determine whether or not a word contains a prefix, check in a dictionary.

Check It Out Examine these words and their definitions.

> inapplicable—"not applicable; not suitable"
> illiterate—"not knowing how to read or write"

immeasurable—"too large or too much to be measured; vast"
irrefutable—"that which cannot be reputed or disproved"
nontoxic—"not poisonous"
prenuptial—"before a wedding"
miscalculate—"to determine or compute incorrectly"
transfix—"to pierce through, as with an arrow; to make unable to move, as if pierced through"
remodel—"to make over; rebuild"
retake—"to take again; to take back or recapture"
disavow—"to deny knowledge of, approval of, or responsibility for; repudiate"
discourage—"to cause to lose courage or confidence"

• What is the prefix in each? What is the base word?

Try Your Skill Twelve of the following words have prefixes. For each word that has a prefix, write the prefix and its meaning, plus the base word. For example, for the word *incapable* you would write: in (not) + capable.

1. refurnish	6. restful	11. displace
2. nonresident	7. inadmissible	12. transact
3. disobey	8. immature	13. irreversible
4. mission	9. repay	14. misrepresent
5. illegal	10. predetermine	15. inning

Keep This in Mind

• A prefix is a word part with its own meaning added at the beginning of a base word. Learn to recognize common prefixes and their meanings.

Now Write Using a dictionary, find seven unfamiliar words, each of which contains one of the seven prefixes shown in this lesson. List the words, define them, and study them. Then write seven sentences, each using one of the new words you have learned. Label your paper **Up Front** and keep it in your folder.

Afterwards

Recognizing Suffixes

Here's the Idea   A **suffix** is a word part added at the end of a
base word. Like a prefix, a suffix has a meaning of its own that
affects the meaning of the base word. Also like a prefix, a suffix
may have more than one meaning or form. For example, the
suffix *-able* or *-ible* means "can be; having this quality." Thus,
manageable means "that can be managed or controlled" and
reasonable means "having the quality of reason or sense."

However, suffixes are unlike prefixes in one important respect. Sometimes the addition of a suffix changes the spelling of
a base word. A final consonant may be doubled. For example,
run becomes *runner*. The final letter may be dropped. For
example, *sense* become *sensible*. The final letter of the base
word may be changed. For example, *pity* becomes *pitiful*.
Therefore, when you add a suffix to a word, check the spelling of
the word in a dictionary.

Study this list of common suffixes.

Suffix	Meaning	Example
-ful	"full of, having"	shameful
-ous	"full of, having"	mysterious
-y	"tending to be" or "characterized by"	sleepy
-ness	"the state or quality of being"	weakness
-ion	"the act, result, or condition of"	celebration
-ment	"the act, result, or state of"	movement
-less	"without"	weightless

Check It Out   Examine these words and their definitions.

soulful —"full of or showing deep feeling"
malicious —"having malice, the desire to harm another"
catty— "of or like a cat; mean; malicious"
willingness —"the state of being ready to do gladly"
rejection —"the act of refusing to take, use, or believe something"
achievement —"the result of doing something successfully"
tasteless —"without taste or flavor (as for something eaten); also, lacking the ability to judge what is beautiful and appropriate"

· What is the suffix in each? What is the base word?

Try Your Skill   Find the suffix in each of the following words. Write the base word and the meaning of the suffix for each word. For example, for the word *translation* you would write: translate + the act of.

1. nervous	6. spiteful	11. funny
2. wavy	7. tenderness	12. gracious
3. friendless	8. development	13. reflection
4. improvement	9. misty	14. tactless
5. handful	10. correction	15. eagerness

Keep This in Mind

· A suffix is a word part added at the end of a base word. Each suffix has its own meaning. Check the spelling of a word when you add a suffix.

Now Write   Using a dictionary, find seven unfamiliar words, each of which contains a different one of the seven suffixes shown in this lesson. List the words, define them, and study them. Then write seven sentences, each using one of the new words you have learned. Label your paper **Afterwards** and keep it in your folder.

The Centerpiece

Using Roots from Latin

Here's the Idea   As a means of developing an effective vocabulary, you have been studying word parts. You have learned that a prefix, such as *trans-*, can be added to a base word, such as *form*. The new word, *transform*, means "to change the form, appearance, or condition of." You have learned that a suffix, such as *-y*, meaning "tending to," can be added to a base word, such as *art*. The new word, *arty*, means "pretending or trying to be artistic." You have also learned that base words are separate words with their own meanings. What are the base words in *inconsiderate, heaviness,* and *misstatement?*

Some words are formed from a different kind of word part, called a **root.** A root has a particular meaning of its own. Usually, a root is not a word by itself. Instead, a root forms the main part of a word. Since so many words in English come from Latin, the most common roots also come from Latin.

Study these four Latin roots.

Latin Root	Meaning	Example
flect, flex	"bend"	*flex*, meaning "to bend (an arm, leg)"
grat	"thank" or "favor"	*gratitude*, meaning "thankfulness"
gress, grad	"step" or "go"	*grade*, meaning "a step; stage; degree; rating"
rupt	"break"	*abrupt*, meaning "broken off; sudden"

Check It Out   Examine these words and their definitions.

flexible—"able to be bent; adjustable"
deflect—"to bend or turn aside; swerve"
gratuity—"a gift of money for service; a tip"
ingratiate—"to work (oneself) into another's favor"
aggressive—"ready to start fights or engage in direct action"
transgress—"to overstep a limit; to break a law"
disrupt—"to break apart; to disturb the orderly course of"
erupt—"to burst forth, as from some restraint"

- Point out the Latin root in each example. How is the meaning of the root related to the meaning of the whole word?

Try Your Skill   Copy the following pairs of words and circle the Latin roots. Use the meanings of the roots to help you figure out the meanings of the words. Then check the history and the meaning of each word in a dictionary. Finally, use one word from each pair in a sentence of your own.

reflect	congratulate	graduate	interrupt
inflexible	ingrate	progress	rupture

Keep This in Mind

- A root is part of a word and has a meaning of its own. Learn to recognize the many common roots that come from Latin.

Now Write   Using a dictionary, find four new words containing each of the four Latin roots you have studied. List and define the new words. Then use each one in a sentence. Label your paper **The Centerpiece.** Keep your work in your folder.

Classics

Combinations from Greek

Here's the Idea The vocabulary of English is enriched by many Greek words and word parts. Learning the meanings of a few Greek roots will help you to figure out the meanings of many unfamiliar words.

Often, you will recognize only one part of the word. Then add what that part tells you to clues from context. Think about *cardiology* in the following sentence.

> New discoveries in *cardiology* have increased the chances that a person will recover from a heart attack.

If you know that *-ology* means "science," you know something about the word. Context tells you more. *Cardiology* must be the science of the heart or of diseases of the heart.

Study these common Greek roots, their meanings, and examples of words in which they appear. Notice that the forms of some roots may change slightly.

Greek Root	Meaning	Example
micro	"small"	*microfilm*
bio	"life"	*biology*
chrono	"time"	*chronology*
geo (gee)	"earth"	*geology*
tele	"far"	*telephone*
ology	"science"	*bacteriology*
graph	"writing"	*telegraph*
metron	"measure"	*thermometer*
phobia	"fear"	*claustrophobia*
scope	"see"	*microscope*

Check It Out Examine these words and their definitions.

> geophysics—"the branch of physics that investigates natural occurrences on the earth"
> metronome—"a device that keeps a musical tempo"
> hydrophobia—"fear of water"
> microcircuitry—"very small electronic circuits"
> telegraph—"a machine for sending writing across long distances"

- What Greek root or roots are in each example? How is the meaning of each Greek root related to the meaning of the whole word?

Try Your Skill Read the following sentences. Note the italicized word in each sentence. Use the meanings of the Greek roots to help you figure out the meaning of each word. Use context clues as well. Then check each word in a dictionary.

1. Louis had such strong *ailurophobia* that he couldn't even stand being in the same room with a cat.
2. Many *microorganisms*, such as bacteria, cause disease.
3. Instead of letters representing the sounds of words, Chinese uses *ideographs*, which represent ideas or objects.
4. An electrical technician may use an *oscilloscope* to see the activity of electricity in a circuit.
5. We know now that the universe is not *geocentric*; in fact, the earth is far from the center.

Keep This in Mind

- Many English words have Greek roots. By learning Greek roots, you will gain understanding of many unfamiliar words.

Now Write In a newspaper or magazine, find at least five words containing the Greek roots you have learned. List and define the words. Label your paper **Classics.** Save it.

On the Mark

Using Precise Words

Here's the Idea Choosing the right word has two benefits. First, it makes your writing more precise. For example, did the dog *bark* or *snarl?* Was the chore *strenuous* or merely *time-consuming?* Choose a word that expresses the precise meaning you intend. Second, using the right word makes your writing more vivid. For example, avoid using a general word like *said.* Select a more specific word, like *whispered,* or *bellowed.*

To choose the right word, learn to choose among synonyms and antonyms. **Synonyms** are words with nearly the same meaning, like *strong, stout, sturdy, tough,* and *stalwart.* A *synonymy*, a list of synonyms and their shades of meaning, is given at the end of some entries in a dictionary. Synonyms are also given in a reference book called a *thesaurus.* **Antonyms** are words with opposite meanings, like *strong—weak, correct—wrong,* and *rare—common.* Antonyms are given in some dictionaries as well as in a thesaurus.

Check It Out Examine these synonymies.

SYN.—**healthy** implies normal physical and mental strength and freedom from disease, weakness, disorder, etc.; **sound** suggests a condition of perfect health in which there is no sign of disease or weakness; **hale** is close to **sound** in meaning and is used esp. of elderly people who are lively and free from the weaknesses of old age; **robust** implies great bodily health and strength that can be seen in firm muscles, good color, large reserves of energy, etc.; **well** implies simply freedom from illness —*ANT.* **ill, diseased, infirm, frail**

SYN.—**sick** and **ill** both express the idea of being in bad health, having a disease, etc., but **sick** is more commonly used than **ill**, which is somewhat formal [he's a *sick* person; he is *sick*, or *ill*, with the flu]; **ailing** usually suggests poor health that lasts a long time or never improves [she has been *ailing* ever since her operation]; **indisposed** suggests a slight, brief illness or feeling of physical discomfort [*indisposed* with a headache] —*ANT.* **well, healthy**

- Which synonym for *healthy* is the right word to describe an elderly person who is in perfect health?
- Which antonym for *healthy* suggests poor health that lasts a long time?

Try Your Skill   Choose the synonym that best fits the meaning of each sentence. Use a dictionary or thesaurus if necessary.

1. Although Beth (asked, begged, demanded, requested) angrily that her money be refunded, the clerk responded politely.

2. The jackhammers below (trembled, shook, disturbed, upset) the windows of the third-floor apartment.

3. Because I was not used to the standard transmission, the car (lurched, moved, jumped, advanced) forward when I shifted gears.

4. The racers' (silly, foolish, unwise, foolhardy) attempt to sail during the rainstorm ended when the boat capsized.

Keep This in Mind

- Choose precise words. Check their meanings in a dictionary or thesaurus.
- Synonyms are words with similar meanings. Antonyms are words with opposite meanings.

Now Write   Using a dictionary or thesaurus, find four synonyms for one word. Write a separate sentence for each of the four words. Be sure that the sentences indicate the differences of meaning among the synonyms. Then write one sentence using an antonym of one of the words. Label your paper **On the Mark** and put it into your folder.

Extrasensory Details

Building a Vocabulary of the Senses

Here's the Idea In order to present your experiences in the most vivid way, you need to sharpen two skills. First, you must develop an awareness of sensory details. That is, you must train yourself to be aware of the specific sights, sounds, textures, smells, and tastes around you. Second, you must develop a vocabulary to describe sensory details. If something is pleasant to the taste, for example, is it *buttery, sweet,* or *spicy?* Become familiar with sensory words, such as those listed on pages 20 and 21 at the end of this lesson. Select sensory words that describe an experience precisely.

Through the use of sensory details, you can write vividly about familiar experiences or extraordinary ones. For example, notice the use of sensory details in the following paragraphs.

I had been wandering about the fairgrounds for hours, simply following wherever the most interesting sights and sounds had taken me. I drew in a deep breath and held it, savoring the smell of rich earth and sweet, damp hay. I found myself on the edge of a quiet crowd. I craned my neck and glimpsed a pair of horses. I was told that these workhorses were preparing to move a two-ton weight.

Suddenly, at a shrill "Haw!" from their trainer, the horses lunged forward. Straining into the creaking leather harness, they grunted and snorted. Their hooves thundered as the animals drove at the ground. Slowly the horses inched the ponderous weight forward. With a final effort, they dragged the weight across the finish line. I joined the crowd, roaring and clapping in approval.

Check It Out   Examine these examples of sensory words.

Sight: crimson, tapered, mottled, robust
Hearing: screech, bray, whir, guffaw
Touch: tepid, waxy, leathery, gritty
Taste: hearty, bland, tangy, medicinal
Smell: aromatic, briny, acrid, dank

- Which of these sensory words are new to you? What do they mean? Think of something that might be described by each of these words.

Try Your Skill   Think of a specific place that fits one of these general categories. List as many sensory words as you can think of about the place. Be specific. Try to use all of your senses.

a hospital	a park
a shopping center	a bus terminal
a zoo	a busy intersection

Keep This in Mind

- When you write, use vivid sensory details that bring an experience to life. Build a vocabulary of the senses.

Now Write   Think of a place where you would like to be. List as many sensory details about the place as you can. Choose specific words that show the responses of all of your senses. You may want to refer to the sample lists on the following pages. Label your paper **Extrasensory Details** and put it into your folder.

A List of Sight Words

colorless	round	mottled	transparent
white	flat	freckled	sheer
ivory	curved	wrinkled	opaque
yellow	wavy	striped	tall
gold	ruffled	bright	lean
orange	oval	clear	muscular
green	angular	glossy	handsome
olive	triangular	shimmering	robust
turquoise	rectangular	jeweled	fragile
azure	square	fiery	pale
pink	hollow	muddy	small
crimson	wide	drab	tiny
maroon	long	dark	large
lavender	narrow	grimy	massive
purple	tapered	worn	immense
silver	wiry	cluttered	perky
brown	lopsided	fresh	lacy
black	shapeless	flowery	shadowy

A List of Hearing Words

crash	squawk	crackle	chime
thud	whine	buzz	laugh
bump	bark	clink	gurgle
boom	bleat	hiss	giggle
thunder	bray	snort	guffaw
bang	blare	bellow	sing
roar	rumble	growl	hum
scream	grate	whimper	mutter
screech	slam	stammer	murmur
shout	clap	snap	whisper
yell	stomp	rustle	sigh
whistle	jangle	whir	hush

A List of Taste Words

oily	rich	bland	ripe
buttery	hearty	tasteless	medicinal
salty	mellow	sour	fishy
bitter	sugary	vinegary	spicy
bittersweet	crisp	fruity	hot
sweet	savory	tangy	burnt

A List of Smell Words

sweet	piney	acrid	sickly
scented	pungent	burnt	stagnant
fragrant	spicy	gaseous	musty
aromatic	gamy	putrid	moldy
perfumed	fishy	spoiled	dry
fresh	briny	sour	damp
earthy	sharp	rancid	dank

A List of Touch Words

cool	wet	silky	sandy
cold	slippery	velvety	gritty
icy	spongy	smooth	rough
lukewarm	mushy	soft	sharp
tepid	oily	wooly	thick
warm	waxy	furry	dry
hot	fleshy	feathery	dull
steamy	rubbery	fuzzy	thin
sticky	bumpy	hairy	fragile
damp	crisp	leathery	tender

Some Critical Points

Developing a Vocabulary of Criticism

Here's the Idea You may not be aware of it, but you are being critical all the time. You are being critical when you choose a friend, a book, or a TV program. You are being critical when you shop for vegetables, apply for a job, or vote for a political candidate. In these and many other situations, you must be able to judge the good and the bad qualities of what is around you. Moreover, for each of your judgments, you need specific words that can help you to express your findings.

Developing a vocabulary of criticism does not mean merely learning to express an opinion. For example, you may describe a movie as "great." However, by doing so you are merely giving your *subjective*—or personal—opinion of it. That judgment is weak if you have said nothing about why the movie was "great." Such criticism supplies very little information.

The most informative and valuable criticism attempts to be *objective*—fair and impersonal. Objective criticism is concerned with explaining why an opinion is held. Its main purpose is to convey information. Therefore, it is expressed in words that convey information rather than opinion.

Your first step in developing a vocabulary of criticism must be to discard such empty words as *good, okay, great, terrible, terrific,* and *neat.* These are all vague words that tell a reader nothing about what you are evaluating except that you liked or disliked it. Instead, choose specific words that describe the qualities of something in an informative way.

Check It Out Compare the following criticisms.

1   *Presenting the Candidates* was a great TV show. Last night's program was well done. It was interesting and enjoyable. Most important, I learned a lot.

2   *Presenting the Candidates* was an informative and impartial review of the Democratic and Republican presidential candidates. In the first segment of the two-hour special, brief biographies outlined the background of each candidate. Their education and public service records were covered in detail. In the second segment, film clips revealed informal glimpses of the candidates relaxing with their families. In the final and most important segment, each candidate responded in turn to questions about major national issues. This well-organized factual presentation is the most comprehensive television program of its kind shown to date in this campaign.

- Which criticism is subjective? Which is objective?

Try Your Skill   Rewrite the following sentences, which contain empty subjective words. Write sentences that show objective judgments. Invent details if necessary.

1. The party was fun.
2. Mr. Wolfe is a very nice neighbor.
3. The soccer game was interesting.
4. Juan is a good athlete.
5. The play we saw was wonderful.
6. That was the dumbest movie I have ever seen.

Keep This in Mind

- In making judgments, avoid empty, subjective criticism. Use specific words that convey information objectively.

Now Write   Write several sentences that reflect your objective judgment about something that actually exists. It can be a book, a movie, a TV program, a restaurant, a record, a band, a car, or anything else you choose. Use precise, specific judgment words to describe the qualities of your subject. Label your paper **Some Critical Points,** and put the paper into your folder.

The Future Is Now

Future Talk

Here's the Idea   As the interests of people change, the English language changes. As technology leads to new inventions, new processes, and new ways of working and living, new words are needed to name and study the changes.

Entirely new words may be created. New meanings may be added to the meanings of old words. Words that already exist may be combined, either with other existing words or with new ones, to make new terms.

For example, the space industry has added a new vocabulary to English. Some space terminology consists of old words with new meanings. Can you tell what the following words mean in the space industry?

shuttle   booster   attitude   go

Entirely new technological terms are created in several ways. Some are acronyms, some are compounds, and others began as slang terms used by people in the new industry. How many of these terms can you define?

DOS   BASIC   CAT scan   laser

To understand the growing and progressing world, you must keep up with changes in the vocabulary of English. Many dictionaries do not include definitions of the newest terms. Therefore, you must find their meanings from other sources. One good method is to ask people who are familiar with the fields in which the terms are used. Science teachers, for example, are likely to be able to define new terms from science and technology. In addition, recent books on new technological developments are likely to include glossaries of new terms.

Check It Out   All of the following terms have been added to English fairly recently. Each one has a specialized meaning in science, technology, or medicine. In addition, some have older meanings. Study the terms carefully. Find out what all their meanings are.

turbocharger	modem	interface	window
LED	vehicle	deploy	access

- Do you see how English words can acquire new meanings to describe new ideas and inventions?

Try Your Skill   Find each of the following words in a dictionary. On your paper, write one older, more familiar meaning for each word. Then write each word's new meaning in a modern technological field.

keyboard	down	printer	transplant
scroll	nominal	hold	probe

Keep This in Mind

- The vocabulary of English changes to reflect changes in the world. Old words may acquire new meanings, and entirely new words may be added to the language.
- Since dictionaries may not include definitions of the newest terms, you will have to turn elsewhere for their meanings. Ask teachers. Look for glossaries in recent books.

Now Write   Label your paper **The Future Is Now.** Find and list at least ten new technological terms that appear in a newsmagazine or newspaper. Determine the meaning of each term, and write it beside the term. Save your work in your folder.

Developing Dictionary Skills

Readout

Using a Dictionary Entry

Here's the Idea A dictionary is a reference book containing a list of words and information about the words. It is probably the single most valuable reference you can use whenever you are reading or writing.

There are several kinds of dictionaries you may find helpful. Usually you will be able to find what you need in an abridged, or shortened, dictionary. Sometimes you may need an unabridged dictionary, which contains nearly all of the words in a language. In addition, there are some specialized dictionaries that include only words related to a single subject, such as medicine.

You will discover that most dictionaries vary in some ways. Every dictionary organizes information in its own way and uses its own symbols and abbreviations. Read the introduction to a dictionary to find an explanation of its format. Become familiar with the dictionaries you use.

All dictionaries list words in alphabetical order. Also, all dictionaries have two guide words in large, bold print at the top of each page to indicate the words listed on that page. The left guide word is the same as the first word on the page. The right guide word is the same as the last word on the page. To look for a word, flip through the dictionary until you find the page where the word comes alphabetically between the guide words.

Check It Out Examine the portion of the dictionary page at the top of page 29.

- How is each column of words listed? What symbols are used? What words are new to you? What are the guide words? Would you find the word *mosaic* on this page?

mor·tar (môr′tər) *n.* [< OE. & OFr. < L. *mortarium:* for IE. base see MORBID] **1.** a very hard bowl in which substances are ground or pounded to a powder with a pestle **2.** a short-barreled cannon which hurls shells in a high curve **3.** a mixture of cement or lime with sand and water, used between bricks, etc., or as plaster —*vt.* **1.** to plaster together with mortar **2.** to attack with mortar shells

PESTLE

MORTAR

mor·tar·board (-bôrd′) *n.* **1.** a square board with a handle beneath, on which mortar is carried **2.** an academic cap with a square, flat top, worn at commencements, etc.

mort·gage (môr′gij) *n.* [< OFr. < *mort*, dead (see MORTAL) + *gage*, GAGE[1]] *Law* **1.** an agreement in which a person borrowing money gives the lender a claim to a certain piece of property as a pledge that the debt will be paid **2.** the deed, or legal paper, by which this pledge is made —*vt.* **-gaged, -gag·ing 1.** *Law* to pledge (property) by a mortgage in order to borrow money *[they mortgaged* their house to buy a new car*]* **2.** to put a claim on; make risky *[he mortgaged* his future by piling up debts*]*

mort·ga·gee (môr′gə jē′) *n.* the lender to whom property is mortgaged

mort·ga·gor, mort·gag·er (môr′gi jər) *n.* the borrower who mortgages his property

mor·tice (môr′tis) *n., vt. alt. sp. of* MORTISE

☆**mor·ti·cian** (môr tish′ən) *n.* [< L. *mors*, death (see MORTAL) + -ICIAN] *same as* FUNERAL DIRECTOR

Mo·ses (mō′ziz) [LL. < Gr. < Heb. *mōsheh*, prob. < Egypt. *mes*, child] **1.** a masculine name **2.** *Bible* the leader who brought the Israelites out of slavery in Egypt and led them to the Promised Land, and who received the Ten Commandments

☆**mo·sey** (mō′zē) *vi.* [< *vamose*, var. of VAMOOSE] [Slang] **1.** to amble along **2.** to go away

Mos·lem (mäz′ləm, muz′-, mäs′-) *n.* [Ar. *muslim*, true believer < *aslama*, to resign oneself (to God)] a believer in the religion of Islam —*adj.* of Islam or the Moslems: also **Mos·lem′ic** (-lem′ik) —**Mos′lem·ism** *n.*

mosque (mäsk) *n.* [< MFr. < It. < Ar. *masjid* < *sajada*, to pray] a Moslem temple or place of worship

mos·qui·to (mə skēt′ō, -ə) *n., pl.* **-toes, -tos** [Sp. & Port., dim. of *mosca* < L. *musca*, a fly: for IE. base see MIDGE] a two-winged insect, the female of which has skin-piercing, bloodsucking mouthparts: some varieties transmit diseases, as malaria and yellow fever —**mos·qui′to·ey** (-ē) *adj.*

☆**mosquito net** (or **netting**) a fine mesh cloth or a curtain made of this for keeping out mosquitoes

moss (môs, mäs) *n.* [OE. *mos*, a swamp] **1.** a very small, green plant growing in velvety clusters on rocks, trees, moist ground, etc. **2.** any of various similar plants, as some lichens, algae, etc. —*vt.* to cover with a growth of moss —**moss′like′** *adj.*

moss agate agate with mosslike markings

☆**moss·back** (môs′bak′, mäs′-) *n.* [Colloq.] an old-fashioned or very conservative person

☆**moss pink** a hardy, perennial phlox forming sprawling mats with bristly, narrow leaves and white, pink, or lavender flowers

moss rose 1. *same as* PORTULACA **2.** a variety of the cabbage rose with a roughened, mossy flower stalk and calyx

---

Try Your Skill

Look up the following words in a dictionary: *camera, empire, honor,* and *spiral.* Write a definition for each. Then examine the page on which each word is found. For each page, copy the guide words, any special symbols used, and three unfamiliar words.

Keep This in Mind

• A dictionary is a reference book that lists words alphabetically and explains each word. Become familiar with the dictionaries you use.

Now Write

When you are employed, you may hear the following words: *employer, foreman, labor union, manager, pension, promotion, seniority,* and *withholding tax.* Find each word in a dictionary and list the guide words for each page. Read each definition carefully. Then choose four of the words and use them in sentences. Label your paper **Readout** and put it into your folder.

A Grand Entry

Reading a Dictionary Entry

Here's the Idea   You refer to a dictionary most often to find the meanings of words. However, a dictionary entry contains additional information to help you understand a word and use it correctly.

The **entry word** itself appears in bold print and is divided into syllables. The word *environment*, for example, is entered as **en • vi • ron • ment.** Check the entry word when you divide a word at the end of a line of writing.

The **pronunciation** of a word is shown in parentheses. Use the symbols and accent marks to help you sound out an unfamiliar word. The word *mortgage*, for example, is written as (môr′ gij). Refer to the explanation of symbols shown at the bottom of a page or at the front of the dictionary.

The **part of speech** of a word is indicated by an abbreviation in bold print. *Verb*, for example, may be abbreviated **vt.,** for *transitive verb*, or **vi.,** for *intransitive verb*. If a word can be used as more than one part of speech, the other parts of speech will be noted later in the entry. Refer to the list of abbreviations at the front of the dictionary.

If a word has **special forms** or **endings,** these will be included next in the entry. The entry for the irregular verb *write*, for instance, includes the forms **wrote, written, writing.** Plural endings of some nouns are also given. For *cactus*, for instance, the two acceptable plural endings, **-tuses** and **-ti,** are shown.

The **origin,** or **history,** is given next, usually in brackets. Abbreviations, such as *OE.* or *Sp.*, indicate the languages from which words came, such as Old English or Spanish. Refer to the list of abbreviations given at the front of a dictionary.

Definitions are given next. The most common definition is often given first. If a word has a special meaning in a field, that meaning is indicated. One definition of *major* as a noun says "*Educ.* a major field of study [her *major* is history]."

Sometimes a word may have a special meaning in casual conversation and informal writing. This is termed a *colloquial* meaning, and it is usually noted in the dictionary. For example, one definition of *ham* is "[Colloq.] an amateur radio operator." Slang—very informal, spoken language—is also indicated. For example, one definition of *cut* is "[Slang] to stop; discontinue." In many cases, the informal meanings first appeared in the United States. These Americanisms, like the meanings given for *ham* and *cut*, are often noted in the dictionary by a special symbol, such as a star.

At the end of an entry, some dictionaries list **synonyms** and **antonyms**. For example, at the end of the entry for *kind*, the synonyms *kindly, benign,* and *benevolent* are explained, and the antonyms *unkind, unfeeling,* and *cruel* are listed.

Check It Out   Examine this dictionary entry.

fault (fôlt) *n.* [< OFr. *faulte*, ult. < L. *falsus*, FALSE] **1.** a thing that mars or makes something imperfect; flaw; defect **2.** *a)* a misdeed; offense *b)* an error; mistake **3.** responsibility for something wrong; blame [it's my *fault* that he's late] **4.** *Geol.* a fracture or zone of fractures in rock strata along with a shifting of the strata **5.** *Tennis, Squash,* etc. an error in service —*vt.* **1.** to find fault with; blame **2.** *Geol.* to cause a fault in —*vi.* **1.** to commit a fault in tennis, etc. **2.** *Geol.* to develop a fault —**at fault** guilty of error; deserving blame —**find fault (with)** to seek and point out faults (of) —**to a fault** too much; excessively
SYN.—**fault** refers to a definite imperfection in character, but not one which is strongly condemned [her only *fault* is stubbornness]; **failing** implies an even less serious shortcoming, usually one that many people have [*tardiness* was one of his failings]; **weakness** applies to a minor shortcoming that results from a lack of perfect self-control [talking too much is his *weakness*]; **foible** refers to a slight weakness that is regarded more as an amusing peculiarity than an actual defect in character [eating desserts first is one of his *foibles*]; **vice**, although it implies the doing of something morally wrong, does not suggest a serious moral weakness or shortcoming when used as a synonym for any of the preceding terms [a little gambling is his only *vice*] —**ANT.** virtue

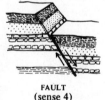

FAULT
(sense 4)

• From what language did *fault* come? As what parts of speech can *fault* be used? What special meanings are given? What is an antonym for *fault*?

Try Your Skill Read this entry and answer the questions.

reg·is·ter (rej′is tər) *n.* [< MFr. < ML. *registrum* < LL. < L. pp. of *regerere*, to record] **1.** *a)* a record or list of names, events, items, etc. *b)* a book in which this is kept [a hotel *register*] *c)* an entry in such a record **2.** registration; enrollment **3.** a device, as a meter or counter, for recording fares paid, money deposited, etc. [a cash *register*] ☆**4.** an opening into a room by which the amount of air passing, as from a furnace, can be controlled **5.** *Music a)* a part of a range of tones of the human voice or of an instrument having a specified quality *b)* an organ stop, or the tone quality it produces **6.** *Printing* exact placing of lines, pages, colors, etc. —*vt.* ☆**1.** to enter in or as in a record or list; enroll [to *register* a birth] **2.** to indicate as on a scale [a thermometer *registers* temperature] **3.** to show, as by a look on the face [to *register* surprise] **4.** to protect (mail) by paying a fee to have its delivery recorded at a post office **5.** *Printing* to cause to be in register —*vi.* **1.** to enter one's name, as in a hotel register, a list of eligible voters, etc. **2.** to enroll in a school, college, etc. **3.** to make an impression —**reg′is·tra·ble** (-trə b'l) *adj.* —**reg′is·trant** (-trənt) *n.*

1. From what language does *register* come?
2. As what parts of speech can *register* be used?
3. Name two specialized fields that use the term *register*.
4. Explain two ways in which a shop owner might use the term *register*.
5. What meanings appear to be Americanisms?
6. Find the definition of *register* that fits its use in this sentence: Kim's face *registered* surprise when she saw the name on the letter.

Keep This in Mind

- A dictionary entry includes the meanings of a word and other useful information. An entry may vary in different dictionaries.

Now Write On your paper list: *Entry word, Pronunciation, Parts of speech, Special forms, Origin, Definition* [*Colloq.*] and *Synonym and antonym.* Using a dictionary, find and copy one example of each kind of information. Use a different entry to illustrate each kind of information. Label your paper **A Grand Entry** and put it into your folder.

More Ways Than One

Finding the Meaning of a Word

Here's the Idea   As you search for words in a dictionary, you will notice that many words have more than one meaning. Therefore, whenever you look up a word, read all of its meanings. Find the meaning that fits the context in which you found the word or intend to use it.

For instance, the simple word *break* has a surprising number of meanings. *Webster's New World Dictionary, Students Edition,* lists thirty-four meanings for *break* as a verb. The same entry includes thirteen meanings for *break* as a noun and twenty meanings of *break* as it is used in phrases. In the following sentences, notice how the context helps you to determine the correct meaning.

1. The cowboy can *break* the wild horse in two weeks.
(In this context, *break* means "to tame an animal, as with force.")
2. We left home at the *break* of day.
(Here, *break* means "a beginning or appearance.")
3. The bushes that Ann landed in *broke* her fall.
(Here, *break* means "to reduce the force of by interrupting.")
4. I can't wait to *break* the good news to Dad.
(Here, *break* means "to make known; disclose.")
5. Meet me in the cafeteria during your *break*.
(Here, *break* means "an interruption of something regular.")

From these few examples, you can understand how many different meanings might be contained in a single entry.

Some words seem to be repeated in more than one entry. For example, you will find the word *key* entered twice: *key*[1], a noun, means "an instrument, usually of metal, for moving the bolt of a lock and thus locking or unlocking something"; *key*[2], also a noun, means "a reef or low island." In each entry, *key* has a different origin. Such words are called *homographs*. Each entry is not a shade of meaning of the word; it is actually a different word. When you notice a word with more than one entry, read all entries to find the meaning you seek.

Check It Out   Examine these dictionary entries.

fair[1] (fer) *adj.* [OE. *fæger*] **1.** beautiful [a *fair* maiden] **2.** unblemished; clean [a *fair* name] **3.** light in color; blond [*fair* hair] **4.** clear and sunny [*fair* weather] **5.** easy to read; clear [a *fair* hand] **6.** just and honest; impartial; specif., free from discrimination based on race, religion, sex, etc. [*fair* employment practices; *fair* housing] **7.** according to the rules [a *fair* blow] **8.** likely; promising [in a *fair* way to benefit] **9.** pleasant and courteous, often falsely smooth [the traitor's *fair* words] **10.** favorable; helpful [a *fair* wind] **11.** of moderately good size **12.** neither very bad nor very good; average [a *fair* chance of winning] —*adv.* **1.** in a fair manner [play *fair*] **2.** straight; squarely [struck *fair* in the face] —**fair and square** [Colloq.] with justice and honesty —**fair to middling** [Colloq.] moderately good; passable —**fair′ish** *adj.* —**fair′ness** *n.*
SYN.—fair implies the treating of both or all sides alike, without showing preference for any side [a *fair* hearing]; **just** implies judgment according to a fixed standard of what is right or lawful [a *just* decision]; **impartial** and **unbiased** both stress being open-minded and free from prejudice for or against any side [an *impartial* referee; an *unbiased* account]; **dispassionate** implies the absence of strong feelings and, hence, suggests cool, reasoning judgment [a *dispassionate* critic]; **objective** implies the viewing of persons or things according to the facts as they really are [an *objective* study of the problems] Basic to all these synonyms is the idea of making judgments without being influenced by one's own feelings or interests —see also SYN. at BEAUTIFUL —**ANT.** prejudiced, biased
fair[2] (fer) *n.* [< OFr. < ML. < LL. < L. *feriae, pl.*, festivals] **1.** orig., a gathering of people at regular times for barter and sale of goods **2.** a carnival where there is entertainment and things are sold, often for charity; bazaar ☆**3.** an exhibition, often competitive (**county fair, state fair**), of farm, household, and manufactured products, or of international displays (**world's fair**), with amusement areas and educational displays; exposition

- What is the origin of *fair*[1]? *fair*[2]?
- Which meanings of *fair*[1] and *fair*[2] are most familiar to you?

Try Your Skill   Read the following dictionary entries. Then determine which meaning of *lean* fits the context of each sentence and write your answer.

lean¹ (lēn) *vi.* **leaned** or **leant, lean'ing** [OE. *hlinian:* for IE. base see CLIENT] **1.** to bend from an upright position; stand at a slant; incline [the old tree *leans* toward the barn] **2.** to bend the body so as to rest part of one's weight upon something [he *leaned* on the desk] **3.** to depend for advice, aid, etc.; rely (*on* or *upon*) [he still *leans* on his parents] **4.** to have a preference; tend (*toward* or *to* a certain opinion, attitude, etc.) —*vt.* to cause to lean [to *lean* a ladder against the house; to *lean* one's head back] —*n.* a leaning; inclination; slant —**lean'er** *n.*

lean² (lēn) *adj.* [OE. *hlæne*] **1.** with little flesh or fat; thin; spare [a *lean* athlete] **2.** containing little or no fat: said of meat **3.** *a)* lacking in richness, profit, etc.; meager [a *lean* year for business] *b)* characterized by being brief, direct, etc. [a *lean* style] —*n.* meat containing little or no fat —**lean'ly** *adv.* — **lean'ness** *n.*

SYN.—**lean** implies a healthy, natural absence of fat or fleshiness; **spare** suggests a muscular frame without any unnecessary flesh; **lanky** implies an awkward tallness and leanness, and, often, loose-jointedness; **skinny** and **scrawny** imply extreme thinness that is unattractive and that indicates a lack of strength and energy; **gaunt** implies a bony thinness such as that caused by a wasting away of the flesh from hunger or suffering —see also **SYN.** at THIN —**ANT. fleshy, fat, stout**

1. The roast beef was *lean* and tender.

2. The birches *leaned* over the road under the weight of the heavy snow.

3. During Ginny's illness, she *leaned* on her family for moral support and encouragement.

4. My Uncle Ed, who sells used cars, told me that this has been a *lean* year for his business.

5. The crowd continued to cheer the winning speed skater after he crossed the finish line and stood up, stretching his strong, *lean* body.

Keep This in Mind

- When you look up an unfamiliar word in the dictionary, determine which meaning fits the context.
- Sometimes a word has more than one entry, with a different meaning and origin for each.

Now Write   Use a dictionary to find one example of a word with many meanings and one example of a homograph. For each example, copy three definitions. Then write a sentence using each of the meanings you have written. Save your paper.

The Right Language at the Right Time

Setting Standards

Standard and Nonstandard English

Here's the Idea If you were writing a note to a friend, would you use the same language you use in reports? Probably not. Instead, you would use language that is more like conversation. In different situations, people use different types of language. Two types of language that you can choose from are standard English and nonstandard English. The following chart describes these two types of language.

Using Standard and Nonstandard English

Definition and Use	Examples
Standard English is language that follows the rules of good grammar and usage. Standard English is acceptable in all situations.	1. Lucas and I want to go. 2. It isn't any good. 3. They don't want any snapshots.
Nonstandard English is language that does not follow the rules of good grammar and usage. Nonstandard English should not be used in most situations, especially in discussions, in speeches, or in most kinds of writing.	1. Me and Lucas want to go. 2. It ain't no good. 3. They don't want no snapshots.

Use standard English whenever you meet new people or when you want to make a good impression. Use standard English on the job, in class discussions, and in compositions, reports, and speeches.

Check It Out Read the following examples.

Standard English	Nonstandard English
1. We don't have any way of knowing.	1. We ain't got no way of knowing.
2. That jigsaw doesn't work.	2. That jigsaw don't work.
3. He and I are store managers.	3. Him and me are store managers
4. He said so himself.	4. He said so hisself.

- What is nonstandard about the sentences in the second column?

Try Your Skill From each of the following pairs, choose the sentence that is written in standard English.

1. This fudge has walnuts in it.
   This here fudge has walnuts in it.
2. It was a real cheerful cottage.
   It was a really cheerful cottage.
3. Let me go to the dance.
   Leave me go to the dance.
4. I got lots of time to read in the summer.
   I have lots of time to read in the summer.

Keep This in Mind

- Standard English follows the rules of good grammar and usage.

Now Write Use each of the following verbs in a sentence. Refer to pages 501–506 of your Handbook. These pages contain rules that will help you to use these verbs correctly.

1. bring	5. lie	9. rise
2. take	6. lay	10. raise
3. learn	7. may	11. sit
4. teach	8. can	12. set

Dressy or Casual

Formal and Informal English

Here's the Idea Whenever you speak or write, you should choose language that suits the occasion. One thing to consider when choosing your language is how formal the occasion is. Formal occasions require formal English. Informal occasions require informal English.

Formal English is language that is right for serious or important occasions. It is the language used in lectures, reports, public speeches, and official documents. Formal writing and speech never contain slang or contractions. The sentences used in formal writing and speech also tend to be longer and more complicated. If you were sending an entry to an essay contest, you would use formal English in your cover letter:

> **Formal English:** Dear Ms. Schneider, Please consider the enclosed essay as an entry in your contest. I am a high school senior and plan to attend Clairmont Junior College in the fall.

Informal English is the type of standard English used in everyday situations. It is the language used in conversations, letters to friends, and informal speeches. Informal writing and speech use simpler words, contractions, and a variety of sentence lengths. If you were telling a friend that you had just won an essay contest, you would use informal English:

> **Informal English:** Jill, guess what! Remember that contest I told you about? Well, the sponsor of the contest called, and I've won! Isn't that great?

Check It Out Read the pairs of words on the following page.

1. shouldn't   should not
2. purchase   buy
3. locate   find
4. thing   item

- Which word in each pair would you use in a formal situation? Which would you use in an informal situation?

Try Your Skill   Read the following paragraph from the rough draft of a report. Then, revise the paragraph. Replace all informal English with formal English.

The cuscus is a small, catlike animal that lives in New Guinea, Indonesia, and Australia. It has woolly fur, short ears, and its eyes are really neat. They're *so* big and beautiful! The female's got a plain white coat, but the male's coat has some red thrown into it. The cuscus climbs trees all its life and never comes down to the ground. Isn't that weird? Most cuscuses keep to themselves. They don't like hanging around with other animals—not even with each other! In fact, there are only two things a cuscus really likes—munching leaves and taking a snooze.

Keep This in Mind

- Formal English is used for serious or important occasions.
- Informal English is used for letters to friends and casual conversation.

Now Write   Choose a person who has influenced your life in an important way. Write two paragraphs describing the importance of this person in your life. In one paragraph, use language that you might use in describing the person to a friend. In the other paragraph, use language that you might use in a formal report or speech.

Insight and Out of Sight

Using and Misusing Slang

Here's the Idea   Our language is constantly growing. Every day, people invent new words. Some of these words become accepted as standard English. Some never do. Popular words and phrases that are not accepted as standard are known as **slang.**

Most slang terms lead a brief, colorful life. Then, they disappear and are replaced by newer slang. For example, consider the following words:

hoosegow	marvy
out of sight	moolah
gee	hepcat

At one time or another, each of these terms was very popular. Now, they sound odd and outdated. They have been replaced by the slang of today.

Slang is considered nonstandard English because it is temporary and because it is not understood by everyone. Since slang is nonstandard, it is not acceptable in most formal situations. Avoid slang in formal speeches and in most of your writing. Use slang only in casual conversation or in the dialogue of a play or short story. Whenever you write a speech, composition, or report, check your work for slang. Replace any slang that you find. If you are unsure about whether a word is slang, look it up in a dictionary.

Check It Out   Read the following dictionary entries.

☆**gig**⁴ (gig) *n.* [< ?] [Slang] **1.** a job to play or sing jazz, rock, etc. **2.** any stint of work

mooch (mo͞och) *vi., vt.* [ult. < OFr. *muchier*, to hide] [Slang] to get (food, money, etc.) by begging or sponging —**mooch′er** *n.*

- How does this dictionary indicate slang words?
- In what situations would these slang words be appropriate? In what situations would they be inappropriate?

Try Your Skill Find the slang terms in the following sentences. Then, rewrite each sentence. Replace the slang terms with standard words or phrases.

1. The electrician shut off the juice.
2. We shelled out a lot of dough for the decorations.
3. The jeweler showed Jim a rock worth three thousand dollars.
4. After that game, the announcer said the team was washed up for this season.
5. The President put the kibosh on the plans for the new satellite.

Keep This in Mind

- Popular words and phrases that are not accepted as standard English are known as slang.
- Avoid slang in formal writing or speech. Use slang only in casual conversation or in dialogue.

Now Write Rewrite the following sentences. Change the slang terms to standard English.

1. If something goes wrong, don't freak out.
2. Saturday's beach party was a real gas.
3. The D.J. at the dance played nothing but oldies.
4. In the old John Wayne movie, two outlaws bit the dust.
5. We couldn't hear the show because of the people yapping in the audience.

On the Job

Using and Misusing Jargon

Here's the Idea   When you listen to experts talk, you may sometimes have trouble understanding what they are saying. Experts often use words and phrases that are unfamiliar to people outside their fields. These specialized words and phrases are known as **jargon.** The following are some words from the jargon of electronics:

parallel circuit	resistance
positive terminal	alternating current
semiconductor	amperes
frequency	potential energy
hertz	ohms
voltage	circuit breaker

Electricians know the jargon of their field. Therefore, they can use these terms when talking to one another. However, when talking to people outside their field, they must avoid these terms or define them. Otherwise, the listener will not understand what is being said.

By using jargon, experts can communicate with one another quickly and easily. However, jargon must be used only with certain audiences. When you speak or write about a specialized activity, keep your audience in mind. If your audience is not familiar with the activity, avoid using jargon. If you do use a jargon word, define it so that your readers or listeners will not become confused.

Check It Out   Read the following words from the jargon of computer science:

output	byte	array
utility file	menu	work station
mode	library	console

- How many of these words do you recognize?
- How many of these words do you understand?
- How many of these words have other meanings that are not related to computers?

Try Your Skill   The following are jargon words from the vocabulary of the arts. Look up each word in a dictionary. Write the meaning of the word. Also tell which of the arts the word is used in.

1. andante
2. farce
3. entrechat
4. denouement
5. glissade

6. palette
7. blocking
8. allegory
9. aria
10. gesso

Keep This in Mind

- Words and phrases used to describe specialized activities are called jargon.
- When speaking or writing about a specialized activity, keep your audience in mind. If your audience is not familiar with the activity, avoid jargon. If you must use jargon, define each word you use.

Now Write   Choose an activity with which you are very familiar. Make a list of jargon words that you might use to describe this activity. Define each word. Then, use each word in a sentence.

Going Places

Regional Language

Here's the Idea   In different places, people speak and write in different ways. The types of language used in the various areas of the country are called **regional dialects.**

Regional dialects differ in three ways. First, they differ in vocabulary. For example, in some parts of the country, people speak of grocery *bags*. Elsewhere, people speak of grocery *sacks*. Similarly, the vegetables known as *green beans* in some areas of the country are known as *string beans* or *snap beans* in others.

Second, regional dialects differ in pronunciation. For instance, most speakers in the Midwest pronounce the *r* in the middle of words such as *heart*. The word is therefore pronounced "hart." However, in parts of the North and the South, such words are pronounced without the *r*, as in "haht."

Third, regional dialects sometimes differ in grammar. For example, in most of the North and the Northern Midwest, speakers usually say "Where are you going?" In parts of the South, however, many speakers add a preposition to the end of the sentence. Thus the sentence sounds like this: "Where are you going to?"

Because of the influences of television, education, and travel, American dialects are becoming more and more similar. Despite this, there is still no single "correct" dialect of English. Remember, however, that your dialect may be confusing to someone from another part of the country. To avoid causing such confusion, always use language your audience will understand.

Dialects help to make our language interesting. Many fine novels, poems, plays, and short stories are written in the various American regional dialects. For years to come, dialects will continue to add flavor and variety to our language and literature.

Check It Out Read the following words. The words in each column all have a similar meaning.

living room	parkway
parlor	expressway
sitting room	interstate
front room	freeway

- Which of these words are used in your part of the country? How many are not?

Try Your Skill The following passage is from Mark Twain's novel, *The Adventures of Huckleberry Finn*. Read this passage. Find examples of regional dialect and make a list of them.

It's lovely to live on a raft. We had the sky up there, all speckled with stars, and we used to lay on our backs and look up at them, and discuss about whether they were made or only just happened. Jim, he allowed they were made, but I allowed they happened. I judged it would have took too long to make so many. Jim said the moon could a' laid them. Well, that looked kind of reasonable. So I didn't say nothing against it, because I've seen a frog lay most as many, so of course it could be done. We used to watch the stars that fell, too, and see them streak down. Jim allowed they'd got spoiled and was hove out of the nest.

Keep This in Mind

- The types of language used in different parts of the country are called regional dialects.
- Always use language you know your audience will understand.

Now Write Write a conversation between two characters. One character should be from your part of the country. The other should be from another area. Try to recreate the dialects both characters might use.

Writing Effective Sentences

Direct Action

Using Sentences

Here's the Idea   Through your study of vocabulary, you have been learning to use words that are vivid and precise. In order to express an idea, you must learn to combine words effectively. Learn to write good sentences.

A **sentence** is a group of words that expresses a complete thought. A good sentence expresses a complete thought clearly and directly. It also makes a point in an interesting and imaginative way.

Read these examples of effective sentences.

The difficulty in life is the choice.—GEORGE MOORE

Love is love's reward.—JOHN DRYDEN

In the United States there is more space where nobody is than where anybody is.—GERTRUDE STEIN

Things don't change, but by and by our wishes change.
—GEORGE MOORE

To be what we are, and to become what we are capable of becoming, is the only end of life.—ROBERT LEWIS STEVENSON

Notice that each of these sentences expresses an idea in a direct and original way. You can see that a single sentence can be powerful. Whenever you write a sentence, use your imagination to express an idea in an effective way.

Check It Out   Read the following sentences.

1. General Kelly stretched his tired arms over the ledge and lowered the canvas supply bag to Corporal Fellows.
2. The sun dropped behind the hill, setting the clouds ablaze.
3. After you have put the car in gear, release the brake and let out the clutch—slowly.

4. Art should reflect real life.

5. A feature of many American barns is the cupola, a small, domed structure on the roof.

- Does each sentence express a single, complete thought? Is each sentence clear and interesting?

Try Your Skill   Write one sentence in response to each of the following directions. Use real or imaginary details to make your sentences clear and effective.

1. Tell an event that happened in the news this week.
2. Describe a quiet place.
3. Explain how to be happy.
4. Explain why friends are valuable.
5. Explain what courage is.
6. Describe a person whom you respect.
7. Tell one event that you will always remember.

Keep This in Mind

- A sentence is a group of words that expresses a complete thought. A good sentence is clear and interesting.

Now Write   Write five original sentences. One should tell something that happened. One should describe something. One should explain one step of a process. One should explain an opinion. One should explain what something is.

Choose your words carefully. Be specific and direct. Label your paper **Direct Action** and put it into your folder.

Point-Blank

Keeping to the Point

Here's the Idea An effective sentence expresses one idea clearly and directly. Consider these examples.

I read an informative article about careers in electronics.

The Sloans spent an enjoyable vacation in California.

Related details may be added to a sentence. Related details are those that support the main idea. By adding related details, you may add interest and meaning to a sentence. Read these examples.

I read an informative article about careers in electronics in the Sunday *Tribune*.

In this sentence the added detail is related to the *article*.

The Sloans spent an enjoyable vacation at Big Sur in California.

Here, the added detail is related to the *vacation*.

When you include details in a sentence, be sure that they are related to the main idea. Unrelated details confuse the meaning of a sentence. Look at these examples.

I read an informative article that was eight pages long about careers in electronics.

The Sloans, who are our neighbors, spent an enjoyable vacation at Big Sur in California.

In the first example, notice that the added detail adds no real meaning to the main idea of the sentence. In the second example, notice that the added detail is related to the *Sloans*, but not to their *vacation*, which is the main idea.

When you write sentences, keep to the point. Use specific and meaningful details that are related to the main ideas.

Check It Out   Read these sentences.

1. My sister Ginny, who is nearly six feet tall, won three prizes for her oil paintings.
2. Taking a bus to Chicago, which is not the capital of Illinois, is less expensive than taking a plane.
3. Arnold Tyler, who was born in Oklahoma City thirty-eight years ago, announced that he had designed a plan for solving the energy problem.
4. We visited Salt Lake City, which is the largest city in Utah, and we liked the city very much.

- In each sentence what unrelated detail should be omitted? What related details might you add?

Try Your Skill   Read the following sentences and decide which ones contain unrelated details. Rewrite those sentences, using related details.

1. Weather forecasters were concerned that the cold front would damage the orchards near Jacksonville, where I was born.
2. Jill Roberts, president of the amateur sports club, told us about opportunities in athletics for young men and women.
3. The *Voyager I* spacecraft sent back to earth pictures of Jupiter, the largest planet in the solar system, and its moons.
4. The members of the photography club, which meets every two weeks, will display their photographs in the auditorium.

Keep This in Mind

- Use related details that add interest and meaning to the main idea of a sentence. Keep to the point of the sentence.

Now Write   Write five effective sentences about subjects that interest you. Use related details that support the main idea of each sentence. Label your paper **Point-Blank,** and put it into your folder.

No-Show

Avoiding Empty Sentences

Here's the Idea Effective sentences express ideas clearly and completely. Some other sentences, however, do not express ideas effectively. Some of these sentences are **empty sentences.** One kind of empty sentence repeats an idea.

> My history teacher aided me and helped me with my report.

To be aided means to be helped. Therefore, the sentence unnecessarily states the same idea twice.

To improve this kind of empty sentence, you must eliminate the repetition. Sometimes you may choose to simplify the sentence. More often, you will want to add related information.

> My history teacher helped me with my report.

> My history teacher helped me with my report by showing me several informative magazine articles.

There is also another kind of empty sentence. This type of empty sentence states a strong but unsupported opinion. A strong statement is made, but no reasons or facts are presented to explain it. Because the opinion is not supported, the sentence is incomplete and empty of meaning for a reader.

> Spring is a fascinating season.

To improve this kind of empty sentence, you must add supporting evidence that completes the idea. Supporting evidence may be given in the same sentence or in another sentence.

> Spring is a fascinating season because it is a time of continual awakening in nature.

> Spring is a fascinating season. It is a time of continual awakening in nature.

Check It Out   Read these empty sentences.

1. The book was dull because it seemed boring.
2. Craig's personality is pleasant, and he is always nice.
3. Camping is the ideal hobby.
4. Susan is talented and can do many things.
5. Cities are dangerous.
6. Melinda's clothes are fashionable and she dresses stylishly.

- Which sentences repeat an idea? Which state an unsupported opinion? How would you improve each of these empty sentences?

Try Your Skill   Rewrite each of these empty sentences.

1. Margaret Mead wrote an autobiography of her life.
2. Biology is the most interesting science.
3. Individual sports are better than team sports.
4. You have been given the wrong information, and you are misinformed.
5. Define each word and tell what it means.
6. The United States is a strong country.

Keep This in Mind

- Sentences that repeat ideas or state unsupported opinions are empty sentences. Improve a sentence that repeats an idea by simplifying it or by adding related information. Improve a sentence with an unsupported opinion by adding reasons or facts that support the opinion.

Now Write   Label your paper *Empty Sentences*. Write, or find, three examples of each kind of empty sentence. Improve the sentences by avoiding repetition or by including supporting evidence. Keep your work in your folder. Continue to check for empty sentences in your writing.

Battle of the Bulge

Avoiding Padded Sentences

Here's the Idea An effective sentence contains no more words than are necessary. A **padded sentence** contains useless phrases that bury the main idea. Phrases that signal padded sentences should be avoided. Study these examples.

what I mean is	well, you see
what I'm saying is	you know
the reason that	in my opinion, I think
my feeling is that	because of the fact that
the point is	owing to the fact
the thing is	on account of the fact that

Usually you can improve a padded sentence simply by eliminating the unnecessary expressions. Sometimes, however, you will need to revise the sentence completely.

Padded In my opinion I think that television programing should be improved.

Improved Television programing should be improved.

Padded Ann's help was valuable to the success of the program on account of the fact that she had experience as a fund-raiser and she was willing to volunteer her time.

Improved Ann's experience as a fund-raiser, and her willingness as a volunteer, contributed a great deal to the success of the program.

Some groups of words using *who is, which is,* or *that is* may also be used unnecessarily in sentences. Use such expressions only when they add to the meaning of the sentence.

Padded Cara, who is my best friend, is moving to Iowa.

Improved My best friend, Cara, is moving to Iowa.

Check It Out   Read these padded sentences.

1. Mom will be late for work due to the fact that she overslept.
2. Early covered wagons were called Conestoga wagons because of the fact that they were built at Conestoga, Pennsylvania.
3. What I wish is that I could go with you.
4. It seems to me that some people are always complaining about the weather although it is one of those things that they can't do anything about anyway.

• How would you improve these padded sentences?

Try Your Skill   Rewrite these padded sentences. Improve them by eliminating useless phrases or by revising the sentence completely.

1. For three years we lived in New Orleans, which is, as you know, in the state of Louisiana.
2. I think that Gwen should be elected because she is, in my opinion, the most qualified of the candidates running for treasurer.
3. Hal is a dependable employee owing to the fact that he is always at work on time.
4. What I mean is I like ice skating on account of the fact that it makes me feel as if I'm flying.

Keep This in Mind

• Sentences that include unnecessary phrases are padded sentences. Improve a padded sentence by eliminating the useless expression or by revising the sentence totally.

Now Write   Label your paper *Padded Sentences*. Write, or find, five examples of padded sentences. Improve the sentences by deleting useless phrases or revising the sentences completely. Keep your paper in your folder. Check for padded sentences in your writing.

Think Small

Avoiding Overloaded Sentences

Here's the Idea Sentences containing too many ideas are
overloaded sentences.

Overloaded sentences usually contain several thoughts
loosely joined by *and*. The word *and* is used incorrectly when it
is used to connect ideas that are not closely related.

> Carrots are a practical vegetable to buy, and they are inexpen-
> sive and they are a good source of Vitamin C, and they can be
> eaten raw or cooked in a variety of ways, and there are many
> recipes for delicious carrot cakes.

From this example, you can see how confusing an overloaded
sentence is. Too many ideas run together. Which is the main
idea? It is difficult to tell. You should avoid such confusion.
Separate an overloaded sentence into several shorter sentences.

> Carrots are a practical vegetable to buy. They are inexpensive
> and a good source of Vitamin C. In addition, they can be
> eaten raw or cooked in a variety of ways. There are even
> recipes for delicious carrot cakes.

There may be times when you need to express a complex idea
in writing. However, be sure that a single sentence contains
only one main idea or related ideas.

Check It Out Read this overloaded sentence.

> Overloaded On the first day of our trip, we crossed the Mis-
> sissippi River into St. Louis, and just as we were
> about to stop for the night our car sputtered and
> stopped, and we located a mechanic, and he said
> that it would take two days to fix the car and we
> did some unexpected sightseeing in St. Louis.

Improved   On the first day of our trip, we crossed the Mississippi River into St. Louis. As we were about to stop for the night, our car sputtered and stopped. We located a mechanic, who told us that it would take him two days to fix the car. As a result, we did some unexpected sightseeing in St. Louis.

• How has this overloaded sentence been improved?

Try Your Skill   Improve the following overloaded sentences.

1. I searched everywhere for my missing wallet and I looked in the house, outside, and in the car and then I retraced my steps and finally found the missing wallet in a drawer of my desk at work.

2. The horseshoe crab is found on the eastern shores of the United States and it has a large, rounded body and a stiff, pointed tail, and it is also called "king crab."

3. The Cheshire cat is a fictional character, and it is always grinning, and it gradually disappears with only its grin remaining visible, and the cat is in the book *Alice's Adventures in Wonderland,* and it is written by Lewis Carroll.

4. Some people think that the federal government should deregulate oil prices and that would probably cause gas and oil prices to rise, but if gas and oil prices rose, then people would buy less, and the country would have to import less, and maybe that would help control inflation.

Keep This in Mind

• Sentences that contain too many ideas are overloaded sentences. Improve an overloaded sentence by separating it into shorter sentences.

Now Write   Label your paper *Overloaded Sentences.* Write four examples of overloaded sentences. Improve them by separating the main ideas into several shorter sentences. Keep your paper in your folder.

Balance of Power

Making Sentences Parallel

Here's the Idea   When you write a sentence, you must express a complete thought. You should also keep to a point, avoid repetition and unnecessary phrases, and limit the number of ideas in the sentence. In addition, you should join the parts of the sentence in a smooth and balanced way.

Usually, the word *and* is used to join similar sentence parts. These equal sentence parts should be in the same form. When they are, they are **parallel.** Sentences containing parts that are not parallel are faulty. These faulty sentences are awkward and confusing. Look at the following sentence.

Maria is intelligent, ambitious, and likes to study.

The parts *intelligent, ambitious,* and *likes to study* serve the same function in the sentence. They name qualities that Maria possesses. Therefore, these three parts should be in the same form. The sentence is improved when the parts are parallel.

Maria is intelligent, ambitious, and studious.

Many sentences with faulty parallelism can be corrected in more than one way, although one change will probably sound most natural. Compare these examples.

Faulty   Making the team requires skill, practice, and you have to want to.

Parallel   Making the team requires you to be skillful, to practice, and to want to make it.

Parallel   Making the team requires skill, practice, and desire.

Notice that both sentences with parallel structure are correct. However, the shorter parallel sentence sounds more natural. Thus, that sentence is more effective.

Check It Out Compare the following pairs of sentences.

Faulty   We are going to take a vacation by bus, train, or fly.

Parallel   We are going to take a vacation by bus, train, or plane.

Faulty   The referee explained the rules that he would follow and that he would use certain signals.

Parallel   The referee explained the rules that he would follow and the signals that he would use.

- How has each faulty sentence been made parallel? Can either sentence be corrected in a different way?

Try Your Skill Rewrite the following sentences, making the similar parts parallel.

1. The dogs in the show are judged on their appearance, their breeding, and how they behave.

2. The teacher explained the lesson and that the assignment was due in two days.

3. I like movies with suspense, dramatic music, and filled with colorful scenery.

4. For the part of the mother, we need a person with some acting experience and who has an alto voice.

Keep This in Mind

- Sentence parts serving the same function should be parallel. Many sentences with problems in parallel structure can be corrected in more than one way.

Now Write Write, or find, four examples of sentences containing similar parts that are not parallel. Rewrite the sentences, making the parts parallel. Be sure that your revised sentences are clear and smooth. Label your paper **Balance of Power** and keep it in your folder.

Variations on a Theme

Varying Your Sentences

Here's the Idea   Any sentence idea may be stated in a variety of ways. You must decide which way expresses most precisely the particular idea you mean.

In a series of sentences, variety becomes especially important. When you write a series of sentences that are too similar, your writing seems monotonous and ineffective. To strengthen your writing and make it lively, add variety. Vary the order in which you present ideas. Vary the ways in which you combine ideas. Vary the length of your sentences.

One way to vary sentences is to rearrange the word order. For example, use different beginnings. Read the following sentences. The first sentence is written in the most common order. The other sentences express the same idea but with a variety of beginnings.

> Leo practiced the guitar faithfully for two hours each day.
> For two hours each day, Leo faithfully practiced the guitar.
> Faithfully, Leo practiced the guitar for two hours each day.
> Each day, Leo practiced the guitar faithfully for two hours.

Another way to strengthen your writing is to vary the structure of sentences. For example, the two ideas *Carla got up early* and *she wanted to be on time* can be combined into an effective sentence in a variety of ways.

> Carla wanted to be on time, so she got up early.
> Wanting to be on time, Carla got up early.
> Because she wanted to be on time, Carla got up early.
> Carla wanted to be on time; therefore, she got up early.

A series of sentences of the same approximate length can be monotonous. Try to vary sentence length.

Check It Out   Read the following paragraph.

When Linda bought her first car, she didn't realize the extent of her financial responsibility. She had thought only about keeping the gas tank filled and about enjoying the convenience. However, Linda soon learned otherwise. Filling the tank every week cost more than she had expected. Oil changes and tuneups added a great deal to the cost of maintaining the car. Since she was under twenty-five, her insurance bill was considerable. As soon as Linda had paid that bill in full, she received another one for excise tax. After six months, Linda sold her car and began taking the bus.

· How have these sentences shown variety?

Try Your Skill   Rewrite each of the following sentences or pair of sentences. Use a variety of beginnings and structures to express these ideas. Invent necessary details.

1. We had dinner late. The traffic delayed us.
2. I was disappointed when I heard the bad news.
3. Mark worked hard at his first job. Mark was successful.
4. I stepped off the curb. I fell down.
5. The President repeatedly urged adoption of price controls.
6. Many people today are finding jobs in the field of computer technology.
7. In A.D. 79 Mt. Vesuvius erupted, pouring molten lava down the mountainside. The lava destroyed the city of Pompeii.

Keep This in Mind

· A sentence idea can be expressed in more than one way. Sentences can be varied by using different beginnings, structures, and lengths.

Now Write   Write three original sentences. Rewrite each of your sentences in two different ways, striving for variety. Label your paper **Variations on a Theme.** Put it into your folder.

Sentence Combining

Togetherness

Combining Sentences

Here's the Idea A paragraph or composition is made up of a great many ideas. Sometimes two closely related ideas appear as separate sentences. By combining these sentences, you often can make the relationship between the ideas clearer. Sentences can usually be combined if they state ideas of equal importance.

Two sentences may state similar ideas of equal importance. Such sentences can usually be joined with a comma and the word *and*.

> We visited the Great Meteor Crater of Arizona. I walked down into it.
>
> We visited the Great Meteor Crater of Arizona, and I walked down into it.

Two sentences may also state contrasting ideas of equal importance. Such sentences can usually be joined with a comma and the word *but*.

> Amy loves the novels of Steinbeck. I prefer the novels of Roth.
>
> Amy loves the novels of Steinbeck, but I prefer the novels of Roth.

Finally, two sentences may offer a choice between ideas of equal importance. Such sentences can usually be joined with a comma and the word *or*.

> Is there gas in the tank? Should we stop at a station on our way?
>
> Is there gas in the tank, or should we stop at a station on our way?

Check It Out Read the following sentences.

> 1. Lindbergh landed, and the crowd ran to greet him.
> 2. Am I early, or have the others already left?

3. We won the game, but we could have played better.

- Which sentence combines contrasting ideas of equal importance?
- Which combines similar ideas of equal importance?
- Which sentence combines ideas of equal importance and offers a choice between them?

Try Your Skill Combine each pair of sentences.

1. Our cat climbed up the fire escape. She could not get back down. (Join with **, but.**)
2. A truck broke down in the center lane. Traffic came to a standstill. (Join with **, and.**)
3. Meteors are solid. Comets are not. (Join with **, but.**)
4. Trucks may use gasoline. They may use diesel fuel. (Join with **, or.**)
5. The mother wolf growled softly. The tiny cubs sprang immediately to her side. (Join with **, and.**)

Keep This in Mind

- Combine sentences that state similar ideas of equal importance with a comma and *and*.
- Combine sentences that state contrasting ideas of equal importance with a comma and *but*.
- Combine sentences that offer a choice between ideas of equal importance with a comma and *or*.

Now Write Combine each pair of sentences using **, and** or **, but** or **, or**. Label your paper **Togetherness**. Save it.

1. Drought dried the earth. Winds blew the topsoil away.
2. Lightning causes some fires. People cause far more.
3. Will you join us for dinner? Have you already eaten?
4. The actor forgot his line. The audience didn't notice.

In Part

Combining Sentence Parts

Here's the Idea Instead of joining entire sentences, you can sometimes join parts of sentences. For example, some sentence parts state similar ideas of equal importance. Such parts can be joined with *and*.

> Mars is riddled with craters. *Mars is* covered by sand dunes.
>
> Mars is riddled with craters and covered by sand dunes.

Combining sentence parts allows you to drop any repeated words. Notice how the repeated words shown in italics were dropped in the example above.

Some sentence parts state contrasting ideas of equal importance. Such parts can be joined with *but*.

> Shonda knows the tap routine. *Shonda* hasn't practiced it.
>
> Shonda knows the tap routine but hasn't practiced it.

Sentence parts may also offer a choice between ideas of equal importance. Such parts can usually be joined with *or*.

> Are gibbons New World monkeys? *Are gibbons* Old World *monkeys?*
>
> Are gibbons New World or Old World monkeys?

Check It Out Read the following sentences.

1. Most reptiles lay eggs. Some mammals lay eggs.
   Most reptiles and some mammals lay eggs.

2. Did the officials close the factory? Did they leave it open?
   Did the officials close the factory or leave it open?

3. The material for the space suit is very light. The material for the space suit is very strong.
   The material for the space suit is very light but very strong.

- Which sentence contains contrasting parts of equal importance?
- Which contains similar parts of equal importance?
- Which sentence combines parts that offer a choice between ideas of equal importance?

Try Your Skill   Combine each pair of sentences by following the directions in parentheses. Leave out the italicized words.

1. The votes were counted. *The votes were* stored on computer tape. (Join with **and**.)
2. The plane lost an engine. *The plane* landed safely. (Join with **but**.)
3. Can we ski on this lake? *Can we* fish *on this lake?* (Join with **and**.)
4. Is the car you bought new? *Is the car you bought* used? (Join with **or**.)

Keep This in Mind

- Use *and* to join sentence parts that state similar ideas of equal importance.
- Use *but* to join sentence parts that state contrasting ideas of equal importance.
- Use *or* to join sentence parts that offer a choice between ideas of equal importance.

Now Write   Combine each pair of sentences. Use *and, but,* or *or* to join sentence parts. Label your paper **In Part**. Save it.

1. Will the new school be bigger? Will it be the same size?
2. Cocker spaniels are beautiful dogs. Golden retrievers are beautiful dogs.
3. The crust was somewhat dry. The crust was still tasty.
4. Ivy can grow in sunlight. Ivy can grow in shadow.

Added Ingredients

Adding Single Words

Here's the Idea   You have seen that closely related sentences can often be combined. Sometimes a pair of sentences is very closely related indeed. In such pairs, one sentence states a main idea. The second sentence adds only one important word to this main idea. You can often combine such sentences by adding the one important word to the main idea sentence.

> A yellow car with a vinyl roof crashed through the gate. *The vinyl roof was* white.
>
> A yellow car with a white vinyl roof crashed through the gate.

Notice that the word *white* was added to the first sentence. The words in italics were dropped.

When you add a word to a sentence, you may sometimes have to change its form. You may have to change the ending of the word by adding *-ing, -ed,* or *-ly.*

> Build the second level of the set on a platform. Raise *the platform.*
>
> Build the second level of the set on a raised platform.
>
> The sign said to beware of the rocks. *The rocks might* fall.
>
> The sign said to beware of the falling rocks.
>
> One day, Mr. Jones disappeared. *The disappearance was* mysterious.
>
> One day, Mr. Jones mysteriously disappeared.

Check It Out   Study the following examples.

> 1. The gymnast threw herself into the air. *The gymnast's movement was* sudden.
>
> The gymnast suddenly threw herself into the air.

2. The wind buffeted the tiny boat. *The wind* howled.
The howling wind buffeted the tiny boat.
3. Add chestnuts to the stuffing. Roast *the chestnuts*.
Add roasted chestnuts to the stuffing.

- What word has been added to each sentence?
- How was each word changed before it was added?

Try Your Skill Combine each pair of sentences by adding the important word. Leave out the italicized words.

1. The biplane trailed a banner. *The banner* fluttered. (End the important word with **-ing.**)
2. Donna trudged up the steps. *Donna was* weary. (End the important word with **-ly.**)
3. Put some cheese on the pizza. Grate *the cheese*. (End the important word with **-ed.**)
4. Marcus described the plans for the trip. *Marcus was* enthusiastic. (End the important word with **-ly.**)

Keep This in Mind

- Sometimes two sentences can be combined by moving a word from one sentence to the other.
- Before adding a single word, you may have to change its ending to *-ing, -ed,* or *-ly.*

Now Write Choose the important word from the second sentence in each pair. Add this word to the first sentence. Remember that you may have to change the ending of the added word. Label your paper **Added Ingredients.** Save it in your folder.

1. Insert the letter into the envelope. Fold the letter.
2. "We'll win the game," said Coach Malone. She seemed confident.
3. Garfield looked at Jon. His look was disapproving.
4. Sugar cane has an outer layer. The outer layer is tough.

Group Work

Adding Groups of Words

Here's the Idea   As you have learned, you can sometimes combine sentences by adding single words. Sentences can also be combined by adding an important group of words.

> This box contains glassware. *The glassware is* from Bolivia.
> This box contains glassware from Bolivia.

Sometimes the important group of words gives more information about a person or thing. If this is true, add the group near the words that name the person or thing.

> The teacher sprained an ankle. *She was the teacher* of the aerobics class.
> The teacher of the aerobics class sprained an ankle.

The important group of words may also describe an action. If this is true, add the group as near as possible to the words that name the action.

> The horse and rider jumped. *They jumped* over the fence.
> The horse and rider jumped over the fence.

Sometimes the group of words refers to the entire main idea of the other sentence. If this is true, you may add the group of words in any of several places.

> Doctors worked to eliminate smallpox. *Doctors worked* for years.
> For years, doctors worked to eliminate smallpox.
> Doctors worked for years to eliminate smallpox.

Check It Out   Study the following sentences.

1. Geologists are searching for oil.

Geologists are searching along the north coast.
Geologists are searching along the north coast for oil.

2. We watched a very funny movie.
The movie was on channel five.
We watched a very funny movie on channel five.

- What words were added or dropped?

Try Your Skill   Combine each group of sentences. Leave out the italicized words.

1. Did you see the bald eagle? *The bald eagle is* at the zoo.
2. The new player kicked the football. *The football went* between the goalposts.
3. The fireworks were beautiful. *The fireworks were* after the concert.
4. A young man left a package for you. *The young man was dressed* in a checkered suit.
5. The ship sank. *This happened* during the night.

Keep This in Mind

- Sometimes sentences can be combined by adding a group of words.
- Add a group of words next to the person, thing, or action that the group of words describes.
- If the group of words describes the entire main idea of another sentence, you may add the group of words in more than one place.

Now Write   Combine each pair of sentences by adding words to the first sentence. Leave out any unnecessary words.

1. Marseille is a seaport. Marseille is in Southern France.
2. The book was listed in the card catalog. It was listed under "Lincoln" and "Sandburg."
3. The river was rapid. The river was above the falls.

Who's That?

Combining with *Who, Which,* and *That*

Here's the Idea   When you add a group of words that describes a person, you may have to begin the group with *who.*

> The woman was a reporter. *The woman* sat in the back row.
>
> The woman who sat in the back row was a reporter.

Notice that the word *who* took the place of the words in italics.
   To add a group of words that describes a thing, you may have
to use *that.*

> The story was hard to believe. Jean told *the story.*
>
> The story that Jean told was hard to believe.

Again, notice that the word *that* replaced the words in italics.
   In the above examples, the words added to the first sentence
in each pair are necessary. The added words make clear which
woman and which story are meant. In some sentences, the
added words are not necessary. They do not tell which person,
place, or thing is meant. Instead, they just add more information. When you add words that just give more information, use
, who instead of *who* and *, which* instead of *that.*

> Lucy scored two goals. *Lucy* missed the last game.
>
> Lucy, who missed the last game, scored two goals.
>
> Grains provide protein. *Grains* are grown worldwide.
>
> Grains, which are grown worldwide, provide protein.

Check It Out   Study the following examples.

> 1. A man *who* comes from my town is running for senate.
>   Ted Mitchell, *who* comes from my town, is running for the
> senate.

74

2. The shades *that* the Bernsteins ordered have arrived.
Window shades, *which* come in many styles, can lower cooling costs.

- Why do the two sentences in each pair use different methods of adding information?

Try Your Skill Combine each pair of sentences. Follow the directions in parentheses. Leave out the italicized words.

1. Andorra has a population of 25,000. *Andorra* lies between France and Spain. (Combine with , which.)
2. The director was John Ford. *The director* made this classic western. (Combine with who.)
3. Calcium is a metal. Calcium develops strong bones. (Combine with that.)
4. The black-eyed Susan is a wildflower. The flower has yellow petals and a brown center. (Combine with that.)

Keep This in Mind

- When you add a group of words, you may have to begin the group with *who*, *which*, or *that*.
- When the words make the meaning clear, combine with *who* or *that*. When the words just add information, combine with , *who* or , *which*.

Now Write Combine each of the following pairs of sentences. Decide on your own how to combine them. Save your paper.

1. I caught the donkey. The donkey broke the fence.
2. Mark Spitz became a dentist. Mark Spitz had won nine Olympic gold medals in swimming.
3. The exhibit arrived in the United States today. The exhibit has never before left Europe.
4. The singer received the most applause. The singer was Irene Cara.

Winning Combinations

Using Combining Skills in Writing

Here's the Idea In this chapter you have learned the following ways to combine related ideas in sentences:

1. Combine sentences with , *and*, , *but*, or , *or*.
2. Combine sentence parts with *and*, *but*, or *or*.
3. Add single words.
4. Add groups of words.
5. Add groups of words that begin with *who, which,* or *that*.

Use what you have learned about sentence combining whenever you revise your writing. Remember that by combining sentences, you can make the relationships between your ideas clearer. Combining sentences can also add interest to your writing. It does this by varying the length of your sentences.

Check It Out Study the following paragraphs.

1   The direct route ran through the valley. The scenic route wound up Bear Mountain. The scenic route offered a view of the whole valley below. Ignoring our schedule, we chose the scenic route. Our schedule was tight. We ate sandwiches. This was at a rest area. We had packed the sandwiches that morning.

2   The direct route ran through the valley, but the scenic route wound up Bear Mountain and offered a view of the whole valley below. Ignoring our tight schedule, we chose the scenic route. At a rest area, we ate the sandwiches that we had packed that morning.

- In which paragraph are related ideas combined?
- How was each pair of sentences combined?

Try Your Skill Improve the following paragraph by combining each pair of sentences. Follow any directions given in parentheses. Leave out the words in italics.

1. Young dragonflies live in water. *Young dragonflies* are called "nymphs." (Combine with **, which**.) 2. They breathe through gills. *The gills are* tiny. (Add the important word.) 3. Most dragonfly nymphs eat water insects. Some eat young fish. (Combine the sentences with **, but**.) 4. The nymphs stay in the water. *They do this* for one to five years. (Add the group of words.) 5. Eventually, they leave the water. *They* develop into adults with beautiful, fragile wings. (Join the sentence parts using the word *and*.)

Keep This in Mind

- Combining skills are useful for revision.
- By combining sentences, you can make the relationships between your ideas clearer.
- Combining sentences also adds variety to your writing.

Now Write Revise the following paragraph by combining the sentences.

Are you looking for a job? Should the job be rewarding? We need volunteers at Heritage Housing. This is housing for the elderly. You may run errands. These errands could be at supermarkets. These errands could be at shopping centers. You might get books from the library. You might help to run our movie projector. If you are interested, call Heritage Housing at 555-6767. Ask for Mr. Thom.

Analyzing the Paragraph

Make a Stand

Defining a Paragraph

Here's the Idea You have analyzed words and sentences. Now you are ready to analyze paragraphs. A **paragraph** is a group of sentences dealing with one main idea. For example, notice how the sentences in each of these groups work together.

1   Last Saturday I took my date to the new Takahashi Restaurant. It was my first Japanese meal. I ordered sukiyaki, and a young woman in a black and white kimono brought us a platter of thinly sliced meat, onions, and other vegetables. She quickly grilled these items at our table and filled our plates with the hot foods. Then she broke a raw egg into a bowl, handed it to me, and stepped back, waiting. I didn't know what to do. In desperation, I nodded in thanks and picked up a spoon to sip the egg. When my date giggled, I looked up. Then, the waitress explained to me how to dip the hot food into the egg. The meal was delicious, but I vowed to ask questions before I try another new dish.

2   The near-empty auditorium echoed. The only sounds were the whispers of the few campaign workers too exhausted to move. Crushed paper cups and shreds of paper streamers covered the floor. Scattered amid the debris were dozens of discarded campaign buttons. Suddenly, the door opened and the candidate herself entered the room. Her disappointed supporters clapped, but Ellen Collins looked truly defeated.

3   Taxes keep rising in our city, and taxpayers keep complaining. However, the higher taxes have bought us improved services. We are able to maintain our good schools, a well-equipped fire department, and a municipal pool. A great deal of money is needed continually. If residents want lower taxes, they will have to learn to do without many services. Taxpayers simply cannot demand something for nothing.

Check It Out Examine the three groups of sentences. The first group tells a story. The second group describes a scene. The third group explains an opinion.

- Are these groups of sentences paragraphs? Does each group of sentences deal with one idea?

Try Your Skill One of these groups is a paragraph. One is not. For the group that is a paragraph, write the main idea. For the group that is not a paragraph, explain why.

1   During periods of warm weather, many people wish they owned a motorcycle. Of course, it is precisely at such times that most motorcycle owners do not want to sell. Therefore, it makes more sense to buy a motorcycle during the winter. The prices of used motorcycles are lower then, and there are more vehicles for sale. In addition, it is most sensible to shop by searching through the classified ads. Once I found a good used bicycle through the classified ads, and last winter I found a part-time job there, too.

2   The United States is a nation of watchers. Of the sixty million homes in the United States, ninety-five percent have televisions. One out of every four homes has more than one set. The average television set is turned on five and three-quarter hours per day. An American child can expect to view enough television to total nine years of his or her life. On a winter evening, half of all Americans are at home in front of their television sets. Television-watching seems to be a national addiction.

Keep This in Mind

- A paragraph is a group of sentences dealing with one main idea.

Now Write Analyze the group of sentences in **Try Your Skill** that is not a paragraph. Rewrite it so that it is. Label your paper **Make a Stand,** and put it into your folder.

In Unison

Recognizing Unity in a Paragraph

Here's the Idea A paragraph is an organized unit of sentences. When all the sentences of a paragraph work together and relate to one main idea, a paragraph has **unity.**

Notice how these sentences relate to an experience.

> I had been nervous about entering my drawings in the Seattle spring art show. However, I was even more nervous when I walked into the lecture hall at the museum where the entries were being displayed. I pretended to study them, but I was really only looking for my own work. I was too excited to concentrate anyway. By the time I had worked my way halfway around the room, I was truly upset. I could not find my drawings. Had someone lost them? I finished my search in despair. My work was definitely not there. Gathering my courage, I asked one of the judges whether all entries were displayed. She pointed across the hall to a door. Then I saw the sign over the door. It read: Award-Winning Drawings.

Check It Out Read this paragraph.

> Thousands of years ago, sometime after the end of the Ice Age, tribes of people came to the New World from Asia. They traveled across the Bering Strait into Alaska and by the fifteenth century they had spread throughout all of North and South America. These people were hunters, fishers, and food-gatherers. They wandered around the land to find food, and they developed many cultures and many languages. By the time Christopher Columbus arrived in the New World there were over thirteen million Indians there. The approximately one million Indians of North America lived in seven major areas: the Eastern Woodlands, the Southeast, the Plains, California, the Southwest, the Northwest Coast, and Alaska.
>
> —ROSEBUD YELLOW ROBE

- Do all of the sentences relate to one main idea? Does the paragraph have unity?

Try Your Skill   Read the following paragraphs. Decide if each has unity. If a paragraph does not have unity, write the sentence or sentences that do not belong.

1   A recording artist does not always make a lot of money by making a record. When a record is purchased, only about ten percent of the price goes to the artist. The artist must split that money with managers, producers, arrangers, and any backup musicians. Barry Manilow was once a backup musician for Bette Midler. Nevertheless, because an album can easily sell ten million copies, huge profits are possible.

2   There are many kinds of microphones used in radio broadcasting today. There are microphones that pick up all the sounds in an area, and others that absorb only the sound of the announcer's voice. There are also microphones for interviews, and remote microphones for news reports. Many people rely on the radio for daily news updates.

3   Mimes are trained in the art of portraying characters through movement. They use a combination of acting and dancing, but they never speak any lines. They work without props and in simple costumes. Mimes tell stories that can be understood by anyone from any country because these artists speak through body and facial expressions rather than words.

Keep This in Mind

- All the sentences in a paragraph should relate to one main idea. Then a paragraph has unity.

Now Write   Name a public figure you respect. Write one sentence that sums up your thoughts about him or her. Below that sentence, list five more sentences related to the main idea. Label your paper **In Unison.** Keep your work in your folder.

What's the Point?

Using a Topic Sentence

Here's the Idea The **topic sentence** of a paragraph states the main idea in a clear, direct, and interesting way. Because it tells what a paragraph is about, the topic sentence is often the first sentence in a paragraph. Placed in this position, it prepares a reader for what is to follow. However, the topic sentence may be placed anywhere in a paragraph where it expresses the main idea most effectively.

The topic sentence must state an idea that can be developed by the other sentences in the paragraph. Suppose you were writing a paragraph about Boston. The sentence "Boston is the capital of Massachusetts" is too limited to be a good topic sentence. It makes a simple statement of fact that cannot be developed meaningfully. A more effective topic sentence might be "Boston, Massachusetts, is known as the 'Cradle of Liberty.' " This topic sentence offers an idea that promises more. A sentence like this could be developed by other sentences.

Check It Out Read the following paragraph.

Some animals are associated with a particular character trait. For example, a dolphin is associated with intelligence and a fox with slyness. An animal that has a reputation for fierceness is the mongoose. Mongoose is the name given to several related animals native to Africa and southern Asia. The common mongoose is only about sixteen inches long with a slender body and a long tail. This small, speedy animal is most noted for its ability to fight and kill poisonous snakes like the cobra. This ability makes the mongoose a fierce enemy.

- Which is the topic sentence? Is it too narrow? State the main idea of the paragraph.

Try Your Skill Read each paragraph below. Write the topic sentence. If the topic sentence is too limited, label it *Narrow*. Then rewrite it so that it is a better topic sentence.

1   Charlie Chaplin wore a derby hat. One of the most famous stars in movie history, Chaplin was called "the funniest man in the world" during the era of silent comedies. The character he made famous was "the Tramp." He always wore a coat that was too small and baggy pants that were too large. The little Tramp was usually penniless, but he was always spirited and ready for mischief.

2   Many American portrait painters in the eighteenth century had a practical approach to painting. The artists traveled with canvases that were painted with bodies, but without heads. When customers wanted their portraits painted, they simply chose from the bodies available, and the painter would fill in the face while the customer waited. This unusual method offered convenience to the customer and increased sales for the painter.

3   Cloves were once thought to be a cure for headaches. These dried flower buds, used most often as spices, were also used as breath fresheners. Chinese messengers once had to place cloves in their mouths before speaking to their emperors. This nail-shaped spice has even been suggested as a cure for toothaches and for coughs.

Keep This in Mind

- A topic sentence states the main idea of a paragraph. The sentence should deal with an idea that can be developed in a meaningful way.

Now Write Think of three topics that you might develop in paragraphs. For each one, write a topic sentence that states the main idea you have in mind. Label your paper **What's the Point?** Keep your work in your folder.

Multiple Choice

Ways of Developing a Paragraph

Here's the Idea A paragraph can be developed with sensory details, specific examples, facts and statistics, and incidents or anecdotes.

Use **sensory details** to make a subject come alive.

> The man came out of the house and stood quite still, listening. Behind him, the lights glowed in the cheerful room, the books were neat and orderly in their cases, the radio talked importantly to itself. In front of him, the bay stretched dark and silent, one of the countless lagoons that border the coast where Florida thrusts its green thumb deep into the tropics. It was late in September. The night was breathless; summer's dead hand still lay heavy on the land. —ARTHUR GORDON

Use **specific examples** to develop a general statement.

> Most construction workers specialize in certain building materials. For example, carpenters use wood in constructing buildings and such building features as floors and frames. Metalworkers perform such jobs as pipe fitting and welding. They also install plumbing, heating, and air-conditioning systems.
>
> —*The World Book Encyclopedia*

Use **facts and statistics** to make an idea or an opinion clear.

> Lions are among the largest members of the cat family. An adult male usually weighs about 400 pounds. Some males, however, weigh up to 500 pounds. Most male lions are nine feet long from nose to tail. Females are somewhat smaller and usually weigh about 300 pounds.

Use an **incident** or an **anecdote** to illustrate a point.

> President Kennedy had the ability to inspire people wherever he went. When he visited West Berlin in 1963, he knew

the people were afraid. The government of East Berlin had erected a wall to divide the city. West Berliners feared that the city might be cut off from the free world. Kennedy spoke to a huge crowd of West Berliners at the wall. He ended his speech with the words, "Ich bin ein Berliner," which means, "I am a Berliner." The crowd cheered wildly.

Check It Out   Read the following paragraph.

As Chris entered the forest, he was surrounded by sound. A stream of water gurgled over the rocks. Branches of birch trees clacked together in the wind like gossiping neighbors. The older limbs of the stately evergreens creaked as they bent. Nearby, a woodpecker drilled a message into the bark of a tree. The forest seemed a lively, noisy place.

• How is this paragraph developed?

Try Your Skill   What is the main idea of this paragraph? Copy the topic sentence. Tell how the paragraph is developed.

Long before the metric system was developed in Europe, kings could set their own standards of measurement. One king's foot was used as a measure for length. One king's favorite cup was the standard measure for liquids. In England, a yard was the distance from the tip of King Edgar's nose along his outstretched arm to the tip of his middle finger.

Keep This in Mind

• The main idea of a paragraph may be developed by sensory details, by specific examples, by facts and statistics, or by incidents or anecdotes.

Now Write   Take out your paper labeled **What's the Point?** Choose one of your three topic sentences. List details, examples, facts and statistics, or an incident or anecdote to develop the main idea stated in the topic sentence. Save your work.

The Name of the Game

Recognizing Three Kinds of Paragraphs

Here's the Idea   Every paragraph—whether it is about something real or something imaginary—is either a story, a description, or an explanation. Each kind of paragraph deals with an idea in a different way.

A **narrative** paragraph tells a story or relates a sequence of events. All events are usually told in the order in which they happened.

A **descriptive** paragraph is a word picture of an object, a scene, or a person. Its sensory details usually create a particular mood.

An **explanatory** paragraph explains something. It may explain a process, state an opinion, or state a definition. This kind of paragraph is also called an *expository* paragraph.

Check It Out   Read the following paragraph.

1   Mr. Sherlock Holmes was leaning back in his chair, unfolding his morning paper in a leisurely fashion. Suddenly our attention was caught by a tremendous ring at the bell. This sound was followed immediately by a hollow drumming sound, as if someone were beating on the outer door with his or her fist. As it opened, there came a noisy rush into the hall. Rapid feet clattered up the stair, and an instant later a wild-eyed and frantic young man—pale, disheveled, and trembling—burst into the room.   —SIR ARTHUR CONAN DOYLE

2   One cloudy winter evening I sat in the corner of a second-class car of a Tokyo train and waited for the starting whistle. In the car there was no passenger but myself. On the platform, there was not a single person who had come to bid someone good-bye. The only sound was that of a puppy whining sadly from time to time. All of these things seemed wholly suited to my mood. Fatigue and boredom surrounded me with their dull

and heavy shadows, like a gray and shadowy sky. With both hands deep in my pockets, I didn't even feel like taking the evening paper out of my pocket. —RYUNOSUKE AKUTAGAWA

3   We put together a unique example of Americans. There were Jews, Catholics, Protestants, agnostics, white men, black men. The only thing we had in common was an Irish name— The Celtics. We did the Irish name proud. Through it all we never had a quarrel. We simply considered ourselves a proud group of men who bore the distinction of being something no one else could be in basketball—the champions of the world.

—BILL RUSSELL

- Which paragraph is narrative? Which is descriptive? Which is explanatory?

Try Your Skill   As you read these possible topic sentences, decide what kind of paragraph they would most likely be part of.

1. Many adolescents develop poor eating habits.
2. My desk looks chaotic, but it is actually a masterpiece of organization.
3. A hush fell over the crowd as the stage curtain rose.
4. The first step in baking is to assemble all the ingredients.

Keep This in Mind

- A narrative paragraph tells a story or relates a sequence of events.
- A descriptive paragraph creates a word picture.
- An explanatory paragraph explains a process, states an opinion, or states a definition.

Now Write   Review your work labeled **Multiple Choice.** Write which of the three kinds of paragraphs you would use for this topic. Explain why this choice seems best. Label your paper **The Name of the Game.** Keep your work in your folder.

Writing a Paragraph

What's Your Plan?

Writing as a Process

Here's the Idea   When you write a paragraph, you must follow a plan. This plan, called *the process of writing*, contains three stages. These are pre-writing, writing the first draft, and revising.

Pre-writing is the stage in which you plan what you are going to write. In this stage, you choose a topic and narrow it. Then, you gather and organize the ideas and details you will use to develop your topic.

Writing the first draft is the second stage of the process. During this stage, you turn your pre-writing notes into sentences and paragraphs.

Revising is the final stage in the writing process. In this stage, you work to improve your language, content, and organization. You make sure that your ideas are well organized. You also proofread to correct errors in grammar, usage, or mechanics.

Check It Out   Read the following pre-writing notes and paragraph. Notice how the writer followed the steps of the process of writing.

General Topic	themes of folk tales
Narrowed Topic	folk tales about returning after an absence
Pre-Writing Notes	people who return after a long absence known as *revenants*
	tales about returning home after an ordeal
	–after war, long journey, shipwreck
	tales about returning from the grave
	–to visit loved ones

First Draft   Many folk tales are about revenants. A revenant is someone who returns after a long absence. Some of these tales are about people returning home to their families. Often these people have been through terrible ordeals, such as shipwrecks or wars. Other tales of this type tell about people who return from the grave. Again, these people usually return to their loved ones. Both types of tales reflect a common need—the desire to seek comfort after difficult experiences.

- What stage of the process of writing does this writer still have to complete?

Try Your Skill   On a piece of paper, tell which stage of the writing process each of the following steps belongs to.

getting your ideas down on paper

narrowing your topic

gathering details

correcting errors in spelling and punctuation

organizing your notes

revising your content

Keep This in Mind

- The three stages of the process of writing are pre-writing, writing the first draft, and revising.

Now Write   One of the hardest parts of writing is finding a good idea to write about. However, this can be made much easier by keeping a journal. A journal is a notebook in which you record your thoughts, observations, and experiences. Keeping a journal also gives you a chance to practice your writing.

Start keeping a journal today. Begin by writing about an interesting experience you've had this week. Place this entry and all your journal entries in a separate notebook or folder.

Decisions, Decisions

Pre-Writing: Choosing a Topic

Here's the Idea A paragraph can be written on any topic that interests you. As you search for an idea for a paragraph, use the following sources:

Journals In your journal, you record your experiences, thoughts, and feelings. By checking your journal, you can find many ideas to write about.

Brainstorming Another way to find ideas for paragraphs is through brainstorming. To brainstorm, begin with a general idea such as *movies* or *crafts*. Then, write down everything that comes to mind about this subject.

Clustering One form of brainstorming is called *clustering*. To use this method, write a general idea on a piece of paper. Circle it. Then write a related idea, circle it, and connect it to the general idea. Continue to write down ideas and to connect these to the general idea and to the other related ideas.

Interviews and Discussions Other people can also supply you with good writing ideas. For example, you might find a topic by interviewing someone who has done something interesting. You might also find a topic through an interesting class discussion.

Reading Other sources of good topics include books, magazines, newspapers, and reference works. When you read something that interests you, make a note about it in your journal.

Check It Out Here are some ideas that one student got by skimming the front page of a newspaper:

Fire in an office building
  –Heroism of fire department
  –Dangers of very tall buildings

Education bill passed
   –Is more money needed for schools?
   –How can schools be improved?

 • What other parts of a newspaper might supply excellent
   writing ideas?

Try Your Skill   Study the following example of clustering
based on the idea "deserts." Using this example, write three
good topics for paragraphs.

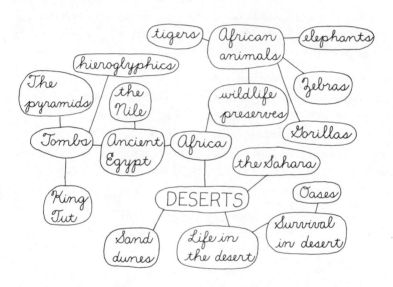

Now Write   Make a list of five good topics for paragraphs. To
find ideas, use the methods described in this lesson. Save your
topics in your folder.

A Perfect Fit

Pre-Writing: Narrowing a Topic

Here's the Idea To write an effective paragraph you must begin with a specific topic. A topic as general as "travel," for example, can only lead to a paragraph that is vague and dull.

> Traveling can be an educational experience. Going to a foreign country is certainly educational. Visiting an area with a different climate within your own country can be instructive, too. It is good to see how people work and live in other places.

However, if you narrow a topic, you can write a lively and informative paragraph. One simple way to narrow a general topic is to ask questions about it. Begin your questions with *who, what, where, when, why,* and *how.*

For example, to narrow the topic *travel,* you could ask a question beginning with *where.* By doing this, you might come up with topics such as these:

a trip to Arizona   hiking in Canada   riding by train across
                                              Canada

To narrow your topic even further, you might ask questions like these:

Who traveled?	my family and I
When did this happen?	last July
Why did we go?	to visit cousins
What did we see?	deserts, the Colorado River
How did we feel?	hot—temperatures between 108 and 120 degrees

By asking questions such as these, you might come up with a good topic: *What I learned about Arizona during a family trip.* These questions will also help you find specific details to include in your paragraph.

Check It Out   Read the following paragraph.

My favorite geography lesson was a two-week family trip to Yuma, Arizona. Last July we traveled to visit cousins who live in that desert community. As a native of Maine, I was fascinated by the southwestern United States. I saw desert areas surrounded by low, barren mountains. I saw lush green areas irrigated by the Colorado River and planted with vegetables, fruits, and cotton. I endured the region's intense summer heat, with highs between 108 and 120 degrees Fahrenheit. For the first time, I realized the powerful effect of geography on our daily lives.

- Why is this paragraph more interesting than the one in **Here's the Idea?**
- How did asking specific questions help this writer to narrow the topic of travel?

Try Your Skill   Choose two of these general topics. Write each topic on a piece of paper. Below each, write questions beginning with *who, what, where, when, why*, and *how*. Then, on a separate piece of paper, write two narrowed topics for each general topic you chose.

jobs   hobbies   winners   space   superstitions

Keep This in Mind

- To narrow a topic, ask questions beginning with *who, what, where, when, why*, and *how*.
- Make sure your topic is specific enough to be covered completely in a single paragraph.

Now Write   Choose one of the topics you wrote for **Now Write** in the previous lesson. Narrow this topic by asking questions about it. Write your questions, your answers, and your narrowed topic on a piece of paper. Save this paper in your folder.

On Target

Pre-Writing: Purpose and Audience

Here's the Idea   Before you begin to write, you must ask yourself two important questions:

What is my purpose?
Who are the people in my audience?

These questions will help you to focus your ideas. In other words, they will help you to decide what information to include in your paragraph. They will also help you to write in a way that is suited to your readers.

The **purpose** of a paragraph is what you want the paragraph to accomplish. A paragraph may serve any of the following purposes:

1. It may tell a story.
2. It may describe a person, place, thing, or event.
3. It may explain a process.
4. It may support an opinion.
5. It may define a word or phrase.

The **audience** of a paragraph includes all the people who will be reading it. Always think of the ages and interests of these people. Also think of how much your readers already know about your subject. Suppose, for example, that you are writing about how to plant a rose bush. If your readers were other experienced gardeners, you could include very specific, complex information. However, if your readers were unfamiliar with gardening, you would have to keep your explanation simple.

Check It Out   Read the following pre-writing notes for a paragraph on San Francisco's cable cars.

Possible Purposes:	to describe a cable car
	to explain how cable cars work
	to tell about my first ride on a cable car
	to persuade someone that cable cars are safe
Possible Audiences:	residents of San Francisco
	people who have never seen cable cars
	people who know a great deal about how machines operate
	people who do not know a great deal about machines
	a very nervous friend

- How would each purpose and audience affect the details that could be included in the paragraph?

Try Your Skill   Choose a subject you are very familiar with. The subject may be a hobby, a sport, or something you have learned in school. Imagine that you are going to write paragraphs for two different audiences. One is very familiar with your subject already. The other knows nothing about your subject. Write a narrowed topic and a list of details for each audience. Make sure that your topics and details suit the audience you are writing for.

Keep This in Mind

- Your purpose is what you want your writing to accomplish.
- Your audience is all the people who will read your writing.

Now Write   At the top of a piece of paper, write the narrowed topic you chose in the previous lesson. Below this, write the purpose of the paragraph you plan to write. Then, describe your audience. Save these notes in your folder.

What To Expect

Pre-Writing: A Good Topic Sentence

Here's the Idea You have learned that a topic sentence states the main idea of a paragraph. To be effective, a topic sentence must be informative, direct, and interesting.

An informative topic sentence is one that states the topic clearly and completely. Avoid vague, general topic sentences such as the following:

Cactuses are desert plants.

Instead, write a topic sentence that tells the reader exactly what to expect from the paragraph:

Cactuses come in many sizes, shapes, and colors.

To make a topic sentence direct, get to the point quickly. Avoid using unnecessary words to introduce the subject. Introduce the topic, not yourself. Do not begin with such phrases as "I think . . ." or "This paragraph is about . . . ."

I'd like to write about cactuses, which grow so well in a sunny window in my apartment.

Instead, write topic sentences that are direct:

Cactuses are easily cared for.

Cactuses, with their striking shapes, are among the most beautiful of desert plants.

To make a topic sentence interesting, find a striking or unusual way to express the main idea. There may even be ideas that you want to express in a humorous way.

A cactus is a prickly, peculiar, living sculpture.

Check It Out   Read the following topic sentences.

1. My first driving lesson was almost my last.
2. The first course, mud-colored soup, was the highlight of the meal.
3. I'm going to tell you why school is important.
4. This paragraph is about building a glider.

- Which of these sentences are informative and direct? Which sentences state the main idea in an interesting way?

Try Your Skill   Rewrite these eight topic sentences. Use real or imaginary details. Make each sentence informative, interesting, and direct.

1. I am going to tell you about the first meal I ever cooked.
2. This paragraph will tell you how to get a good job.
3. Molly, my sister who was thirteen in May, broke her arm.
4. I would now like to describe my invention.
5. The purpose of this report is to argue for a lower speed limit on superhighways.
6. Many people are interested in daredevil activities, and one such activity is parachuting.
7. I know what patriotism is.
8. There are many sports to play, but baseball is my favorite.

Keep This in Mind

- Write topic sentences that are informative, interesting, and direct.

Now Write   Write several topic sentences. Each should state the main idea of the topic you narrowed in Part 3, **A Perfect Fit.** Try to express your main idea in several different ways. Make sure your sentences are informative, interesting, and direct. Save your topic sentences in your folder.

A Gathering

Pre-Writing: Developing a Paragraph

Here's the Idea At this point, you have completed several steps in the process of writing a paragraph. You have chosen and narrowed your topic. You have identified your purpose and audience. You have also written a topic sentence that states your main idea. Now you are ready to develop this main idea with specific details. These details will be part of the pre-writing notes for your paragraph.

The types of details you will use depend on the type of paragraph you are writing. If you are writing a description, you will use **sensory details.** These are details that tell how a subject looks, sounds, tastes, feels, and smells. If you are writing a story, your details will be a list of **incidents,** or events. If you are supporting an opinion, you may use **facts and statistics.** You may also tell a very short story, or **anecdote,** to prove your point. Finally, if you are explaining or defining a word or phrase, you may decide to give **specific examples.**

To gather the details you need, use any of the following methods: observation, interviewing, discussion, reading, brainstorming, clustering, and research.

Make sure you choose a method that suits your purpose. Suppose that you want to describe a park. One way to gather the information you need would be to go to the park. Once there, you could observe the sights, sounds, tastes, smell, and feel of the things around you. If you want to explain how a motorcycle engine works, you might do some research in the library. You might also interview a motorcycle mechanic.

When choosing sources of information, always make sure that your sources are reliable. For more information on choosing sources, see Section 21, **Critical Thinking,** on pages 281–299.

Check It Out   Read the following paragraph.

A mosaic is a kind of decoration made by fitting together pieces of colored glass or stone. The pieces of glass or stone are called "tesserae." They are set in cement to form a design or picture. Usually, mosaics are made on flat surfaces such as floors, walls, and ceilings. Mosaics are not very common today. However, they were very popular among many ancient cultures. The mosaics of the ancient Greeks, Romans, and Mayans are particularly beautiful.

· What kinds of details does the paragraph include?
· Where might the writer have found these details?

Try Your Skill   Here are three possible topic sentences. Tell what kind of details you might use to develop each one.

1. The first computer bore little resemblance to the sleek, compact models of today.
2. The last time I went fishing, I almost ended up as bait.
3. An amoeba is a tiny animal that looks like water with a wall around it.

Keep This in Mind

· To develop a paragraph, use sensory details, incidents, facts and statistics, anecdotes, or specific examples.
· Gather details through observation, brainstorming, interviewing, discussion, clustering, research, and reading.

Now Write   Decide what kind of details you will need to develop your paragraph. Then, use the sources mentioned in this lesson to gather the details you will need. Save your prewriting notes in your folder.

The Way It Goes

Pre-Writing: Organizing a Paragraph

Here's the Idea The information in a paragraph must be arranged logically to be understood. There are several different methods of organization that may be used to arrange ideas in paragraphs.

Chronological order is used to tell a story, give directions, or to explain how something happens or is done. When using chronological order, present events as they occur or should occur.

Spatial order is used to present the details of a description. It shows how the things you are describing are related in space.

Order of importance is used to present the reasons, facts, or examples that support an opinion. When using order of importance, begin with the least important idea and move toward the most important.

General to specific order is used in some types of explanatory paragraphs. Begin with a general statement. Then add specific details to develop the main idea.

Most familiar to least familiar order is used for defining or describing things. Begin with details that are familiar to your readers. Then introduce less familiar details.

Comparison and contrast is used to show similarities or differences between two subjects. You can compare and contrast two subjects point by point. Or you can write first about just one subject and then about the second subject.

Check It Out Read the following poorly-organized paragraph.

A dangerously worn and tattered rope bridge spanned the river. When Jerry reached the other side, he felt relieved to be safely across the bridge. Jerry had always been afraid of heights. As he crossed the bridge, he felt a deep fear grip his stomach. When he looked down, he broke into a sweat. Halfway across the bridge, his knees began to shake. It was all he could do to keep going. The water raged angrily below.

- What is the purpose of this paragraph?
- What method of organization would best suit this purpose?
- How could this paragraph be improved?

Try Your Skill   The following is a list of topics for paragraphs. Tell what method of organization would best suit each of these topics.

1. The flying dragon is the oddest-looking creature on earth.

2. Taking good photographs can be quite easy if you follow a few simple guidelines.

3. Both trout and pike are fish native to northern waters, but their habits are very different.

4. There are many excellent reasons for studying a foreign language.

5. One lazy afternoon last summer, a car drove into our living room.

Keep This in Mind

- Arrange the details of a paragraph in a clear, logical order.
- Choose a method of organization that suits the purpose of your paragraph.

Now Write   Following the guidelines presented in this lesson, organize your pre-writing notes. Use a method of organization that suits the purpose of your paragraph. Save your organized notes in your folder.

At First Sight

Writing the First Draft

Here's the Idea Organizing your pre-writing notes is the last step in the pre-writing stage. After this step, you are ready to write your first draft. Do this by turning your pre-writing notes into sentences. Most paragraphs should contain sentences of the following kinds:

1. a topic sentence that states the main idea
2. several sentences that develop the idea presented in the topic sentence
3. a sentence that sums up the ideas presented in the rest of the paragraph

Some narrative paragraphs do not contain a topic sentence. In such paragraphs, the first sentence simply tells the first event in the story. However, all other paragraphs should contain an interesting and informative topic sentence.

As you write your first draft, concentrate on your organization and content. At this point, do not be too concerned with errors in grammar, usage, and mechanics. You will be able to correct these errors at a later time.

As you write, try to make sure that your readers will understand how the ideas in your paragraph are related. To do this, use transitional words and phrases. Choose transitions that suit the organization of your paragraph. If your paragraph is arranged in chronological order, use transitional words and phrases that express time. If your paragraph is arranged in spatial order, use transitional words and phrases that show place or position.

Check It Out   Read this descriptive paragraph.

The interior of Bonnie's Theatrical Supplies was strange and wonderful. The air smelled of greasepaint and powder. Glass display cases ran the length of the store on either side. Inside these cases were dozens of latex noses and chins. There were also assorted tubes and tins of makeup and rows of beards, mustaches, and wigs. On the walls hung costumes and masks. Some were covered with rhinestones, some with spangles or beads. A few were made of gold or silver lamé.

- What transitional words and phrases did the writer use?

Try Your Skill   Rewrite this paragraph. Add transitional words and phrases to show the kind of order being used.

The concert was a disaster. The crew set up the instruments and amplifiers. One of the amps blew up and had to be replaced. The crowd grew impatient. The band came to the stage. They started the first song. The lead guitarist broke a string. A stagehand brought out a new guitar. The band started to play the same song. The microphones went dead. The concert hall manager came out to the stage to apologize.

Keep This in Mind

- In your first draft, put your pre-writing notes into sentence form.

Now Write   Read your organized pre-writing notes. Then write the topic sentence and the body of your paragraph. In the next lesson, you will write an ending for your paragraph. Save your work in your folder.

The Last Word

The First Draft: Ending a Paragraph

Here's the Idea Every paragraph should end with a strong concluding sentence. The purpose of this sentence is to sum up or tie together the ideas in the rest of the paragraph. In this way, the ending sentence helps readers to understand the ideas presented.

A good ending makes a clear, final statement that works with the other sentences in the paragraph. A good ending should not introduce new information. In fact, often an ending may simply restate the idea of the topic sentence in a slightly different way.

A good ending should also be interesting. Sometimes it may be appropriate for an ending to be surprising or humorous. In every paragraph you write, try to express your idea in an ending sentence that is clear and effective.

Check It Out Read this paragraph.

I left home this morning as usual, never suspecting anything was wrong. However, a group of schoolchildren who passed me on the sidewalk turned and ran. Then the clerk at the newsstand stared at me, horror-stricken. Alarmed, I raced home, slammed the door, and dashed to the bedroom mirror. When I saw my face, I tried to scream. No sounds came out. Only the buzzing of my alarm clock rescued me from this nightmare.

• Is the ending sentence of this paragraph effective?

Try Your Skill Read these paragraphs with ineffective ending sentences. Rewrite or replace the endings. Make your endings clear and interesting.

1   It is difficult to believe that the ostrich and the hummingbird belong to the same family. They are both birds, but they represent the extremes of the species. An ostrich can stand as tall as eight feet and can weigh as much as 300 pounds. Its clumsy size prevents it from flying. On the other hand, the hummingbird is the smallest of birds. This agile creature weighs less than a penny. *There are both tiny and huge members of the monkey family, too.*

2   We were pleased when the branch of First Bank opened near our apartment building. However, the convenience of its location was overshadowed by inconvenience at first. At the main bank, I had been accustomed to instant recognition. At the branch, none of the tellers knew me. Every time I cashed a check, I had to show a pocketful of identification and account numbers. *The bank certainly has a strong security system.*

3   I hope to be the engineer who designs the perfect car. The body of my car would be completely rust-proof. The tires would never wear out, and they would be as safe on icy roads as on dry ones. The frame of the car could withstand a severe crash with only minor damage. Best of all, the car would run on a small electric battery that would require recharging only once a year. *Maybe the perfect car will be developed soon.*

Keep This in Mind

- A good ending sentence should tie together the related ideas of a paragraph. It should also be clear and interesting.

Now Write   Review the topic sentence and body of your first draft. Think about what you have written. Then write an ending that sums up your main idea in an interesting way. Save your completed first draft in your folder.

One More Time

Revising a Paragraph

Here's the Idea   The last stage in the process of writing is revising. When you revise a paragraph, you read it carefully to see what improvements need to be made. Then, you make changes until the paragraph is the best it can be. These changes may be in content, presentation, or style.

Content refers to the ideas and details in your paragraph. To revise your content, check your topic sentence. Make sure it is informative, interesting, and direct. Then, check the paragraph as a whole for unity. A paragraph has unity if all its details are related to the main idea given in the topic sentence. Finally, check to make sure you have developed your main idea completely. If necessary, add more details to support your main idea.

Presentation refers to the way in which your ideas are organized. To revise your presentation, check your paragraph for coherence. A paragraph is coherent if its ideas are arranged in a clear, logical order. The reader should be able to move smoothly from one idea to the next. The method of organization should be clear and should suit your purpose.

Style refers to the language you have used in your paragraph. Always make sure that your words are right for your audience and purpose. Check for words that are dull or uninteresting. Replace these with strong, specific verbs, adjectives, and adverbs.

Finally, you must proofread your paragraph. Find and correct any errors in grammar, capitalization, punctuation, and spelling. When this is done, make a final copy and proofread this copy one last time.

Check It Out Read this revised paragraph.

Flies are *well named. They are* among the best fliers, *in the animal kingdom.* around. When you ~~here~~ *hear* a house fly buzzing, you are actually h*e*ring its wings, ~~B~~eating at the *incredible* rate of two hundred times a second. Being able to fly this fast enables the housefly to escape from *enemies such as frogs and* people. The housefly ~~flies~~ *can travel* at ~~great~~ *a* speeds, *of over four and a half miles per hour.*

- What changes were made in the content, presentation, and style of this paragraph?

Try Your Skill Revise this first draft. Follow the guidelines presented in this lesson.

In my opinion, we should start a class in first aid at our school. Most importantly, we could learn teckniques to save a persons life. Second a person trained in first aid can give imediate help to victems of accidents. Before professional help arrives. For example someone who knows how to apply first aide to a burn could prevent infection from setting in. My sister Sandra knows first aid. A first aid course would give students pracktical knowledge that they would have forever.

Keep This in Mind

- To revise a paragraph, check for ways to improve your content, presentation, and style. Then, proofread your work.

Now Write Revise your first draft. Follow the guidelines presented in this lesson. Proofread your revised draft. Then make a clean, neat final copy. Save your finished paragraph in your folder.

The Process of Writing

The Process of Writing

Throughout the rest of this book, you will be practicing many different kinds of writing. You will write narratives, descriptions, explanations, and a research paper. Although the kind of writing you do will change, one aspect of your writing will remain the same. You will always use the three stages of the process of writing—pre-writing, writing the first draft, and revising—to plan, write, and improve your paragraphs and compositions.

Pre-Writing   The planning stage of the process of writing is called pre-writing. During pre-writing, you will complete the following activities.

1. Choose and narrow a subject. Look for a subject that interests you and that you know something about or want to learn about. You can find interesting writing ideas through brainstorming, clustering, reading, research, interviewing, discussing, and looking in your journal. Then narrow your subject so that it is specific enough to be covered well in a paragraph, a composition, or a research paper.

2. Define your purpose. Why are you writing? Do you want to tell a story, describe something or someone, explain a process, express an opinion, or define something? Knowing your purpose will help you to focus your writing.

3. Identify your audience. Who are your readers? What are their interests and opinions? How old are they? How much do they know about your subject? If you know your audience, you can suit your writing to your readers.

4. Gather details. Look for ideas to support and develop your topic. You can use sensory details, specific examples, facts and statistics, or incidents or anecdotes. You can use the same techniques to gather information that you used to choose a topic.

5. Organize your information. You must arrange the details you have gathered into a logical order. You might choose chronological order, spatial order, the order of importance, general to specific order, most familiar to least familiar order, and comparison and contrast. Whichever method you choose, be sure that it suits the type of writing you are doing.

Pre-Writing

You list possible topics and select one.

first day on the job   trip to Museum of Art

the homecoming dance   renting roller skates

⑤ pouring water on Mrs. Jackson

president of bank

② water boy, Chez Leslie

very expensive

a real disaster

① uniform lost

white satin/red velvet

organ grinder's monkey

④ car backfires

had to get work permit

③ bumping into waiter

great tasting food

⑥ tripping over chair

soaking wet

You list details, choose those that develop your topic, and organize them.

You identify your purpose and audience.

Writing the First Draft   When you have finished all of your planning, you are ready to write your first draft. When you write a first draft, concentrate on turning your details into sentences and paragraphs. Follow your organized pre-writing notes as you write, but don't be afraid to experiment with the order of your ideas. Let your ideas flow naturally as you write. Don't interrupt this flow by questioning your grammar, capitalization, punctuation, or spelling. You will have time later to correct any mistakes you make.

Writing the First Draft

You write a paragraph about your topic.

> The first day of my job was a disaster. My problems began when I got there. I was a water boy at the restaurant Chez Leslie. My uniform was lost. So I had to get another one. The white satin pants were short. The velvet jacket was tight. I looked like an organ grinders monkey. I bumped into a waiter. The waiter was carrying a tray of dishes. The dishes and the waiter crashed to the floor. I helped the waiter clean up. I went back to filling glasses. I was pouring water for Mrs. Jackson. A car backfired. I poured half a glass of water into Mrs. Jacksons lap. I apologized. I backed into a chair and fell to the floor. I thought, things can't get any worse.

Revising   A first draft is just a rough version of your written work. During the third stage of the process of writing, called revising, you smooth out the rough edges. You work to improve what you have written.

When you revise, you should pay attention to the content, presentation, and style of your writing.

Content refers to the ideas and details you have presented. To check the content of your writing, ask yourself these questions.

1. Does each topic sentence express the main idea of a paragraph?
2. Do all of my details relate directly to my main idea?
3. Have I included enough details to develop my main idea fully?
4. Does my conclusion sum up my ideas?
5. Have I fulfilled my purpose?

Presentation refers to the way your writing is organized. The following questions will help you to check your presentation.

1. Does my writing have a clear beginning, middle, and ending?
2. Have I arranged my details in a logical order?
3. Does my method of organization suit the kind of writing I am doing?
4. Do my ideas flow smoothly from one to another?

Style refers to the way you have expressed yourself in your writing. Most writers have different styles. Still, there are some examples of good style that are common to all writers.

1. Is each topic sentence interesting enough to capture a reader's attention? Is each topic sentence direct, not wordy?
2. Have I used lively, vivid language?
3. Is my language well suited to my audience?
4. Have I included transitional words and phrases to help the reader see how my ideas are connected?

Proofreading When you are satisfied with the content, presentation, and style of your writing, proofread your work. Look for and correct any errors in grammar, capitalization, punctuation, and spelling.

As you revise your first draft, use the following proofreading marks to show your corrections and changes.

Proofreading Symbols

Symbol	Meaning	Example
∧	add	would ∧gone *have*
≡	capitalize	United ≡states
/	make lower case	our club /President
∾	reverse	th∾e∾r
ℛ	take out	finished (the) the race
¶	make new paragraph	....be over.¶New ideas
⊙	period	....and stop⊙Before we
∧	add comma	Red, blue ∧and green are

Revising

You rewrite. You express your idea in a different way.

The first day ∧at ∧of my ∧new job was a disaster. ¶My problems began when I got there. I was ∧a ∧the new water boy at the ~~restaurant~~ Chez Leslie. ∧the most expensive restaurant in town My uniform ~~was lost,~~ ∧had been So I had to ~~get anoth-er one.~~ ∧replacement. ∧wear a The white satin pants were ∧short, ∧and The ∧red velvet jacket ~~was tight,~~ ∧so I looked like an organ grinder's monkey. ∧Clutching my crystal water pitcher, I bumped into a waiter, ~~The waiter was~~ carrying a tray of dishes. The dishes and the waiter crashed to the floor. ∧After I helped the waiter clean up, I went back to filling glasses. ∧As I was pouring water for Mrs. Jackson. ∧the president of the bank, A car backfired ∧outside. I poured half a glass of water into Mrs. Jacksons ~~lap. I apologized.~~ ∧Stammering an apology, I backed into a chair and ∧tumbled ~~fell~~ to the floor. ∧After tonight, I thought, things can't get any worse.

The Final Copy When you have finished revising and proof-reading your writing, copy it in its final form. Write carefully. Make your work as neat as possible. Proofread your final copy. Neatly correct any errors you find.

Final Copy

The first day at my new job was a disaster. I was the new water boy at Chez Leslie, the most expensive restaurant in town. My problems began immediately. My uniform had been lost, so I had to wear a replacement. The white satin pants were so short and the red velvet jacket so tight, I looked like an organ grinder's monkey. Clutching my crystal water pitcher, I bumped into a waiter carrying a tray of dishes. The dishes and the waiter crashed to the floor. After I helped the waiter clean up, I went back to filling glasses. As I was pouring water for Mrs. Jackson, the president of the bank, a car backfired outside. I poured half a glass of water onto Mrs. Jackson. Stammering an apology, I backed into a chair and tumbled to the floor. I was soaked from head to toe. After tonight, I thought, things can't get any worse.

The Narrative Paragraph

In Any Event

Pre-Writing: Developing a Narrative

Here's the Idea   Every kind of paragraph has a different purpose. Therefore, each kind of paragraph is developed and organized differently.

One kind of paragraph is called a *narrative paragraph*. The purpose of a narrative paragraph is to tell a story. The story you tell may be something that actually happened to you or someone else. For example, you could write about your first day at your new job or the time you took your driving test. The story may also be imaginary. Whether it is real or imaginary, a narrative paragraph may be serious or humorous.

The first step when you begin a narrative paragraph is to choose a topic. You might look through your journal for ideas. Also, think about favorite family stories. Search your imagination—is a good story idea waiting there? Once you have selected a topic, narrow it. That is, make it specific enough so that it can be developed completely in just one paragraph. Remember, the story you choose to tell should be interesting. It should also have a clear beginning, middle, and ending.

The next step is to gather details for the paragraph. An interesting narrative is made up of many separate events. It also contains vivid sensory and descriptive details. If you are writing a true story, you will recall these events and details from your memory. If you are writing an imaginary story, you will use your imagination to invent the events and details. One method of gathering details is to ask yourself questions about the story you are going to tell. Ask *who, what, when, where, why,* and *how* questions about the people, the places, and the things that are a part of your story. Answer each question with a specific detail. These details will enable you to write an interesting, vivid narrative.

Check It Out   Here are some pre-writing notes for a *narrative* paragraph.

Who?   Alan and Ramona
What?   found a sick bear cub—brought cub to forest service vets who saved its life
When?   last summer, during August heat wave/drought
Where?   Yellowstone National Park
How?   working as junior forest rangers

- How will the answers to these questions help the writer to develop the narrative?

Try Your Skill   Look at the notes in **Check It Out**. Add some sensory details to these notes. Use your imagination to make a list of five to ten sensory details. These details might relate to the cub, the park, the time of year, or any other aspect of the story. Compare your details with those of your classmates.

Keep This in Mind

- A narrative paragraph tells a brief real or imaginary story.
- A narrative is developed with details that tell *who, what, when, where, why,* and *how.*
- Include specific and sensory details in a narrative paragraph.

Now Write   Think of an interesting story that would make a good narrative paragraph. Narrow your topic so that it is specific enough to be completely developed in one paragraph. Gather specific and sensory details for your story. Save your pre-writing notes in your folder.

Timely Advice

Pre-Writing: Using Chronological Order

Here's the Idea   After gathering details for your narrative paragraph, the next step is to organize your pre-writing notes. You need to arrange the incidents and details of your story into an order that makes sense. Begin with the first thing that happened. Then continue with the next event, and so on, until you reach the last thing that happened. When you do this, you are arranging your notes in *chronological order*. *Chronological* means "arranged in the order of time." This is the best order to use when you tell a story. Read the following narrative paragraph. Notice how the author presents the incidents in chronological order.

> Very early in the morning George's father got up to go to work in a fish market. Sophie left at about eight for her long ride in the subway to a cafeteria in the Bronx. George had his coffee by himself, then hung around in the house. When the house, a five-room railroad flat above a butcher store, got on his nerves, he cleaned it up—mopped the floors with a wet mop and put things away. But most of the time he sat in his room. In the afternoons he listened to the ball game.
>
> —BERNARD MALAMUD

Check It Out   Read this narrative paragraph.

> When he had dropped out of sight over a little dip in the road, Mama turned to the black ones, but she spoke to herself. "He is nearly a man now," she said. "It will be a nice thing to have a man in the house again." Her eyes sharpened on the children. "Go to the rocks now. The tide is going out. There will be abalones to be found." She put the iron hooks into their hands and saw them down the steep trail to the reefs. She

brought the smooth stone metate to the doorway and sat grinding her corn to flour and looking occasionally at the road over which Pepe had gone. The noonday came and then the afternoon, when the little ones beat the abalones on a rock to make them tender and Mama patted the tortillas to make them thin. They ate their dinner as the red sun was plunging down toward the ocean. They sat on the doorsteps and watched a big white moon come over the mountaintops. —JOHN STEINBECK

- How does this paragraph show chronological order?

Try Your Skill Here is a list of notes for a narrative paragraph. Notice that these events are out of order. Arrange these notes in chronological order.

five miles out to sea—anchored boat, donned wet suits
dawn—Maria, Franco sail out of harbor
they swim deeper—Maria sights masts of sunken ship
radio location to Coast Guard, then dive into icy water
swim back to surface, excited at great discovery
exploring ship, discover sea chest filled with silver/gold

Keep This in Mind

- Organize the incidents and details for a narrative paragraph in chronological order.

Now Write Read the pre-writing notes you made for your narrative paragraph. Arrange these notes in chronological order. Save your organized notes in your folder.

•

The Mind's Eye

Pre-Writing: Choosing a Point of View

Here's the Idea   Suppose you were planning to write a narrative paragraph about the night a neighboring apartment building burned down. In addition to deciding what details to include in your story, you must also decide who your narrator is going to be. Will it be someone who is a character in the story, such as a firefighter or fleeing resident? Or will it be someone outside the story, a nonparticipant who simply reports the action? Your choice of a narrator depends on your choice of point of view. **Point of view** means the eyes and mind through which something is written.

When you choose the **first-person point of view,** the narrator is a character in the story. The narrator is identified by the first-person pronoun *I*. *I* tells what he or she sees, hears, and thinks. This point of view makes the reader feel like a part of the story. This is because a first-person narrator seems to be speaking directly to the reader.

When you choose the **third-person point of view,** the narrator is an outsider. This point of view uses the third-person pronouns *he, she,* and *they.* If you choose the **third-person limited** point of view, the narrator sees and hears everything that happens. The narrator cannot, however, tell what any character is thinking or feeling. If you choose the **third-person omniscient** point of view, the narrator *can* tell what the characters think and feel. The word *omniscient* means "all-knowing." This point of view allows the reader to see into the hearts and minds of the characters.

Check It Out   Read this paragraph.

Arnold sat in the rocker until the last man had filed out. While his family was out in the kitchen bidding the callers good

126

night and the cars were driving away down the dirt lane to the highway, he picked up one of the kerosene lamps and slipped quickly up the stairs. In his room he undressed by lamplight, although he and Eugie had always undressed in the dark, and not until he was lying in his bed did he blow out the flame. He felt nothing, not any grief. There was only the same immense silence and crawling inside of him; it was the way the house and fields felt under a merciless sun. —GINA BERRIAULT

• From what specific point of view is this paragraph written? How do you know?

Try Your Skill   Rewrite the paragraph in **Check It Out**. Use the first-person point of view.

Keep This in Mind

- Point of view shows through whose eyes a story is told.
- With the first-person point of view, the narrator, *I*, reports what the characters say and do.
- With the third-person limited point of view, the narrator is an outsider. The narrator reports what the characters say and do, but not what they think or feel.
- With the third-person omniscient point of view, the narrator is "all knowing." The narrator reports what the characters say, do, think, and feel.

Now Write   Review your organized pre-writing notes and decide on a point of view for your narrative paragraph. Choose whichever point of view seems best suited to the story you are telling. At the end of your notes write *first-person, third-person limited,* or *third-person omniscient*. Save your notes in your folder.

Take Time

Writing the First Draft

Here's the Idea   By now you have completed all of the prewriting steps in the process of writing a narrative paragraph. You have selected and narrowed your topic. You have listed your details and organized them in chronological order. You have chosen a point of view. Now you are ready to turn your notes into a first draft. Remember that at this stage of the process you do not have to make your work perfect. Write your story freely. Follow your notes, and add any new thoughts that occur to you. You may also leave out ideas that no longer seem to develop your main idea.

Because a narrative paragraph tells a story, you do not have to begin with a topic sentence that states the main idea. Instead, you can write an opening sentence that either sets the scene or tells about the first event.

When you write a narrative, it is important to give your reader a clear idea of what happened when. The order of the events in your story can be made clear by using words and phrases that signal the passing of time. Here is a list of transitional words and phrases that will help you make the order of events in your narrative paragraph clear to the reader.

first	now	when	at the same time
then	before	soon	by the time
next	earlier	suddenly	at the beginning
while	after	immediately	in the middle
last	later	finally	at the end

Sometimes you may need to use more specific transitions than these. For example, you may want to say *after two hours, at noon,* or *in 1982.* Use a variety of transitional words and phrases in your narrative.

Check It Out   Now read this paragraph.

Eric blew his whistle and waited by the side of the boat. Soon, in an explosion of warm ocean water, Lily appeared. Laughing, Eric dived into the water beside the trained dolphin. For a while, they swam and floated and practiced diving together. Now and then Lily would leap high above Eric into the air. Suddenly, Lily uttered a series of barks and clicks. Eric answered immediately with his whistle. He let Lily know that he had understood her warning about the shark. By the time Eric was safely back on board the boat, Lily was nowhere in sight.

- Point out the transitional words and phrases that help to show chronological order.

Try Your Skill   Rewrite the following paragraph. Add transitional words and phrases that show chronological order.

The pulsing blue light sped across the horizon. We saw it pass overhead. We jumped into the car and tried to follow it. The light hovered above Tower Hill. It seemed to settle to the ground. We sped toward the hill. A police officer pulled us over to the side of the road. We told her about the light, but she didn't believe us.

Keep This in Mind

- In a narrative paragraph, include transitional words and phrases to show chronological order.

Now Write   Write the first draft of your narrative paragraph. Use transitional words and phrases to make the order of events clear to the reader. Save your first draft in your folder.

Your Best Shot

Revising Your Narrative Paragraph

Here's the Idea   You are now ready to complete the final stage in writing your narrative paragraph. You will be looking now at the details of your narrative, improving your paragraph word by word. As you revise, keep these questions in mind.

1. Have I written a good opening sentence? Will it capture the reader's interest?
2. Have I included vivid sensory details that bring the incidents and characters to life?
3. Have I arranged the incidents in chronological order?
4. Have I used one point of view throughout the paragraph?
5. Have I used transitional words and phrases that show chronological order?

As you revise your paragraph, pay special attention to the verbs you have used. Avoid using too many state-of-being verbs like *is*, *seems*, or *become*. They are weak. Instead, use action verbs. For example, instead of saying "The lion *was* behind a rock," say "The lion *crouched* behind a rock." Your sentence will immediately become more interesting.

Also, try to replace general verbs with specific verbs. Instead of using a vague word like *went*, think about exactly how the lion moved. Did he *creep* or *sneak*, *leap* or *pounce?*

The final step of revision is to proofread for errors in grammar, capitalization, punctuation, and spelling. Correct any error that you find.

Check It Out   Read the following paragraph.

The thunder rumbled louder, sending the barnyard chickens into a flurry of flapping and squawking. Black storm clouds piled ever higher as the winds raged, flattening the field of wheat. Finally the rain came, driving hard, to hammer the windows, rattle the gate, and scour our dusty corner of the earth.

- Point out the strong, specific verbs in this paragraph.

Try Your Skill Revise the following paragraph. Improve it by adding transitions and by replacing the verbs in italics with stronger, more specific verbs.

Rob *got* out of bed. A loud noise *was* in the house. Rob thought, "The smoke alarm!" He *left* his room and began *knocking* on other bedroom doors. His sister *came* out of her room. She *went* to the phone. Smoke began to *go* into the hallway. She dialed the fire department. Rob took his parents and younger brother downstairs and out the door. They heard a siren. Two fire trucks *came* to a stop. Rob's sister *came* out of the house. The firefighters *went* into the house. Fortunately, the fire was small. It was out in no time. The family *went* back in to begin cleaning up the mess.

Keep This in Mind

- Revise your narrative paragraph to make it clear, lively, and interesting.
- Include specific, sensory details.
- Keep the same point of view throughout the paragraph.
- Use transitional words and phrases to show chronological order.
- Replace weak verbs with strong and specific ones.

Now Write Revise your narrative paragraph following the guidelines in this lesson. Then make a final copy. Proofread your paragraph one last time. Save your narrative in your folder.

The Descriptive Paragraph

Impressions

Pre-Writing: Gathering Sensory Details

Here's the Idea Have you ever been somewhere or seen something so special that you had to tell someone about it? Describing is something that you do all the time. You can preserve your memories by writing a descriptive paragraph.

The purpose of a descriptive paragraph is to describe a person, place, or thing as clearly as possible. When you write a descriptive paragraph, you are trying to share an experience with your reader.

To develop an effective descriptive paragraph, you must use sensory details. Sensory details describe things that can be *seen, heard, felt, smelled,* and *tasted.*

Once you have chosen a subject for your paragraph, make a list of sensory details that will help you to describe your subject. Look for details that appeal to as many of the five senses as possible. The best way to gather sensory details is to make notes as you are observing your subject. You can also gather sensory details by searching your memory. Picture in your mind the person, place, or thing that you want to describe. Select specific sensory words that will bring the subject to life for your readers. Notice the sensory details in this description.

> In my Wisconsin, the leaves change before the snows come. In the air there is the smell of wild rice and venison cooking. When the winds come whispering through the forests, they carry the smell of the leaves. In the evenings, the loon calls, lonely. Birds sing their last songs before leaving. Bears dig roots and eat late fall berries, fattening for their long winter sleep. Later, when the first snows fall, one awakens in the morning to find the world white and beautiful and clean.
>
> —THOMAS S. WHITECLOUD

Check It Out   Read the following description.

Evenings were spent mainly on the back porches where screen doors slammed in the darkness with those really very special summertime sounds. And, sometimes, when Chicago nights got too steamy, the whole family got into the car and went to the park and slept out in the open on blankets. Those were, of course, the best times of all because the grownups were invariably reminded of having been children in the South and told the best stories then. And it was also cool and sweet to be on the grass and there was usually the scent of freshly cut lemons or melons in the air. Daddy would lie on his back, as fathers must, and explain about how men thought the stars above us came to be and how far away they were.

—LORRAINE HANSBERRY

· Point out the sensory details in the paragraph. Which senses does the writer appeal to?

Try Your Skill   Think about the last sporting event you attended as a spectator. Make a list of sensory details to describe the event. Try to choose details that appeal to all five senses. Compare your list with those of your classmates.

Keep This in Mind
· Use sensory details to create a vivid description.
· Gather details from direct observation or from memory.

Now Write   Choose a person, place, or thing to describe. List as many sensory details about your subject as you can. Save your list in your folder.

In Place

Pre-Writing: Using Spatial Order

Here's the Idea An effective description creates a vivid impression through the use of sensory details. An effective description is also well organized. If the details are presented in a haphazard order, your description will not be vivid and clear.

A description can be organized in a number of ways. When you are deciding how to arrange your details, remember that your purpose is to share an experience with your readers. Organize your description so that your readers will see as you saw, hear as your heard, feel as you felt, and so on.

One clear way to organize a descriptive paragraph is to use spatial order. **Spatial order** shows how the various parts of a subject are related to each other in space. Start with the most important or obvious detail. Then list the other details in the order they are related to the first detail. You could describe a subject from left to right, from top to bottom, or from near to far. Choose a pattern of spatial order that suits your subject. For example it would make more sense to describe a beach scene from near to far than from top to bottom.

Another way to organize a description is to arrange the details in the order that you want the reader to notice them. Suppose you were describing a crowded store during the holiday shopping season. You might first describe the noise in the store, then describe the way the crowd looks, and finally describe the way the crowd acts.

However you choose to organize the details for a descriptive paragraph, choose an order that is well suited to the subject of the description.

Check It Out   Read this description.

Lined up across the stage stood ten finalists. Smiling nervously, they were avoiding looking at the front row of seats
where the group of judges sat huddled. Instead, those dancers
who had survived the final audition stared straight ahead. They
watched the orchestra directly in front of them filling the tense
moments with soft music. Sometimes, their eyes wandered
over the heads of the musicians to the sea of faces filling the
hall. There they hoped to spot the warm, encouraging smile of
a mother or cousin or friend.

- How does this description use spatial order?

Try Your Skill   Make a list of sensory details that describe
the contents of your school locker. Then arrange these details
logically. Arrange the details in some form of spatial order or in
the order that you want a reader to notice them. Compare your
notes with those of your classmates.

Keep This in Mind

- Organize the details for a descriptive paragraph
  logically. Choose some form of spatial order, or
  arrange the details in the order a reader should
  notice them.

Now Write   Take out the pre-writing notes you've gathered
for your descriptive paragraph. Organize your notes logically.
You might want to try two or three different ways of arranging
them until you find the order that works best for your subject.
Save your organized notes in your folder.

What's in a Word?

Pre-Writing: Creating Mood

Here's the Idea   When you write a descriptive paragraph, you share an experience by including details that will bring the experience to life for your reader. Another way you can share an experience is through mood. **Mood** is the particular feeling suggested by a piece of writing.

A writer expresses mood through language. Nouns, verbs, adjectives, and adverbs can all suggest mood. The two paragraphs below describe the same scene, but suggest very different feelings. Compare the nouns, verbs, adjectives, and adverbs used in the two paragraphs.

> The deserted beach was littered with broken shells and dead fish. An overturned, rotting rowboat lay half-buried in the sand. Sea gulls cried mournfully above the gray, lifeless sea. I shivered as I wandered in the damp, chilly air.

> The beach was bathed in a light morning mist. A bright yellow sailboat bobbed on the waves, and sea gulls wheeled overhead and dove for their breakfast. The salt spray in my face made me feel alive as I jogged along the white sand.

As you plan your descriptive paragraph, consider what mood you want to create. Then think of the nouns, verbs, adjectives, and adverbs that will help you to suggest that feeling.

Check It Out   Read this paragraph.

> Robin awoke feeling as if she were inside a blast furnace. The blinding glare of the noonday sun forced her to close her eyes. The intense rays were scorching her skin. Her throat was parched, and she was drenched with sweat. Robin watched the intense waves of heat flickering around her like the breath of an angry dragon. The gritty sand sizzled under her feet as she searched for shelter.

- What mood has the writer created?
- Which specific words help to create that mood?

Try Your Skill Read the following description. Imagine that the scene being described is a stormy and cold day in the middle of winter. Change the words in italics to create the mood suggested by a cold, stormy, winter day.

When I reached the top of the mountain, I scanned the horizon. It was a *bright, beautiful* afternoon. The wind *slipped quietly* through the trees, and clouds *drifted lazily* across the sky. Everywhere I looked I saw the *soft green* of *springtime*. I felt *relaxed* and *peaceful*.

Keep This in Mind

- Mood is the particular feeling suggested by a piece of writing.
- Nouns, verbs, adjectives, and adverbs help to create mood.

Now Write What kind of mood would you like to express in the descriptive paragraph you are planning? List nouns, verbs, adjectives, and adverbs that will help you create that mood. Save your list in your folder.

Get the Picture

Writing the First Draft

Here's the Idea   You have listed sensory details to describe a certain subject, and you have arranged the details in a logical order. You have also made a list of words that will help you to express a particular mood or feeling. Now you are ready to turn your pre-writing notes into the first draft of your descriptive paragraph.

As you write, keep your subject clearly in mind. To help your reader experience your subject as clearly as you did, include transitional words and phrases. Transitions in a descriptive paragraph tell *where*. Notice these transitional words and phrases.

> *Around* the woman's waist was a wide embroidered sash. *On* her *left* wrist dangled three silver bracelets, and a checkered cloth lay *over* the basket *in* her *right* hand.

Here is a list of transitional words and phrases that you can use in your descriptive paragraph.

above	beside	in the center	over
across	between	near	side by side
against	by	next to	south
ahead of	down	north	throughout
at the end of	east	on	to the left
at the top	facing	on the bottom	to the right
around	in	on the corner	under
behind	in back of	on the edge	up
beneath	in front of	outside	west

Check It Out   Read this descriptive paragraph.

> The farmers drew up their chairs around the immense harvest table. At the end nearest the kitchen door there was a platter piled high with sliced ham. Next to it was an even larger

platter of fried chicken. Just past these platters were the bowls of mashed potatoes and gravy, and to the right of them the sliced tomatoes, green beans, and corn on the cob—a mountain of corn! At the base of the mountain was a dish of fresh, sweet butter. In the middle of the table sat plates of homemade bread and hot biscuits, and farther along to the right were large compotes of honey and preserves. At the far end of the table was an array of fragrant fruit pies and several cakes.

- Point out the transitional words and phrases in the paragraph. How do they help to make the description clear?

Try Your Skill   Add transitional words and phrases to the following paragraph to show spatial order. Try to create a clear mental picture for the reader.

The detective's room was a peculiar, triangular room. It had an old, musty odor to it. In the room, there was a painting of two dueling swordsmen. There was also a big oak chest and some lamps made of iron. The detective had a hand-carved wooden desk. It was obviously very old and nearly priceless. There was a window made with leaded glass panes. The door was on one wall.

Keep This in Mind

- In a descriptive paragraph, use transitional words and phrases that tell *where* to show spatial order.

Now Write   Write the first draft of your descriptive paragraph. Use transitional words and phrases to make your description clear. Save your work in your folder.

A Different Light

Revising Your Descriptive Paragraph

Here's the Idea   Now it is time to look over your first draft and see how it can be improved. You want to make your description clearer and more interesting. As you revise your work, keep these questions in mind.

1. Is the topic sentence clear and interesting? Does it introduce the subject of the description?

2. Have I developed the description with vivid sensory details? Have I used as many of the five senses—sight, sound, taste, touch, and smell—as possible?

3. Are the details arranged in a logical order?

4. Have I used specific nouns, verbs, adverbs, and adjectives to create a particular mood?

5. Have I used transitional words and phrases that tell *where* to make the order of the details clear?

When you have finished revising your paragraph, proofread it for errors in grammar, capitalization, punctuation, and spelling.

Check It Out   Notice how this writer improved his descriptive paragraph by revising it.

My friend's room is a *an electronic* jungle. *Her desk* There is always a pile of parts that *belong* go to some *broken* radio or tape deck that she is fixing for someone. Her stereo equipment lines the *west* wall, and the speakers *sit underneath* are in a *small color* cabinet. A TV sits on her bureau against the *north* other wall, and in a *pine* box *by her bed* are assorted head phones and video games. Her computer sits on a table *by the window.*

Try Your Skill   Revise this descriptive paragraph to make it clearer and more interesting. Pay special attention to the topic sentence, transitions, and word choice.

The island is not too big. No one lives there, but you can camp on it. There are lots of trees and undergrowth. You can take one of the paths if you want to hike. We fish there sometimes and eat our catch for supper. The fish tastes good cooked over a campfire. At night when the stars come out it's peaceful. You can hear some sounds. That's because there are some animals on the island.

Keep This in Mind

- Include strong sensory details in your description.
- Arrange your details in a logical order.
- Use transitional words and phrases to show spatial order.
- Select nouns, adjectives, verbs, and adverbs to suggest mood.

Now Write   Use the guidelines in this lesson to revise your first draft. When you are satisfied with your work, make a final copy. Proofread your descriptive paragraph one final time. Save it in your folder.

The Explanatory Paragraph

Explaining a Process

How About That?

Pre-Writing: Explaining a Process

Here's the Idea   A third kind of paragraph is the *explanatory paragraph*. The purpose of an explanatory paragraph is to explain something. For example, you may have written a paragraph for your science teacher explaining what *photosynthesis* means. You may have written a letter to the editor of your local newspaper expressing your opinion on some important issue.

One kind of explanatory paragraph explains a process. There are two types of processes that can be explained. The first type tells how to do something. For example, you could explain how to prepare a microscope slide for viewing. The second type of process tells how something happens or how something works. For example, you could explain how crop rotation protects the soil or how a microwave oven works.

After you have chosen a process to explain, remind yourself that the purpose of the paragraph is to explain something so clearly and accurately that your readers will understand it as well as you do. Begin by making a list of all of the steps in the process. Express each step clearly and simply. Be careful to include *all* of the important steps. Imagine the reader looking over your shoulder as you write your pre-writing notes. The reader would probably ask, "How does the process begin?" or "How do I start?" The next questions might be "What happens next?" or "Then what do I do?" Be sure your pre-writing notes answer questions like these.

Check It Out   On the next page are some pre-writing notes for a paragraph that explains a process.

Topic   How to grill corn on the cob

Steps   peel back outer layers of husks; remove all of the corn silk; carefully replace the husks; soak corn in water for one hour; remove corn, shake it to remove excess water; place on a hot charcoal grill; roast 30 minutes, turning 2 or 3 times

- Are these notes complete? Could you write a clear explanatory paragraph from these notes? Explain your answer.

Try Your Skill   Read this explanatory paragraph. Tell what is wrong with it.

This is how to frame a picture. Just measure how high it is. Decide where you want to hang it. Over your bed would be nice, or in the living room. Choose any kind of wood you want. I like oak, myself. Cut it and nail it together. Have the glass cut. Then put the picture in and attach a wire to the back for hanging. Make a nice mat first. That's all there is to it.

Keep This in Mind

- An explanatory paragraph can explain how to do something or how something happens or works.
- The steps in an explanatory paragraph that explains a process should be expressed clearly and simply. All of the important steps should be included.

Now Write   Think about a process you would like to explain. Be sure your topic is one that you can explain well in a single paragraph. List all of the important steps of your process. Save your pre-writing notes in your folder.

Step Forward

Pre-Writing: Using Step-by-Step Order

Here's the Idea Have you ever read an explanation of some process and found yourself getting more and more confused? Perhaps the writer had left out an important step or mixed up the order of the steps. Whatever the case, the result was an unclear explanation.

You can avoid making the same mistake by including all of the important steps in the process you are explaining and being sure they are well organized. The best way to organize a paragraph that explains is to use **step-by-step order.**

Step-by-step order is very much like chronological order. Begin by writing down the first step. Then list the rest of the steps in the order that they happen. If you discover that you left out a step, add it to your notes in the proper order.

Check It Out Read the following explanatory paragraph.

> You can make rusty lawn furniture look new again. It is a rewarding project if you follow the right steps. First, sand off all the old rust from the tables and chairs. If the rust is severe, use a chemical rust remover. After sanding, a primer coat is important. If you are painting indoors, be sure to have sufficient ventilation. Paint the furniture carefully with the primer. Usually one coat of primer is enough. After the primer has dried, which should take about one day, paint the furniture with the color of your choice. Spray paint works very well and can be applied more easily than brushed-on paint. When using spray paint, be sure not to spray too much paint. This will result in drips. Let the paint dry. Then apply a second coat. Use two or

three coats of paint to ensure proper coverage without drips. After the final coat has dried, prepare some favorite foods and have a picnic on your newly painted outdoor furniture!

- What process is explained in this paragraph?
- Has the author used step-by-step order? How do you know?

Try Your Skill The following is a list of steps for making adobe bricks. Reorder the steps so that they are in correct step-by-step order.

1. Set the bricks in the sun to dry.
2. Mix the clay and water together.
3. Collect a pail-full of clay.
4. Add more clay to make a stiff mixture and form this mixture into brick shapes.
5. Fill the hole with water.
6. Make a pile of clay with a hole in the middle.
7. Into this wet, soupy mixture add pieces of dry grass or straw.

Keep This in Mind

- Use step-by-step order to organize the steps in a paragraph that explains a process.

Now Write Read the pre-writing notes you made in the last lesson. Organize the notes into step-by-step order. Once again check to see that no important steps are missing. Save the newly organized notes in your folder.

Clear the Way

Writing the First Draft

Here's the Idea Every step in your explanatory paragraph must be stated clearly and simply. If the steps are also organized in step-by-step order, your reader should have no trouble understanding your explanation.

When you write the first draft of your paragraph, follow your pre-writing notes carefully. The topic sentence of your paragraph should tell your reader what process you are explaining. Make sure that all steps are included and that they are presented in the right order.

As you turn your notes into sentences, use transitional words and phrases to make your explanation as clear as possible. The right transitions will help your reader see how the steps in the process are related to each other. Here is a list of transitional words and phrases that you might use in your explanatory paragraph.

first	then	at first
second	now	to start with
third	when	after that
fourth	while	at the same time
next	until	the next step
last	finally	at last

Check It Out Read this explanatory paragraph.

The artist first prepared her canvas by painting it with "magic white" paint. When it was dry, she used a pencil to sketch in a background and some figures. Next, she mixed together several colors of paint on her palette. Then, she began applying paint to the canvas with a palette knife, starting with the background. As soon as the background was completed, she began adding details. While she worked, she added highlights and shading to make her work look more realistic. When the painting was finished, she let it dry. Finally, she sealed the painting with a spray shellac. At last her work was done.

- Point out the transitional words and phrases in the paragraph. How do they help make the explanation clear?

Try Your Skill   Add good transitional words and phrases to the following paragraph. Compare your rewritten paragraph with those of your classmates.

To reach our cabin, take Mountain View Road out of town. Go north for about five miles. You'll see a large fish hatchery on your right. Turn right on Summit Drive and follow it uphill for half a mile. Look for a redwood sign that says Timber Lane. Turn left down the dirt road. At the end of the road park your car. Walk up the path through the woods. Pass two cabins on your left. You'll see ours, right by the creek.

Keep This in Mind

- In a paragraph that explains a process, include transitional words and phrases that will make your explanation clear.

Now Write   Write the first draft of your explanatory paragraph. Use transitional words and phrases to make your explanation clear. Save your first draft in your folder.

First Finished

Revising Your Explanation

Here's the Idea When you write a paragraph that explains a process, your goal is to make your explanation as easy as possible for your reader to understand. After finishing your first draft, reread it carefully to see if you have met this goal. As you examine your paragraph, ask yourself the following questions.

1. Does my topic sentence present the process I intend to explain? Will it also capture my readers' attention?
2. Did I organize the steps in a natural step-by-step order? Have I included all the necessary steps of the process?
3. Did I explain each step simply and clearly?
4. Did I include transitional words and phrases to show the order of the steps and to help my readers move easily from one idea to the next?

Before proofreading your paragraph, have someone else read your explanation. Ask your reader if your explanation is clear or if it needs improvement. Follow your reader's suggestions for improving your paragraph.

When you are pleased with the ideas, organization, and word choice of your explanation, proofread it. Look for and correct any errors in grammar, usage, and mechanics.

Check It Out Read the following explanatory paragraph.

- How has this paragraph been improved through revision?

You can ~~make~~ *create personalized* gifts by learning *the art of* decoupage. Decoupage is the art of decorating with paper cut outs. *First,* Cut out the design or pictures to be used. *Excellent* Selections can come from magazines, greeting cards, photographs, or wrapping paper. *Second,* Sand the outside of the object to be decorated. *Then* Coat the cut out with a sealer *and* Glue it to the object. *Next,* Apply many coats of varnish. *Finally,* Wax and polish the last coat. You can turn ~~many objects~~ *lamps, small boxes, and trays* into works of art through decoupage.

Try Your Skill Reread the poorly written explanation in **Try Your Skill** in the first lesson. Revise it, following the guidelines in this lesson. Compare your revision with those of your classmates.

Keep This in Mind

- An explanatory paragraph should have an interesting and informative topic sentence.
- Include all the necessary steps of the process in step-by-step order.
- Use transitional words and phrases to help your readers follow the steps.

Now Write Using the guidelines in this lesson, revise your explanatory paragraph. Be sure to proofread your paragraph for errors in grammar, usage, and mechanics. When your revision is complete, make a final copy and save it in your folder.

The Explanatory Paragraph

Presenting an Opinion

Personally

Pre-Writing: Developing an Opinion

Here's the Idea In the last chapter, you learned to write a paragraph that explains a process. In this chapter you will write a different kind of explanatory paragraph—one that states an opinion. The purpose of an explanatory paragraph of this type is to express an opinion about a particular subject and to support that opinion with logical reasons or accurate facts. For example, you might write a paragraph explaining why you are the most qualified candidate for class president or why every home should have a smoke detector. Both of these topics require you to explain your opinion.

When you have chosen a topic, write a sentence that clearly states your opinion. Writing this sentence will help you to focus your opinion, to make it more specific. Later, when you write a first draft of your paragraph, this sentence can serve as the basis for your topic sentence.

Whatever opinion you choose to present in your explanatory paragraph, build strong support for it by collecting good, logical reasons and accurate facts. The more unpopular or unusual your opinion is, the more convincing your support will have to be. Make a list of all the important ideas that support your opinion. If necessary, look up facts or statistics in a reference source.

Check It Out Read these pre-writing notes.

- Has the writer clearly stated an opinion?
- Has the writer listed strong supporting ideas?

Opinion   Everyone should become more involved in recycling.

Reasons   recycling reduces litter
          —cities becoming choked with garbage
          recycling saves money
          —corporations save on production costs
          —savings passed on to consumers
          recycling extends earth's resources
          —saves trees, barrels of oil, other natural resources

Try Your Skill   Think about these general topics. Choose one that you have some strong feelings about. Focus your feelings until you have developed a specific opinion about the subject. Then write a sentence that clearly states your opinion. Finally, make a list of logical reasons or accurate facts to support your opinion.

women's rights   auto safety   working   voting

Keep This in Mind

· An explanatory paragraph may present an opinion.
· Support an opinion with logical reasons and accurate facts.

Now Write   Consider some subjects about which you have strong feelings. Focus your feelings until you develop a specific opinion you would like to write about Be sure it is an opinion you can explain well in a single paragraph. Write a sentence that clearly states your opinion. Then make a list of logical reasons and accurate facts to support your opinion. Save your notes in your folder.

The Big Build Up

Pre-Writing: Organizing an Opinion

Here's the Idea   An avalanche begins as a small trickle of snow. Slowly it builds until, finally, it is so powerful that nothing can stand in its way. That's the kind of impact you want your explanatory paragraph to have. You can achieve that impact by organizing your supporting ideas in the **order of importance**.

An explanatory paragraph should begin with a statement of your opinion. Then you must explain why you hold that opinion. To do this, you give reasons and facts. The best way to present them is from the least important idea to the most important. In other words, you start with the weakest reason and build toward the strongest reason. That way your explanation, just like the avalanche, will pick up power as it moves along. Also, your readers will have the best argument fresh in their minds when they finish reading the paragraph.

For example, suppose an ecologist intends to write an editorial explaining why the wooded areas around your town must be saved. The ecologist might include these reasons:

1. Thousands of people picnic, hike, and camp in the area every year.

2. The forest harbors endangered woodland animals.

3. If the woodland areas are destroyed, there will be no natural woodland left in the country.

Notice that the reasons have been listed from the least important idea to the most important idea.

Check It Out   Reread the pre-writing notes from **Check It Out** in the last lesson.

- Are the supporting reasons arranged in the order of their importance? Explain your answer.

Try Your Skill   Rewrite the following explanatory paragraph so that the supporting reasons are arranged in the order of their importance. Compare your rewritten paragraph with those of your classmates.

> Running is the best form of aerobic exercise. First of all, running strengthens your cardio-pulmonary system. A healthy heart and strong lungs mean a longer and more enjoyable life. More important, running is a very popular sport. More people enjoy running than any other form of exercise. Finally, running is relatively inexpensive. All you really need is a good pair of shoes and you're off!

Keep This in Mind

- Organize the ideas that support an opinion in the order of their importance. Start with the least important idea and move toward the most important.

Now Write   In the last lesson you chose an opinion to write about, and you made a list of pre-writing notes to support it. Now arrange your reasons in the order of their importance. Save your organized list in your folder.

Perfectly Clear

Writing the First Draft

Here's the Idea When you write your first draft, the first sentence of your paragraph will be your topic sentence. The topic sentence of your explanatory paragraph should state your opinion directly. Do not begin your topic sentence with *I think, In my opinion,* or *I believe.* Instead, make a direct statement. Simply say, "Car insurance is too expensive," instead of "*I think* car insurance is too expensive."

As you continue writing your first draft, use good transitional words and phrases to make your opinion clearer and to help the reader follow your ideas. In a paragraph that presents an opinion, two kinds of transitions will be especially helpful. One kind helps you to present your reasons by showing how one idea is related to another. The other kind shows the order of your supporting ideas. Here are some transitions that you might use:

State Reasons and Facts	because, so, since, therefore, as a result, if. . . then. . . , for example
Put in Order of Importance	first, the first reason, second, more important, most important, finally

End your explanatory paragraph with a strong concluding sentence that sums up your opinion and your supporting ideas.

Check It Out Read the following paragraph.

Every responsible citizen should become more involved in recycling. Let us all save newspapers, aluminum cans, and glass bottles. First of all, every city is becoming choked with litter. Recycling would greatly reduce the amount of trash and clutter now needing disposal. More important, by reusing materials, corporations can save money on production costs, and can pass this saving on to the consumer. Most important, as a result of widespread recycling, the nation will slow its consumption of natural resources. For example, we will save huge numbers of trees and barrels of oil now needed to make paper and aluminum. Recycling can help guarantee a more abundant future for everyone.

- Identify the topic sentence. Does it clarify and directly state an opinion?
- Identify the transitional words and phrases.
- Does the concluding sentence sum up the opinion?

Try Your Skill Read the following topic sentences. What is wrong with them? Rewrite each sentence so that it states an opinion clearly and directly.

1. I really think that fall is the nicest season.

2. I don't know, but maybe we should all learn a foreign language.

3. In my opinion, everyone should visit our nation's capital, Washington, D.C.

Keep This in Mind

- State your opinion in a clear, direct topic sentence.
- Use transitional words and phrases to help you present your reasons and to show the order of their importance.

Now Write Following your organized pre-writing notes, write the first draft of your explanatory paragraph. Follow the guidelines in this lesson for a strong topic sentence, transitional words and phrases, and an effective concluding sentence. Save your first draft in your folder.

Another Chance

Revising Your Explanation

Here's the Idea   As you revise the first draft of your explanatory paragraph, keep your readers in mind. Your purpose is to make your opinion clear so that your readers can understand and accept it. Remember that all of the sentences must work together to help convince your readers that your opinion is reasonable and well-supported. Ask yourself the following questions as you revise your explanatory paragraph.

1. Does the topic sentence state my opinion clearly and directly?

2. Did I present strong support for my opinion?

3. Are my reasons logical? Are all of the facts accurate?

4. Did I arrange my supporting ideas from the least important idea to the most important?

5. Did I use appropriate transitional words and phrases to state and organize my reasons?

6. Does my concluding sentence sum up my opinion and supporting ideas?

After revising your paragraph, proofread it. Correct any errors in grammar, capitalization, punctuation, and spelling.

Check It Out   Imagine that someone you know wrote this paragraph and has asked you whether it needs revision.

> I think the idea of turning the Pirelli farm into a shopping center is bad. It should be made into a park instead. It should have recreation facilities. The community needs swimming pools and a skating rink. It needs tennis courts and a performing arts center. It doesn't need another bunch of stores. All my friends agree. We have enough shopping centers already.

- What revising suggestions would you make to the writer of the paragraph?

Try Your Skill   Revise the paragraph above in **Check It Out.** Follow the guidelines in this lesson. Be sure the paragraph is well organized and has a strong topic sentence. Use your imagination to add any necessary details. Compare your revision with those of your classmates.

Keep This in Mind

- State your opinion clearly and directly in your topic sentence.
- Use logical reasons and accurate facts to support your opinion.
- Use transitional words and phrases to help state your reasons and show their order of importance.
- Make sure your concluding sentence sums up your opinion.

Now Write   Revise the first draft of your explanatory paragraph. Follow the guidelines presented in this lesson. Proofread your paragraph for correct grammar, usage, and mechanics. Neatly rewrite your revised paragraph and save this final copy in your folder.

The Explanatory Paragraph
Stating a Definition

A Definite Answer

Pre-Writing: Stating a Definition

Here's the Idea   Throughout the day, in school and at home, you are often asked to explain what something is. In other words, you are asked to give a definition. Your teachers might ask you to define *synapse* or *Monroe Doctrine*. Your kid brother might want to know what *extra sensory perception* is.

In this chapter you will learn to write an explanatory paragraph that states a definition. You may define a real thing or object, such as *pesticides* or *calculator*. You may also define a term or an idea, such as *patriotism, inflation*, or *intuition*.

A good definition does three things. First, it gives the subject to be defined. Next, it puts that subject in the general class to which it belongs. Then, by giving specific characteristics, it shows how the subject is different from all other members of its class.

Suppose you want to define *lemon*. What is a lemon? A lemon is a citrus fruit. That shows how a lemon is different from apples, berries, or bananas. Because there are several other citrus fruits, such as oranges and grapefruit, you might add that a lemon is small and tart in flavor. Because the lime is also a small, tart citrus fruit, you need to state that the lemon is yellow. Now you have a complete definition. You might state your complete definition as follows: A lemon is a small citrus fruit with a yellow rind and a tart flavor.

If you were to develop this definition into a paragraph, you would expand the general definition of lemons with additional information. You might tell where and how they are grown and cultivated. You might also write about the uses of lemons, from hair rinses to lemon meringue pie.

Check It Out Read the following paragraph.

An ambulance is a motorized vehicle used for transporting the sick or injured. Modern ambulances are equipped with specially designed stretchers to prevent jarring. They also contain medical supplies and equipment, such as oxygen, blood-transfusion equipment and heart-monitoring equipment. Ambulances are used mainly to take patients to a treatment center or hospital, but they can also be used to move a patient back home or to another health care facility. There are both civilian and military ambulances. Civilian ambulances are constructed to be fast and comfortable. They usually hold one or two patients. Military ambulances, sometimes used on rough terrain, must be sturdy rather than speedy. These larger ambulances can hold four to six patients and more equipment for immediate emergency treatment.

- What subject is being defined in this paragraph?
- To what general class does the subject belong?
- What are some of its particular characteristics?

Try Your Skill Choose three of the following objects, terms, or ideas. For each one, write a good three-part general definition.

wrench	bog	a la carte	novel
barge	cold water	family	success

Keep This in Mind

- An explanatory paragraph can state a definition.
- A good definition names the subject, puts the subject into its general class, and shows one or two of the subject's particular characteristics.

Now Write Make a list of five or six words that you could define and explain in a paragraph. You might find some interesting words in one of your textbooks. Save your list in your folder.

What Do You Know?

Part 2

Pre-Writing: Developing a Definition

Here's the Idea As you learned in the last lesson, a good definition has three parts. It names the subject to be defined, it puts the subject in its general class, and it gives one or two characteristics that set the subject apart from other members of the same class. The topic sentence of your explanatory paragraph should do those three things.

In the rest of the paragraph, you will develop that general definition as clearly and completely as possible. Gather some specific details to expand your definition. Depending on the subject you have chosen, you might develop your definition with facts and statistics. For example, a computer term such as *down time* would probably be developed with factual information. Encyclopedias and other reference books are good sources for this kind of information.

Some subjects can be developed best with specific examples from your own experience. For example, if you chose to define an idea like *honor*, you would probably use specific examples to show what honor means to you.

Your pre-writing notes must be well organized if you want your readers to understand your explanation. Most definitions begin with a general statement followed by specific details. You might begin by saying, "A sundial is an ancient time-keeping device." Then, you would present specific details to expand your readers' knowledge of sundials.

Check It Out Read this explanatory paragraph.

"D-Day" was the name given to that date in World War II when an incredible military operation was launched. The day

168

was June 6, 1944, and the operation was the invasion of Europe by the Allied forces in World War II. On D-Day, over 10,000 planes and over 4,000 ships left England for the Normandy coast of France. Within a week, the Allies occupied a strip of beach 60 miles long. During the first hundred days following D-Day over two million men landed in France to free that country from German occupation. D-Day marks the major turning point in World War II.

- Does the paragraph clearly define the term?
- Did the writer develop the definition with facts and statistics, or with specific examples from his own experience?

Try Your Skill Choose one of the words for which you wrote a general definition in the last lesson. Make a list of specific details you could use to develop that general definition. Use either facts and statistics or specific examples.

Keep This in Mind

- A paragraph that states a definition can be developed with facts and statistics or with specific examples.
- Organize a definition from the general to the specific.

Now Write Choose and narrow a topic for an explanatory paragraph that defines. Make a list of facts and statistics or specific examples to develop your topic. Then organize your notes from the general to the specific. Save your organized notes in your folder.

Definitely So

Writing the First Draft

Here's the Idea When you write the first draft of your explanatory paragraph, begin with a strong topic sentence. Remember, your topic sentence should be a three-part general definition of the subject of your paragraph. First, name the subject. Then, put the subject into its general class. Finally, show the specific characteristics of the subject that set it apart from all others in its class.

Here is an example of a good topic sentence for an explanatory paragraph that defines.

> Cape Cod is a peninsula that juts into the Atlantic from southeastern Massachusetts like a bent finger.

Once you have defined your topic, proceed to develop the definition with specific details in the body of your paragraph. Use facts and statistics or specific examples from your prewriting notes. Each sentence should increase your readers' understanding of the subject you are defining.

Finish your paragraph with a strong concluding sentence that sums up your definition. Try to leave your readers with an interesting thought about your topic.

Check It Out Read these two paragraphs.

> Cape Cod is a peninsula that juts into the Atlantic from southeastern Massachusetts like a bent finger. The cape was named in the 1600's for the abundance of codfish, which was important to the local economy. During the next two hundred years, Cape Cod became the center of an important whaling industry. Today its economy is based on a tremendous tourist trade. People come to visit the sunny beaches and tour the old

homes and sailing ships of the cape's past. From its humble start as a fishing center, Cape Cod has become one of the most popular tourist spots in the country.

A hydrofoil is a kind of motorboat. It is built out of lightweight materials and is medium-sized. It is called a hydrofoil because it has big wing-like things called hydrofoils. They lift it out of the water. Then it can ride on top of the water and go faster.

- Explain why one of these paragraphs is better than the other. What does the poor paragraph need to become a good definition?

Try Your Skill Read the following sentences. Follow the guidelines in this lesson and turn each sentence into a good topic sentence for a definition.

1. A grizzly bear is a big animal.
2. A piano is a kind of musical instrument.
3. Courage is something we all want to have.
4. A microphone is a thing that people sing into.

Keep This in Mind

- Begin your explanatory paragraph with a three-part general definition of your subject.
- Develop your definition with facts and statistics or specific examples.

Now Write Write the first draft of your explanatory paragraph. Follow the guidelines in this lesson. Save your first draft in your folder.

In Other Words

Revising Your Explanation

Here's the Idea   When you revise any explanatory paragraph, your goal is to make it clearer. This is expecially important when you are writing a definition. Read your explanatory paragraph thoughtfully. Ask yourself these questions as you work to improve your first draft.

1. Does my topic sentence state a good, three-part general definition of my subject?
2. Did I include enough facts and statistics or specific examples to develop my definition fully?
3. Does my definition move from the general to the specific?
4. Does my ending sentence leave the reader with an interesting thought about my subject?

When you finish revising your content and organization, proofread your paragraph. Look for and correct any errors in grammar, usage, and mechanics.

Check It Out   Notice how this definiton has been revised.

Arobatics is an exciting sport. *involving airplanes.* The airplanes are specially designed to do tricks. *such as* Like flying up side down, barel rolls and diving. The planes *might* can be jets or, *brightly colored biplanes.* old time planes. The pilots who fly *these planes* them are very good. They must have nerves of steel. Arobatic meets are held all around the country. With *and* prizes *are* given to the best flyers. Arobatics is *truly* a high adventure.

• How has this paragraph been improved?

Try Your Skill   The paragraph in **Check It Out** was revised, but it was not proofread. Proofread the paragraph. Correct any errors in grammar, capitalization, punctuation, and spelling.

Keep This in Mind

• Begin your paragraph with a three-part general definition of your subject.
• Organize your definition from the general to the specific.
• Leave the reader with an interesting thought about your subject.

Now Write   Following the guidelines in the lesson, revise your explanatory paragraph. Be sure to proofread for errors in grammar, capitalization, punctuation, and spelling. When you have finished revising, make a final copy and save it in your folder.

Writing a Composition

Voyage of Discovery

What Is a Composition?

Here's the Idea Some topics are too broad to develop completely in a single paragraph. If you wish to write about such a topic, you must write a composition. A **composition** is a group of paragraphs that deal with a single main idea.

Compositions vary in content. Some are narratives, some are descriptions, and some are explanations. However, all compositions have a beginning, a middle, and an end. These parts are called the introduction, the body, and the conclusion.

The **introduction** is the first paragraph of the composition. It tells the reader what the composition is about.

The **body** follows the introduction. It contains several paragraphs that completely develop the main idea. If the composition is a narrative, the body will relate a series of events. In a descriptive composition, the body will present sensory details. In an explanation, the body will contain facts or directions.

Sometimes a composition contains different types of body paragraphs. For example, a composition that *tells a story* may contain paragraphs that *describe*.

The **conclusion** is the last paragraph of the composition. It sums up the ideas presented in the introduction and body.

Check It Out Read the following composition.

A Driving Ambition

Getting my driver's license was more difficult than I had expected. Instead of taking the easy, automatic way out, I had decided to learn how to drive a car with a manual transmission.

My driving instructor was Mrs. Marion McKenna, a teacher at my high school. She began my lessons with a lecture on the use of three basic pedals—the gas, the clutch, and the brake. It was the clutch that did me in. I couldn't seem to balance the tension between the clutch and the gas pedal.

Several weeks later, I had gained the skill and confidence I needed to apply for my license. I passed my written exam and faced the final hurdle—the road test. Suddenly, I realized that I would be using a different car, not the usual training car. However, I felt confident and ready to go.

The driving examiner climbed into the car. I sat waiting, anxious to start the engine. Instead, I was told to turn on the windshield wipers. For the first time I noticed the dashboard. Four unmarked knobs faced me. I pushed one. Nothing happened. I tried pulling instead, and the wipers started waving. The examiner smiled and told me to start the car.

- Is this composition a narrative, a description, or an explanation? Explain your answer.

Try Your Skill   Read the following paragraph from a composition. Is it from the introduction, body, or conclusion?

As a child, I was very fond of stories about King Arthur and the Knights of the Round Table. The bravery, gentleness, and nobility of these knights appealed strongly to my youthful idealism. However, ideals are made to be broken, and stories are often untrue. The actual knights of the Middle Ages were vastly different from their counterparts in legends and myths.

Keep This in Mind

- A composition is a group of paragraphs dealing with a single main idea.
- A composition may be a narrative, a description, or an explanation.
- A composition must have an introduction, a body, and a conclusion.

Now Write   Write a paragraph comparing compositions and paragraphs. Show their similarities and differences.

Chart Your Course

Pre-Writing: Choosing a Topic

Here's the Idea   Good compositions are full of interesting details. Gathering details for a composition is easier if you are already familiar with your topic. Therefore, begin your search for a topic by thinking about your own experiences and interests. The following questions will help you.

1. What people, places, things, and events are important in my life?
2. What sports, hobbies, and other activities do I enjoy?
3. Who are the most interesting people I've met?
4. What people or events have influenced or interested me most?
5. What opinions, beliefs, or values do I have? Which do I feel most strongly about?
6. What skills have I acquired in school and elsewhere?
7. What unusual experiences have I had or heard about?
8. What would I like to learn more about?

Another way to find a topic is to look through your journal. You can also get composition ideas by watching movies or television shows. Magazines, newspapers, and books may also provide ideas. Other good sources of topics include brainstorming, clustering, class discussions, and interviews.

After you have chosen a topic, narrow it to fit the size of the composition you want to write. If your topic is very general, make it more specific by asking questions about the topic. Begin these questions with *who, what, where, when, why,* and *how.* See pages 96–97 for more information on how to narrow a topic.

Check It Out   One general topic for a composition might be "baseball." Read the questions that follow this topic.

Baseball

Who is the most promising new player in baseball?
How did the various baseball teams get their names?
What became of the great baseball players of the
    Negro leagues?
Why does football get more air time than baseball?

- Did you see how asking questions can help you to find specific topics?
- What other topics can you add to this list?

Try Your Skill On a piece of paper, answer the questions in **Here's the Idea.** Make your answers as specific as you can. Think of at least two answers to each question. Then, choose two possible topics for a composition. Narrow them by asking *who? what? where? when? why?* and *how?* questions.

Keep This in Mind

- Choose a composition topic that you know about or that interests you.
- Use the following sources to find composition topics: your journal, books, magazines, brainstorming, clustering, class discussions, and interviews.
- Narrow your topic to fit the size of your composition.

Now Write Look at the list of answers you have in **Try Your Skill.** Also check the other sources of topic ideas mentioned in this lesson. Based on these sources, choose a topic. Then, narrow the topic by asking questions. Make sure the topic is specific enough to be developed completely in a few paragraphs. Save your work in your folder.

Gather Supplies

Pre-Writing: Organizing Ideas

Here's the Idea   After narrowing your topic, gather details to develop that topic. The types of details you must gather depend upon the type of composition you want to write.

A **narrative composition** tells a story. For this sort of composition, you will need a list of events. You will also need specific information about your setting and characters.

A **descriptive composition** paints a picture of a person, place, or thing. For a composition of this kind, you will need a list of sensory details that describe your subject.

An **explanatory composition** supplies information. For a composition of this type, you may use any of the following: facts, statistics, and specific examples. You can also use sensory details, incidents, or anecdotes. If your composition will explain a process, your details may be a list of the steps in the process you want to explain.

After you have gathered your details, organize them logically. Cross out any details that are not related to your main idea. Then, study the notes that remain. Try to group them around three or four main ideas. Sometimes these main ideas will be part of your notes. At other times, you will have to decide what main idea a group of notes suggests.

Finally, decide upon the order in which you want to present your groups of details. Also organize the details within each group. Use any of the following methods of organization.

chronological order	spatial order
order of importance	general to specific order
most familiar to least familiar order	comparison and contrast

See pages 104–105 for more information on organizing details.

Check It Out   Read these pre-writing notes.

Topic   walking as a form of exercise

Details   doesn't require special equipment
exercises the heart, is safe for the young
doesn't have to be done in a special place
is safe for many people who cannot do other
   types of exercise
burns up calories, expands the lungs
gives people a chance to relax and think
doesn't require a special outfit
is safe for people who are out of shape and want
   to start an exercise program

- What type of composition are these notes for?
- Do you see how these details might be grouped?

Try Your Skill   The pre-writing notes in **Check It Out** can be grouped around three major ideas.

1. Walking doesn't require special equipment or a special location.
2. Walking is safe for most people.
3. Walking offers many physical and non-physical benefits.

Write these three headings on a piece of paper. Then, write each pre-writing note under the correct heading.

Keep This in Mind

- To develop a composition, gather plenty of details.
- Group your details around several main ideas.

Now Write   Think about the topic you chose in the last lesson. Gather appropriate details to develop your topic. Organize these details into idea groups. Then, arrange the idea groups and the details within them in a logical order. Save your work.

Anchors Away

Writing the First Draft

Here's the Idea   When you write the first draft of a composition, concentrate on your content and organization. At this stage, do not worry about the details of grammar, capitalization, punctuation, and spelling. Instead, use the drafting stage to get your ideas down on paper.

Begin by writing your introduction. In the introduction, state your topic as clearly as you can. Experiment with various introductions. Find one that will capture your readers' interest.

Next, write the paragraphs of the body. Base the paragraphs on your organized pre-writing notes. Make certain that every paragraph has a strong topic sentence. In each paragraph, present details that support the topic sentence. Make sure that these details are logically organized.

Finally, write your conclusion. End your composition in a way that suits the type of composition you are writing. You may tell the last event in a story. You may summarize your major points and restate your main idea. You may also draw a lesson from the ideas presented in the rest of the composition. Make certain that your conclusion brings the composition to a satisfying close.

Check It Out   Read this first draft. It was written from the pre-writing notes in the last lesson.

Walking for Exercise

I'd like to tell you about the advantages of walking. In the last few years, a physical fitness craze has started. People are exercising a lot more. Everyone, it seems, is jumping on the fitness bandwagon. This is great! Nonetheless, one simple method of exercise is being ignored. This is walking.

No type of exercise is as easy as taking a walk. Walking is safe for the young, the not-so-young, the strong, and the not-so-strong. It also requires no special location. Walking can be done almost anywhere.

In addition, walking is one of the safest forms of exercise. In most sports, beginners have to see if they are fit enough to take up the activity. Medical checkups are suggested and caution is advised. However, almost anyone can walk without worrying about it.

And this is real important. Walking offers lots of phisical and sycological benifits. It helps the heart, helps the lungs. And you weigh less. Walking also gives people the chance to think and to relax. This helps to make people feel better at the end of a long hard day.

Walking in short, is good exercise. It is safe and easy to do. It is also good for you.

- Does this composition have an introduction, body, and conclusion? Does each part fulfill its purpose? Explain your answers.

Try Your Skill Discuss with your classmates the composition given in **Check It Out**. Identify its strengths and weaknesses. Then, point out ways to improve it.

Keep This in Mind

- A first draft should have an introduction, a body, and a conclusion.
- When writing your first draft, concentrate on content and organization.

Now Write Write the first draft of your composition. Use the pre-writing notes that you made in the last lesson. Also follow the guidelines given in this lesson. Save your first draft in your folder.

Trim Your Sails

Revising: Content and Organization

Here's the Idea   A sailor cannot simply climb into a boat and expect it to go in the right direction. Winds and seas change constantly. Therefore, a sailor must make adjustments.

When you write, you must also make adjustments. You must add or change ideas to make your writing the best it can be. You may make some additions and changes as you write your first draft. However, you will make most of them as you revise.

To revise a composition, read your first draft several times. Pay attention to the content and organization of this draft.

Content refers to the ideas and details used to develop your main idea. Ask yourself these questions about content:

1. Is my introduction interesting? Is my main idea clearly expressed?

2. Does each paragraph have an interesting and informative topic sentence? Is this sentence supported by details?

3. Have I included enough details to develop my main idea?

4. Have I chosen the right kinds of details for the type of composition I am writing?

5. Does my composition have *unity?* That is, do all my details help to support and develop my main idea?

Organization refers to how you have arranged your ideas. When revising the organization ask these questions.

1. Does my composition have an introduction, body, and conclusion?

2. Is my composition coherent? That is, are all the ideas arranged in a clear, logical order?

3. Have I chosen a method of organization that suits the type of composition I am writing?

Check It Out   Study this revised paragraph from the composition given in Part 4. Notice the changes that have been made in content and organization.

> ~~I'd like to tell you about the advantages of walking.~~ In the last
> few years, a physical fitness craze has ^(swept across America.) ~~started.~~ People are
> *jogging, swimming, dancing, and lifting weights* everywhere
> ~~exercising a lot more.~~ Everyone, it seems, is ~~jumping on the~~ ^(trying to get fit. However,)
> ~~fitness bandwagon. This is great!~~ ~~Nonetheless,~~ one simple
> method of exercise is being ignored: ~~This is~~ walking.

- What changes have been made in the content and organization of this paragraph?
- Why was the first sentence taken out?

Try Your Skill   Read the following first draft of a paragraph from a composition. Then, revise the paragraph to improve its content and organization.

It was a really nice day. The sun was shining and the trees were beautiful. I decided to go for a walk. Then, it started to rain. That was after I had fallen asleep in the park.

Keep This in Mind

- When you revise, look for ways to improve your content and organization.
- *Content* refers to the ideas and details in your composition.
- *Organization* refers to how ideas are arranged in your composition.

Now Write   Revise the content and organization of your composition. Follow the guidelines in this lesson. Save your work.

Shipshape

Revising: Word Choice and Proofreading

Here's the Idea As you write, you should try to make your composition as interesting as possible. Use vivid nouns, verbs, adjectives, and adverbs. Also try to choose words that will strengthen the mood of your composition. As you revise, look for dull, uninteresting words and phrases. Also look for words that do not suit the mood. Notice how the following sentences have been improved by adding precise details.

1. The box had tools in it.
   Beneath the workbench sat a large, red box full of hammers, screwdrivers, drill bits, and other tools.
2. The man started the ride.
   The carnival worker yanked at the long lever and watched with interest as the Ferris wheel began to turn.

You can also improve **dialogue,** or conversation between characters, by using precise language. When revising dialogue, make sure your characters sound real. If a character is young, use language that a child would use. If a character is angry, use language that shows this anger. Another way to improve dialogue is to use dialogue tags that tell how a character sounds or feels. Instead of "he said" or "she replied," use language that is more specific, such as "he groaned" or "she demanded."

Transitional words and phrases can also improve your writing. They lead your readers from one idea to the next. They show how your ideas are related. For example, you can use them to show how people or things are related in space or in time.

Once you have revised the content, organization, and word choice of your composition, proofread carefully. Find and correct any errors you have made in grammar, usage, capitalization, punctuation, or spelling.

Check It Out   Here are the last two paragraphs of the composition on walking. Notice how they have been revised.

~~And~~ *Finally,* ~~this is real~~ *most* important, ~~Walking~~ *(ly,)* offers ~~lots of~~ *many* ~~phisical~~ *(ly)* and *psych-* ~~seycological~~ *(ie)* benifits. It ~~helps~~ *strengthens muscles, exercises* the heart, ~~helps~~ the lungs, *expands* ~~And~~ *burns up calories.* ~~you weigh less.~~ Walking also gives people the chance to ~~think~~ *collect their thoughts, to reflect,* and to relax. *relieve the stress that many* This helps to ~~make people feel better~~ at the end of *people* a long, hard day. *feel*

   Walking, in short, is ~~good~~ *the ideal* exercise. It is safe and easy to do. It is ~~also good for you.~~ *beneficial to both the body and mind.* *Perhaps in the future many people will drop their weights and rackets and learn to walk all over again.*

Try Your Skill   Revise the following dull, uninteresting sentences. Add details to make the language more specific.

1. Anne liked being on the beach.
2. We went to a movie, but it was boring.
3. Enrico looked upset.
4. The woman carried the pieces of furniture up the stairs.

Now Write   Revise the language of your composition to make it more specific. When this is done, proofread your revised draft and correct any errors you find. Then, make a final copy and proofread your composition one last time. Save your work.

The Masthead

Choosing a Title

Here's the Idea   Often, a reader will judge the quality of a composition by its introduction and title. The title is, of course, the first part of your composition that the reader will see. Therefore, you want to make the title interesting enough to capture your reader's attention. Your title should also suggest what your composition will be about.

Explanatory compositions often have simple informative titles such as "How To Care for a Kitten." Such titles tell exactly what information will be presented in the composition. However, narrative and descriptive compositions usually have titles that are more creative. Some titles suggest strange or marvelous events:

The Day the Earth Stood Still
The Secret Lives of Plants

Others use rhyming words or repeated sounds:

"The Pit and the Pendulum"
"Riki Tiki Tavi"

Some use parts of complete sentences:

And They Dance Real Slow in Jackson

Others use common sayings, or cliches:

You Can't Take It with You
Our Town
The Way of the World

These are just a few of the many ways to write a title. Pay attention to the titles that you come across every day. When you find a title that catches your eye, ask yourself why the title appeals to you. For more information on titles, see pages 655 and 695 in your Handbook.

Check It Out Read the following titles of stories and poems you may have read.

"O What Is That Sound"   "Dream Deferred"
"Harrison Bergeron"   "The Rocking Horse Winner"
"The Fifty-First Dragon"   "Thinking Like a Mountain"
"Say It with Flowers"   "Time to Talk"

- What techniques described in **Here's the Idea** are used in these titles? Are these good titles? Why or why not?

Try Your Skill Choose four of the following possible topics for a composition. For each topic, write two titles.

1. a narrative about working as a short-order cook
2. a description of a flooded town
3. an explanation of how to care for contact lenses
4. an explanation of why the U.S. needs the draft
5. an explanation of what black holes are
6. a report on careers in fashion designing
7. a story about a boating experience
8. a report on solar energy
9. a description of a mountain cabin
10. a report on the Olympic games

Keep This in Mind

- A title should capture the reader's interest. It should also suggest what the composition will be about.

Now Write Read the material on punctuating and capitalizing titles given in your Handbook on pages 655 and 695. Then, write a title for your composition. Make sure this title is both interesting and informative. Write the title at the top of your revised draft. Save your composition.

Safe Harbor

Guidelines for Writing a Composition

In this chapter you have learned a great deal about writing compositions. First, you learned how to choose and narrow a topic. Then, you learned how to gather and organize details to develop a main idea. Finally, you learned how to write and revise a rough draft.

In the next few chapters, you will learn how to write different kinds of compositions. As you learn about these types of compositions, bear in mind that the process of writing is the same for each type. Whatever kind of composition you are writing, follow these guidelines:

Guidelines for Writing a Composition

Pre-Writing

- Choose a topic that interests you and that you know something about. Narrow the topic so that you can cover it well in the assigned length of your composition.
- Identify your purpose and your audience.
- Gather details to develop your topic.
- Group similar details around two or three main ideas.
- Organize your details into an order that suits the type of composition you are writing.

Writing the First Draft

- Begin your composition with an interesting introductory paragraph that tells your reader what your composition is about.

- After your introduction, write the body of your composition. Use your organized details to develop your topic. Each group of details will become a paragraph in the body of your composition.
- Use transitional words and phrases to lead your readers from one idea to the next.
- Add, take out, and reorganize your ideas as needed.
- End your first draft with a concluding paragraph that sums up your ideas.
- Add an interesting title to your composition.

Revising

- Be sure your composition has an introduction, a body, and a conclusion.
- Check to see that you have included enough details to develop your topic.
- Organize the paragraphs and the ideas within them logically.
- Be sure the topic sentence of each paragraph presents the main idea of that paragraph.
- Use effective transitional words to make your ideas flow smoothly.
- Make sure you have used vivid language. Use language that suits the audience you are writing for.
- Proofread to find and correct errors in grammar, capitalization, punctuation, and spelling.

Final Copy

- Rewrite your composition neatly in ink on white, lined paper, or type your composition, double-spaced, on plain white paper.
- Write your name, subject, and the date in the upper righthand corner of your paper.
- Proofread your final copy one last time. Neatly correct any errors you find.

The Narrative Composition

Imagine That!

Pre-Writing: Planning a Story

Here's the Idea A **narrative composition** is a story. The story may be about real or imaginary events. Every narrative composition has these parts:

1. The **setting** tells when and where the story takes place. When planning the setting, choose a specific time and place. Then, list details that will make this time and place seem real.

2. The **characters** are the people or animals in the story. When planning characters, decide *how* you want each character to look, act, and speak. Also decide *why* your characters look, act, and speak as they do. Use details taken from real life.

3. The **theme** is the point that you want to make with your story. Every story should contain one major theme. A theme might be that being honest is sometimes difficult. It might also be that hard work usually pays off in the end.

4. The **plot** is the series of events in your story. Stories usually begin with events that introduce a conflict. A **conflict** is a problem faced by the main character. The body of a story shows how the conflict grows. The conclusion shows how the conflict is solved. When planning the plot of a story, first choose a conflict to write about. Then name the event that introduces the conflict. Also list the events that happen after the conflict is introduced. Finally, add the event that solves the conflict.

Check It Out Read the following introduction to a narrative.

Kate Shelley and the Midnight Limited

Kate Shelley stood by the front window of her Iowa farm home and watched the storm raging outside. It had been pouring all day—all week, really—and listening to the wind and rain beating against the sill, Kate knew it wouldn't let up tonight. A real summer storm, this one.

She moved restlessly away from the window. Supper was over and the four youngest Shelley children were tucked snugly in bed, and now Kate and her mother sat up alone listening to the downpour. The pounding rain wasn't so bad, but the loud roar of nearby Honey Creek made Kate uneasy. Their house stood on a knoll and so was safe from the threat of flooding, but the barn was on lower ground, and if the small river overflowed its swollen banks, the livestock would be in trouble.

Finally, when the clock on the mantel struck ten, Kate decided to check the animals. She put on her heavy coat and an old hat and stepped out into the night.

- What is the setting of this story?
- Who is the main character?

Try Your Skill   Study the introduction given in **Check It Out.**

1. What details are used to describe the setting of this story?
2. What conflict is suggested by this introduction?

Keep This in Mind

- A narrative composition tells a story.
- A story has a setting, characters, a theme, a plot, and a conflict.

Now Write   Begin thinking about ideas for a story. You can write about real events or imaginary ones. To come up with a good story idea, try asking questions beginning with *What if*. For example, you might ask the following questions:

What if I were taking a driver's test and the brakes failed?
What if someone went to sleep in modern day America and woke up in ancient Egypt?

Make a list of your story ideas and of any details that occur to you. Save this list.

Conflicting Stories

Pre-Writing: Developing a Plot

Here's the Idea   To develop a story, you must first choose a conflict to write about. This conflict may be internal or external. An **internal conflict** takes place in the mind of a character. For example, a character might have to choose between pleasing a friend and doing what is right. An **external conflict** takes place between a character and some outside force. The force may be something in nature, another character, or a social custom or rule. For instance, a character might be in conflict with a raging river or with an unjust law.

Once you have chosen your conflict, you can list the events that will make up your plot. The plot should contain three parts.

1. The **opening** tells about the event that introduces the conflict.

2. The **body** tells about the events that occur as the main character or characters deal with the conflict.

3. The **conclusion** tells about the event that ends the conflict.

In your pre-writing notes, list the events of your plot in chronological order. Vary from this order only when you want to insert a flashback. A **flashback** interrupts the normal chronological order of a story to describe an event that happened earlier. Writers use flashbacks to explain how certain things in their stories came to be.

Check It Out   Continue reading this narrative.

Hard work around the farm had matured fifteen-year-old Kate, had given her strength and energy. Since her father's death in a railroad accident three years before, Kate had taken care of the farm while her mother managed the house and the younger children. In a quiet and efficient way, Kate had learned to handle the hoe and the plow, the livestock and the dozens of odd jobs found on a farm in 1881. She was used to doing what had to be done.

So what she saw outside the house that night did not frighten her, although the pouring rain and howling wind were even worse than she had imagined from inside. Mud and water were everywhere, and sure enough, Honey Creek was out of its banks and running wild. Soon the flood waters would reach the barn.

- What does this flashback reveal about the main character?

Try Your Skill   Review the discussion of setting, characters, and theme in Part 1. From your list, choose one idea that interests you. Then, make pre-writing notes for the setting, characters, theme, and conflict of your own narrative composition. Include all the details that occur to you. Tell whether your conflict will be an internal conflict or an external one. If your conflict is external, tell what your main character will be in conflict with.

Keep This in Mind

- A conflict may be internal or external.
- A plot is a series of events. These events show how the conflict begins, develops, and ends.
- The events in a story are in chronological order.
- Flashbacks may be used to explain the present situation in a story.

Now Write   Continue your pre-writing notes by listing the events that will make up your plot. Include the event that introduces your conflict and the events that develop the conflict. Then add the event that ends the conflict. Put these events in chronological order.

Who's Watching?

Pre-Writing: Choosing a Point of View

Here's the Idea Before you can write your narrative, you must choose a point of view. **Point of view** refers to how the story is told.

If a character within the story describes the action, the story is told from the **first-person point of view.** In stories of this kind, the narrator can use pronouns such as *I, me, we, our, my,* and *mine.* The reader sees everything through the eyes of one character, the narrator.

If someone outside the story describes the action, the story is told from the **third-person point of view.** In stories of this kind, the narrator can only use pronouns such as *he, she, it,* and *they.*

If you decide to write in the third person, you will have to make yet another choice. You can choose to write from the **third-person limited point of view.** If you write in this way, your narrator will report only what the characters say and do. You can also choose to write from the **third-person omniscient point of view.** *Omniscient* means "all-knowing." If you write in this way, your narrator can tell what all the characters say, do, think, and feel.

Check It Out Read the following paragraphs from two short stories.

1   Dad used to tell me stories about the trees that still existed when he was a boy. There weren't very many even then, with the urbanization program in full swing, but most people had seen at least one tree by the time they started school. It wasn't like nowadays, at any rate. Oh, I've seen the plastic trees; practically every street has a few of them. But you can tell the plastic ones are artificial just from looking at pictures in the microdot library. And now, after seeing a real tree, I can say for sure that the artificial ones aren't the same at all. —A. LENTINI

2   The orchard was most wonderful, for instead of mere apples, its trees bore oranges, lemons, limes, and all sorts of tropical fruits whose names he did not know. There were melons and pineapples growing, and plantains and avocados. Better still, he saw the lady in her white and gold waiting at the end of an alley and was able to draw near enough to speak to her.—JOAN AIKEN

- Which of these paragraphs is told from the first-person point of view?
- Which is told from the third-person point of view? How can you tell?

Try Your Skill   The following passage is from the story you have been reading. Read this passage and tell whether it is written from the first-person or third-person point of view. Then, rewrite the passage using the other point of view.

Kate made her way across the yard and let out the pigs, cows, and their one horse so they could get to higher ground. Then she looked again at Honey Creek. Even as she watched, she could see the swirling water rise along the piers of the railroad bridge spanning the river. The bridge carried the steel rails of the Chicago and North Western Railroad, and Kate knew that in less than two hours the Midnight Limited, with its 200 passengers, would come pounding down onto the bridge. She hoped the rain would have let up by then.

Keep This in Mind

- Point of view refers to how the story is told.
- You can tell a story from the first-person, third-person limited, or third-person omniscient point of view.

Now Write   Decide upon a point of view for your story. Include this point of view in your pre-writing notes. Save these notes in your folder.

The Whole Story

Writing the First Draft

Here's the Idea   A story is only as good as the pre-writing notes that go into it. As you write, follow your pre-writing notes. Stick to one point of view and to one central conflict. However, feel free to add new events and details that will add interest to your story.

Begin by writing your introduction. In the introduction, describe your setting and present your major character or characters. Also describe the event that introduces the central conflict.

After your introduction, write the paragraphs of the body. Develop your conflict by showing how it affects your characters. Describe the events that occur as your main character or characters struggle with the major problem or difficulty in the story. Let the actions, speech, and thoughts of your characters show your readers what is happening.

To end your story, describe the event that settles the conflict. Do not simply tell your readers what happens to end the conflict. Instead, show the readers what your main character does to end it.

Check It Out   Read these paragraphs.

Back inside the house, Kate and her mother sat quietly in the candlelight and listened to the wails and shrieks of the storm. The clock was just striking eleven when they heard a shriek that was louder than the wind and recognized it as the whistle of a railway engine. They hurried to the window that overlooked the bridge approach and saw the headlight of an engine cutting a path of light through the rain. It was too early for the Midnight Limited, but they both knew what was happening. A yard engine had been sent out to test the tracks before the passenger train came along.

As Kate and her mother watched, the test engine moved slowly onto the bridge, and almost instantly the span collapsed with a thunderous crash. Beams and timbers splintered and ripped apart, and there was a tremendous splash and hiss of steam as the engine plunged into the swirling waters below. Then it was dark again.

For several moments the women stood frozen at the window, speechless with horror. Then Kate came to life, Once more she pulled on her old coat. Grabbing her father's railroad lantern, she lighted it and rushed out of the house. Everywhere the flooding was deeper now, but Kate managed to find a way to the railroad tracks. She ran along them until she reached what was left of the bridge, and then, half-afraid of what she might find, she looked down to see the wheels of the engine sticking out of the churning water far below.

- How is the conflict developed in this narrative? What new struggles are faced by the main character?

Try Your Skill Imagine that you are writing a story for children. The story will tell about the struggle of a mouse to escape from a laboratory. Write the introduction to this story. In your introduction, describe the setting, present your main character, and show what the central conflict of the story will be.

Keep This in Mind

- The introduction to a narrative presents the setting, the characters, and the central conflict.
- The body develops the plot and the conflict.
- The conclusion shows how the conflict is ended.

Now Write Using your pre-writing notes, write the first draft of your introduction. In this introduction, present your setting, characters, and central conflict. Save your work in your folder.

Telling Remarks

Part 5

The First Draft: Dialogue

Here's the Idea   One way to bring your characters to life is to have them talk to each other. Conversation between characters is called **dialogue.** Dialogue can serve two important purposes. It can show what events are happening in your story. It can also reveal the thoughts and feelings of your characters.

Try to make your dialogue as realistic as possible. Remember that different people use the language in different ways.

Whenever you give the exact words of a speaker, use quotation marks around these words. Start a new paragraph for each new speaker. Use dialogue tags to show who is speaking and how the words are being said. A **dialogue tag** is an expression such as *Chris said* or *Aretha sighed.* Dialogue tags can be used to show how a character is feeling. For instance, if you want to show that a character is upset, you can write *he bellowed.* If you want to show that a character is amused, you can write *she chuckled.* For more information on writing dialogue, see pages 691–693 in the Handbook.

Check It Out   Read the following passage from a story.

> The bird-walkers drew to a halt respectfully and stood in silence. They stood and stood. It was not good form even to whisper while fellow bird-walkers were logging a victim, but after quite a long time, the Leader, whose feet were flat and often hurt her, whispered impatiently, "Haven't you got him logged yet?"
>
> "You drove him away," Eileen replied sternly. "It was a yellow-billed cuckoo."
>
> "A yellow-billed cuckoo?" cried the Leader incredulously.
>
> "Well," Eileen said modestly, "at least I think it was." Then, with many a pretty hesitation and thoughtful pause, she recited

the leading features of the yellow-billed cuckoo, as recorded in
Bird Life for Children.

The Leader was terribly impressed.　　—RUTH McKENNEY

- What hints do you have that Eileen is not telling the truth?
- What dialogue tags are used in this passage? What do they tell you about the characters?

Try Your Skill　　Read this passage from the narrative about Kate Shelley. Rewrite it using dialogue between Kate and the railroad men.

> Kate shouted down into the pit. Surprisingly, a voice came back to her, faintly, saying that two men had managed to catch hold of a tree and were alive. The rest of the crew were dead.
>
> Kate wasted no time. She knew that the midnight passenger train had to be stopped before it reached the smashed bridge. Assuring the men below that she would get help, Kate set out for Moingona, about a mile away. Only a mile—but what a mile! Between Kate and the Moingona railroad station the Des Moines River roared on its way to the Mississippi. To reach the Moingona side of the river, Kate would have to cross a wooden railroad trestle nearly 200 yards long. There was nothing on the trestle but rails and ties—no footwalk and no railing.

Keep This in Mind

- You can bring your characters to life by writing conversation, or dialogue.
- Dialogue can reveal the personalities of your characters. It can also advance the action of your story.

Now Write　　Keep working on the first draft of your narrative composition. Use dialogue to bring your characters to life. Refer to the guidelines for writing dialogue in this lesson and in Chapter 14 of your Handbook. Save your work in your folder.

Story Time

The First Draft: Transitions

Here's the Idea   As you have learned, a narrative composition presents a series of events. These events should be told in chronological order. To do this, use transitional words and phrases that tell *when*. Use these words and phrases both within and between paragraphs. Notice their use in the following passage.

> *When* the cubs went into the bush, they *often* had adventures. *One morning*, I was following them, for I had given them a worming powder and wished to see the result. I saw them a little way off, asleep. *Suddenly*, I noticed a stream of black soldier ants approaching them.   —JOY ADAMSON

When you write flashbacks, be particularly careful to use transitions. Always begin a flashback with a transition such as "on the previous Thursday" or "an hour earlier." Then, when the flashback is over, use another transition such as "now" or "at present."

Check It Out   Reread the flashback given in **Check It Out** on pages 196–197.

  • What transitions signal the beginning and the end of the flashback?

Try Your Skill   Read the following passage. Then, copy all the transitions that are used to show when events occur.

> Many thoughts raced through Kate's mind at that moment, but she didn't hesitate. The Midnight Limited had to be warned, and she was the only one who could do it. Fighting her way through the rising storm, she finally reached the trestle and stepped onto the first slippery ties. Rain tore at her angrily,

and after the first few steps, the gale knocked her over, smashing her lantern.

From then on, Kate crawled over the widely spaced ties on her hands and knees. Sometimes she flattened out on her stomach to inch her way forward through the pitch-black downpour. The rough wooden ties skinned her knees, and splinters sharp as needles stabbed her hands. Rail spikes ripped her clothes. The wind buffeted her so that she was afraid she might lose her balance and fall between the ties into the raging river.

Kate lost track of time as she struggled, inch by inch, across the seemingly endless trestle. Was the Midnight Limited already due to approach the crossing? She had no light. If the train caught her on the trestle, there was no hope that the engineer would see her in time. Desperately, Kate pressed on.

At last, after what seemed like hours, Kate made it to the end of the trestle. Barely pausing to catch her breath, she staggered on the rest of the way to the Moingona depot, listening all the while for the shriek of a train engine above the wailing of the wind.

When the depot finally appeared through the blinding storm, Kate was just able to stumble into the room and deliver her message: *Honey Creek bridge down, stop the train!* Then she fell to the floor, exhausted, still clutching the broken lantern.

Keep This in Mind

- Use chronological order when describing a series of events.
- Use transitional words and phrases to make the order of the events clear.

Now Write Finish the first draft of your narrative. Use transitional words and phrases within and between paragraphs. In the conclusion of your narrative, tell about the event that ends your conflict. Save your work in your folder.

Tell It Again

Revising Your Narrative

Here's the Idea   When your first draft is finished, you are ready to revise your composition. As you revise, draw upon your experience of what makes a good story.

Begin your revision by rereading your story several times. Imagine that you are a reader of the story, not its author. Would everything in the story be clear to you? Would you have a sense of a definite time and place? Would the characters seem real? Find ways to improve your narrative by asking the following questions.

1. Does the story have a theme? Is the theme clear?
2. Does the introduction present the setting, the characters, and the conflict?
3. Does the story seem complete? Do more events or more details need to be added?
4. Are the events arranged in chronological order?
5. Do flashbacks help to explain the situation in the story?
6. Is the conflict clear? Does the body of the story develop the conflict in an interesting way?
7. Have you kept a single point of view throughout?
8. Does the story use dialogue to relate events and to reveal the thoughts and feelings of the characters? Are dialogue tags used to tell who is speaking?
9. Does the story use transitions within and between paragraphs?
10. Does the conclusion show how the conflict is solved? Is the conclusion effective and interesting?

Once you have finished your revisions, proofread your narrative. Find and correct any errors in grammar, usage, and mechanics. Then, make a final copy.

Check It Out   Review the guidelines for revising given in **Here's the Idea**. Then, read the following conclusion.

Kate Shelley had done what she set out to do. The Moingona station master and his red lantern did the rest, and on July 6, 1881, the Midnight Limited, with its crew and cargo and two hundred passengers, was saved from certain disaster.

Kate's courage did not go unnoticed. Stories and photographs describing her daring rescue appeared in newspapers around the country, and she became a national heroine. She was awarded medals and given a college scholarship; songs and stories were written about her bravery. The Chicago and North Western Railroad rewarded her with a lifetime pass to ride their trains and a job as station agent at Moingona, where she stayed until she died in 1912.

The last, and possibly the greatest, honor came after Kate's death. In 1926 the old wooden trestle she had crawled across on that wild night many years before was torn out and replaced by a huge steel span. It was called the Kate Shelley Bridge.

—JON WATERS

- Does the story you have been reading meet the guidelines given in **Here's the Idea?**

Try Your Skill   Following the guidelines given in this lesson, revise the introduction to your narrative. Proofread your revised draft for errors in grammar, usage, and mechanics.

Keep This in Mind

- When revising a narrative, imagine that you are reading the story for the first time. Make sure that every part of the story is interesting and clear.

Now Write   Finish revising your narrative composition. Make sure to find and correct any errors in your revised draft. Then, make a final copy. Save your work in your folder.

The Descriptive Composition

Setting the Scene

Pre-Writing: Planning a Description

Here's the Idea   In a **descriptive composition**, you paint a picture in words. Your purpose is to bring an experience to life for your reader. To do this, you must use **sensory details**. These are details of sight, hearing, touch, taste, and smell. If you choose your details well, you will create vivid images in your reader's mind. These images will communicate both information and emotions about your subject.

To plan a descriptive composition, first choose a subject that appeals to the senses. Your subject may be a person, place, or thing. The next step is to gather details that show how your subject looks, sounds, feels, tastes, and smells. Gather as many sensory details as you can.

Once you have enough details for a composition, organize these details into groups of related ideas. For instance, suppose you are writing about an amusement park. Some of your details might deal with the rides. Some might deal with the games. Others might deal with the food and refreshments. To organize this composition, you would divide your details about the amusement park into three groups. Then, you would use each of these groups of ideas in a separate paragraph of the composition.

Once you have grouped your details, decide upon the order in which you want to present them. In most descriptive compositions, details are presented in spatial order. Spatial order shows how the details are related in space. See pages 136–137 for more information on using spatial order.

Sometimes details do not fit into any obvious spatial order. If this is so, arrange your details in the order in which you want your reader to notice them.

Check It Out   Read the following pre-writing notes.

Topic	Sal's Diner
Introduction	busy city block at morning rush hour; Central Street, Somerville; new, commercial area; one exception—Sal's
Body	diner is old-fashioned; wooden, rectangular; shabby, peeling paint; squeaky old door
	breakfast; noisy, friendly; heaping plates
	neighborhood gathers; buzz of conversations; flow of customers
Conclusion	Sal's offers more than its appearance shows; old-fashioned hospitality; good food, conversation

- What details will describe the diner?
- What senses do these details appeal to?

Try Your Skill   Make a list of details you could use to write a composition describing where you live. Divide this list into three groups. The first should contain details about the buildings and streets. The second should contain details about the people. The third should contain details about the activities. Put the details in each group in a logical order. Save these notes.

Keep This in Mind

- To write a description, first gather sensory details.
- Divide these details into groups of related ideas.
- Organize these idea groups and the details within them.

Now Write   Think of a topic for a descriptive composition. List the sensory details that you can use in your description. Then, place these details into groups of related ideas. Finally, organize your idea groups and the details within them. Place these ideas and details in a logical order. Save your notes.

The Whole Picture

Writing the First Draft

Here's the Idea When writing the first draft of your composition, work from your pre-writing notes. However, continue to develop your ideas. Feel free to change or add ideas as you write.

Keep in mind that a descriptive composition should create a definite mood. Choose nouns, verbs, adjectives, and adverbs that will suggest a specific mood to your readers. Also remember to use transitional words and phrases. Such words and phrases include *above, below, further out, in front of, to the left, closer,* and *on top.*

Begin with a one-paragraph **introduction**. In this introduction, state your topic. Try to introduce the topic in a way that will make your readers want to learn more about it.

Next, write the **body** of the composition. In the body, present the details you gathered in your pre-writing notes. Use one of your groups of details for each paragraph of the body.

Finally, write a **conclusion**. In the conclusion, sum up the feelings and ideas presented in the rest of the description.

Check It Out Read the following introduction and body of a description.

> Every morning I get off the Number Twelve bus on the same busy city block. As Somerville has grown, this block has changed from a quiet old neighborhood to a busy commercial area. Sleek skyscrapers reach up towards the sunlight—with one exception. Sal's Diner was here long before any of these new structures and still remains the heart of the neighborhood.

Sal's Diner is a tiny, rectangular wooden structure that looks like a railroad car. Its yellow paint is peeling. The roof is missing a few shingles. At the right side of the diner, two worn stone steps lead to a glass door, which squeaks and sags on its hinges. To the left of the door are three small windows. Under each window is a flower box.

Whenever I open the door and step inside, a tinkling bell sounds. Sal glances out from the grill window, smiling broadly to welcome me, as she does to each of her customers. Then she quickly turns her attention to the waiting breakfast orders. Silverware rattles and dishes clatter. Waitresses place heaping plates on the counter and empty ones into the tub of dirty dishes underneath. Bacon and eggs sizzle on the grill.

Every morning I see the same people sitting in the red vinyl booths and at the counter. Customers come and go, often leaving behind sections of the morning paper. On their way out, they wave at Sal. Then they rejoin the working world.

- Does the introductory paragraph present the subject?
- Does the body paragraph present sensory details? Does it use transitions to show spatial order?

Try Your Skill   Reread the notes you made for **Try Your Skill** in Part 1. Choose one of the idea groups you developed. Use the notes from this idea group to write a descriptive paragraph. Begin your paragraph with a topic sentence. Use transitions to show the order of the details you present. Save your work.

Keep This in Mind

- Choose the language of a description carefully.
- Use transitional words and phrases to show the order of your details.

Now Write   Complete the introduction and the body for the first draft of your descriptive composition. Save your work.

Wrapping It Up

The First Draft: Ending a Description

Here's the Idea   Imagine that you are at a play given by the Drama Club at your high school. At intermission, you get up to stretch your legs. When you return, you find that the rest of the play has been cancelled. How would you feel about this? You would probably be upset. Every play should have an ending that ties together the rest of the story.

A conclusion is also important in a descriptive composition. The conclusion of a description should tie together the ideas presented in the rest of the composition. The conclusion should be a single paragraph. This paragraph should follow naturally from what has come before it. In other words, the conclusion should have the same mood as the introduction and body. If, for example, your introduction and body present a peaceful scene, your conclusion should emphasize once again the peacefulness you have described.

When writing a conclusion for a description, first read over the rest of your rough draft. Ask yourself the following questions: What ideas and details have I presented? How can I summarize my feelings about these ideas and details? What mood have I created? What lasting impression do I want my readers to have when they finish my composition? Answering these questions will help you to bring your work to a satisfactory close.

Check It Out   Review the descriptive composition about Sal's diner that is shown in the last lesson. Notice how the description is organized. Then read the following conclusion and title.

Sal's Diner looks out of place among its towering new neigh-bors. It doesn't seem to belong, it's true. Despite its old-fashioned appearance, however, Sal's continues to offer a pleas-ant haven. Whenever I walk by, I can't seem to resist stopping in for a cup of coffee and a bit of cheerful conversation. Most of the neighborhood shares my feelings and my routine. Sal's is the busiest spot on this busy block, and will probably remain so for quite some time.

Title: A Taste of Home

- Does this conclusion summarize the ideas presented in the rest of the composition?
- What is the mood of this conclusion? Does this mood fit the rest of the composition? Why or why not?

Try Your Skill   Reread the notes you wrote for **Try Your Skill** in Part 1. Next, reread the paragraph you wrote for **Try Your Skill** in Part 2. Then, write a conclusion for a composition about your neighborhood. Remember to sum up the ideas in your composi-tion and to keep the same mood.

Keep This in Mind

- The conclusion of a description should summarize the ideas presented in the rest of the composition.
- The conclusion should show how you feel about your subject.

Now Write   Reread the introduction and body of the descrip-tive composition you have been writing. Then, write a conclu-sion that summarizes your ideas and feelings. Save your first draft in your folder.

A Clearer View

Revising Your Descriptive Composition

Here's the Idea   Once your first draft is completed, you are ready to begin revising. As you revise, put yourself in your reader's place. Revise your composition until it presents as clear a picture as possible. Use these questions as guidelines for revising.

1. Does the introduction tell the reader what the subject is?
2. Do the paragraphs in the body have good topic sentences?
3. Did I include interesting sensory details?
4. Did I use transitional words and phrases to make the order of the details clear?
5. Does the description create a strong mood or feeling?
6. Does the conclusion sum up the ideas and feelings in the rest of the composition?

When you have finished revising your content, organization, and language, proofread your composition. Find and correct any errors in grammar, capitalization, punctuation, and spelling.

Check It Out   Notice how the following introduction to a description has been revised.

Nothing remains
~~Not much is left~~ of the family farm ~~on which I was born.~~ *where I spent my youth.*
The state of Kentucky
~~People~~ bought the land years ago and replaced the hog lots and tobacco fields with a ~~highway.~~ *four-lane interstate. Now* ~~Things are really different now.~~
~~Cars zip by~~ *on the way to somewhere else* ~~with business elsewhere~~ or stop at the new ~~disco by~~ *shopping center outside of town.*
~~the road.~~ I have~~n't~~ been back there for a while. ~~I cannot go back by car.~~ Instead, I ~~just have~~ *visit my past through* my memories.

- Has this paragraph been improved? What new sensory details have been added?
- What is the mood of this paragraph? Have the revisions made this mood more obvious?

Try Your Skill   Revise this paragraph. Following the guidelines presented in **Here's the Idea**. You may also want to combine sentences and ideas. Feel free to invent details to make the paragraph more vivid.

The farmhouse was one of them kinds you see all over. It had a roof of tin. When it rained, it would make a lot of noise. Outside, the house had tar paper walls and two doors. There is a porch attached in front with four pillars on it. The porch is old. The porch is rickety. On the porch were a swing and a chair. On the porch was also a bucket for water and a hollowed-out gourd for drinking. The water came from a well. The well was on the front lawn. Beyond this well was a sycamore tree. And a bed of flowers. The flowers were forget-me-nots and bleeding hearts.

Keep This in Mind

- After finishing your rough draft, revise your composition.
- Make sure your readers will be able to picture your subject clearly.

Now Write   Revise the descriptive composition that you have been writing. Follow the guidelines presented in this lesson. Make sure to proofread your work carefully. When you have finished, give your composition a title and make a clean, neat final copy. Proofread this copy as you did your revised draft. Make your corrections as neatly as you can. Save your work in your folder.

The Explanatory Composition

Explaining a Process

How So?

Pre-Writing: Planning an Explanation

Here's the Idea There are two types of compositions that explain processes. One type explains the process of making or doing something. It gives directions. A composition of this kind might explain how an animated cartoon is made or how to tune up a car. The other type tells how things work or happen. This sort of composition might explain how a video camera works or how caterpillars turn into butterflies.

Every process involves a series of steps. To write a composition that explains a process, you must explain each step simply and clearly. To do this, present each step in the order in which it happens or should be done.

Begin by choosing and narrowing a topic. To find a topic, think about your own interests and experiences. If you have experience as an actor, you might describe the process of putting on makeup for a show. Choose a topic with which you are already familiar. This will make it easier for you to explain the process completely.

After you have chosen a topic, write the steps of the process in your pre-writing notes. Make sure to include all the steps of the process. Describe each step clearly and simply. Include any tools, ingredients, or materials that are used in the process.

Check It Out Read these pre-writing notes.

How To Trace Your Family Tree

1. Collect facts from those living: write down what you know, interview parents, grandparents, relatives

2. Sort notes: begin a file for each person, compare information gathered, try to clear up confusion
3. Search family records: photograph albums, legal and personal documents, personal documents of other relatives
4. Check public records: organizations, library records, town records, newspapers

- What process is explained in these notes?
- Do the notes clearly list the steps in the process?

Try Your Skill Review the examples of processes given in **Here's the Idea**. Then, do some brainstorming about processes. Come up with a list of ten processes that would make good topics for an explanatory composition. Save your list in your folder.

Keep This in Mind

- There are two types of compositions that explain processes. One type gives directions. The other shows how something happens or works.
- In your pre-writing notes, list the steps in the process.
- Include in your notes any tools, ingredients, or materials used in the process.

Now Write Choose a topic for a composition that explains a process. This may be one of the topics you developed in **Try Your Skill**. Make pre-writing notes for your composition. List all the steps in the process. Also include necessary tools, ingredients, or materials. Save these notes in your folder.

Watch Your Step

Pre-Writing: Using Step-by-Step Order

Here's the Idea A composition that explains a process must be complete and well organized. If it is not, the reader may have trouble understanding the process. To avoid confusing your readers, make sure your pre-writing notes contain all the steps in the process. Then, arrange the details in your notes in step-by-step order. This is the order in which the steps in a process happen or are done.

Begin by organizing the details you will use in your introduction. The first detail should be a topic sentence that tells what process you are going to explain.

Next, organize the details you will present in the body of your composition. Check your pre-writing notes and find the main steps in the process. Then, identify the smaller steps that are part of each main step. Place these smaller steps under each main step. When this is done, you will have several groups of details. Each of these groups will become a paragraph in your first draft.

Finally organize the details you will present in your conclusion. In the conclusion, you may explain the last main step and describe the result of the process or you may summarize or review the process as a whole. You may also tell your readers why learning about this process is important or valuable.

When you have finished organizing your notes, check them once again. Make sure you have included every step. Also make sure that each step is in its proper order.

Check It Out Read the body of the following explanatory composition about the process of tracing a family tree.

Jot down where and when you were born, your parents' names, your mother's maiden name, and the schools you have attended. Then, interview the older members of your family. Find out where and when they were born and where they went to school. Also ask where they worked and when they were married. Then interview your grandparents or gather information about them from other relatives.

Next, sort your notes and file them properly. You may wish to make separate files of notes for each person.

Once you have exhausted your family's records, move on to public records. You may find information in newspapers, in library or city records, and in church or synagogue records.

· What steps are explained in these paragraphs?

Try Your Skill The following are pre-writing notes for two compositions. Write the titles of these compositions. Then, list the steps under each title in step-by-step order.

How To Write a Composition	**How To Bake a Cake**
Revise your first draft.	Assemble ingredients.
Choose a topic.	Add eggs to butter and sugar.
Organize your information.	Spoon batter into pan.
Proofread your revised copy.	Put batter into hot oven.
Narrow your topic.	Add dry ingredients last.
	First, preheat oven.

Keep This in Mind

· When writing a composition to explain a process, organize your details in step-by-step order.

Now Write Use step-by-step order to organize the pre-writing notes that you wrote in the last lesson. Decide which notes will go in the introduction, the body, and the conclusion. Save your organized notes in your folder.

Signs of the Times

Writing the First Draft: Using Transitions

Here's the Idea   When you write the first draft of your explanatory composition, follow your organized list of pre-writing notes. First write your introduction. This should be a single paragraph that states your main idea and captures the attention of your readers. Then, write the paragraphs of the body. In each paragraph of the body, present one major step from your pre-writing notes. Also include the smaller steps that are part of each major step. When the body is finished, write your conclusion. The conclusion may explain the last step, summarize the entire process, or tell why the process is important.

As you write, use transitional words and phrases to show *when* each step happens or is done. The following are some transitional words and phrases that tell *when*:

first	after	when	the next step	finally
next	while	before	as soon as	later

Check It Out   Read the following introduction and conclusion of the composition on tracing your family tree.

Introduction   From ancient times to the present day, people have asked themselves "Who am I?" One way to begin answering this question is to trace your family tree.

Conclusion   Finally, you should be able to use the information from your notes to write about your family tree. Begin with yourself and go backwards. This tracing of your family tree will reward you by giving you a better sense of who you are.

- What transitions are used within these paragraphs?
- What transition links the conclusion to the body of the composition?

Try Your Skill   Read the following explanation for the process of making a woodcut. The steps are presented in the correct order. Rewrite the paragraph. Add a topic sentence. Also add transitional words and phrases that tell *when*.

Assemble your tools and materials. You will need a soft lead pencil, a woodblock, and woodcutting tools. You will also need a bottle of ink, an ink tray, a roller, and clean white paper. All of these materials can be found in an art supply shop. On the woodblock, make a sketch of the subject you want to print. Use the pencil to darken all the areas that you want to appear white in your final print. Carve out these darkened areas with your woodcutting tools. Pour ink into your ink tray. Use the roller to ink the top of your woodblock. Place a piece of plain, white paper on top of the block. Press evenly against the back side of the paper. Peel the paper off the block and allow the finished print to dry.

Keep This in Mind

- When writing a composition that explains a process, use transitional words and phrases that tell *when*.

Now Write   Write the first draft of your composition. In the introduction, state your topic. In the body, present the steps given in your pre-writing notes. Make sure each paragraph of the body has a topic sentence. Use transitions within and between paragraphs. End with a conclusion that states the last step in the process, summarizes the entire process, or tells why the process is important. Save your work.

A Job Well Done

Revising Your Explanation

Here's the Idea   A composition that explains a process must be clear and thorough. No step in the process can be missing, out of order, or poorly explained. If one is, readers of the composition may become confused. To avoid confusing your readers, revise your composition carefully. Ask yourself the following questions as you revise.

1. Does my introduction tell what process the composition will explain? Does it capture the interest of the reader?

2. Have I included *all* the steps in the process?

3. Are these steps presented in step-by-step order?

4. Does each body paragraph contain a main idea and supporting details?

5. Have I used transitional words and phrases that tell *when?* Do these transitions appear both within and between paragraphs?

6. Does my conclusion explain the last step in the process, summarize the process, or tell the reader why the process is important?

After you have revised the content, organization, and language of your composition, proofread your revised draft. Find and correct any errors in grammar, capitalization, punctuation, and spelling.

Check It Out   The following paragraph is from the rough draft of a composition that explains a process. Notice how this paragraph has been revised.

- How has this paragraph been improved?
- Has the paragraph been proofread? How do you know?

Some fossils are the result of traps set by nature. For example, ~~Here's how some fossils are formed.~~ A long time ~~ago~~ *ages* a bee got stuck in the sap of a tree. *(Soon around its prisoner)* ~~The sap dried and hardened. It~~ *honey* *The sap hardened into resin called amber. When decomposed,* ~~became~~ a clear yellow~~-colored stuff~~. The tree died and ~~fell to~~ *amber* ~~the ground~~. The piece of ~~yellow-colored stuff~~ was buried. ~~This~~ *under layers of* *dirt and decaying plant matter. Recently, this* ~~stuff is known as amber. The~~ piece of amber ~~has been found~~. *was uncovered by scientists.* Inside it ~~is~~ *crested* the perfect body of the *by preserved* bee. *honey*

Try Your Skill The following paragraph is from the body of a composition about how to plan a vacation. Revise this paragraph. Follow the guidelines presented in this lesson.

> Find out about the place your going too before you set out. Do this by going to the library or calling there to the Chamber of Commerce. Look at a map. If you are planning to go by car. Plan the route you will take. The Chamber of Commerce in the city or town you are going to can tell you lots of things. Like where you can eat and about motels and stuff to do while you're their.

Keep This in Mind

- When revising a composition that explains a process, make sure that each step in the process is presented clearly and logically.

Now Write Revise your explanatory composition. Make sure you have included *all* the steps in the process you are explaining. Also make sure that these steps are presented in a logical order. Rewrite any parts of your composition that are unclear or confusing. When your revision is finished, proofread your composition. Then, write a title. Save the completed composition.

The Explanatory Composition
Presenting an Opinion

You Be the Judge

Pre-Writing: Stating an Opinion

Here's the Idea   No two people have exactly the same opinions. Because this is so, you will sometimes have to explain your opinions to others. One way to explain an opinion is to write an explanatory composition. In this type of explanatory composition, you state an opinion and then support it. In other words, you give your readers reasons for believing as you do.

It is not difficult to find a topic for a composition that presents an opinion. Think about what is happening in your school, your neighborhood, your city, and your nation. What issues do you feel strongly about? Also think about the beliefs you hold.

After you have chosen a topic, write a sentence that states your opinion. This sentence will serve as the topic sentence of your paragraph.

The next step is to gather details that support your opinion. These details may be facts or statistics. They may also be specific examples, anecdotes, or personal experiences. You can find these details in reference works, books, and newspaper or magazine articles. You can also find support in your own experiences or in the experiences of others.

Check It Out   Read these pre-writing notes.

Topic   All people who drive should learn how to maintain and repair their cars.

Reasons   1. not difficult to learn how
cars easy to understand
interesting and rewarding to learn about

2. saves money
   spend less on routine upkeep
   spend less on major repairs
   spend less to buy new cars
3. prevent problems
   avoid chances of car not working when
      needed
   avoid breakdowns
   avoid mechanical failure while car is
      in motion

- Is the topic a clearly expressed opinion?
- Is the opinion supported by reasons?

Try Your Skill   Choose three of the following subjects. For each subject, write a sentence that states an opinion.

college education	nuclear energy	computers
national parks	jobs for teenagers	space program

Keep This in Mind

- An explanatory composition can present an opinion.
- State the opinion in a single sentence.
- Gather facts, statistics, examples, and anecdotes to support the opinion.

Now Write   Choose a topic for an explanatory composition that presents an opinion. Your topic may be one you developed in **Try Your Skill**. It may be any other topic about which you feel strongly. On a piece of paper, write a sentence that states your opinion. Then write a list of reasons that support your opinion. These reasons may be facts, statistics, examples, or anecdotes. Save these notes in your folder.

The Evidence

Pre-Writing: Organizing an Opinion

Here's the Idea   An opinion is one person's feelings about a subject. Therefore, an opinion cannot be proved true or false. Because this is so, some people believe that one opinion is just as good as another. However, this is not the case. Some opinions are better than others because they are more carefully supported and presented.

For example, think about the opinion "Everyone should use seat belts." This is a sound opinion because it is supported by facts. Statistics show that people who wear seat belts are more likely to survive accidents.

When you write about an opinion, you must support your ideas with strong reasons. This is why you gather details during the pre-writing stage. It is not enough to collect a number of supporting details, however. You must also present these details so that they will have an impact on your reader.

To present your material well, begin by organizing your information. Study your pre-writing notes carefully. Group your details around two or three major ideas. These ideas will be the main reasons you will use to support your opinion.

The next step is to put your idea groups into a logical order. Usually, this means putting your reasons in the order of their importance. Begin with the group that presents the least important of your reasons. Follow this with the next most important group of reasons. Continue in this way until you reach the group of ideas that explains the strongest reason of all.

Finally, organize the details within each idea group. You may use order of importance here, too. You may also choose comparison and contrast or any other method of organization that suits your material.

Check It Out Read this paragraph from the body of an explanatory composition. The paragraph was developed from the pre-writing notes given in the last lesson.

There is an even more important reason for learning how to repair a car. By recognizing and correcting problems, you can avoid many annoying and possibly dangerous situations. Your car will be in better working order. As a result, it will start and run when you need it. More importantly, the car will be less likely to break down while you are driving. Avoiding such breakdowns will save you time and towing bills and may even save your life.

- What is the main idea of this paragraph?
- Is the main idea supported with reasons?
- Are the reasons organized from least important to most important?

Try Your Skill Choose one of these opinions to support. List at least three reasons to support the opinion. Then, place these reasons in a logical order. Begin with the least important reason. End with the most important.

1. Community colleges are valuable institutions.
2. There should be more public facilities for the handicapped.
3. Students should learn how to use the library.
4. Parents should supervise the television viewing of children.

Keep This in Mind

- A sound opinion must be supported by facts.
- Organize the reasons in an explanatory composition from the least important to the most important.

Now Write Organize the pre-writing notes that you made in the last lesson. Save these notes in your folder.

Trial Run

Writing the First Draft

Here's the Idea   Begin your first draft with an introduction. This should be a single paragraph. In the introduction, include a topic sentence that states the opinion you want to support. Also, include details that will capture the interest of your readers. If the issue is very complicated, you may also wish to provide some background information.

Follow your introduction with the paragraphs of the body. In each paragraph, include a topic sentence that states an important reason for accepting your opinion. Also include the details that support each topic sentence.

Then, write your conclusion. This should also be a single paragraph. In the conclusion, restate your opinion using different words. You may also summarize your reasons for holding this opinion.

Within and between paragraphs, use transitional words and phrases to tie your ideas together. The following words and phrases can be used to show the relationship between your ideas:

> most importantly   first   another reason   finally

These transitional words can be used to present reasons and facts:

> consequently   since   if
>   therefore   because   as a result

Check It Out   Read the following conclusion from an explanatory composition.

There are therefore many good reasons for learning how to work on cars. First, working on cars can be an enjoyable and satisfying experience. Second, learning to do routine maintenance and repairs can save money. Third, by learning about cars, people can avoid many problems and dangers.

- Does the conclusion restate the opinion in other words? Does it summarize the argument?

Try Your Skill Read the following pre-writing notes. Use the notes to write a paragraph that presents an opinion. Feel free to add details. Also add transitions to help state reasons or to show the order of the ideas.

The government should continue the space program.
The space program appeals to our spirit of adventure.
The space program helps us to learn about the unknown.
The space program has given us useful inventions such as communications satellites.

Keep This in Mind

- In the introduction of an explanatory composition that presents an opinion, state an opinion clearly and directly. Also capture the interest of the reader.
- In the body, present the supporting evidence.
- In the conclusion, summarize the argument.
- Use transitions to state reasons and to show the order of ideas.

Now Write Write the first draft of your composition. As you write, use transitional words and phrases to present your ideas and to show how they are related. Save your work in your folder.

Order in the Court

Revising Your Explanation

Here's the Idea   When you have finished your first draft, reread your composition. Look at it as though you were a reader who is hard to convince. Make certain that your evidence shows why your opinion is sound. Also make sure you have presented your evidence in a logical order. Ask yourself the following questions as you revise:

1. Did I express my opinion clearly in the introduction? Is my introduction interesting?
2. Have I used strong, specific reasons, facts, statistics, examples, and anecdotes. Do these support my opinion?
3. Did I support my opinion with enough details?
4. Did I use transitional words and phrases both between and within paragraphs?
5. Are my major ideas and the details supporting them arranged logically?
6. Does my conclusion restate my opinion and summarize my reasons for holding it?

Revise your organization and content. Then, proofread your revised draft. Find and correct all errors in grammar, capitalization, punctuation, and spelling.

Check it Out   The following paragraph is from the composition about why people should learn about cars. Notice how this paragraph has been revised.

- In what ways has this paragraph been improved? Give specific examples?

repair and maintenance

Learning about cars, is not difficult. The biggest surprise is
how simple auto repairs and ma̤tenance really, is. ~~Manuals~~ *are* *Many* *in*
are available that ~~explain how to do~~ *routine maintenance such as oil changes.* ~~everything.~~ ~~They~~ also explain how to do such
repairs as changing brake shoes or replacing the starter. *These manuals* Your
car will, be in excellent shape. *always* *More importantly, If you learn these simple procedures,* Once you've finished with a job,
you'll have the satisfaction of knowing you did it yourself. *In fact,* If a
person thinks of, it as a process of discovery, it can be both *learning about cars*
interesting and surprizing.

Try Your Skill   Revise the following paragraph.

School ought to teach people how to type good. Most
important students need to know how to type for there
classes. Also they should know how to type for jobs such as
office and business. And for a career as an editor or writer.
Letters are also typed when applying for jobs or to colleges.

Keep This in Mind

- When revising a composition that presents an opinion, check your organization and content. Make
sure you have presented enough evidence to support your opinion.

Now Write   Revise your explanatory composition. Follow the
guidelines presented in this lesson. Then, proofread your revised draft. Find and correct any errors in grammar, usage,
capitalization, punctuation, or spelling. Save your final copy in
your folder.

The Explanatory Composition
Stating a Definition

What in the World?

Pre-Writing: Developing a Definition

Here's the Idea   Suppose that you want to explain the game of basketball to a friend. You would have to explain the rules of the game. You would also have to describe the positions and duties of the players. One way to do this would be to write an **explanatory composition that defines.**

Many kinds of subjects lend themselves to this type of composition. The subject could be any term that requires a long definition, such as *science fiction, telescope,* or *macramé.*

The subject may also be an unfamiliar person, place, or idea, such as *lobbyist, mesa,* or *courage.*

Once you have chosen your subject, write a sentence that defines it. This sentence should do three things. It should tell what term is being defined. It should then put the term into a general class. Finally, the sentence should show how the subject differs from other members of its class.

A <u>telescope</u> is a <u>scientific instrument</u>
   | term | | general class |
<u>used for making distant objects seem nearer and larger</u>.
      | particular characteristics |

The next step is to gather specific details about the subject. If you are defining a thing, gather facts, statistics, and sensory details. These can be found through personal observation. They can also be found by checking dictionaries, encyclopedias, and other reference works. If you are defining an idea, you may want to gather specific examples or anecdotes. These can be found through research. They can also come from interviews.

When you gather details to use in your definition, think of your audience. If your audience is not familiar with your topic, keep your explanation simple. If your audience already knows about your topic, you may provide more detailed information.

Check It Out Read these pre-writing notes.

Topic bluegrass music—folk music that includes traditional Appalachian elements

Details developed in Kentucky/spread across country
Bill Monroe—creator of bluegrass music
songs about many subjects
familiar instruments used in bluegrass—guitars, banjos, fiddles, mandolins, string basses
developed from folk music of England, Ireland, and Scotland
uncommon instruments used in bluegrass—washboards, autoharps, dulcimers, jugs, dobros
instrumental music fast-paced and exciting—hand clapping and foot stomping
titles of songs—"Tea for Texas," "Salty Dog"
music got its name from a type of Kentucky grass

- Do these details help a reader understand "bluegrass music"?

Try Your Skill Choose three of the following subjects. For each subject, write a one-sentence definition. In your definition, name the subject you are defining. Then, place the subject in a general category or class. Finally, show how the subject differs from other members of its class.

fear   porpoise   jazz   word processer

> ### Keep This in Mind
> - In a composition that defines, you explain a term clearly and completely.

Now Write Choose and narrow a topic for a composition that defines. Write a definition of your subject. Then gather details to develop your definition. Save your pre-writing notes.

Made to Order

Pre-Writing: Organizing a Definition

Here's the Idea   Whenever you write a composition that defines, you must arrange your details logically. Begin by organizing the information for your introduction. The introduction should include your one-sentence definition of your topic. It should also include details that will capture your reader's interest.

Next, organize the information for the body of the composition. Study your pre-writing notes. Look for relationships between the ideas in these notes. Find or think of two or three major ideas to which your details are related. Arrange your notes into groups of related details. These idea groups will become separate paragraphs in your first draft.

Finally, decide upon a logical order for your ideas. Choose methods of organization that suit the details you are using. For example, in one paragraph you might describe your subject. Therefore, you might organize the details in spatial order. In another paragraph, you might tell the history of your subject. In this paragraph, you might use chronological order. There are many other methods you could use. You may choose to present your information in order of importance or in order of familiarity. You may also organize your ideas from the most general to the most specific.

Check It Out   Read these pre-writing notes.

Topic   Mummies

Introduction   mummy—body preserved by the method of embalming used by the ancient Egyptians
people's fascination with mummies in museums
people's fascination with mummies in horror films

Body 1. what a mummy looks like—
carved, jeweled coffin
body covered with strips of cloth
face mask under the strips of cloth
2. how mummies were made—
internal organs, except heart, removed
chemical called "hatron" put in and on body
body wrapped with strips of linen
linen strips glued together with resin
finished mummy placed inside elaborate coffin

- Do the notes for the introduction include a complete one-sentence definition? Do they include details that will interest readers?
- Are the notes in the body paragraphs organized logically? What methods of organization are used in these notes?

Try Your Skill Look again at the notes given under **Check It Out** in the previous lesson. Find three major ideas to which the details in these notes are related. Write these ideas on a piece of paper. Then, write the details that belong under each major idea. Finally, arrange the idea groups and the notes beneath them in logical order. Be prepared to explain the methods of organization you have used.

Keep This in Mind

- Arrange, in a logical order, the details in a composition that defines.

Now Write Organize the pre-writing notes you have made for your composition that defines. Choose two or three major ideas. Then, group the remaining details under these ideas. Finally, place your idea groups and details in a logical order.

On the Whole

Writing the First Draft

Here's the Idea After you have organized your pre-writing notes, study them carefully. Make sure you have enough information to define your subject completely. If any part of your notes is incomplete, gather additional information. Then, begin writing. As you write, concentrate on your organization and content. At this point, do not be too concerned with grammar, usage, or mechanics.

Start with your introduction. In this paragraph, include the one sentence definition that tells your main idea. Also include details that will make your readers want to learn more about your topic.

Next, develop your definition in the paragraphs of the body. In each paragraph, present one major idea that helps to define your subject. Use the details from your pre-writing notes to explain or support this major idea.

Finally, write your conclusion. In the conclusion, sum up the major parts of your definition. Then add a sentence that brings the composition to a satisfying close.

Check It Out Read this introduction and body of a composition that defines.

Bluegrass is a type of folk music that uses traditional Appalachian instruments, lyrics, and melodies. The music takes its name from the bluegrass country of its native state, Kentucky. Like blues, bluegrass music is distinctly American.

Bluegrass music developed in Kentucky in the 1930's and 40's. The creator of this music was Bill Monroe. He and his band, the Bluegrass Boys, performed many Appalachian folk tunes. Many of these tunes were based upon the folk tunes of England, Ireland, and Scotland. To this music, Bill Monroe added fast-paced picking, beautiful vocal harmonies, and his own high-pitched lead vocals. These became the essential elements of bluegrass.

Much of bluegrass music is instrumental. It is played by a band that includes a guitar, a banjo, a mandolin, and a string bass. Some bluegrass bands add a fiddle and a harmonica. Others use less familiar instruments, such as dobros, autoharps, dulcimers, zithers, and washboards. The music played on these instruments is almost always high-spirited and energetic.

Vocal music is also an important part of bluegrass. Some bluegrass songs are light and comic. Such songs include "Salty Dog" and "Up on Cripple Creek." Other bluegrass songs are sad or tragic. "Pretty Polly" and "Blue Moon of Kentucky" are songs of this kind.

- Does the introduction contain a one-sentence definition of the subject?
- Does each body paragraph deal with a single main idea? Do the details in each paragraph relate to this idea?

Try Your Skill   Reread the composition in **Check It Out**. Then write a satisfying conclusion.

Keep This in Mind

- The introduction of a composition that defines should contain a one-sentence definition of the subject.
- The body should develop the definition with specific details.
- The conclusion should summarize the main points of the definition.

Now Write   Write the first draft of your composition that defines. Follow your organized pre-writing notes. Also follow the guidelines in this lesson. Save your work in your folder.

New and Improved

Revising Your Explanation

Here's the Idea   To please their customers, companies always look for ways to improve their products. In order to please your readers, you must look for ways to improve your writing. The process of improving your writing is called revising.

To revise a composition that defines, read the composition several times. Make certain that your ideas are clear and well organized. Also make sure that your language is interesting and exact. As you revise, ask yourself the following questions:

1. Does the topic sentence of my introduction define the subject?

2. Does my one-sentence definition name the subject? Does it place the subject in a general class? Does it name some characteristics that make the subject different from other things in its class?

3. Do the paragraphs of the body develop my definition with specific facts, statistics, details, examples, or anecdotes?

4. Is my composition organized logically?

5. Does the conclusion summarize the main points of the definition?

6. Is my language interesting, clear, and simple? Will the audience be able to follow my ideas?

Once you have checked your ideas, organization, and language, proofread your composition carefully. Check for errors in grammar, capitalization, punctuation, and spelling. Correct any that you find.

Check It Out   Notice how this conclusion to the composition about bluegrass music has been revised.

First Draft Bluegrass is very popular. Bluegrass festivals are held all over. Lots of people go to here it. These people love good bluegrass.

Revised Draft Every year, hundreds of bluegrass festivals are held throughout the country. The festivals bring together people of all ages and backgrounds. These people have one thing in common: their love for the best in traditional music and song.

- How has this conclusion been improved?
- What specific improvements have been made?

Try Your Skill   Read the following one-sentence definitions. Each was taken from the first draft of an introductory paragraph. Find what is wrong with each definition. Then, revise each sentence, correcting any errors it contains.

1. A *ferret* is a small animal.
2. A *meteor* is a chunk of rock or metal.
3. *Boredom* is a familiar feeling.
4. *Evergreens* are different from other trees.
5. A *belief* is a thing you believe.

Keep This in Mind

- When revising your composition that defines, check your content, organization, and language.
- Make sure your definition is clear and complete.

Now Write   Revise your composition that defines. As you revise, follow the guidelines presented in this lesson. Proofread your revised draft. Then make a final copy and save it in your folder.

The Research Paper

Is That a Fact?

Developing a Research Paper

Here's the Idea   In this section you will be learning about the **research paper,** a special kind of composition. In some ways, the research paper is just like any other composition. It has an introduction, a body, and a conclusion. It presents information about a single, specific topic.

However, there are important differences between research papers and other compositions. A research paper is never written from the first-person point of view. Also, a research paper never includes the personal opinions of the writer.

A research paper is written from facts—statements which can be proved to be true. To gather facts for a report, you must look to sources outside your own knowledge and experience. These outside sources may include books, encyclopedias, magazines, or newspapers. Sources may also include atlases, almanacs, and pamphlets. Non-print materials, such as interviews, recordings, television programs, and films, can also be used.

When choosing a topic for a research paper, begin the process much as you would for any other composition. Think about a general subject that interests you and spend time reading about it in the library. Be sure that your subject is one that can be developed with facts. As you read, you will likely discover some specific topics that especially interest you.

Suppose, for example, that you are assigned the general subject of environmental issues to investigate. You need to survey available information and select a specific aspect of the subject.

Choose an environmental issue about which you will be able to find enough information. Jot down a few environmental concerns that interest you. Go to the library. Look through the card catalog for the subject cards *Environment* and *Ecology.* Look in the nonfiction section for books on the environment.

Search also throughout the reference section. Here you will find a variety of sources, including encyclopedias. Magazines and the pamphlets found in the vertical file are also good sources of information to check, as are local and national newspapers.

Here is a sample list of sources you might check to find general information about environmental issues.

1. "Environmental Pollution" in *The World Book Encyclopedia*, 1982 ed.

2. *Clean Water for Us All*, U.S. Environmental Protection Agency, June, 1977

3. "Nature and Cities," by J. M. McCloskey in *Sierra* magazine, April, 1978, pages 14–16

4. "Preserving Wildlife—A Worldwide Struggle," *U.S. News and World Report* magazine, April 17, 1978, pages 62–65

5. "Acid Rain Hard to Quantify" in the *New York Times*, March 27, 1983

After you have considered environmental issues in general, focus on a particular issue. Consider your interests and particular environment. You will write your best about an issue that affects you. Make sure that the issue you choose is not too broad to be developed in the assigned length of your research paper.

Once you have chosen a particular environmental issue to investigate, search again in the kinds of sources already mentioned. Look for additional material as well. If possible, talk to someone with special knowledge in the area you have chosen. Be sure to record each source of your information in your notebook. Record titles of books, encyclopedias, pamphlets, and magazine articles. Also write the volume and page number of the encyclopedias you may decide to use and the dates of the magazines.

Check It Out   Examine this list of sources for a research paper about the wildlife conservation efforts of zoos.

- Is this a varied and specific enough list of sources for a research paper?

1. *Encyclopedia Americana*, 1982 ed.

2. *Zoo Animals, People, Places*, a book by Bernard Livingst[e]

3. *Saving the Animals: The World Wildlife Fund Book of Conservation*, a book by Bernard Stonehouse

4. *Newsweek* magazine, May 31, 1982, pp. 58-61

5. *Science Digest* magazine, (Sept., 1978), pp. 34-38

Try Your Skill Choose one of these issues to research. Narrow the subject to a specific issue. Then find and list four sources of information about this specific issue.

air pollution	soil pollution	nuclear radiation
water pollution	wildlife conservation	recycling

Keep This in Mind

- A research paper is developed with facts gathered from outside sources.
- With a general subject in mind, search through books, magazines, and other reference works to find a specific, limited subject for a report.
- With a specific subject chosen, begin your research by looking for sources of information. Keep a list of the sources.

Now Write Choose an environmental issue to investigate. Then go to the library. Check the reference shelves, the card catalog, the *Readers' Guide*, and the vertical file. Find as many sources about your subject as you can. Note the call numbers, the book titles, the magazine issues, or the vertical file references. Write down all this information.

Report Cards

Taking Notes

Here's the Idea   When you have located a variety of sources about your topic, you must begin reading them and writing down the important information that you find. Before you begin this task, you may want to prepare a preliminary outline.

A **preliminary outline** is a list of the aspects of your topic that you want to cover in your paper. Once you know what to write about, you can direct your research to those specific subjects.

When you write a research paper, you must give credit to your outside sources. **Bibliography cards** contain all the publication information you will need to properly credit your sources. Here is the kind of information you will need.

Book	author, title, publisher, date published, city in which published
Magazine	author of article (if there is one), title of article, name of magazine, date published, page number of article
Encyclopedia	author of article (if there is one), name of encyclopedia, volume number, page number of article, date published
Newspaper	author of article (if there is one), title of article, name of newspaper, date published, section, page, and column number of article

When you make bibliography cards, assign each source a number. Write this number in the upper right-hand corner of the card. Write down the place you located the source as well as other identifying information, such as a call number.

As you read about your topic, write the information on **notecards**.

1. Use a separate 3″ × 5″ note card for each fact or idea.
2. Write a key phrase at the top of each card. This key phrase

should tell the main idea of the note. As you work, you may want to keep cards with similar key phrases together.

3. Label each note card with the number given to that source on its bibliography card. Include the exact page number.

4. Take notes in your own words. Copying another writer's words is called **plagiarism**. Plagiarism is a serious offense. When you want to quote a source directly, use quotation marks to enclose the writer's words. Copy the words exactly as they are given.

Check It Out   Examine the sample cards on page 255.

- What information does each bibliography card contain?

Try Your Skill   Read the following information. Make a bibliography card and a note card based on it.

Pesticides and herbicides have, without doubt, allowed farmers to produce more crops and livestock than they could have done without these chemical aids. . . . However, pesticides and herbicides also have undesirable effects on soils.

from a book called *Shadow Over the Land*, by J. J. McCoy. The Seabury Press, New York, 1970, on pages 56 and 57, with library call number 628.5 Mcc

Keep This in Mind

- Make bibliography cards that contain basic information about all sources for your report.
- Write note cards. Each card should contain one fact or idea.

Now Write   In the last lesson, you listed at least four sources suitable for a report. Take that list and a stack of 3″ × 5″ note cards with you to your library. Make bibliography cards for all suitable sources. Then, read through those sources and make note cards. Follow the guidelines in this lesson. Save your cards.

Carpenter, Mary
"Zoos: Last Hope To Preserve
Vanishing Species,"
Science Digest, Vol. 84
Sept., 1978   pp. 34-38
                        public library

(1)

Bridges, William
"Zoological Gardens"
Encyclopedia Americana, Vol. 29

pp. 800-804   New York, copyright 1982

                        school
                        library

(2)

Stonehouse, Bernard.
Saving the Animals: The World
Wildlife Fund Book on Conservation
New York, Macmillian
copyright 1981
                    public library

333.95
STO

(3)

educational benefits:

"Zoos are educational... often
giving people their only chance
to see exotic animals."

                            page 68

(3)

Order Please

Organizing Information

Here's the Idea If you plan a research paper thoughtfully, you will be able to write the paper much more easily. An essential step in planning is to organize the information you have gathered.

Begin by reading through your note cards. Separate them into several piles, each dealing with one general idea. The key phrase you wrote at the top of each note card will help you to complete this step. Try to group the cards around four or five main ideas.

For instance, if you were writing about the role of zoos in wildlife conservation, you might find that all your information could be organized into four main ideas. You might have found facts about zoos of the past, facts about modern zoos, facts about what zoos can do to protect animals, and facts about what zoos can do to educate the public.

If you find cards that do not belong with any others, you may want to omit these ideas from your report. Save these cards, however. They may contain information you can use in your introduction or conclusion.

When all of your cards are separated into piles, write a topic sentence for each group of cards. This sentence should state the main idea of the cards in that group. You can use these topic sentences when you write the first draft of your paper.

Finally, you must put your notes in order. First, arrange the groups of cards in the order that you want to write about them. Then arrange the cards in each group in a logical order. For information on different types of organization, see pages 104–105.

Check It Out Read the following sentences. They describe the main ideas for a research paper on wildlife conservation.

1. In zoos of the past, animals were kept for various human purposes.

2. Modern zoos reflect an interest in animals for their own sake.

3. Many modern zoos are working to conserve endangered species.

4. Modern zoos are working to educate the public to support wildlife conservation efforts.

· Is one main idea stated clearly in each sentence?

Try Your Skill   Organize the following environmental issues into four separate groups of four issues each. For each group, write one sentence that expresses the main idea.

the blue whale	traffic sounds	construction noise
paper recycling	plastics recycling	the California condor
open dumps	compacting	ocean dumping
incineration	glass recycling	the whooping crane
airport noise	the Bengal tiger	metal recycling
very loud music		

Keep This in Mind

· Organize your note cards into separate piles. Group together cards with the same main idea. Write a topic sentence stating the main idea of each group. Arrange the groups and the cards within them into a logical order.

Now Write   Take out the note cards you have written for your report. Organize them into four or five main groups. Write a topic sentence for each group. Then arrange the sentences and the notes that go with them in a logical order. Save your notes.

Numbers and Letters

Making an Outline

Here's the Idea   After you have listed the main ideas for your paper, make an outline. By making an outline, you will be organizing your notes in a more detailed way. You will be deciding where each individual note card with its one idea fits into your paper. In this way, you will be making a plan to follow when you write your first draft.

Each main idea will become a main topic in your outline. The related facts on your note cards will become subtopics and details of the outline. Each main idea, subtopic, and detail will be stated in a word or phrase.

All outlines follow the same form, which you must follow whenever you make an outline. An outline begins with a title. Below that, first in importance, are the main ideas, shown by Roman numerals. Under main ideas, next in importance, are the subtopics, shown by capital letters. Under subtopics are the details, shown by Arabic numerals. If more specific details must be shown, small letters are used. In an outline, you must have no fewer than two main topics or subtopics.

Each part of the outline is indented from the one above. However, each symbol is in a straight line with the others like it. Each kind of symbol is followed by a period, although the words of the outline are not to be followed by periods. In a completed outline, the first word and all important words are capitalized in every line, as well as in the title.

Check It Out   Examine this outline.

- What ideas and details explain the role of zoos in wildlife conservation? Point out how the form for outlining has been followed correctly.

I. Introduction
   A. Effects of people on environment
   B. Attitudes towards animals measured by zoos
II. Zoos of the past
   A. Animals kept for human purposes
      1. Chinese Garden of Intelligence, for observation
      2. Egyptians, for prestige
      3. Romans, for sporting contests
      4. Europe in Middle Ages, for gifts
   B. Needs of animals not met
III. Modern zoos
   A. Interest in animals for themselves
      1. First zoos in U.S. in Philadelphia, New York, Chicago
      2. Reflected gains in scientific knowledge
   B. For entertainment and education also
   C. More understanding of animals
      1. New, natural exhibits
      2. More freedom for animals
IV. Commitment to conservation
   A. Zoo as "repository for vanishing species"
   B. Breeding in captivity
      1. 85% of all exhibited animals
      2. Formosan deer
      3. Animals saved from extinction
V. Educating the public
   A. Increase environmental awareness
   B. Teach about specific animals and problems
   C. Develop concerned citizens
      1. 115 million zoo visitors each year in U.S.
      2. To support wildlife conservation

Try Your Skill Outline the information stated in the following paragraph from *The Wounded Earth* by Carl Marzani.

The dictionary defines garbage as any waste parts of food—animal or vegetable—that are thrown away. In general usage the word includes trash, such as glass, paper, plastics, which is collected by the sanitation services. In the large cities, such as New York and Chicago, the sanitation services collect broken-down furniture, refrigerators, air conditioners, among other items. Increasingly, they also have to do something about old cars abandoned on the streets. Ecologists call all this solid waste. It costs us some three billion dollars a year to get rid of the two billion tons of waste produced every year—including seven million junked cars, twenty million tons of paper, forty-six billion cans. Fifteen percent of total solid waste is household trash and garbage, and it works out to three-and-one-half pounds a day per family.

Keep This in Mind

- Use your notes to write an outline of the ideas and details to be presented in your report. Follow the correct form for making an outline.

Now Write Take out your organized note cards. Make an outline, using your list of main ideas and your note cards.

When your outline is written in its final form, arrange the cards in the order in which they appear in the outline. Save your work in your folder.

Put It in Writing

Writing the Introduction

Here's the Idea   Writing a research paper is much like writing a composition. Each has three parts—an introduction, a body, and a conclusion—and the function of each part is similar. The introduction introduces the main idea of your subject. The body develops the main idea with supporting ideas and details. The conclusion summarizes the important information.

However, there is an important difference between a composition and a research paper. A research paper, unlike a composition, must never be written from the first-person point of view. You should not use the words *I*, *me*, or *my*. Your personal opinion has no place in a factual paper.

When you write the introduction to your paper, be sure to state what the paper is about. Sometimes you will want to present certain facts in the introduction. At other times you will want to keep the introduction brief and general.

As you write your first draft, refer to your outline and your note cards. Use each of the main topics of your outline as a guide to writing the topic sentence of each paragraph. Use the subtopics of your outline and the facts from your note cards to develop each paragraph in a detailed way.

As you write, keep reading and reviewing your ideas. Are they clearly expressed? Are they organized logically? Is your writing detailed and interesting? Take time to think about how you can best express the information you have gathered.

Check It Out   Read the first draft of the introduction and the first paragraph of the body of the report about wildlife conservation on page 262.

- How does this first draft use the information shown in the outline on page 259?
- What main idea is presented in the introduction?

Human beings, ~~have many effects on their environment~~, affect their environment in many ways that range from the most negative to the most positive. Throughout history, one ~~big~~ major way people have affected their environment is through their attitudes toward wildlife. Perhaps these attitudes, especially those toward animals, can best be ~~studied~~ measured by the ~~zoos~~ zoological gardens—or zoos that have been created.

The purposes of ~~zoological gardens~~ zoos have changed ~~a great deal~~ remarkably over the course of the last two thousand years. A Chinese ruler once created a Garden of Intelligence ~~for~~ that kept animals in ~~their~~ natural surroundings. (Anceint Egyption) rulers kept animals ~~for~~ in order to glorify their own reputations. Romans kept animals for ~~sports~~ sporting contests. ~~In~~ In Europe in the Middle Ages, heads of state ~~had~~ kept collections of exotic animals to give as gifts. ~~In~~ Generally, in zoos of the past, the needs of animals were not understood. Many animals died, ~~and were~~ only to be replaced by others trapped in the wild.

Try Your Skill   On page 263 there is part of an outline for a research paper on recycling. Some of this information would fit nicely into the introduction to such a report. Use the information from this outline to write an introductory paragraph for a report on recycling.

I. Advantages of recycling aluminum cans

   A. Environmental cost of producing new cans

      1. About 15,000 kilowatt-hours of electricity to produce one ton of aluminum from bauxite ore

      2. About three tons of mineral wastes for each ton of aluminum produced

      3. About one million tons of aluminum thrown away each year

   B. Environmental savings from recycling old cans

      1. About 450 kilowatt-hours of electricity to obtain one ton of aluminum through recycling

      2. Almost no mineral wastes

      3. Fewer problems with solid waste disposal

Keep This in Mind

- Use your outline and note cards to write the first draft of a report.
- A report, like a composition, has an introduction, a body, and a conclusion. In an introduction, be sure to state your topic clearly.

Now Write Read your outline and note cards. Think about whether to introduce the environmental issue you have researched in a general or a detailed way. Decide how to state the main idea of your information about this issue.

Using both your outline and your note cards, write the introduction to your report. Try to present your ideas clearly. Your first draft, however, need not be perfect. When you have finished the introduction, save your work in your folder.

The Mainspring

Writing the Body and the Conclusion

Here's the Idea   The main part of your research is presented in the body of a research paper. When you write the body, follow your outline. The topic sentence of each paragraph in the body will correspond to a main topic in your outline. The note cards will supply the details to develop each paragraph. Use those details, specific examples, and quotations that will add the most to your paper.

Be sure to use quotation marks when you use the words of another writer. When you prepare your final copy, you will give that writer credit in the correct way. To keep track of information that must be credited, use the source numbers on your note cards. Write the source number after any sentence that contains a direct quote or any other information that must be credited.

A research paper, like a composition, should come to a logical ending. It should have a clear conclusion in which you tie ideas together naturally. You may include additional facts about the topic. However, your most important purpose is to summarize the information presented in the paper.

Check It Out   Read the rest of the body and conclusion of the research paper on wildlife conservation on pages 265–266.

- Compare this first draft with the outline for the paper on page 259. What details, examples, or direct quotations are used to develop the body?

Try Your Skill   Read the conclusion to the research paper on page 266. Explain why the conclusion is a good ending for the paper.

In contrast, the

~~The~~ purposes of modern zoos have arisen from an interest in animals for their own sake. ~~themselves~~. In the United States, the first zoos reflected this interest. They were opened in Philadelphia, Chicago, and New York, beginning in the 1860's. Entertainment and education were major functions of these zoos, and remain so today. However, gains in scientific knowledge are reflected in striking ~~created~~ changes being made in the ways that zoos exhibit animals. Stone barred, cages are being replaced with natural, living environments that allow animals greater freedom. Lions, for example, may live in an open area surrounded by a deep moat; birds may live in a tree-filled, climate-controlled building.

Many modern ~~Modern~~ zoos are now committed to ~~have~~ a policy of conserving animal species. About eighty-five percent of exhibited animals are being born in captivity. William G. Conway, director of the Bronx zoo, expects that this trend will continue. He has said, "The zoo of the future is an environmental park. It should be, among other things, a repository for vanishing species." In fact, at ~~At~~ the same time that the government of Taiwan declared the Formosan deer extinct, the Bronx Zoo had fifty ~~50~~ of them. It is generally agreed that several other animals, including the Père David deer and the Hawaiian Goose, would also be extinct if it were not for zoos. "Although the broad purpose of a zoo's existence is still to entertain and educate the public, breeding previously wild species in captivity will be the major thrust over the next ten years".

Modern zoos also educate the public ^to the needs of ~~about~~ animals. Zoos increase environmental awareness by exhibiting animals in their natural surroundings. Many zoos teach the public directly about specific animals by presenting various special programs. ^Through educational programs, ^these visitors ~~people~~ will become aware of public laws and policies that affect wildlife. ^A Knowledgeable public ~~People~~ will support more humane laws dealing with wildlife conservation. ^Human beings and animals can benefit only by sharing their surroundings.

"Each year over 115 million visitors come to the 130 zoos in the United States — more than the combined attendance at all U.S. professional basketball, football, and baseball games."

Keep This in Mind

- Use your outline and note cards to develop the body of a research paper.
- Write a conclusion that summarizes the information presented in the paper.

Now Write Take what you have written for your own research paper about an environmental issue. Review your outline and your notes, and write the first draft of the body and conclusion of your paper. Make sure you use quotation marks if you use other writers' words. When you are finished writing, save your work.

Inspection

Revising Your Research Paper

Here's the Idea   A research paper is a bit more complicated to plan and write than any other kind of composition. Therefore, you must take more care when revising a research paper.

Reread your first draft carefully. You may find that some of your ideas need to be expressed more clearly. A particular paragraph might need more details to develop its main idea fully. You may want to improve your word choice, perhaps adding transitional words and phrases to help the reader move from one idea to the next. However you decide to improve your work, don't feel discouraged if your first draft needs more work than you thought. Remember, your first draft was just a beginning.

As you revise your research paper, here are some questions to ask yourself.

1. Is the introductory paragraph direct and informative? Will it catch the reader's attention?

2. Does the first draft follow the outline I developed?

3. Are all of my facts accurate? Have I spelled all proper names and special words correctly?

4. Have I included enough information to develop my topic thoroughly?

5. Does each paragraph develop just one main idea? Does each paragraph have a strong topic sentence?

6. Do all the facts and ideas in each paragraph work to develop the main idea of that paragraph?

7. Did I use effective transitions between sentences and paragraphs?

8. Does my conclusion summarize the main ideas in my research paper?

267

When you are satisfied with the presentation of your ideas, proofread your first draft. Look for and correct any errors in grammar, usage, and mechanics.

Check It Out   Read this first-draft paragraph from a research paper about drilling for oil.

> After geolgists have got a good spot for driling, big trucks bring in the steel and other stuff to build the oil derick. The derick is a tower that will stand 100 to 200 foot high. Depending on the depth of the oil well. It is built with heavy steel beems, and girders. The derick is for a system of pulleys that that lifts the drill in and out of the well. I guess it's got to take alot of pressure and vibrations as the drill cuts into the bedrock.

• How can this paragraph be improved?

Try Your Skill   Use your revising skills to improve the paragraph in **Check It Out**. Be especially careful when proofreading the paragraph. Compare your revisions with those of your classmates.

Keep This in Mind

• When you revise your research paper, try to improve your ideas, your organization, and your word choice.
• Check your facts for accuracy. Also, check the correct spelling of proper names and special words.

Now Write   Revise the first draft of your research paper. Take your time and work carefully. Follow the guidelines in this lesson. Remember to proofread your paper. Give your paper a good title. Save your work in your folder.

The Last Word

Footnotes and Bibliography

Here's the Idea   Because your research paper is written with information gathered from outside sources, you must give credit to those sources in your paper.

A **footnote** gives credit to a writer whose words, facts, or ideas you have used. A direct quotation requires a footnote. So does a statistic. So do any ideas not common knowledge.

To prepare proper footnotes, follow these steps.

1. Look through your paper for any material that needs to be footnoted. Follow each direct quote, statistic, or idea with a number. The number should be written slightly above the line, like this: [1]. The numbers should run in order, with the first piece of text to be footnoted numbered *1*.

2. On a separate page at the end of your paper, make a list of the sources from which your footnoted material was taken. The order in which the footnotes appear in your paper and the order of the footnotes on the footnote page should be the same.

3. To write your footnotes, look for the source number you wrote after each piece of text you wanted to footnote. If you didn't write these source numbers when you wrote your first draft, look through your note cards for the card that contains the information you are footnoting. That note card should contain the proper source number. Then locate the bibliography card with the same number. This bibliography card, together with the page number from the note card, will give you all of the information you need to write your footnote.

To find the proper footnote form for the source you are footnoting, see pages 272–273.

Finally, prepare your **bibliography,** which is a complete list of sources you used to prepare your research paper. A bibliography usually appears on a separate, final page. Each entry contains the information from your bibliography cards, except for the source number and library location. The form for a bibliography entry differs slightly for books, magazines, encyclopedias, and other sources. See pages 274–275 for the proper forms.

Check It Out   Study the form of the footnotes and bibliography for the research paper on wildlife conservation.

Footnotes

¹William Bridges, "Zoological Gardens," *Encyclopedia Americana*, 1982 ed.

²Bernard Livingston, *Zoo Animals, People, Places*, (New York: Arbor House, 1976), p. 263.

³Mary Carpenter, "Zoos: Last Hope To Preserve Vanishing Species," *Science Digest*, Sept. 1978, p. 34.

⁴Carpenter, p. 38.

Bibliography

Bridges, William. "Zoological Gardens," *Encyclopedia Americana*, 1982 ed.

Carpenter, Mary. "Zoos: Last Hope To Preserve Vanishing Species," *Science Digest*, Sept. 1978, pp. 34-38. 978),

Livingston, Bernard. *Zoo Animals, People, Places*. New York Arbor House, 1976.

Stonehouse, Bernard. *Saving the Animals: The World Wildlife Fund Book of Conservation*. New York: Macmillian, 1981.

- Identify the information listed for each footnote.
- Identify the information in each bibliography entry.

Try Your Skill   Write a footnote and a bibliography entry for the following passage. See pages 272–275.

Few modern families can grow their own apples, produce their own milk, fell their own timber, reprocess their own sewage, or do any of the many other things that would help to cut down waste and reduce pollution. What we can do, however, is continually press for and support the social changes that will help to bring about environmental improvement. . . . 'Putting things in the wrong place,' is, after all, one possible definition of pollution even if it does not tell the whole story.

from page 125 of a book titled *Earth in Danger: Pollution* by Ian Breach, published in 1976 by Doubleday & Company, Inc., in Garden City, New York

Keep This in Mind

· Use footnotes to give credit to writers whose words, or ideas you include in a research paper.
· Prepare a bibliography to show your sources.

Now Write   Make a final copy of your research paper. Include your footnotes and a bibliography. Insert the numbers for your footnotes into the first draft of your paper. Find the information you need for your footnotes on your bibliography cards. Copy it in the correct form on a separate page labeled *Footnotes*. Write a bibliography entry for each source you used. Copy the entries in alphabetical order onto a separate page labeled *Bibliography*. Use the proper form.

For help in preparing the final copy of your pages, see Handbook Section 16, **The Correct Form for Writing.**

Also, examine the final copy of the paper on wildlife conservation shown on the following pages.

Basic Forms for Footnotes

A. A book with an author:

[1]Robyn Davidson, Tracks (New York: Pantheon Books, 1980), p. 62.

B. A book with no author:

[2]Degolyer Institute for American Studies. Oral History Collection: on the Performing Arts in America (Dallas: Southern Methodist University, 1981), p. 17.

C. A book with an editor:

[3]Keith Muckleroy, ed., Archaeology Under Water: An Atlas of the World's Submerged Sites (New York: McGraw Hill, 1980), p. 97.

D. An encyclopedia article:

[4]"Canyons, Submarine," Encyclopedia Britannica, 1981 ed.

E. A magazine article with an author:

[5]Barbara Goldstein, "Washed Up on the New Wave," Progressive Architecture, September 1981, p. 161.

F. A magazine article without an author:

[6]"Who Has the Upper Hand?" Time, 16 July 1984, p. 30.

G. A newspaper article:

[7]Malcolm Moran, "First Women's Olympic Marathon to Benoit," New York Times, 6 August 1984, p. 1, cols. 2–4, p. 31, col. 5.

H. An interview:

[8]Personal interview with E. Talbot Donaldson, Distinguished Professor Emeritus, Department of English, Indiana University, 26 Sept. 1978.

I. A film:

[9]Alfred Hitchcock, dir., <u>North by Northwest</u>, with Cary Grant and Eva Marie Saint, M.G.M., 1959.

J. A television or radio program:

[10]"A Desert Blooming," writ. Marshall Riggan, <u>Living Wild</u>, dir. Harry L. Gorden, prod. Peter Argentine, PBS, 29 April 1984.

K. A report or a pamphlet:

[11]American Medical Association, <u>Medical Relations Under Workmen's Compensation</u> (Chicago: American Medical Association, 1976), p. 3.

If the report is by an individual author rather than by an association or committee, begin with the author's name.

Sources Already Footnoted

To refer to sources already cited, use a shortened form.

A. In most cases, the author's last name, followed by the relevant page numbers is sufficient.

[12]Susan Sontag, <u>Illness as Metaphor</u> (New York: Farrar, Straus and Giroux, 1978), p. 50.

[13]Sontag, pp. 79–80.

B. If more than one work by the same author has been referred to, you should write the author's last name and the title. The title may be in shortened form.

[14]Will Durant, <u>The Pleasures of Philosophy: A Survey of Human Life and Destiny</u> (New York: Simon and Schuster, 1953), p. 179.

[15]Will Durant, <u>The Story of Philosophy: The Lives and Opinions of the Great Philosophers of the Western World</u> (New York: Simon and Schuster, 1961), p. 209.

[16]Durant, <u>Story of Philosophy</u>, p. 49.

Basic Forms for a Bibliography

The entries in a bibliography are arranged alphabetically according to the author's last name. When there is no author, use the first important word of the entry to determine the correct place in the bibliography for that entry.

A. A book with an author:

Davidson, Robyn. Tracks. New York: Pantheon Books, 1980.

B. A book with no author:

Degolyer Institute for American Studies. Oral History Collection: on the Performing Arts in America. Dallas: Southern Methodist University, 1981.

C. A book with an editor:

Muckleroy, Keith, ed. Archaeology Under Water: An Atlas of the World's Submerged Sites. New York: McGraw Hill, 1980.

D. An encyclopedia article:

"Canyons, Submarine." Encyclopedia Britannica. 1981 ed.

E. A magazine article with an author:

Goldstein, Barbara. "Washed Up on the New Wave." Progressive Architecture, September 1981, p. 161.

F. A magazine article without an author:

"Who Has the Upper Hand?" Time, 16 July 1984, p. 30.

G. A newspaper article:

Moran, Malcolm. "First Women's Olympic
Marathon to Benoit." <u>New York Times</u>,
6 August 1984, p. 1, cols. 2-4,
p. 31, col. 5.

H. An interview:

Donaldson, E. Talbot. Distinguished Professor Emeritus, Department of
English, Indiana University. Personal Interview. 26 Sept. 1978.

I. A film:

Hitchcock, Alfred. dir., <u>North by North-
west</u>, with Cary Grant and Eva Marie
Saint, M.G.M., 1959.

J. A television or radio program:

"A Desert Blooming." Writ. Marshall Riggan. <u>Living Wild</u>. Dir. Harry L.
Gorden. Prod. Peter Argentine. PBS,
29 April 1984.

K. A report or a pamphlet:

American Medical Association. <u>Medical Relations under Workmen's Compensa-
tion</u>. Chicago: American Medical
Association, 1976.

If the report is by an individual author rather than by an association or committee, begin with the author's name.

Sarah Hoyle

English 401

March 8, 1985

Wildlife Conservation

Human beings affect their environment in many ways that
range from the most negative to the most positive. Throughout
history, one major way people have affected their environment
is through their attitudes toward wildlife. Perhaps these
attitudes, especially those toward animals, can best be
measured by the zoological gardens—or zoos—that have been
created.

The purposes of zoos have changed remarkably over the
course of the last two thousand years. A Chinese ruler once
created a Garden of Intelligence that kept animals in natural
surroundings. Ancient Egyptian rulers kept wild animals in
order to glorify their own reputations. Romans kept animals
for sporting contests. In Europe in the Middle Ages, heads of
state kept collections of exotic animals to give as gifts.[1]
Generally, in zoos of the past, the needs of animals were not
understood. Many animals died, only to be replaced by others
trapped in the wild.

276

In contrast, the purposes of modern zoos have arisen from an interest in animals for their own sake. In the United States, the first zoos reflected this interest. They were opened in Philadelphia, Chicago, and New York, beginning in the 1860's. Entertainment and education were major functions of these zoos, and remain so today. However, gains in scientific knowledge are reflected in striking changes being made in the ways that zoos exhibit animals. Barred, stone cages are being replaced with natural living environments that allow animals greater freedom. Lions, for example, may live in an open area surrounded by a deep moat; birds may live in a tree-filled, climate-controlled building.

Many modern zoos are now committed to a policy of conserving animal species. About eighty-five percent of exhibited animals are being born in captivity. William G. Conway, director of the Bronx Zoo, expects that this trend will continue. He has said, "The zoo of the future is an environmental park. It should be, among other things, a repository for vanishing species."[2] In fact, at the same time that the government of Taiwan declared the Formosan deer extinct, the Bronx Zoo had fifty of them. It is generally agreed that several other animals, including the Père David deer and the Hawaiian goose, would be extinct if it were not for zoos. "Although the broad purpose of a zoo's existence is still to entertain and educate the public, breeding previously wild species in captivity will be the major thrust over the next ten years."[3]

Modern zoos also educate the public to the needs of animals. Zoos increase environmental awareness by exhibiting animals in their natural surroundings. Many zoos teach the public directly about specific animals by presenting various special programs. "Every year over 115 million visitors come to the 130 zoos in the United States—more than the combined attendance at all U.S. professional basketball, football, and baseball games."[4] Through educational programs, these visitors will become aware of public laws and policies that affect wildlife. A knowledgeable public will support more humane laws dealing with wildlife conservation. Human beings and animals can benefit only by sharing their surroundings.

Footnotes

[1] William Bridges, "Zoological Gardens," Encyclopedia Americana, 1982 ed.

[2] Bernard Livingston, Zoo Animals, People, Places (New York: Arbor House, 1976), page 263.

[3] Mary Carpenter, "Zoos: Last Hope To Preserve Vanishing Species," Science Digest, Sept. 1978, p. 34.

[4] Carpenter, p. 38.

Bibliography

Bridges, William. "Zoological Gardens," Encyclopedia Americana, 1982 ed.

Carpenter, Mary. "Zoos: Last Hope to Preserve Vanishing Species." Science Digest, Sept. 1978, pp. 34–38.

Livingston, Bernard. Zoo Animals, People, Places. New York: Arbor House, 1976.

Stonehouse, Bernard. Saving the Animals: The World Wildlife Fund Book of Conservation. New York: Macmillan, 1981.

Critical Thinking

Get the Facts

Facts and Opinions

Here's the Idea   Some of the learning you do takes place in school. However, a great deal of learning also takes place in everyday life. On a job, for example, you learn new skills and ideas. Then, you use what you have learned to accomplish specific tasks. To be successful on a job, you must therefore be able to learn quickly and easily. One way to develop your ability to learn is to study critical thinking. Critical thinking is the process of interpreting, judging, and using information.

Information comes to you in the form of statements that you read or hear. These statements may be facts or opinions. To judge the truth or value of a statement, you must first decide what sort of statement it is.

A **fact** is a statement that can be proved true. You can use any of the following methods to prove a fact:

1. You can make a personal observation.
2. You can ask an expert.
3. You can check the fact in a reference work. (a dictionary, encyclopedia, almanac, or book written by an expert)

For instance, the statement "Kangaroo rats live in the deserts of Arizona" is a fact. The statement can be proved by making personal observations in the deserts of Arizona. It can also be proved by reading about kangaroo rats in an encyclopedia or in a book written by an expert.

An **opinion** is a statement that cannot be proved. "The films of George Lucas are the best in the world" is a statement of opinion. The statement simply tells how someone feels about the films of George Lucas. Another person might disagree with this statement. If so, there would be no way to prove which person was right.

Though opinions cannot be proved, they can be supported. A sound opinion is one that is supported by facts. An unsound opinion is one that is not supported by facts.

Check It Out Read the following statements.

Susan Sarandon is a marvelous actress.
Susan Sarandon is an actress.

- Which of these statements is a fact? Which is an opinion? How do you know?

Try Your Skill Check the following statements of fact. Use the reference works listed in parentheses. Tell whether each statement is true or false.

1. Texas is known as "The Lone Star State." (encyclopedia or almanac)
2. Georgia was named after King George II of England. (dictionary or encyclopedia)
3. San Diego is located in northern California. (atlas)

Keep This in Mind

- Facts are statements that can be proved.
- Check facts by observation, by asking an expert, or by reading in a reference work.
- Opinions are statements that cannot be proved.
- Check opinions by seeing whether they can be supported by facts.

Now Write Write three opinions that you hold. Then write two statements of fact to support each opinion. Choose one of your statements of opinion and use it as the topic sentence of a paragraph. In the body of the paragraph, present the facts that support your opinion.

What Do You Think?

Types of Opinions

Here's the Idea   Many of the statements you read and hear are opinions. There are three main types of opinions. They are judgments, predictions, and statements of obligation.

A **judgment** tells how a speaker or writer feels about a subject. The following statement, for example, is a judgment:

> Rugby is an interesting game.

This statement is a judgment because it tells how the writer feels about rugby. You can recognize opinions of this kind because they use judgment words. Examples of such words are *interesting, boring, good, bad, terrific, terrible, wonderful,* or *awful.*

A **prediction** makes a statement about the future. The following statement is a prediction:

> Within the next hundred years, the world's oil supplies will be completely used up.

You can recognize opinions of this kind because they tell about future events.

A **statement of obligation** tells what one should or should not do. The following is a statement of obligation:

> You ought to take up jogging.

You can recognize opinions of this kind because they use words such as *should, ought to,* and *must.*

Whenever you express judgments, predictions, or statements of obligation, remember that these are opinions. Therefore, they must be supported by facts.

Check It Out   Read the following statements.

1. People should not eat between meals.

2. A new orbiting telescope will be launched during the 1990's.

3. Langston Hughes was a marvelous poet.

- Which of these opinions is a judgment? Which is a prediction? Which is a statement of obligation? How do you know?

Try Your Skill   Tell whether the following opinions are judgments, predictions, or statements of obligation.

1. Soon every American family will have a videotape player.

2. You should always take a jacket with you when you go to night games.

3. Nylon tents are much better than canvas ones.

4. Mr. Sanchez will probably win reelection in the fall.

5. Companies ought to provide day-care centers for employees with small children.

Keep This in Mind

- A judgment tells how a speaker or writer feels about a subject.
- A prediction tells about the future.
- A statement of obligation tells what should or should not be done.

Now Write   Read the following pairs of statements. Tell which statement is an opinion and which is a fact. Then use one pair of sentences as the basis for a paragraph.

1. In recent years, home computer sales have increased. Soon, every family will own one of these useful machines.

2. Texas is a beautiful state. It is also the second largest state in the nation.

3. Some used cars have mechanical problems that cannot be easily detected. Therefore, you must be careful when shopping for one of these cars.

Feelings Run High

Avoiding Loaded Language

Here's the Idea No two people are exactly alike. As a result, differences of opinion sometimes arise. To settle such differences, people must offer facts to support their opinions. Then they can see which opinion is better supported by the facts.

You cannot support an opinion simply by stating it forcefully. Loud or emotional language will not show that one opinion is more sound than another. Therefore, when supporting your opinions, try to avoid language that expresses strong emotions. In other words, avoid **loaded language.**

There are two common types of loaded language: snarl words and purr words. A **snarl word** is one that expresses negative feelings. A **purr word** is one that expresses positive feelings. Read the following examples.

Snarl words: Andrew is *very picky*.
That place offers *handouts* to *freeloaders*.

Purr words: Andrew is a *perfectionist*.
That place offers citizens a
helping hand.

Loaded language expresses personal feelings, not facts. Therefore, avoid using loaded language to support an opinion.

Check It Out Read the following descriptions.

1. Mr. Tares is just the mayor's puppet.
2. Mr. Tares is a loyal supporter of the mayor.

- How do these two statements differ? How are they alike? What snarl words and purr words do they contain?

Try Your Skill   Find the snarl words and purr words in the following sentences.

1. Felicia has drive and determination.
2. Felicia is pushy.
3. Benedict Arnold was a British patriot.
4. Benedict Arnold was an American traitor.

Keep This in Mind

- Loaded language is made up of words and phrases that express strong feelings.
- Snarl words express negative feelings.
- Purr words express positive feelings.
- When supporting opinons, do not use loaded language in place of facts.

Now Write   Study the pages of a local newspaper. Find an important issue that is in the news. Write two statements of opinion about this issue. In the first opinion, use snarl words. In the second, use purr words. Then, rewrite each opinion, avoiding loaded language completely.

Not So Fast

Errors in Reasoning

Here's the Idea   Unsound opinions may result from errors in reasoning. In this lesson you will learn about some of the most common of these errors.

Overgeneralization occurs when a person makes a statement about an entire group based on too few examples. The following is an overgeneralization:

> The fruits and vegetables I saw at the grocery store the other day looked terrible. That's why you should buy fruits and vegetables only at a fresh produce stand.

This is an overgeneralization because it is based on too few examples. The speaker would have to examine the fruits and vegetables at many grocery stores before he or she could assume that all grocery store produce looked "terrible."

Try to avoid making overgeneralizations when you write and speak. Don't make broad statements about an entire group unless you are quite familiar with that group and are certain that your statement applies to all members of that group. Also, avoid using absolute words such as *all, everyone, nobody,* and *never.* Instead, use qualifying words such as *many, some, often,* and *rarely.*

A **stereotype** is an overgeneralization about an entire group of people. Suppose you encounter a rude car salesperson. If you then decide that all car salespersons are rude, you are guilty of stereotyping. Stereotypes are illogical, unreasonable, and sometimes harmful. They are often directed against the members of racial, ethnic, political, or religious groups. Avoid stereotyping in your speaking and writing.

A third error in reasoning is called the **bandwagon.** Bandwagon occurs when you assume that an action is right because many

people are doing it. For example, imagine that a clothing manufacturer tells you to buy her work-out apparel because "everyone is buying them." This manufacturer is asking you to "jump
on the bandwagon."

Snob appeal is similar to the bandwagon. This error in reasoning asks you to take some action because supposedly intelligent,
fashionable, or rich people do it.

Check It Out   Read these unsound opinions.

All science fiction movies are boring.
These sunglasses are neat. They must be, because all the jet-
setters are wearing them.

· What is wrong with each of these opinions?

Try Your Skill   Each of the following statements contains an
error in reasoning. Choose the type of error from those given in
parentheses.

1. All the people at the phone company are unreasonable.
   (bandwagon, stereotyping, snob appeal)
2. New Laurel perfume is the ultimate; specially made for
   those who must have the very best. (stereotyping, bandwagon, snob appeal)
3. Anyone who sleeps late is lazy. (overgeneralization, bandwagon, snob appeal)

Keep This in Mind

· Common errors in reasoning include overgeneralization, stereotyping, bandwagon, and snob appeal.

Now Write   Errors in reasoning often appear in television and
print advertisements. Using these sources, find an example of
each of the four errors in reasoning discussed in this lesson.
Write a brief paragraph that describes each advertisement. Tell
what error in reasoning the advertisement is guilty of.

False Moves

More Faulty Reasoning

Here's the Idea   People often use their powers of reason to figure out why something *is* or why something happened. People are always looking for the causes of events in their lives. Whenever you reason about causes, be careful to avoid two common errors. These errors are called false-cause reasoning and only-cause reasoning.

When one event happens right after another event, people often decide that the first event must have caused the second event. This is **false-cause reasoning.** They draw this conclusion even though there is no proof that the two events are connected. Superstitions are often based on false-cause reasoning. For example, suppose that if you walk under a ladder or break a mirror, you then have some bad luck. You might conclude that walking under ladders or breaking mirrors causes bad luck. Actually, the two events are unrelated.

Only-cause reasoning occurs when a person assumes that an event has just one cause when, in fact, it has many causes. Suppose you water a houseplant a great deal and it dies. You might conclude that the plant died from overwatering. It is entirely possible, however, that the plant may have died from too little light, bugs, or a combination of these causes.

Check It Out   Read these two paragraphs.

My friend, Loni, had a terrible day. First she lost her house keys and had to have the locks changed. Then, when she decided to begin studying for her history test, it took her two hours to find her notes. While she was ironing her favorite shirt, she accidently scorched the back. I had told her to be careful—it was Friday the thirteenth!

Bob's grades have started to slip. He used to be a straight B student. Lately, however, he hasn't been doing nearly as well. I told him if he would just quit the track team, his grades would improve.

- Which of these paragraphs contains the false-cause error in reasoning? Which contains the only-cause error? Explain your answers.

Try Your Skill Tell which of the following are examples of false-cause reasoning and which are examples of only-cause reasoning.

1. Rick is healthy because he takes vitamin C daily.
2. Marilyn lost her rabbit's foot key ring three days ago. Since then, she's had one disaster after another.
3. Too much sun causes headaches. I know, because after a day at the beach I got a terrific headache.
4. Tina won the award because her father knows the head of the awards committee.

Keep This in Mind

- False-cause reasoning is the error of mistaking an unrelated event for a cause.
- Only-cause reasoning is the error of believing that an event has only one cause when it actually has many causes.

Now Write Think of three different sayings, statements, or stories that you've heard recently that are examples of false-cause or only-cause reasoning. Write them down and explain the error in reasoning.

In the Final Analysis

Drawing Conclusions

Here's the Idea   Every day, you draw conclusions from facts. A **conclusion** may be a judgment, a prediction, an interpretation, or a decision. As you study the facts, you try to see how they are related. When you find a relationship, you state it in a sentence. This sentence is your conclusion.

There are two ways of drawing conclusions. You may draw a conclusion by observing specific facts. For example, suppose that you are listening to a radio station one morning. At seven o'clock, a news program comes on. The next morning, you listen to the same station and the same program comes on at seven. After several mornings of this, you can make a general conclusion. This station broadcasts the news every morning at seven.

Another way to reach a conclusion is by observing a general fact and a related specific fact. For instance, suppose that you read in an almanac that all teachers in your state are required to have a Master's degree. You then learn that your new neighbor is a teacher. You put together the general fact about teachers and the specific fact about your neighbor. You can then draw a specific conclusion. Your new neighbor has a Master's degree.

Check It Out   Read these sentences.

All Presidents have to swear an oath to defend the Constitution of the United States. Jimmy Carter was a President.

- What conclusion can you draw from these facts?

Try Your Skill   The following graph presents many separate facts. Study this graph. Then, answer the questions that follow by drawing conclusions.

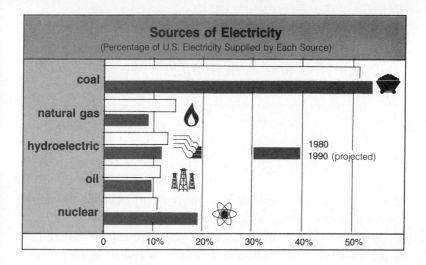

Sources of Electricity
(Percentage of U.S. Electricity Supplied by Each Source)

coal
natural gas
hydroelectric
oil
nuclear

1980
1990 (projected)

0   10%   20%   30%   40%   50%

1. Of the many sources of electricity, which does the United States depend on most?
2. Is use of nuclear power expected to increase or decrease in the next ten years?
3. Which source of electricity do we now use least?

Keep This in Mind

• Draw conclusions by observing facts.

Now Write   Read the following passage from a short story. Notice the many facts presented in the passage. Then, make a list of conclusions you can draw about the character whose actions are described.

Darrell lived in an old, old house. At night, the wind would whisper into the eaves. At such times, Darrell would sit upright and listen. Soon, he would go to the window, checking the night to see what might be there. If the moon were out, he would see the persimmon tree. At times the branches would move, and Darrell would run and hide under the covers. The tree would appear again that night in his dreams.

Two of a Kind

Synonyms and Antonyms

Here's the Idea   Critical thinking skills affect every part of your life.

Because critical thinking is so important, schools and businesses often test applicants on these skills. One of the skills most often tested is the ability to recognize similarities and differences. Studying synonyms and antonyms can help you to develop this skill.

Synonyms are words that are very similar in meaning. Pairs of words such as *run* and *jog*, *stumble* and *trip*, and *faithful* and *loyal* are examples of synonyms. You can tell whether words are synonyms by writing a sentence that uses one of the words. Then, substitute the other word in the same sentence. Both sentences should make sense. The meaning of the sentence also should not change. If this is so, then the words are synonyms.

Antonyms are words that have opposite meanings. Words such as *sweet* and *sour*, *nervous* and *calm*, and *wise* and *foolish* are examples of antonyms.

You will find test questions involving antonyms on the SAT. These initials stand for the Scholastic Aptitude Test. An antonym question begins by giving you a single word. It then asks you to choose from a list of words the one that is most opposite in meaning.

An antonym question looks like this:

> PORTION: (A) height   (B) large   (C) whole   (D) bit
> (E) pieces

To answer an antonym question, use this method:

1. Think about the meaning of the given word.

2. Place the word *not* before the given word.

3. Find the word from the list that means the same as *not* plus the given word. For example, whole is the correct answer to the sample question because it means *not a portion*.

Check It Out   Read the following pairs of words.

1. sorrow   unhappiness   3. honor   shame
2. obey   rebel   4. trick   deceive

   • Which of these words are antonyms? synonyms?

Try Your Skill   Look at the following questions. They are like the antonym questions found on the SAT. Choose the word in lowercase letters that is most nearly opposite the first word.

1. DESTROY: (A) leave   (B) create   (C) waste
                 (D) decorate   (E) loosen
2. STRENGTH: (A) weakness   (B) ability   (C) lift
                 (D) power   (E) giant
3. THOUGHTFULLY: (A) tactfully (B) slowly (C) speedily
                 (D) angrily   (E) carelessly

Keep This in Mind

   • Synonyms are words that are similar in meaning.
   • Antonyms are words that are opposite in meaning.

Now Write   Choose the correct antonym for each word given in capital letters.

1. PRAISE: (A) sing   (B) criticize   (C) thank
                 (D) speak   (E) impress
2. ALERT: (A) awake   (B) nervous   (C) careful
                 (D) animal   (E) unaware
3. FRIGHTENED: (A) brave   (B) scared   (C) trembling
                 (D) hero   (E) coward

More of the Same

Analogies

Here's the Idea   Look at the following pairs of words. How are the two pairs similar?

   wolf/pack   horse/herd

You probably realized that both pairs include a member of a group and the group itself. The ability to see this kind of relationship is an important critical thinking skill. Working with analogies can help you develop this skill. An *analogy* is a comparison of two things that are not exactly alike.

Questions using analogies are included in SAT tests. In an analogy question, you are given two words that are related in some way. You must decide how the two words are related. Then, you must choose a second pair of words that are related in the same way. An analogy question looks like this:

   BIRD: FLY::   (A) boat: water   (B) bear: cave   (C) fish: scales
                 (D) fish: swim   (E) sparrow: wings

Use the following method to answer analogy questions:

   1. Study the first pair of words. Find the relationship between the words by using both of them in a sentence. (A bird can fly.)

   2. Next, find a second pair of words that you can put in place of the first pair. (A fish can swim.)

Check It Out   Read the following pairs of words. Also read the sentence next to each one.

   1. painter: brush   A *painter* uses a *brush.*
   2. satin: smooth   *Smooth* is a characteristic of *satin.*
   3. flute: woodwind   A *flute* is a type of *woodwind.*
   4. carpenter: house   A *carpenter* builds a *house.*

- Do you see how sentences can help show how words are related?

Try Your Skill

Complete each analogy. Choose the pair of words that shows the same relationship as the first pair.

1. FRAGILE: DELICATE:: (A) glass: china (B) smooth: rough (C) brush: painting (D) close: near (E) musician: melody
2. PETAL: FLOWER:: (A) house: cabin (B) stem: trunk (C) star: moon (D) river: fish (E) finger: hand
3. MICROSCOPE: MAGNIFY:: (A) examine: study (B) crane: lift (C) museum: exhibit (D) telescope: star (E) pulley: ropes

Keep This in Mind

- An analogy is a comparison between things that are not exactly alike.
- To answer analogy questions, use the first pair of words in a sentence. Then find another pair that you can substitute for the first pair.

Now Write

Complete these analogies. Then choose any five pairs of words. Write sentences that show you understand how the words in each pair are related.

1. SECRETARY: TYPEWRITER: (A) mechanic: car (B) teacher: class (C) photographer: camera (D) clerk: filing (E) librarian: library
2. BOXER: RING:: (A) ball: bat (B) referee: basketball (C) actor: stage (D) football: field (E) singer: choir
3. SHOES: LEATHER:: (A) dress: clothing (B) statue: marble (C) helmet: protection (D) gloves: hands (E) iron: steel

Blank Checks

Sentence Completion

Here's the Idea   Imagine that you are having a conversation with a friend. In the middle of a sentence, she suddenly stops talking. She can't find the right word to say what she means. However, you find you are able to supply the word for her.

You have probably had this experience many times. You are able to complete a sentence because you can see the relationships between the words. This critical thinking skill is tested by the sentence completion questions on the SAT. Here is an example of this type of question:

> After the _____ pace of the city, Steve appreciated the _____ of the river when he went canoeing.
> (A) quick . . wetness   (B) frantic . . excitement
> (C) familiar . . current   (D) hectic . . tranquility
> (E) quiet . . scenery

To answer sentence completion questions, use the following method:

1. Read the incomplete sentence carefully. Note any key words. Look for words that state contrasts (*however, but, on the other hand*). Also look for words that signal similarities (*also, another, like, similarly*). Finally, note words that signal cause and effect (*because, since, therefore*).

2. Try each choice in the sentence. Do not be misled by answers that have only one word that works well in the sentence. In the sample question, answer D is the only choice in which both words make sense.

Check It Out   Read the following incomplete sentences.

1. Cheryl _____ the test because she did not study.

2. He stamped his feet and acted very _____.
3. Despite the _____, we all enjoyed our day at the beach.

* What words could complete these sentences?

Try Your Skill Choose the pair of words that best completes each sentence.

1. Good writers develop their _____ so that they can express their ideas _____.
   (A) stories . . carefully (B) characters . . perfectly
   (C) vocabularies . . clearly (D) penmanship . . neatly
   (E) plots . . smoothly
2. As the argument continued, Jim got _____ but Maria became _____.
   (A) angrier . . calmer (B) irritated . . annoyed
   (C) pleasant . . finer (D) arguments . . clever
   (E) awards . . upset

Keep This in Mind

* Sentence completion questions test the ability to recognize relationships between words in sentences.

Now Write Complete each sentence with a pair of words. Make sure that the sentence makes sense when you are done.

1. The English _____ told his students that poetry was meant to be _____.
   (A) book . . written (B) language . . rhymed
   (C) teacher . . enjoyed (D) class . . studied
   (E) teacher . . verses
2. Julian had always been _____ of snakes because he thought they were all _____.
   (A) proud . . poisonous (B) fearful . . right
   (C) interested . . reptiles (D) afraid . . poisonous
   (E) nervous . . colors

Developing Library Skills

Special Arrangements

Finding What You Need

Here's the Idea A library is a treasury of information and ideas. There you will find sources of factual information on a variety of subjects. There you will also find books and magazines describing a variety of imaginary experiences. To find what you need, you must first learn how your school or public library is organized.

All library books are classified into two general groups, fiction and nonfiction. **Fiction** books are arranged alphabetically according to the author's last name. For example, the novel *Ethan Frome,* written by Edith Wharton, would be filed under *W*.

Nonfiction books are arranged according to their subjects on a separate section of shelves. Many libraries use a system called the **Dewey Decimal System.** This system groups nonfiction books into ten numbered categories.

000-099	**General Works**	(encyclopedias, almanacs)
100-199	**Philosophy**	(ethics, psychology, occult)
200-299	**Religion**	(the Bible, mythology)
300-399	**Social Science**	(economics, law, education, government)
400-499	**Language**	(languages, grammar, dictionaries)
500-599	**Science**	(mathematics, biology, chemistry)
600-699	**Useful Arts**	(farming, cooking, sewing, television, business)
700-799	**Fine Arts**	(music, painting, dance, photography, sports)
800-899	**Literature**	(poetry, plays)
900-999	**History**	(biography, travel, geography)

On the spine of every nonfiction book is its **call number,** The call number, which includes the Dewey Decimal number and other useful information, identifies a single book. Some libraries add the letter *B* to the call number of a biography or the letter *R* to the call number of a reference work, such as an encyclopedia.

Examine this model of a nonfiction book.

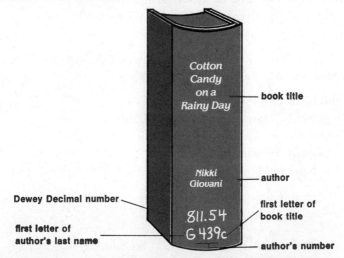

Cotton Candy on a Rainy Day — book title

Nikki Giovani — author

Dewey Decimal number

first letter of author's last name

.811.54
G439c

first letter of book title

author's number

Check It Out   Examine the books represented here.

Walking Tours of America	The Great Gatsby	Survive the Savage Sea	Nineteen Eighty-Four	WORKING	Gone with the Wind	We Have Always Lived in the Castle	All Creatures Wise and Wonderful
Louise Feinsot	F. Scott Fitzgerald	Dougal Robertson	George Orwell	Studs Terkel	Margaret Mitchell	Shirley Jackson	James Herriot
917.304 WAL		910.09164 R545s		331.209 TER			636.089 H435aw

- Which books are fiction and which are nonfiction?
- What is the general category of each nonfiction book?

Try Your Skill Write the answers to the following questions.

1. Under what letter on the library shelves would you find the following fiction books?

Billy Budd by Herman Melville
Song of Solomon by Toni Morrison
The Time Machine by H. G. Wells
Catch-22 by Joseph Heller
The Crystal Cave by Mary Stewart

2. In which categories of the Dewey Decimal System would you find information on these subjects?

the history of television
a guide to low-cost travel in the U.S.
some recipes for canning vegetables
a play by William Shakespeare
the legal rights of consumers

Keep This in Mind

- In the library, fiction books are filed alphabetically by the author's last name.
- Nonfiction books may be classified in ten major categories of the Dewey Decimal System. Each nonfiction book has a call number.

Now Write As your teacher directs, become familiar with the organization of your school or public library. Learn the locations of fiction and nonfiction books, reference books, magazines, and special collections.

On your visit to the library, find four fiction books and four nonfiction books that you might enjoy reading. In fact, you may want to check out one or more of these books. On your paper, write the titles, authors, and call numbers of the books you find. Label you paper **Special Arrangements,** and put it into your folder.

On File

Using the Card Catalog

Here's the Idea   In every library, you will find a file called the card catalog. The card catalog contains basic information about all the books in the library. In fact, each book is listed three times—by its author, by its title, and by its subject.

All three cards—author card, title card, and subject card—contain the same information. However, on each card the information is arranged under different headings. In this way, you are able to locate a book in one of several ways.

All three cards list the author, title, publisher, date of publication, and number of pages in the book. There is a notation if the book has illustrations or maps. There may also be a description of the book or a list of related books. In addition, all three cards list the call number of a nonfiction book in the upper left-hand corner. This is the same number that appears on the spine of the book.

On an **author card,** the author's name is given at the top, last name first. Author cards are filed alphabetically by the author's last name. If there is more than one author, the card is filed by the name of the author whose name is shown first in the book.

On a **title card,** the title appears on the top line, with only the first word of the title capitalized. Title cards are filed alphabetically by the first word of the title. However, if *A, An,* or *The* appears as the first word in a title, look for the card under the first letter of the second word in the title.

On a **subject card,** the subject appears on the top line. The subject may be written in capital letters or in red. Subject cards are filed alphabetically by the first letter of the subject.

You will also notice some cards that say *See* or *See also.* These **cross reference cards** refer you to other subject headings that are related to the one you want.

Searching the card catalog will be quicker if you use the **guide cards.** These blank cards have tabs on which are written general subject headings. The headings help you to follow the alphabetical arrangement of the card catalog.

Check It Out   Examine the three sample cards on page 307.

- Under what letter would each card be filed? Where would you find more books by Daniel S. Halacy? Where would you find other books about alternative energy sources?

Try Your Skill   Suppose you are doing research on the subject of voting in the United States. Go to your school or public library and find a subject card, a title card, and an author card for books about voting. Copy the important information as it appears on each card.

Keep This in Mind

- Every book in a library is listed in the card catalog on three separate cards—author, title, and subject. Each card shows the author, title, publisher, date of publication, number of pages, and other useful information. Cards for a nonfiction book also list its call number.

Now Write   Select an interesting subject that you can research at the library. Use the card catalog to find at least three nonfiction books about your subject. Copy the important information from the author, title, and subject cards. Label your paper **On File** and keep it in your folder. Also, choose the most interesting book you find, check it out of the library, and bring it to class.

333.7
H128e
    Halacy, Daniel Stephen

        Earth, water, wind, and sun: our
energy alternatives / D. S. Halacy,
Jr. — New York : Harper & Row,
c1977.
      186 p. : ill.; 22 cm.

      Includes index.
      Bibliography: p. [179]-180.
      ISBN 0-06-011777-X : $8.95

333.7
H128e
    Earth, water, wind, and sun

        Earth, water, wind, and sun: our
energy alternatives / D. S. Halacy,
Jr. — New York : Harper & Row,
c1977.
      186 p. : ill.; 22 cm.

      Includes index.
      Bibliography: p. [179]-180.
      ISBN 0-06-011777-X : $8.95

333.7
H128e
    ENERGY

        Earth, water, wind, and sun: our
energy alternatives / D. S. Halacy,
Jr. — New York : Harper & Row,
c1977.
      186 p. : ill.; 22 cm.

      Includes index.
      Bibliography: p. [179]-180.
      ISBN 0-06-011777-X : $8.95

To Know Better

Using an Encyclopedia

Here's the Idea   You may not always need to read an entire book on a subject you want to know more about. Sometimes you only need to read a short article containing basic information. The place to find such articles is in an encyclopedia. An encyclopedia is a general reference work that contains much information on many subjects. The articles are arranged in alphabetical order by subject from the first volume through the last. On the spine of each volume is either a single letter or a set of guide letters noting what is included.

In a large library, you will find several sets of encyclopedias, many at different reading levels. Be sure to choose one that you can read easily. Select a suitable encyclopedia for your work by skimming through several or by asking a librarian for assistance. You may select *The World Book Encyclopedia, Collier's Encyclopedia,* or the *Britannica Junior Encyclopaedia,* for example.

To find an article on a topic, you need to find the right heading. To do this, determine the key words of your topic. Often there will be more than one key word and more than one heading under which you might find information on your topic. For example, you might find information on pollution under "Environmental Pollution" or "Ecology." Select the appropriate volume and look under both headings. Guide words at the top of each page will help you find the headings quickly.

An encyclopedia article on an important subject is usually presented in parts, each with a subtitle. An article on "Environmental Pollution," for example, may include such parts as "Kinds of Pollution," "Causes of Pollution," "Controlling Pollution," and "History." Depending on the purpose of your research, you may need to read all of the article or only parts of it.

At the end of a major article you will find additional information to guide your research. For example, you may find lists of related articles in the encyclopedia, an outline of information on the subject, books for further reading, or a study guide.

Most encyclopedias also include an index, usually the first or last volume in a set. Some encyclopedias also publish yearbooks that contain up-to-date information.

Check several encyclopedias, as well as other kinds of reference books. In addition to general encyclopedias, you may want to check some of the specialized encyclopedias that provide information about one subject only. For example, you may need an encyclopedia that includes information on art or animals. Try to use the most recent or most reliable reference. Be sure that you identify every source you use.

Check It Out   Look at the encyclopedia shown below.

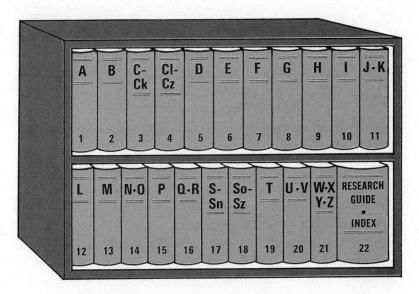

- In what volume, and under what key word, would you find information on American poets? causes of inflation? freedom of the press? the Nobel Prize? the novels of John Steinbeck? rules for playing soccer? the Swiss Alps?

Try Your Skill   As your teacher directs, use an encyclopedia to answer the following questions.

1. Name three of the most heavily populated cities in the world.
2. What are the colors of roses?
3. What is the capital of the Netherlands?
4. In what year of the Civil War did the Battle of Gettysburg take place?
5. Where is the Taj Mahal?
6. Who was President of the United States during World War I?
7. Which native American Indian tribes have lived in Florida?
8. Who is the god of thunder in Norse mythology?
9. What musical instruments are commonly used in African music?
10. Name two important French directors of motion pictures.

Keep This in Mind

• An encyclopedia is a general reference work containing information on many different subjects. Articles are arranged alphabetically in numbered volumes. Examine a variety of encyclopedias, and select one that is suitable for you and the purpose of your research.

Now Write   Choose a subject that interests you, and look up that subject in two encyclopedias. List a few of the most important facts that you find in each, and compare them. Be sure to identify each source completely. List the names of the encyclopedias, numbers of the volumes, page numbers of the articles, and include several titles of other related articles or books mentioned. Also, name the encyclopedia you prefer, and briefly explain your choice. Label your paper **To Know Better** and put it into your folder.

References on Request

Using Reference Works

Here's the Idea Every library has a reference section with a collection of sources to help you research subjects in many different areas. Some reference works contain a range of general information, while others are more specialized. Few of these valuable references can be taken out of a library. In addition to dictionaries and encyclopedias, with which you are already familiar, you will find several other standard references useful.

Atlases are books of maps. Many atlases also contain information about the earth's population, weather, and geologic structure. Among the most·widely used atlases are the *National Geographic Atlas of the World, Rand McNally Picture Atlas of the World,* and the *Atlas of World History.*

Almanacs and **yearbooks,** published each year, are the most useful sources of up-to-date facts and statistics. For example, in these references you will find information about current world events, governments, populations, products, and awards. You may want to use the *World Almanac and Book of Facts,* the *Information Please Almanac, Atlas, and Yearbook,* the *Statesman's Yearbook,* or the *Guinness Book of World Records.*

Biographical references contain information about important people. Useful reference works include the *Dictionary of American Biography, Current Biography, Who's Who, Twentieth Century Authors,* and *The Book of Presidents.*

A **vertical file** is the name of a library's collection of assorted pamphlets, catalogs, handbooks, and clippings. The collection is usually kept in a file cabinet, but its contents differ from library to library. It may include information about local events and schools, for example.

311

Magazines are valuable sources of information about a wide range of subjects. To locate specific information in magazines, learn to use the *Readers' Guide to Periodical Literature*. The *Readers' Guide* contains the titles of articles, stories, and poems published in more than a hundred major magazines. One hardcover volume of the *Readers' Guide* covers material published during a year. Several shorter paperback volumes cover material for shorter time periods.

Become familiar with these standard references. Each contains an explanation of how its information is organized and what symbols and abbreviations are used. Often a sample entry is presented. Before you use any reference work for the first time, examine these explanations.

Check It Out   Study this model of a section from the *Readers' Guide to Periodical Literature*.

Travel agencies and agents
The airline confusion has travel agents flying blind. il
Bus Week p43 O 17 '83

date of magazine _____

Travel agent exclusivity bill support grows [airline
tickets] *Aviat Week Space Technol* 119 34 O 10 '83

volume number _____

Travel consultants *See* Travel agencies and agents
Travel folders *See* Travel literature
Travel literature
   See also
   Guidebooks
   Travel. P. Zweig. il *N Y Times Book Rev* 88:15+ D 4 '83

name of magazine _____

Travel photography
Travel in focus. M. Grimm and T. Grimm. See alternate
issues of Travel Holiday

Anecdotes, facetiae, satire, etc.
Snapshots. R. Baker. il *N Y Times Mag* p20 O 9 '83

author _____

Travel regulations
   See also
   Passports

cross reference _____

Travel with children
How to survive baby's first flight. il *Glamour* 81:44 D '83

title of article _____

Travelers' checks
   See also
   American Express Co.
La traviata [opera] See Verdi, Giuseppe, 1813-1901
La traviata [film] See Motion picture reviews—Single
works
Travolta, John
        about
   Animal magnetism. C. Arrington. il pors *People Wkly*
20:110-11+ D 19 '83

page reference _____

- Read one unmarked listing in this sample and explain all the information given. What other kinds of references are in the reference section of your school or public library?

Try Your Skill Write the name of a reference work other than an encyclopedia that you might use to find the following information. If magazines would be the best source, write *Readers' Guide.*

1. Name five poems written by Langston Hughes.
2. What vocational schools and colleges are located in your area?
3. What countries share borders with Yugoslavia?
4. How were Presidents John Adams and John Quincy Adams related?
5. What is the average daily summer temperature in the Sahara Desert?
6. What is the current population of the United States?
7. Name two famous American composers.
8. Who are the present U.S. Senators representing Ohio?
9. What was Mark Twain's real name?
10. What national projects deal with wildlife conservation?

Keep This in Mind

- There are several kinds of useful specialized references. Learn to use those available in your library.

Now Write Choose a well-known person or place that interests you. Use several specialized references to research your subject. Skim each source and jot down several of the most interesting facts. Identify your sources by listing the titles, call numbers, and volume and page numbers of the sources you find most informative. Label your paper **References on Request** and put it into your folder.

Study and Research Skills

Before You Begin

Understanding Your Assignments

Here's the Idea   To complete an assignment, first, make sure you understand the directions. Then, complete each step in the directions.

Recording Directions Whenever you are given an assignment, record the directions in an assignment notebook. Be thorough. Include the subject or class, the date of the assignment, and the due date. Record each step in the directions for the assignment. Write down any page numbers for assigned reading. Also list any materials you will need and the form your final product should take.

Following Directions Sometimes you will have to listen to directions. As you listen, write each step in the assignment. Keep the steps in order. Underline key words such as *read* and *explain*.

At other times you will follow written directions. Always read these carefully. Divide the assignment into separate steps. Then, put the steps in the order in which you must do them.

If you have any questions about an assignment, ask your teacher. Then, when you are ready to do the assignment, gather any materials and supplies that you will use.

Check It Out   Read the following entry.

Subject	Assignment	Date Given	Date Due
Government	Read Chapter 5, "The Executive Branch." Answer questions on pp. 210-211.	Nov. 28	Dec. 1

- What does this assignment ask you to do?
- What action words are used in the assignment?
- What materials will you need?
- What will your final product be?
- When is the assignment due?

Try Your Skill   Read the sample assignment below. Then, answer the questions that follow the assignment.

Using tracing paper, copy the diagram of the underside of a car given on page 63 of your textbook. Label the following parts of your diagram: the oil filter, the drive shaft, the muffler, the tie rods, and the catalytic converter. Use a black pen to make your diagram and a red pen to label it. Then, on a separate piece of paper, list each part shown on your diagram. Describe each part and tell what purpose it serves. Turn in your diagram and your list of terms on Friday.

1. What steps are included in this assignment?
2. What action words are used in this assignment?
3. What materials will you need?
4. What will the final products be?
5. When is the assignment due?

Keep This in Mind

- Record all the details of your assignments in an assignment notebook.
- Read or listen to the directions for assignments very carefully.

Now Write   Begin an assignment notebook. Use a different section of the notebook for each of your classes. Use the notebook to record your assignments. When recording assignments, follow the model given in **Check It Out.**

A Studied Approach

A Studied Approach

Using SQ3R

Here's the Idea Many assignments involve reading. Even difficult reading assignments can be completed successfully if you use the right study method. One such method is called **SQ3R**. SQ3R includes five steps: **S**urvey, **Q**uestion, **R**ead, **R**ecite, and **R**eview.

Survey Look over the reading material. Get a general idea of its content. Notice titles, subtitles, and illustrations. Read the introduction and summary.

Question Make a list of study questions. Include any questions you think you should be able to answer after reading the material. Also include any study questions in the book and any given to you by your teacher. Use titles, headings, pictures, maps, or charts as sources of questions.

Read Read the assignment closely. Look for answers to your questions. Also look for main ideas and supporting details. Make notes. Pay attention to definitions, topic sentences, and chapter headings.

Recite Say the answers to your questions to yourself. Make notes to help you to remember the answers.

Review Try to answer your original questions without looking at your notes. If necessary, look over the selection again to find the answers. Read your notes over several times to help you remember.

Check It Out Look at these headings from a literature textbook. Read the questions that can be made from these headings.

Chapter Heading	Questions
The Romantic Revolt	1. What does the word "romantic" mean here?

2. Who revolted? Against what?

The Development of the Sonnet
1. What is a "sonnet"?
2. How has the sonnet changed over time?

- How can such questions help you to study the material?

Try Your Skill   Study the following selection. Use the SQ3R study method. Write your questions and the answers to them.

The Origins of the Circus

Beginnings in Europe. The circus developed from traditions established centuries ago. The ancient Greeks performed stunts on horseback. The ancient Romans were entertained by acrobats and trained animals. In the Middle Ages, jesters, jugglers, and tightrope walkers performed throughout Europe. Some of these performers used trained animals.

Development of the Modern Circus. Modern circuses began in England. However, by the late 1700's, circuses had become popular in America. The first circuses in this country were fairly small. These circuses had clowns, jugglers, and riding acts. Musicians and fireworks were soon added.

The Golden Age of Circuses. By the late 1800's, there were about ten large circuses in America. These circuses traveled from city to city and performed under tents. They were popular well into the twentieth century. The most famous show to come out of this period was the Ringling Brothers and Barnum & Bailey Circus. This circus still exists.

Keep This in Mind

- Use the SQ3R method whenever you study reading assignments.

Now Write   Use the SQ3R method to study the front page of a current newspaper. Save your questions, answers, and notes.

To Make a Story Short

Taking Notes

Here's the Idea When you take notes, you make a simple record of something you have heard, or seen, or read. You should take notes when you listen in class or do assigned readings. You should also take notes when you do research or conduct interviews. Notes can be used to review for tests and quizzes. They can also be used to record information for a composition or report. The following guidelines will help you.

1. **Keep a notebook.** For each class, use a separate section of a notebook. Whenever you begin a page of notes, write the date and the name of the class at the top of the page.

2. **Take notes as you read.** Include in your notes the questions and answers you write while using the SQ3R study method. Also include key words, definitions, and ideas from your reading.

3. **Take notes as you listen.** Listen for clues that tell you what information is important. Such clues may be phrases like *most importantly*, *remember this*, and *in summary*. Clues may also be found in the speaker's delivery. For instance, a speaker may emphasize a point with a gesture, or by pausing or slowing down.

4. **Write neatly.** Make sure you will be able to read your notes.

5. **Use a rough outline form.** Record main ideas and supporting details. Write main ideas at the left margin. Begin each main idea with a capital letter. Under each main idea, write any supporting examples or details.

6. **Use phrases, abbreviations, and symbols.** Do not write complete sentences. Instead, save time by using short phrases, abbreviations, and symbols.

If you wish to do so, add your own abbreviations to this list. Make sure that the abbreviations you use are clear.

w/ with	info. information
w/o without	Eng. English
+ and	tho. though
* important idea	def: definition
M memorize this	= equals
Amer. American	ex: example

Check It Out   Read the following notes.

Congress

Powers of Congress
—levy taxes
—borrow money
—declare war
—regulate commerce

- Which is the main idea?
- Which are the supporting details?

Try Your Skill   Take notes on the selection about circuses given in Part 2. Use the guidelines given in this lesson.

Keep This in Mind
- Take notes in class or when reading.

Now Write   Start a notebook for use in your classes. Label a section of the notebook for each class.

The Changing Pace

Adjusting Your Reading Rate

Here's the Idea   When you read, you must choose the right tools. The tools you have to choose from are the different types of reading. The types of reading include in-depth reading, skimming, and scanning. Each type of reading is used for different purposes.

In-depth Reading   Use in-depth reading for studying new or difficult material. Follow the steps of the SQ3R study method. Survey the material. Make a list of study questions. Move your eyes slowly across every line. Look for main ideas. Then, for each main idea, look for supporting examples or details. Note definitions, topic sentences, key words, titles, and headings.

Fast Reading   Use fast reading when you want to survey or review written material. Two useful types of fast reading are **skimming** and **scanning.**

Skimming is used to gain a general overview of material. When you skim a selection, do not read every word. Instead, glance at titles, subtitles, headings, pictures, and graphic aids. Also look at the first and last sentences in paragraphs. If you are skimming a book, glance at the table of contents.

Use skimming to survey materials as the first step in the SQ3R study method. Also use skimming when you need to get a general idea of the content of a selection. When doing research, for example, you will sometimes need to find out whether a source contains information on your topic. You can use skimming to do this.

Scanning is used to find specific information. To scan, move your eyes quickly across each line or down each page. Again, do not read every word. Instead, look only for words or phrases that relate to the specific information you need. Once you spot a key word or phrase, stop scanning and start to read more slowly.

Check It Out Study the following list of reading tasks.

1. Looking for information on the backstroke in an encyclopedia article on swimming
2. Glancing through a new novel to find out what it is about
3. Studying a chapter in a government text

- Which of these tasks involves skimming? Which involves scanning? Which involves in-depth reading?

Try Your Skill Study the following situations. In which cases would you use skimming? scanning? in-depth reading?

1. Studying a driver's manual in preparation for a license exam
2. Looking through a book about computers to see if it contains information about several computer languages
3. Looking for a number in a telephone directory
4. Surveying material as part of the SQ3R study method
5. Looking for the date of the first day of winter in an almanac
6. Reading a very complicated set of written instructions

Keep This in Mind

- Use different types of reading for different purposes.
- Use in-depth reading to study new or difficult material.
- Use skimming to survey material.
- Use scanning to find specific information.

Now Write Choose an article in a magazine. Skim the article to find out what it is about. Write a list of study questions about it. These should be questions that you think should be able to answer after reading the article. Then, scan the article to find the answers to your questions. Write your questions and answers on your paper.

Figure It Out

Drawing Conclusions from Graphic Aids

Here's the Idea   Not all information is presented in written form. Textbooks and other materials often present information through **graphic aids.** Common graphic aids include diagrams, illustrations, maps, tables, charts, and graphs. These are some guidelines to follow when studying graphic aids:

1. Read all titles, captions, legends, or labels given.
2. Decide what specific facts are shown by the graphic aid.
3. Ask yourself how these specific facts are related.
4. Try to draw conclusions about the facts based on the relationships. Write your conclusions in your notes.

Check It Out   Study these graphic aids.

Circles equal total work in U.S. in 1850 and 1980

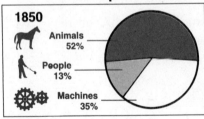
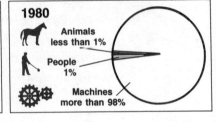

- In these graphs, what does each circle represent?
- In 1850, what percentage of work in the U.S. was done by animals? In 1980, what percentage of work was done by animals?
- How has our dependence on animal labor changed over the years?

Try Your Skill   Study the following graphic aids.

1. Leading Tea-Growing Countries

India	
	1,246,000,000 pounds
China	
	780,420,000 pounds
Sri Lanka	
	462,970,000 pounds
Russia	
	297,620,000 pounds

2. The World's Longest Rivers

Africa	Nile 4,145 miles
South America	Amazon 4,000 miles
Asia	Chang Jiang 3,915 miles
North America	Mississippi 2,348 miles

1. What facts are being compared in Graph 1?
2. What two countries might be called world tea capitals?
3. According to Graph 2, what is the longest river on earth?

Keep This in Mind

- Decide what facts are presented a graphic aid. Look for relationships between these facts.

Now Write   Make a list of the specific facts presented by the following graphic aid. Then, write one general conclusion that you can draw from these facts.

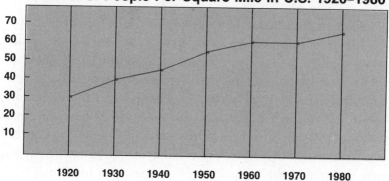

Number of People Per Square Mile in U.S. 1920–1980

Test Case

Preparing for and Taking Tests

Here's the Idea As you already know, tests are very important to success in school. Tests are also important in work. To enter many fields, you must first pass a test. Tests are also used by employers to screen people for jobs or for promotions.

Preparing for Tests Before studying, find out exactly what the test will cover. If you are unsure about this, ask the person giving the test. Try to study the same material several times before the test. Follow these guidelines when you study.

1. **Make a list of study questions.** Include any questions that you wrote while using the SQ3R study method. Also include any study questions given in your textbook or by your teacher.

2. **Review the materials covered by the test.** Skim your notes, textbook chapters, and other reading materials. Write the answers to your study questions.

3. **Find a study coach.** Give your list of study questions to a relative or friend. Ask this person to quiz you.

4. **Review problem areas.** Go over the questions that you missed when being quizzed by your relative or friend.

5. **Make a list of important names, dates, definitions, events, or formulas.** Quiz yourself on these, or ask someone to quiz you.

6. **Eat and sleep properly before the test.**

Taking the Test Begin by skimming the test. This will tell you what kinds of questions you will have to answer. Decide on the order in which you will answer the questions on the test. Start with the easiest questions. Next, read all directions and test questions carefully. Make sure you understand the directions before you answer any question. As you work, budget your time carefully. Do not spend too much time on any one part of the test. Allow extra time for long or difficult questions. After you have completed the test, check for unanswered questions.

Check It Out Read the following questions from a test. Study the notes written in the margins.

1. The branch of business that deals with managing money matters is called _*finance*_

check 2. The branch of business that deals with packaging, advertising, and selling is called ~~*sales*~~ *marketing*

? 3. The branch of business that deals with producing goods is called _____

- How did this student indicate that a difficult question had been skipped?
- How did this student indicate that an answer should be checked again before the test is turned in?

Try Your Skill Suppose that you are going to take a quiz over the information given under **Check It Out** in Part 5. Make a list of study questions you could use to prepare for your quiz.

Keep This in Mind

- Prepare for tests by reviewing your materials carefully.
- Read all the directions before answering any test question.
- Budget your time.
- Save time at the end of the test period for review.

Now Write Choose a time when you did well on a test. Write a paragraph about your experience. Explain what you did to prepare for the test and why you did so well.

You're Right!

Answering Test Questions

Here's the Idea   There are basically two kinds of tests: objective and written. **Objective tests** may contain true/false, matching, or multiple choice questions. **Written tests** may contain completion, short answer, or essay questions. For each of these types of tests, there are some simple guidelines you can learn to improve your scores.

True/False Remember that if any part of a statement is false, the entire statement is false. Also remember that words like *all, always, only, never,* and *everyone* often appear in false statements. Words like *some, often, a few, most,* and *usually* often appear in true statements.

Matching First check the directions. See if each item is used only once. Also check to see if some are not used at all. Read all items in both columns before starting. Match those you know first. Cross out items as you use them.

Completion, or **Fill-in-the-Blank** If several words are required, give all of them. Write neatly. Use good grammar, punctuation, and capitalization.

Short Answer Use complete sentences. Answer the question completely. Use correct grammar, capitalization, punctuation, and spelling.

Essay Look for action words like *explain* and *compare.* These are words that tell you what to do. Make a list of the details you will need to answer the question. Make a rough outline of your essay on a separate sheet of paper. Make sure each paragraph contains a topic sentence. Proofread your completed essay.

Multiple Choice Read all of the choices before answering. Eliminate any obviously incorrect answers first. Choose the answer that is most complete or accurate. Pay particular attention to answers such as *none* or *all of the above.*

Check It Out   Read the following test questions.

1. In a paragraph, explain each step in the SQ3R study method.

2. Diagrams, illustrations, maps, charts, and graphs are types of graphic aids. (true or false) _____

3. Assignments should be recorded in an _____
_____ .

4. Match the following types of reading with their uses.
a. skimming ____   1. surveying material
b. scanning ____   2. studying reading assign-
                             ments
c. in-depth reading ____ 3. finding specific informa-
                             tion

- Can you tell what types of test questions are shown above?

Try Your Skill   Copy the questions given in **Check It Out** onto your own paper. Then, answer each question.

Keep This in Mind
- True/false, matching, and multiple choice questions are found on objective tests.
- Completion, short answer, and essay questions are found on essay tests.
- When answering test questions, follow the guidelines in **Here's the Idea.**

Now Write   Review the material in Part 1, **Before You Begin.** Then, copy the following essay question onto a piece of notebook paper. Circle the key words that tell you what to do. Make a rough outline of your answer. Then, write your answer.

Essay Question:
Briefly explain what information you should include when recording an assignment.

High Standards

Preparing for Standardized Tests

Here's the Idea   One type of objective test is the **standardized test.** There are two kinds of standardized tests. One kind measures basic skills. The other measures knowledge of specific subjects. To enter many schools and apprenticeship programs, you must first take a standardized test. Standardized tests are also required in order to get a license to perform many jobs.

Two common standardized tests are the **Scholastic Aptitude Test** (the SAT) and the **American College Testing Program Assessment Test** (the ACT). Many colleges require these tests as part of their admission procedures. If you plan to go to college, ask your guidance counselor whether you must take one of these tests. A guidance counselor can tell you how to sign up for these tests.

Follow these guidelines whenever you take a standardized test:

1. Learn about the types of questions that will appear on the test. Also find out what materials the test will cover.

2. Use the practice materials supplied by the testing organization. Also study the test-taking manuals available in many libraries and bookstores.

3. Learn how to answer the types of questions that will be on the test. (See Part 9.)

4. Eat and sleep properly before the test.

5. Take steps to overcome nervousness about the test. If you can, do some light exercise an hour or so before the test begins. Exercising will relieve tension. It will also clear your mind.

Check It Out   Read the following passage.

LeRoy decided that he wanted to attend Indiana University. He went to the library for a copy of the Indiana University college catalog. The catalog said that he would have to take the SAT. Therefore, LeRoy went to his guidance counselor. LeRoy's counselor signed him up for the PSAT. The PSAT is a practice SAT test. LeRoy took this practice test. He also studied a manual on taking the SAT that he had bought at the bookstore.

- How did LeRoy prepare for the SAT?
- What else could he have done?

Try Your Skill Imagine that you are going to take the SAT. The SAT has sections that test basic English skills. It also has sections that test basic skills in math. Make a list of the steps you could take to prepare for this test.

Keep This in Mind

- Standardized tests are required by many employers, colleges, vocational schools, and apprenticeship programs.
- Studying practice materials can help you to prepare for standardized tests.
- Studying the types of questions asked on the test can also help you to prepare.

Now Write To enter many jobs in the health industry, you must first pass a standardized test. All of the following must take standardized tests to obtain their licenses:

Nurses   Nuclear Medicine Technicians
X-Ray Technicians   Respiratory Therapists

Choose one of these job titles. Do some research. Find out the duties of the job. Also find out what training and tests are required to enter this field. Write a composition reporting your findings.

Right Again!

Answering Standardized Test Questions

Here's the Idea   One way to prepare for a standardized test is to learn about types of standardized test questions. Antonyms, analogies, and sentence completion questions are discussed in Parts 7–9 of Section 21, **Critical Thinking.** In this part you will learn about sentence correction and reading comprehension questions.

Sentence correction questions measure your ability to find errors in sentences. In these questions, all or part of a sentence is underlined. If the underlined material is free of errors, you mark "A." If the underlined material does contain an error, you choose the answer that corrects the error in the sentence.

> EXAMPLE: Sentence Correction
>
> The coach presented the awards to Sarah and I.
>
> (A) I   (B) myself   (C) me   (D) mine

Follow these guidelines when answering correction questions:

a. Look for the error before looking at the answers.
b. Check for errors in grammar, usage, and mechanics. Also check the underlined material for awkwardness.
c. Check your answer by placing it into the sentence and reading the sentence to yourself.

The correct answer for the sample question is C.

Reading comprehension questions measure your ability to understand short reading passages. To answer such questions, first skim the questions below the reading passage. Then, read the passage carefully. Look for relationships between the ideas discussed in the passage. Before choosing an answer, read the question and all the choices. If necessary, scan the passage again to find the right answer.

Check It Out   Read the following passage.

The Pacific Ocean is larger than the entire land surface of the Earth. Across the Pacific are scattered thousands of islands.

The Pacific islands can be divided into two types—high islands and low islands. The high islands are usually of volcanic origin. Some have very high mountains. They are usually well watered and heavily forested. They also have good soils.

The low Pacific islands are often made of coral rock. They usually are much smaller than the high ones and have little water and poor soils.

According to this passage, the low Pacific islands are often made of

(A) sand   (B) mountains   (C) coral rock   (D) volcanoes

•   What is the correct answer to this question?

Try Your Skill   Review the standardized test questions covered in Parts 7–9 of Section 21, **Critical Thinking.** Then, choose the correct answers for the following questions.

1. TREE : TRUNK ::   (A) flower : petal   (B) garden : gardener   (C) flower : stem   (D) plant : leaf

2. HELP : (A) assist   (B) hinder   (C) gain   (D) aid

3. When the zookeeper returned, the chimpanzees <u>was gone.</u>
   (A) was gone (b) are gone (C) were gone (D) is gone

Keep This in Mind

•   Study the various types of standardized test questions before taking a standardized test.

Now Write   Reread the sample reading comprehension passage in **Check it Out.** Write five reading comprehension questions based on this passage. Exchange your questions with a classmate. Answer your classmate's questions.

Letters and Applications

Dear Friend

Writing Personal Letters

Here's the Idea   A **personal letter** is informal and friendly. It is usually handwritten. Personal letters allow you to stay close to friends or to express feelings in a certain social situation. Personal letters contain five parts.

The **heading** consists of three lines: one line for your street address; one for the city, state, and ZIP code; and one for the date. Do not abbreviate any of this information. Place the heading at the top right corner of your letter.

The **salutation** is your greeting, which you generally begin with *Dear*. Write the salutation on the next line below the heading at the left margin. Place a comma after the greeting.

The **body** of the letter is the main part. Write what you want to say in a detailed and conversational way. Begin on the line following the salutation. Indent each paragraph of the body.

The **closing** is your "goodbye." You may write *Love,* or *Your friend,* for example. Write the closing on the line below the last line of the body, placing a comma after it. Align the first word of the closing with the first words of the heading.

Your **signature** is the last part of the letter. Skip a line after the closing, and sign your name in line with the first word of the closing. Usually, you need only sign your first name.

Some personal letters are written for special occasions. These social notes include invitations and thank-you notes. On these notes, the heading may be shortened to the date only.

If you send an **invitation,** include specific information about the event. If you receive an invitation, reply immediately.

You may also send **thank-you** notes. Write a thank-you note after you receive a gift. Also write a thank-you note to thank someone for his or her hospitality if you stayed overnight as a guest. Be sure to write any thank-you note promptly.

1012 Ocean Way
San Francisco, California 94109
March 15, 1985

Dear Rudy,

Today at a basketball game I saw your cousin Paul, who told me that your Grandfather Lane had died last week. I am writing to tell you how sorry I am. I know what a great friend he was to you. I remember the time when Mr. Lane took us camping and canoeing. Do you remember how he talked your mother into letting us go hiking? I will never forget that he said I could borrow him as my grandfather if I needed one.

Maybe, if you can visit again this summer, we can go fishing together at the pond where he used to take us. Since I can't be with you now, please know I'm thinking about you. Try to think about how lucky you have been to have had such a fine man for a grandfather.

Sincerely,
Joe

- Identify the five parts of the personal letter on page 337.
- Is this a well-written letter? Why or why not?

Try Your Skill   Arrange the following information in the correct form for a personal letter. Add the information and details necessary to make it a good letter. Use capital letters and punctuation correctly.

106 willow st., flatbush, kans. 67052, september 16, 1985, dear aunt lois and uncle vic, thank you for inviting me to your farm this summer. I had a wonderful time. I thought the country fair was especially exciting. I'd love to come back again soon. love, julia

Keep This in Mind

- Write personal letters that are conversational, detailed, and neat. Be sure that the heading, salutation, body, closing, and signature follow the correct form.
- Social notes are short forms of personal letters. Write invitations that are specific and thank-you notes that express your appreciation.

Now Write   Write a personal letter. Use your own address and today's date in the heading. The body of the letter may be based on either real or imaginary events. Be sure all parts of your letter are in the correct form. Label your paper **Dear Friend,** and put it into your folder. Make a copy of your letter that you could send, and save that also.

First Class

Preparing Letters for the Mail

Here's the Idea   After you have written a letter, prepare it correctly for mailing. Begin by folding the letter neatly and selecting an envelope that matches the width of the stationery. Insert the folded letter and seal the envelope.

To make sure that your letter reaches its destination without delay, prepare the envelope accurately and neatly. First, address the envelope. Be sure to include your ZIP code. (You may review the correct use of ZIP codes and state abbreviations by turning to page 341.) Next, double-check all numbers to make sure they are correct. Then, put a stamp on the envelope. Be sure you have used enough postage for the letter. Finally, check every envelope for accuracy. If you need any more information, call your local post office.

Check It Out   Examine the envelope below.

Bill Garber
3128 Eagle Boulevard
Denver, CO 80201

Ms. Sylvia Rosso
1915 Maple Avenue #111
New Orleans, LA 70140

- Who wrote the letter? Who will receive it? What state abbreviations are used? How could you check all of the information?

339

Try Your Skill   Rewrite each of these jumbled addresses as it should appear on an envelope. Also write a return address. You may need to refer to the list of correct state abbreviations on page 341.

1. Henry Wright, 27 Rose Circle, Tucson, Arizona 95703
2. 5138 Enfield Avenue, Lincoln, Nebraska 68501, Nina Trovato
3. Miami, Florida 33116, 2241 M Street, Albert Vega
4. 9942 Long Road, St. Louis, Missouri 63114, Jan Weissburg
5. Isabel Saez, P.O. Box 2216, Vieques, Puerto Rico 00765
6. Dr. J. C. Chua, 14943 18th Street, N.W., Washington, D.C. 20036
7. Betty Casali, 645 Crain Street, Portsmouth, New Hampshire 03801
8. San Diego, California 92109, Dennis Boyd, 22 Parkway Drive
9. 1417 Greenwood Avenue, Michigan City, Indiana 46360, Leona Corby
10. Linda Rooney, Clarkston, Georgia 30021, 243 Elm Road

Keep This in Mind

- Prepare letters for the mail carefully. Check all information for accuracy.

Now Write   Take out your personal letter labeled **Dear Friend.** On the other side of that paper, write the title of this lesson, **First Class.** Draw a rectangle to represent an envelope. Address it as if you were going to mail it to your friend or relative. Put this paper into your folder.

Copy your work onto a real envelope. Fold the copy of the letter that you can send and put it into the envelope. Add a stamp and mail your letter.

Zip Codes and State Abbreviations

In order to make sure that your letter reaches its destination, check the address, including the ZIP code. The ZIP code is very important today. It enables the postal department to sort your letter for delivery as rapidly as possible. If you don't know a ZIP code, call your post office. Someone will give you the correct ZIP for any address in the United States and the territories.

The United States Postal Service has created a list of approved state abbreviations to be used on all envelopes and packages. You must use the ZIP code with these abbreviations.

Abbreviations of State Names

Alabama	AL	Montana	MT
Alaska	AK	Nebraska	NE
Arizona	AZ	Nevada	NV
Arkansas	AR	New Hampshire	NH
American Samoa	AS	New Jersey	NJ
California	CA	New Mexico	NM
Canal Zone	CZ	New York	NY
Colorado	CO	North Carolina	NC
Connecticut	CT	North Dakota	ND
Delaware	DE	Ohio	OH
District of Columbia	DC	Oklahoma	OK
Florida	FL	Oregon	OR
Georgia	GA	Pennsylvania	PA
Guam	GU	Puerto Rico	PR
Hawaii	HI	Rhode Island	RI
Idaho	ID	South Carolina	SC
Illinois	IL	South Dakota	SD
Indiana	IN	Tennessee	TN
Iowa	IA	Trust Territories	TT
Kansas	KS	Texas	TX
Kentucky	KY	Utah	UT
Louisiana	LA	Vermont	VT
Maine	ME	Virginia	VA
Maryland	MD	Virgin Islands	VI
Massachusetts	MA	Washington	WA
Michigan	MI	West Virginia	WV
Minnesota	MN	Wisconsin	WI
Mississippi	MS	Wyoming	WY
Missouri	MO		

Office Hours

Writing Business Letters

Here's the Idea   In many situations, you will need to write
business letters. You may want to write to a school or college. You
may need to write a letter seeking employment. You may have
to write to an organization requesting information. You may
have to write to a company to order a product or to complain
about one. You may wish to write to the editor of a newspaper or
to an elected official about issues that affect your life. In all of
these situations, your letters will be most effective if you follow
the correct form for business letters.

To make the best impression, your business letters must be
neat. Use plain white paper, 8 1/2 x 11 inches. Type your letters,
if possible. Although you are not required to type a business
letter, you create a better impression if you do so.

You may write any business letter following one of two
standard forms. One form is the **block** form, which should be
used only if you type a letter. Using the block form, begin every
part of a letter at the left margin. Leave two lines of space
between paragraphs and do not indent them. A second form, the
modified block, may be used either for handwritten or typewritten letters. In this form, place the heading, closing, and
signature at the right side of the page. Indent the paragraphs
and do not leave extra space between them.

Every business letter has six parts—the five parts of a
personal letter, plus an **inside address.** The inside address is the
name and address of the company to which you are writing.
Whenever possible, include the name of an employee or department within the company. Place the inside address at the left
margin, below the heading and above the salutation.

The language of business letters is more formal than that of
personal letters. For the salutation, use Dear *Mr., Mrs., Miss,*

or *Ms.* with the name of an employee. Otherwise, use a general greeting, such as *Dear Sir or Madam.* Place the salutation two lines below the inside address and use a colon (:) after it.

For the more formal closing, write *Sincerely, Yours truly,* or *Very truly yours,* followed by a comma. If you type a letter, leave four lines of space between the closing and your typed signature. Then write your signature in the space.

Be sure a business letter is polite, specific, and neat. Keep a copy of each business letter you write.

Check It Out   Read this business letter.

```
        64 Vernon Street
        St. Paul, Minnesota   55107
        February 2, 1986


        The St. Paul Repertory Theater
        178 Summit Avenue
        St. Paul, Minnesota   55101


        Dear Sir or Madam:


        My neighborhood drama group is interested in
        attending your production of Dracula next month.
        There will be about fifteen of us.  Please send
        information on ticket prices for this show and a
        schedule of performance dates.  If you have group
        rates, please let me know.


        Sincerely yours,

        Lois Gordon


        Lois Gordon
```

- What is the purpose of the business letter on page 343?
- In what form is this letter?

Try Your Skill Write a letter from Herbert Stann to Sheila Troy, Sales Manager of Soundwave Records, Incorporated. Have Herbert ask why his order for the "Golden Hits of the 70's" album has not yet been filled after eight weeks. Invent other necessary details. For the purpose of this exercise, use the block form, even though your letter will be handwritten.

Keep This in Mind

- You may write a business letter to apply to a school, to seek employment, to request information, or to ask about a product. Whether you write or type a business letter, be polite, specific, and neat. Keep a copy of every business letter.
- Use either the *block* or *modified block* form for a business letter. Either form has six parts, including an inside address.

Now Write Write or type a business letter to a real organization regarding a product or requesting information. Draw an envelope and address it. Label your paper **Office Hours.** Keep it in your folder.

Take the Credit

Completing a Credit Application

Here's the Idea *Credit* means "trust in a person's integrity in money matters and his or her ability to meet payments when due." At some time, you may want to borrow money from a bank for a large purchase, such as a car or house. You may want to borrow money for tuition. You may want a credit card. You may want check-cashing privileges at a local supermarket. In these situations, you will need to complete a credit application.

A credit application has two major parts, one in which the business gives information, and one in which you give information. The company's part of an application is perhaps the more important part; it states the terms of your agreement. In this section of any credit application, for example, you will find information about billing policies, finance charges, and penalties for failing to make payments. If you are applying for a credit card, you will find a statement of your responsibility if the card is lost or stolen. This section of the application is often difficult to read. It may be complicated or written in small print. Your signature, a requirement on any application, indicates that you have read this information, and that you agree to these policies. Read this section carefully before you sign an application, and keep this information for your records.

You will be asked to give personal information, including your age, social security number, and length of residence at your present address. You will be asked to give employment information, including your salary and length of employment. You will be asked to give credit information, including the status of any monthly payments, loans, or charge accounts. Finally, you will be asked to sign your name. Your signature indicates that the information you have given is true, that you authorize the company to investigate your credit, and that you agree to all policies stated in the agreement.

When you submit a credit application, a business or store will investigate you and your credit history. The business will make a judgment about whether you will be given credit. If you are considered a good credit risk, you will be allowed an amount of credit based on the company's policies.

Check It Out   Examine the credit application shown on page 347.

- What information has the applicant stated? What store policies are stated?

Try Your Skill   Refer to the credit application on page 347 and answer the following questions.

1. Suppose Rafael Ortega had had no previous employer, what would he enter in that blank?
2. If Rafael had no present loan but had just finished paying off a $1500 loan, would this information be relevant?
3. What does Rafael indicate when he puts his signature on the application form?

Keep This in Mind

- On a credit application, you state information about yourself, your employment and income, and your financial obligations. Also a business states information about its policies. By signing an application, you agree to all terms stated.

Now Write   Complete an actual credit application. Use a form given to you by your teacher or one from a business in your town. Read the application thoroughly and then complete the form. Label it **Take the Credit.** Put it into your folder.

APPLICATION FOR CREDIT

J. B. Weber's
708 Fifth Street
Spokane, Washington

PERSONAL DATA

☐ MRS. ☐ MISS ☐ MS. ☒ MR.
Designation of title is optional

FIRST NAME: Rafael
INITIAL: J.
LAST NAME: Ortega

STREET ADDRESS: 1526 Crawford

CITY: Chicago,
STATE: Illinois
ZIP CODE: 60607
HOW LONG: 12 yrs.

☐ RENT ☐ BOARD
☐ OWN ☒ WITH PARENTS
HOME PHONE: 555-9634
AGE: 20
SOC. SEC. NO.: 698-51-7242

NEAREST RELATIVE, NOT LIVING WITH YOU: Juan Ortega Jr.
RELATIONSHIP: Brother

ADDRESS: 914 East Watson
CITY: Chicago, Illinois
STATE/ZIP: 60680

EMPLOYMENT AND INCOME

PRESENT EMPLOYER: Lincoln Federal Bank
PHONE: 555-1600

ADDRESS: 212 Market Square
CITY: Chicago,
STATE: Illinois 60607

POSITION: Teller
SALARY: $900/month
HOW LONG: 1 year

PREVIOUS EMPLOYER: Ferman Drug Store
POSITION: Cashier (part-time)

ADDRESS: 1223 Mason Street
CITY: Chicago,
STATE: Illinois 60607

CREDIT REFERENCES

LANDLORD OR MORTGAGE HOLDER: Mr. Juan Ortega
MONTHLY PAYMENT: 200.00

ADDRESS: 1526 Crawford, Chicago
PHONE: 555-9634

BANK: Lincoln Federal Bank
CITY:
☒ CHECKING
☒ SAVINGS

LOANS OWED TO
1. City National Bank
BALANCE: $1400.
MONTHLY PAYMENTS: $85.00 (car payment)

2.

MONTHLY CHARGE ACCOUNTS
1. Sherman's Dept. Store
ACCT. NO.: 555-613-0987
BALANCE: $23.45

2.

The above information is for the purpose of obtaining credit and is warranted to be true. False or misleading information will cause revocation of any extension of credit.

I hereby authorize J. B. Weber's or any credit bureau employed by them to investigate the references herein listed pertaining to my credit responsibility and to report to proper persons and bureaus my performance of this agreement.

I agree to pay all charges made by any authorized person within fifteen days of statement closing date. This is a 30 day charge account to be paid in full upon receipt of statement, if the account becomes delinquent (60 days overdue), I agree to pay a finance charge of 1½% per month, which is an annual percentage rate of 18% applied to the past due balance after deducting payments or credits.

Credit cards, when issued, are the property of J. B. Weber's and are returnable on request.

The Federal Credit Opportunity Act prohibits creditors from discriminating against credit applicants on the basis of sex or marital status.

I have a copy of this agreement and understand and agree to the terms herein specified.

SIGNATURE OF APPLICANT: Rafael Ortega
DATE: 2/14/85

SEE IMPORTANT INFORMATION ON PAGE 2 OF THIS APPLICATION

May I?

Writing Letters of Request

Here's the Idea Frequently, you will write a business letter to request something from a company or organization. For example, you may need information to write a report or to plan a vacation, or you may want to order a product. **Letters of request** should contain the six parts of a business letter and should follow either the block or modified block form.

When you write a letter of request, follow two important guidelines. First, be specific. Provide all the information needed to fill your request. To request information, state precisely what you need and for what purpose you need it. To place an order, include details about the size, color, cost, or identification number of the product you want. Second, be sure that your letter is courteous. Remember, you are asking someone to help you.

Check It Out Read the letter of request on page 349.

- Is this letter of request courteous, specific, and to the point? Which form does this business letter have?

Try Your Skill Write a letter to one of the following organizations, requesting the information mentioned.

1. National Aeronautics and Space Administration, 400 Maryland Avenue SW, Washington, D.C. 20546. Request information on future plans for a permanently inhabited space station in Earth orbit.

2. American Youth Hostels, National Campus, Delaplane, Virginia 22025. Request information about getting a hostel membership card for a bike trip you are planning this summer.

```
         25 Maple Terrace
         Lansdale, Pennsylvania   19446
         October 22, 1985


         Public Relations
         Wilson Brothers Bakery
         Lansdale, Pennsylvania   19446


         Dear Sir or Madam:


         I understand that you give free guided tours
         through your bakery to groups of twenty or more.
         I am planning to bring a Cub Scout troop on your
         tour.  I will need 25 tickets for any Saturday in
         the month of December.  Please send the tickets
         to the above address.


         Very truly yours,

         Nick Tuminello


         Nick Tuminello
```

Keep This in Mind

- Write a letter of request that is courteous, specific, and to the point. Use either the block or modified block form for this business letter.

Now Write Write a letter to a federal or state government agency requesting information on a topic that interests you. Be sure to ask for specific information, and supply all necessary information. Label your letter **May I?** Put it into your folder. You may want to make a copy of the letter and mail it.

Satisfaction

Writing Letters of Complaint

Here's the Idea When you have spent time and money ordering a product by mail, you hope to be satisfied with it. Similarly, the company from which you purchased the product has an interest in seeing that you are satisifed. However, if you are not satisfied with a product, you should write a **letter of complaint** to the company courteously explaining your problem.

When you write this kind of business letter, you must include all necessary information. Be sure to identify a product completely. State the specific name of the product, its size, color, and identification or catalog number. Mention when and where the item was ordered and the amount you paid for it. It is best to include a photocopy of the order form, of your receipt, or of both sides of the canceled check with your letter.

You must state your complaint specifically. For example, is the item missing a part? Did an item arrive in damaged condition? State precisely how you want the problem to be handled. Are you returning the merchandise for a refund or credit? Do you want it replaced? If you are polite and to the point, most companies will make an effort to solve your problem.

Check It Out Read the letter of complaint on page 351.

- Does this letter of complaint contain specific information about the products and the problems? Is it courteous?

Try Your Skill Write a letter of complaint based on the following situation.

You ordered a subscription to *Indoor Farming* from Halliday Publications, Incorporated at 1424 Wesley Street, St. Louis, Missouri 63190. The subscription cost $6.00, but you have been billed for $60.00.

```
28 Oak Road
Hartfort, Connecticut  06106
January 3, 1985


Kramer Clothes Catalog, Inc.
P.O. Box 140
Walden, North Dakota  58313


Dear Sir or Madam:


On October 4, 1984, I ordered two blue personal-
ized T-shirts (catalog number R-246) and a
personalized sweatshirt (catalog number J-189)
from your fall catalog.  I paid $20.85 for the
order:  $5.95 for each T-shirt, and $6.95 for
the sweatshirt, plus $2.00 for postage and handling.


These items were intended as Christmas presents.
Your catalog states that you guarantee delivery
within six weeks.  It has now been nearly eleven
weeks, and Christmas has passed.  Under the circum-
stances, I would like to have the $20.85 refunded.


Sincerely,

Katie Montel

Katie Montel
```

Now Write   Write a letter of complaint based on a real product. Tell how you want the problem handled. Label your paper **Satisfaction Guaranteed**. Put it into your folder.

The Pen Is Mightier

Writing a Letter-to-the-Editor

Here's the Idea   Writing a **letter-to-the-editor** can be an effective way to air your ideas and feelings on a subject and perhaps to influence public opinion.

When you write a letter-to-the-editor, you are writing a business letter. Thus, you must follow one of the two standard business forms and the related guidelines you have learned. In addition, remember that your letter may be published, becoming a matter of public record.

It is most important that you express your opinion in a reasonable, responsible way. You may be angry or upset about a subject. However, if you want your reader to consider your ideas seriously, you must state your opinion clearly and logically. You must also offer strong supporting evidence. You may find it helpful to remember the skills you learned in writing an explanatory paragraph or composition that states an opinion.

Keep a letter-to-the-editor short. Many letters are not published because they are too long to fit the space limitations of a newspaper. As a rule, a shorter letter has a better chance of being published.

You must always sign your full name and include your address. No responsible newspaper will publish an anonymous letter—no matter how well written it is. If a letter includes personal information, however, you may request that your name be withheld if your letter is printed.

Newspapers, especially the larger ones, often have a policy stating a standard form for letters-to-the-editor. This policy may be stated on the editorial page, along with the address to which you should mail your letter. Read these instructions before you make the final copy of your letter.

Check It Out   Read this letter-to-the-editor.

44 Grove Street
Weston, Alabama 71654
January 15, 1985

Editor
Weston Weekly Post
Sheehan Road
Weston, Alabama 71654

Dear Sir:

I urge the citizens of Weston to vote <u>yes</u> in the upcoming
school tax referendum.

A <u>no</u> vote will mean that each taxpayer saves five to ten
dollars a year. However, a <u>no</u> vote also means no foreign
language program for junior high students, no speech
therapist for the high school, no tennis or soccer teams,
and two fewer school nurses. At the elementary schools, a
<u>no</u> vote means no after-school gymnastics program and no
after-school dramatics or music program.

I urge all Weston voters to think: Are you going to miss
that five dollars as much as we students will miss what it
can buy?

Sincerely,

John Mc Connell

John McConnell

- Is this letter brief and well organized?
- Does the letter state and support an opinion clearly?

Try Your Skill Imagine that your local newspaper has written an editorial supporting one of the following actions. Write a letter-to-the-editor supporting or opposing the action.

1. eliminating a major community program, such as bus service, in order to save money
2. freezing all salaries
3. raising the voting age to 25
4. abolishing the Olympic Games
5. instituting a national lottery to raise money for education

Keep This in Mind

- Writing a letter-to-the-editor of a newspaper is an effective way to express your feelings publicly. State your opinion in a brief, well-organized letter that includes strong supporting evidence.
- For this business letter, also follow any guidelines set by the newspaper about an acceptable form. Always sign your letter, and include your full name and address.

Now Write Borrow or buy a recent issue of your local newspaper. Write a letter-to-the-editor in response to an article, editorial, or letter appearing in the issue. Express your feelings in a strong, well-organized letter that includes factual supporting evidence. Label your paper **The Pen Is Mightier** and put it into your folder.

Be Counted

Writing a Letter to an Elected Official

Here's the Idea   There will probably be times when you will want to write to an elected official. The United States has a form of government in which the power rests with the citizens entitled to vote and is exercised by their elected representatives. Thus, it is only natural that you would want to communicate with an official who represents you. In fact, it is your responsibility as a citizen to do so.

When would you want to write to an elected official? You might want to urge action on an issue or bill or to complain about a situation you want corrected. You might want to express your approval or disapproval of an official's performance. You might also want to apply for an appointment to a military academy, or to request help or information. A letter to an elected official will have more positive results if you write before an action is to be taken than if you write to complain about it after the fact.

First, determine whether the issue you are dealing with is a city, state, or national issue. Then write to the appropriate officials. For a city, or municipal, problem, you should call your city hall to learn which of the city officials you should write to. For a state issue, write to your state representative or senator, or to the governor. Regarding a national, or federal, issue, it is most effective to write to your United States senator or representative, or to the President. You can find the names and addresses of these officials at the library.

When you write a letter to an elected official, use facts to clearly define the issue that concerns you. You must be specific in explaining what action you wish the official to take, if any.

For this kind of business letter, addresses and salutations differ somewhat. On the inside address and on the envelope, use *The Honorable* followed by the official's name and title.

Write, for example, *The Honorable Jane Smith, U.S. Senator.* Use this form of address for all senators, representatives, governors, or mayors. Use *Mr.* or *Ms.* for all other city officials. Use *The President,* for the President of the United States. As a salutation, *Dear Sir* or *Dear Madam* is always acceptable. However, you may prefer a more specific greeting, like *Dear Senator Smith.* In all other parts of the letter, use the standard business letter form you have learned.

Check It Out   Read the letter on page 357.

- Does this letter concern a municipal, state, or federal issue? Is it written to an appropriate official? Does the letter clearly explain an issue and how the writer feels it should be handled? Does the letter include an appropriate salutation and inside address?

Try Your Skill   Write *Municipal, State,* or *Federal* to identify each of the following issues. Then find and write the name of an official to whom you would write.

1. a state highway
2. the voting age
3. school athletics budget
4. defense funding
5. a broken street light
6. a national health plan
7. U.S. energy policy
8. the Equal Rights Amendment

Keep This in Mind

- In expressing your views on municipal, state, and federal issues, write to the appropriate elected officials. Be specific about the issue that concerns you and how you wish it to be handled. Include an appropriate salutation and address for the elected official.

241 Taylor Avenue
Hastings, Virginia 05432
April 8, 1985

Mr. Wayne Dobbs, Alderman
City Hall
1283 Main Street
Hastings, Virginia 05432

Dear Mr. Dobbs:

The intersection at Taylor Avenue and Monroe Street in your district is becoming more and more dangerous. At present only a four-way stop sign directs traffic here. In the past four months alone, there have been three serious accidents at this intersection. These accidents resulted in one fatality, and six people have been hospitalized.

The neighbors of this area would like to see a traffic light installed at this location. The numerous phone calls we have made to the Division of Traffic have brought no response. We would appreciate it if you as our elected representative could take a personal interest in this matter and see that some action is taken before anyone else is injured.

Very truly yours,

Andrea Mason

Andrea Mason, President
Taylor Avenue Neighborhood Association

Now Write Write a letter to an elected official about an issue that interests you. Be specific in expressing your viewpoint. Label your paper **Be Counted** and put it into your folder. You may want to make a copy of the letter and mail it.

Skills for Your Future

Suits Me!

Assessing Your Interests and Skills

Here's the Idea Suppose that you want to join an athletic team at your school. What team would you join? Of course, you would choose a sport that you enjoy and that you are good at. In other words, your decision would be based on your own interests and skills.

The same sort of reasoning should go into choosing a career or a college major. To decide what sort of work you would enjoy, you must examine your own interests. To decide what kind of work you would do well, you must determine what skills you have. You must also determine what skills you can develop. Looking at your own interests and skills will help you to find goals that are suited to you.

Check It Out Read the following questions.

1. What nonpaying jobs have I done in the past?
2. What paying jobs have I done in the past?
3. What skills taught in school am I particularly good at?
4. What skills have I learned from crafts or hobbies?
5. What skills have I learned from club or team activities? from participation in student government?
6. What skills would I really enjoy developing?

- How would you answer each of these questions?
- Are the skills in your answers useful job skills? What jobs could these skills be used in?

Try Your Skill The following questions are from an interest inventory. An **interest inventory** is a list of questions that people use to find out what jobs they might be interested in. Answer these questions. Then, think about your answers. Write a paragraph telling what your answers reveal about the kinds of jobs you would enjoy.

1. Do you prefer working with words or with numbers?
2. Do you prefer working indoors or outdoors?
3. Do you prefer working with people or with machines?
4. Do you prefer mental work or physical work?
5. Are you willing to take additional training after high school?
6. Do you work best by yourself or under the direction of others?
7. Do you prefer living in the city or in the country? Would you take a job in either one of these areas?
8. How much money would you have to make to be satisfied?

Keep This in Mind

- Base your career or college choices on careful study of your own interests and skills.

Now Write Choose a job that matches the interests and skills that you identified in **Check It Out** and **Try Your Skill**. Write a paragraph explaining why this would be the right job for you.

Opportunity Knocks

Exploring Careers

Here's the Idea   The *Dictionary of Occupational Titles* lists over twenty thousand jobs. As this number suggests, there are many careers to choose from. Among them may be several that suit your particular interests and skills. You simply have to do some research to find out what opportunities exist. Here are some sources you can use to find out about possible careers:

   1. Reference works such as encyclopedias and dictionaries
   2. Other people, including counselors, teachers, relatives, and employers
   3. Books on careers such as the *Occupational Outlook Handbook* and the *Dictionary of Occupational Titles*

   To find these sources, check with your guidance office, your public and school libraries, and with the people you know. You may also wish to call or write to the following places:

   1. Technical or trade schools
   2. Community or junior colleges
   3. Apprenticeship training organizations
   4. Armed services recruiting offices
   5. Colleges and universities
   6. Businesses

All of these organizations offer job training programs of various kinds. For example, many businesses have on-the-job training programs. Many unions and professional organizations offer job training in their apprenticeship programs. On-the-job training programs are also found in most branches of the armed services.

Check It Out   On the following page there is a passage from the notebook of a student who is researching possible careers.

Job Title	Hotel Manager
Duties	- Oversee operation of hotel/restaurant
	- Responsible for managing employees, budget, promotions and advertising, daily operations
Working Conditions	- Office atmosphere; Lots of personal contact
	- Pleasant surroundings
Training/ Special Skills Required	- Preferred: degree in Hotel/Restaurant Management
	- Both two- and four-year courses available
	- Some on-the-job training
Possible Earnings	- Beginning salary, trainees: $13,500.00
	- Salary of general managers: $20,000.00 - $80,000.00

- What information does this student have about this job?
- What sources could the student have used?

Try Your Skill   Study the following list of job fields. For each job field, give one job title not already listed.

1. **Agriculture/Natural Resources**
farmer, gardener, forest ranger, fisherman, miner
2. **Business and Office**
personnel director, bank officer, insurance salesperson, accountant

3. **Communications and Media**
projectionist, sound effects technician, proofreader, reporter
4. **Construction**
carpenter, mason, electrician, architect, plumber
5. **Environment**
water quality inspector, fire warden, pest control worker
6. **Fine Arts/Humanities**
stagehand, museum curator, writer, artist, conductor
7. **Health**
nurse, ambulance driver, medical records clerk, veterinarian
8. **Home Economics**
interior decorator, nutritionist, food service worker, designer
9. **Hospitality/Recreation**
travel agent, hotel manager, lifeguard, athletic director
10. **Manufacturing**
mechanical engineer, machinist, millworker, welder, chemist
11. **Marine Science**
hatchery worker, sailor, fishery bacteriologist
12. **Marketing**
stockbroker, buyer, warehouse manager, salesperson
13. **Personal Services**
cosmetologist, funeral director, flight attendant, kennel worker
14. **Public Service**
teacher, police officer, librarian, customs inspector
15. **Transportation**
air traffic controller, dispatcher, pilot, truck or bus driver

Keep This in Mind

- Use the many sources of career information.
- Explore different types of job training.

Now Write   Start a jobs notebook. Label each page as shown in **Check It Out.** Use a separate page for each job. Using the sources mentioned in this lesson, make entries in your notebook for five different jobs.

The Subject Is You

Writing a Résumé

Here's the Idea The time will come when you have to apply for a job or to a school. When you apply, you usually send a letter and a résumé (rez′ · oo · mā′). A **résumé** is a list of information about your education, work experiences, and special skills. Many schools and employers will request that you submit a résumé. Often you will have to do this before you will be admitted or given an interview. Using résumés is one way in which they can narrow a large number of applicants. Remember that the stronger your résumé is, the greater your chances of getting through this initial screening.

No two résumés are exactly alike, but most are one-page long and typewritten. When writing your résumé, use short phrases, not complete sentences. Avoid negative language such as "not familiar with all office machines." Instead, use positive language such as "familiar with postage meters and adding machines." Using positive language will help you to highlight your strengths, not your weaknesses.

Your résumé should begin by identifying you. At the top, state your name, address, and telephone number, including the area code. Below that, state your job objective. Identify the kind of position or general area of work you are seeking.

Next, summarize your education. List your high school, its address, and your date of graduation. Also list any work-related courses you have taken. If you have attended more than one school, list the most recent first.

Summarize your work experience next. Tell the dates of your employment and the name and address of your employer. Also tell the position you held and your duties. Again, list your most recent job first. Also list any work-related volunteer experience you have had.

Then, list your important personal achievements. Mention special skills, such as knowledge of a computer language or office skills. Also mention awards, hobbies, special interests, and offices held in societies or clubs.

Finally, mention your references. You may name two or three people who can give you good character or employment references. You may also simply state that you will supply references upon request. In either case, be sure you have asked people for permission to name them as references.

Check It Out   Examine the résumé on page 367.

- Is this résumé well organized and easy to read? Does it include all the necessary information?

Try Your Skill   Revise the résumé on page 367. Add the following information. Rewrite the appropriate sections.

1. Volunteered as camp counselor in Head Start day camp, Lansing, Michigan 48927. Summer, 1983.
2. Student Council member, 1983–1984.
3. Courses in business English and accounting.

Keep This in Mind

- A résumé summarizes basic information about your life in relation to work.
- Make sure your résumé is clear, well organized, and up to date.
- Include all information necessary to present your skills and experience.

Now Write   Now you are ready to write your résumé. First, jot down notes and organize them in a way that shows your talents best. Then, write a rough draft. Follow the model on page 367. Revise your draft. Print or type a neat final copy.

Ruth Marie Myers

2941 Grove Street
Lansing, Michigan 48927
(317) 555-2549

OBJECTIVE	A summer job as a clerk-typist at Valley Hospital.
EDUCATION	Valley High School Lansing, Michigan Member of senior class graduating June 10, 1986, with courses in typing, business machines, shorthand, and office skills.

WORK EXPERIENCE
Present

Clerk
Valley High School
Lansing, Michigan
After school hours

Duties: answering tele-
phones, filing, typing

Summer, 1984

Typist/Clerk
Municipal License Bureau
Lansing, Michigan
Full-time

Duties: typing of
documents and let-
ters; some customer
service

Skills

Excellent typist (70 wpm); thoroughly familiar
with calculators, dictaphones, and adding machines; good communication skills; knowledge of
standard office practices

PERSONAL

Volunteer Candy Striper, Valley Hospital,
1981—1985. Won first place Typing Award, 1985.
Member of Valley High Business Club.

REFERENCES

Will be provided upon request.

Help Wanted

Discovering Job Opportunities

Here's the Idea   Before you can look for a job, you must know what jobs are available. Here are some of the most important sources of information about job oportunities:

Counselors.   Often the guidance department in your school can give you good advice about what jobs are suited to your interests and skills. A counselor may be able to tell you about specific job openings in your community. He or she may also be able to suggest other sources of information about job openings.

Help-Wanted Ads.   Most newspapers list job openings in their classified ads. These ads are arranged alphabetically by job title. Part-time jobs are usually listed separately from full-time jobs. By reading these ads, you can learn a great deal about the jobs listed in them. A help-wanted ad usually lists the job title, the days or shifts to be worked, and how to contact the employer. It may also list a job description, the skills or experience required, the number of hours to be worked each week, and the salary or wages to be paid.

Employment Agencies.   Many employers list job openings with employment agencies. Check your telephone directory for the addresses and phone numbers of these agencies.

Telephone Directories.   One way to look for possible employers is to check the yellow pages of your local telephone directory. Once you find a possible employer, simply call to see if any openings exist.

Personal Contacts.   Your family and friends may also be able to suggest job opportunities. Always inform these people when you start to look for a job. They may be able to help you in your search.

Check It Out   Read the following help-wanted ads.

ANIMAL CARE–Immediate opening in small animal hospital. Evenings, 10 hrs per week. Exper. with dogs and cats pref. Call 555-2356.

DISPATCHER–Supervise six drivers afternoon and weekends. Prefer course work in transportation but will train. $7.50/hr. Send resume c/o Box 578, *The Plainsville Journal*.

- Which of these jobs might be right for a high school student? Which would not be right? Why?

Try Your Skill   Study the want ads given in **Check It Out.** Then, for each job, answer the following questions.

1. What is the job title?
2. Does the ad tell what the job duties are?
3. Is experience required for the job?
4. What work times are given in the ad?
5. How are you asked to contact the employer?

Keep This in Mind

- Become familiar with the many sources of information about job openings.
- Possible sources include counselors, help-wanted ads, employment agencies, telephone directories, and friends and relatives.

Now Write   Suppose that you want a job working with animals in a kennel, zoo, or veterinary clinic. Using at least two of the sources listed in **Check It Out,** make a list of possible employers in your area. Include telephone numbers and addresses.

Working Papers

Writing Letters to Employers

Here's the Idea   After you have found a promising job opening, you need to contact the employer. There are two ways to do
this. One way is to make a telephone call. The other is to send
the employer a letter and a résumé. If you decide to write a
letter, try to present yourself in the best possible way. Be direct
about stating what you can bring to the job. Your strengths may
include valuable previous experience, reliable work habits, or a
desire to learn. Be sure your letter presents your strengths.

In your letter include certain basic information related to the
job. Tell what job you are seeking. Also tell whether you are
looking for full-time, part-time, or temporary employment.
Mention the particular days or hours that you are willing to
work. Also mention the date when you will be able to begin the
job. Finally, request an interview if the job is in your area.

In addition, include information about yourself. Make a brief
statement about your education and your current situation.
Briefly summarize your qualifications. Be sure to mention any
related work experience or courses taken in school.

If you are sending your letter to a large company, write to the
personnel department. If you are writing to a small company,
write to the owner or manager. If you answer a newspaper
advertisement, follow the instructions on how to reply.

Be sure that your letter follows correct business form. Make
certain that it is informative, neat, and polite. Proofread your
letter before sending it. You want the letter to create a good
impression.

Check It Out   Read the following letter.

2941 Grove Street
Lansing, Michigan 48927
April 14, 1985

Personnel Department
Valley Hospital
1600 Sherman Avenue
Lansing, Michigan 48927

Dear Sir or Madam:

I am interested in applying for a full-time summer job as a clerk-typist in the business office. In 1986 I will graduate from Valley High School. I have had courses in typing, shorthand, and business machines. Last summer I worked full time as a typist at the Municipal License Bureau. I am currently working part time in the school office.

For the past four years I have been a volunteer Candy Striper at Valley Hospital and am very familiar with the institution. I am considering entering nursing school after graduation.

I will be available to work full time from June 15 until Labor Day. I can work any combination of hours, including nights and weekends.

I plan to apply in person next week. I will be available for an interview at your convenience.

Yours truly,

Ruth Myers

Ruth Myers

- Does the letter on page 371 include all the necessary information?
- Is it neat and polite?

Try Your Skill   Write a letter answering one of the following help-wanted ads. Mention any experiences you have had that relate to the job for which you are applying.

1. Wanted: Cafeteria help, 4:30–8:30 P.M. No experience necessary. Write C. R. Industries, P.O. Box 414, Duluth, Minnesota 55806.

2. Wanted: Part-Time Teller. Join organization that promotes from within. Will train. Must type and speak English well. Write to Glenbrook Savings and Loan, 5162 Howard Street, Topsfield, Massachusetts 01983.

3. Deliver suburban newspapers. Early morning hours. Must have valid driver's license. Write *Village News*, 158 Ogden Avenue, Hinsdale, Illinois 60521.

Keep This in Mind

- When you write to an employer, try to create a good impression.
- Your letter should be informative, polite, and neat.
- The letter should include specific information about you and about the job you want.

Now Write   Write a letter seeking employment at a restaurant, store, or business in your community. Ask to be considered for a particular position. Include all the necessary information. Revise and proofread your letter carefully.

Before You Go

Preparing for an Interview

Here's the Idea   To many employers, the most important part of a job application is the interview. An interview gives the employer a chance to observe you firsthand. The following are some of the things that an employer looks for in an interview.

   friendliness and courtesy; self confidence; experience
   good speaking and listening skills; organizational skills
   punctuality; honesty, intelligence, and creativity

  One way to show an employer that you are well organized is to prepare well for the interview. Follow these steps.

   1. Get copies of your résumé to take to the interview.
   2. Find out as much as you can about the job and about the company. Be prepared to talk about both.
   3. Practice introducing yourself to the employer.
   4. Choose clothing that is neat and tasteful.
   5. List some questions to show your interest in the company.
   6. Think about your weaknesses. Do you lack experience? Did you have a problem on your last job? If so, be prepared to talk openly and honestly about these things. Decide what you can say to assure the employer that these weaknesses will not be a problem in the future.
   7. Think about your strengths. Make a list of the valuable skills you can bring to the job. Include any special training or qualifications you have. Be prepared to talk about these.
   8. Anticipate questions that the employer might ask. Practice answering these questions before you go to the interview.

Check It Out   Read the following questions that an employer might ask during an interview.

1. Why did you apply for this particular job?

2. What are your greatest strengths as an employee? What are your greatest weaknesses?

3. Could you work overtime if necessary?

4. What do you do in your spare time?

5. How well do you like school? What do you like most? What do you like least?

6. What are your immediate and long-range career plans?

7. Do you have any special training or skills that you can use on this job?

8. What job experiences have you had?

9. What did you think of your previous job? Did you like your employer? your fellow employees? Why or why not?

- Why would an employer want to know these things?
- What other questions might an employer ask?

Try Your Skill   Imagine that you are applying for a job as a cashier in a grocery store. Prepare for an interview for this job by answering the questions in **Check It Out.** Try to word your answers in as positive a manner as possible. Even negative experiences can be presented positively if you explain what lessons you have learned from them.

Keep This in Mind

- Always prepare well before an interview.
- Think about your strengths and weaknesses.
- Find out about the company and the job. Prepare answers to questions that the employer might ask.

Now Write   Imagine that you will be interviewing students to work in the cafeteria at your school. Make a list of the questions that you might ask in your interviews. Then, pretend that you are applying for this job. Answer your own questions.

Part 7

First Impressions

Having an Interview

Here's the Idea When you go to a job interview, take with you everything you will need. Make sure to take several copies of your résumé. Also take a notebook, a pen or pencil, and any information that you might need to complete an application form. (See Part 8.)

Show the employer that you are punctual by arriving on time or slightly early. When you introduce yourself, be polite. Speak in a clear, confident voice. Use the interviewer's name, if you know it, along with *Mr., Miss, Mrs.,* or *Ms.* For example, you might say something like this:

> Good morning, Ms. Sanchez. I'm David Goodman. It's nice to meet you.

If you do not know the interviewer's name, listen carefully during the introductions. If you do not catch the interviewer's name, ask the interviewer to repeat it.

If you haven't already sent a copy of your résumé to the employer, offer to give one to the interviewer. Sit quietly until the interviewer is ready to speak to you. During the interview, listen carefully. Take the time to think about your answers to the interviewer's questions. Do not be afraid to say, "Let me think about that for a moment." When you do answer a question, be positive. Do not bring up your weaknesses. However, do discuss these if the interviewer brings them up.

Take every opportunity to tell the interviewer what specific skills and qualifications you can bring to the job. Save questions about salary or wages until later. Discuss these only if the interviewer mentions them first. Throughout the interview, keep in mind the guidelines for good listening and speaking given in Section 26, Parts 1 and 2.

The interviewer will usually let you know when the interview is finished. When this happens, express your interest in the job once again. Ask when you can expect to hear from the company. Thank the interviewer for his or her time.

Check It Out   Read the following portion of an interview. The applicant, Hernando, is applying for a summer job as a worker in an auto parts warehouse.

Mr. Trask: What qualifications do you have for this job?

Hernando: I think I have two important qualifications. First, a warehouse worker has to be in good physical shape in order to do all the necessary lifting. You'll find that I can take a lot of hard physical labor. Second, you probably want a worker who is well organized and can follow directions precisely. If you talk to my former employers, you'll find that this is the sort of worker I am.

Mr. Trask: On your previous job, did you get along well with the other employees?

Hernando: Oh, yes. I was able to work with them well and enjoyed being with them outside of work hours.

Mr. Trask: What would you say is your greatest weakness as an employee?

Hernando: Let me think about that for a moment. Well, I like to be constantly busy. This can be a drawback in jobs that call for a great deal of standing around. I sometimes get a little impatient when things are slow.

Mr. Trask: Well, you won't have to worry about that here. Do you know anything about auto parts?

Hernando: Well, I have had a great deal of experience working on my own car. I'm a good mechanic, and what I don't know I can learn pretty quickly.

- How well did Hernando prepare for this interview? How well did he handle himself during the interview?

Try Your Skill   The following questions are often asked by interviewers. Answer these questions.

1. Can you tell me a little about yourself?
2. Where do you see yourself in five years?
3. What jobs have you held previously?
4. What would you do if your supervisor told you to do something that you know should be done in another way?

Keep This in Mind

- Introduce yourself to your interviewer.
- Answer all questions completely and thoughtfully.
- Let your interviewer see your strongest qualities.

Now Write   Imagine that you are an employer looking at your résumé. Make a list of questions that an employer might ask you about your experience, qualifications, and skills. Answer these questions.

Apply Within

Completing a Job Application

Here's the Idea Generally, whenever you apply for a job, you will be asked to complete a job application. The form of the application will vary from business to business. However, you will find many similarities in the information required and in the process you must follow.

You should always be prepared to answer several standard questions. For example, you will be asked to state your address, telephone number, date of birth, social security number, and your citizenship. You will be asked about your education, work experiences, and special skills. You will usually be asked to name references. Choose people best able to evaluate your strengths and abilities. For example, you may name former teachers or former employers. However, list only those people who have given you permission to use their names.

In answering these questions, it is important to be neat. Your application reflects your ability to follow directions and to work neatly. Print your answers carefully, using a pen. Because there is not much space to print information requested, plan your answers. Read all instructions thoroughly, especially those in fine print. If you do make an error, erase it carefully.

In completing an application, fill in every item. There may be questions that do not apply to you. If an item does not apply to you, write "does not apply" on the form.

Finally, you must be honest in completing an application. You will be asked to sign your name to a statement that all information is accurate.

Check It Out Examine the completed job application on page 379.

Valley Hospital

APPLICATION FOR EMPLOYMENT   Date April 22, 1985

Name **Myers, Ruth Marie**   Tel. No. 555-2549
          Last   First   Middle

Present Address **2941 Grove Street, Lansing, Michigan 48927**
              Street   City   State   Zip

Do you rent? ☐   Own your home? ☐   Live with parents? ☒

Previous Address **does not apply**
              Street   City   State   Zip

Soc. Sec. No. **689-31-2182** Date of Birth **8-29-67**   Are you a citizen? Yes ☒ No ☐

Person to be notified in case of accident or emergency **Anita Myers, (mother)**

Address **Same as above**   Phone **Same**

Position applied for **Clerk-typist**   Date available for work? **June 15, 1985**

RECORD OF EDUCATION

School	Name and Address of School	Years Attended	Circle last year completed
Elementary	Wayne Elementary School Lansing, Michigan	1973-81	5 6 7 ⑧
High	Valley High School Lansing, Michigan	1981-Present	2 ③ 4
College			1 2 3 4

Did you serve in the military? Yes ☐   No ☒   Which branch? **does not apply**

Rank **does not apply**   Date of discharge **does not apply**

RECORD OF EMPLOYMENT   (List your last two employers, starting with the more recent one)

Dates	Name and Address of Employer	Salary	Position	Reason for Leaving
1984-85	Valley High School Lansing, Michigan	$4.00 hour	clerk	will graduate
June-August 1984	Municipal License Bureau Lansing, Michigan	$3.50 hour	Typist	to return to school

Check the following office operations with which you have had experience

☒ Adding Machine   ☐ Switchboard   ☐ Shorthand   ☒ Addressograph   Other_____
☐ Proof Machine (IBM) ☒ Dictaphone   ☒ Typewriter   ☒ Bookkeeping Machine   _____

PERSONAL REFERENCES   (Not former employers or relatives)

Name and Occupation   Address   Phone No.

Ms. Martha Scott, Teacher, Valley High School, Lansing, MI 48927 555-7522

Ms. Jane Hamilton, volunteer coordinator, Valley Hospital, Lansing, MI 48926 555-1313

James Milbank, M.D., 14 Hill Street, Lansing, MI 48927   555-4135

I hereby affirm that my answers to the foregoing questions are true and correct and that I have not knowingly withheld any information which would, if disclosed, be considered sufficient cause for dismissal.

In the event of my employment, I promise to comply faithfully with all the rules and regulations presently in effect, or which may hereafter become effective, relating to the conduct and performance of the employees of Valley Hospital.

Applicant's Signature **Ruth Marie Myers**

- Have all items on the form been completed? How might an employer check that the information is correct?
- Has the application been filled in neatly? Have all instructions been followed carefully?

Try Your Skill   Suppose that you are applying to Valley Hospital for a summer job in the business office. You want to work full time and are willing to work weekends. Refer to the application for employment on page 379. On a separate sheet of paper, list the information you would write on the application. Your teacher may give you a copy of this application to complete.

Keep This in Mind

- Answer all items on an application form honestly, correctly, and completely.
- Complete the application by printing neatly, using ink. Work carefully. Read all instructions.

Now Write   Complete an actual employment application. Use a form given to you by your teacher or one from a business in your community. Complete the form, following the guidelines you have learned.

Schoolwork

Writing Letters to Schools

Here's the Idea Before starting a career, you may need to take additional training or schooling. You may want to go to a vocational school or college. You can learn about some schools through a library, where you will find catalogs and scholarship information. You will also find valuable information about our nation's schools, including listings of their addresses, in references like *Barron's Profiles of American Colleges*.

However, the best way to get specific information about a particular school that interests you is to write directly to the school. A letter to a school or college is one type of business letter. Address it to the Admissions Office of the school and follow either of the forms for business letters shown in Section 24, pages 342–344. As in any business letter, you must be specific and to the point. Briefly give the school the information it needs in order to provide you with the information you need.

The school that you may attend will want to know about you. In your letter, include information about the school you are attending, or any you have attended, and the date of your graduation. Include information about your area of interest.

In addition, you want to know as much as possible about a school. Therefore, in your letter also include a request for information about entrance requirements, special progams offered, the size and location of the school, tuition costs, and scholarships. Include a request for a college catalog.

As you may know, the cost of education can be high. Therefore, you may also be interested in information about student loans and scholarships. If so, write also to the Office of Financial Aid. Ask about financial assistance available for the time you plan to enter. The school will send you any information you need.

Check It Out   Read the letter on page 383.

- What specific information does this business letter include? What specific information does it request?

Try Your Skill   Choose one of the following situations and write a letter to the Admissions Office requesting the information mentioned. Add other necessary details. Use correct business letter form.

1. You are a high school graduate interested in becoming a computer technician. Write to the Piedmont Regional Vocational School at 44 Marlboro Street, Peterson, New Hampshire 03233. Ask whether the school offers courses suitable for you and how much these courses cost.

2. You are a high school graduate interested in music. Write to State College, Western Avenue, Plattsville, West Virginia 25426. Inquire about whether the school offers a major in music and what the course requirements are. Ask about entrance requirements, student housing costs, and scholarship availability. Request a copy of the college catalog.

Keep This in Mind

- When you write to vocational schools and colleges, use the correct business letter form.
- Include specific information about yourself.
- Request specific information from the school.

Now Write   Write a letter to a vocational school or college that interests you. Ask about the program in the field of your choice and request a copy of the school catalog. Use correct business letter form.

122 Broadway
Kenvil, New Jersey 07847
March 3, 1986

Admissions Office
Paxton School of Design
Amsterdam, New York 12010

Dear Sir or Madam:

I am a senior and will graduate from Westport Technical
School this coming June. I intend to pursue a career in
fashion designing, and I am most interested in your program. Can I still apply at this time for the fall of 1986,
or will I have a better chance by applying for 1987?

I need to know your entrance requirements to make certain
that I have taken the proper courses. I can plan to attend
summer school if necessary. Also, I have worked part time
for one year for a local dress designing company. I would
like to know if such experience is either required or
helpful for applicants.

Please send me a copy of your catalog so that I may study
the tuition and fees and may investigage your financial
aid programs. Also, I would like descriptions of specific
courses offered in dress designing.

Sincerely,

Brenda Rowlands

Brenda Rowlands

Public Speaking and Discussion

So To Speak

Part 1

Developing Speaking Skills

Here's the Idea Writing is a common method of exchanging ideas. However, speech is even more common. In fact, over half the messages that people give to one another are spoken. Good speech skills are therefore very important. Your success both in school and on the job will partly depend upon how well you speak. The following guidelines will help you to develop the good speaking skills you need. Remember these guidelines whenever you give speeches or take part in conversations, discussions, or interviews.

1. **Appearance.** Wear clothes that suit the occasion. Stand up straight, but do not stand stiffly. Try to look relaxed, confident, and natural.

2. **Eye Contact.** Look directly at your audience. This will help you to hold their attention. If you are giving a speech, do not stare at your notes. If you are speaking to a group, do not look at just one person.

3. **Voice.** Speak in a clear, strong voice. Do not speak too loudly or too softly. Do not speak too quickly or too slowly. Vary your pitch, pace, volume, and tone. Pronounce your words carefully. Do not mumble or speak in a monotone. Make sure that your tone of voice fits what you are saying. Emphasize important points by pausing before them.

4. **Gestures and Facial Expressions.** Use natural gestures and facial expressions. These will help you to appear relaxed and confident. They will also help your audience to understand how you feel. For example, a speaker may emphasize the importance of a point by shaking a fist or by wearing a serious expression.

Check It Out Read the following descriptions.

1. In his auto body repair class, Jim was asked to give a demonstration. He was supposed to show the other students how to use a sander to remove rust. Jim was nervous. During his demonstration, Jim looked only at the car he was working on. He never looked at his audience. He spoke very quickly and loudly. He paused only to check some notes he had made beforehand.

2. Angelita went to an interview for a job in a gift shop. She wore jeans, a T-shirt, and tennis shoes. During the interview, she sat slumped in a chair. She fidgeted with her purse. She also yawned once or twice.

• What mistakes did Jim and Angelita make?

Try Your Skill Suppose that one of your friends is running for student council president. Your friend wants advice about how to look, act, and speak when giving a campaign speech. Make a list of five things you could tell your friend to do. Then, make a list of five things you could tell your friend not to do.

Keep This in Mind

• When speaking in public, dress appropriately. Also, stand up straight and look at your audience.
• Speak in a strong, clear voice. Vary your pitch, pace, volume, and tone. Pause before important points.
• Show your feelings through natural gestures and facial expressions.

Now Write Think of a time when you spoke to a group of people. Write a paragraph describing the situation and your purpose for speaking. Tell how successful your speech was and why. How could you have improved your performance?

Are You Listening?

Developing Listening Skills

Here's the Idea   Listening, like speaking, is a skill that you use all the time. Good listening skills are important in school, on the job, and in your personal life. The following guidelines will help you to become a better listener in all these situations.

1. Give the speaker your full attention.
2. Make the speaker feel comfortable. Show your interest by the expression on your face.
3. Avoid making distracting noises or movements. Do not speak when someone else is speaking.
4. Think about what you are hearing. Listen for main ideas and supporting details. If the situation calls for asking questions or taking notes, do so.
5. Be open-minded. Do not judge the speaker's ideas before you hear how they are supported.

Check It Out   Read the following passage.

> Arlene took a job as a tape librarian in a computer room. On her first day at work, her supervisor showed her around. The supervisor spoke very quickly and covered a great deal of information. Arlene did not understand all that the supervisor said. However, Arlene just kept nodding her head as though she understood everything. Later, Arlene wished that she had at least taken some notes.

   • What did Arlene do wrong in this situation? What problems could result from Arlene's behavior?

Try Your Skill   Choose one of the following pairs of people. Write a paragraph telling why the two people in the pair must listen carefully to one another.

1. a doctor and a patient
2. a teacher and a student
3. an auto mechanic and a customer
4. a basketball player and a coach

Keep This in Mind

- Always try to listen courteously.
- When you listen, pay attention to main ideas and supporting details.

Now Write Think about times when you have been in the audience at a movie, concert, speech, or play. Write a paragraph comparing the best and worst audiences you have seen. Tell what made these audiences good or bad. Be specific.

To Say the Least

Preparing an Informal Talk

Here's the Idea Both in school and out, you will often have to give informal talks. An **informal talk** is a brief speech that presents specific information. The following describe the four major types of informal talks.

1. **Announcements** tell about an event that has happened or that will happen. In an announcement, answer the questions *who? what? when? where?* and *why?* Keep announcements short and simple. Leave out all unnecessary details.

2. **Introductions** present people to an audience. In an introduction, provide information about the person you are introducing. Make this information as interesting as possible. If necessary, gather the information you need by conducting an interview beforehand.

3. **Demonstrations** show how something is done. To prepare a demonstration, break down the activity you wish to demonstrate into separate steps. Perform each step for your audience. Explain each step as you perform it. For example, to demonstrate how to set up and run a movie projector, actually do these things in front of your audience. Explain each step as you do it. If you plan to use props in a demonstration, practice using them before your talk. When giving the talk, keep your props where your audience can see them.

4. **Directions** tell how to do something. Include all necessary or helpful details. Arrange these details in step-by-step order. Do not leave out any steps. Make sure that each step is presented in the right order.

Check It Out   Read the following informal talk.

Attention, seniors! Commencement practice will be held tomorrow afternoon. Please report to the gymnasium at 2:00. Bring your cap and gown.

- What type of informal talk is this?
- Does the talk include all the necessary information? Is it short and simple?

Try Your Skill   Write an informal talk. Look at the suggestions below.

1. A demonstration showing how to make a birdfeeder
2. An introduction presenting a visiting speaker to one of your classes
3. Directions telling how to get from one place in your community to another
4. An announcement telling the results of a competition in your school or community

Keep This in Mind

- Informal talks are short. They are used to present information quickly.
- Four types of informal talks are announcements, introductions, demonstrations, and directions.
- To prepare for an informal talk, gather your information and organize it logically.

Now Write   Choose a second topic from the list given in **Try Your Skill.** Write another informal talk. If your teacher directs you to do so, deliver your talk to your class.

According to Form

Preparing a Formal Speech

Here's the Idea   A **formal speech** presents a subject in detail. Therefore, a formal speech is longer and takes more preparation than an informal talk. Formal speeches are often required in high school and college classes. They are also heard in meetings held by unions, businesses, and political organizations. In your lifetime, you will probably have to present several formal speeches. When you prepare such a speech, follow these steps.

Pre-Writing

1. Choose a topic that interests you. Narrow it to fit the time available.
2. Identify your purpose. The purpose may be to explain, to persuade, or to entertain.
3. Identify your audience. Consider the backgrounds of audience members. Include all the information audience members will need to understand and enjoy your topic.
4. Determine your main idea. Write a sentence stating this idea.
5. Gather supporting information. Use several sources of information. Sources may include personal experience, other people, and reference works.
6. Organize your information. Use spatial order, chronological order, order of importance, or order of familiarity.

Writing

1. In your introduction, state your main idea. Also try to capture the attention of your audience.
2. In the body, develop your main idea. Use facts, details, and examples.
3. Write a conclusion that brings the speech to a satisfying end. If your purpose is to entertain, end on a high note of amusement or interest. If your purpose is to explain or to persuade, end in one of these ways:

a. Repeat the main idea using different words.
b. Draw a lesson or moral from the ideas presented.
c. Make an appeal for action on the part of your listeners.

Revision

1. Check your content. Make sure that all the material in the speech relates to one main idea.
2. Check your organization.
3. Check for errors in grammar and usage.

Check It Out   Read the following description.

Candidate Smith traveled throughout the state before the election. In a farm community, she spoke about price supports for farm products. In a mining community, she spoke about protecting miners from black lung disease.

- What were the topics that candidate Smith talked about?
- Was her purpose in each case to explain, to persuade, or to entertain? Explain your answer.

Try Your Skill   Choose one of the following topics. Narrow the topic for a five-minute speech. Write an introduction. State your main idea and capture the attention of your audience.

1. videos   2. heroism   3. the future

Keep This in Mind

- A formal speech presents a topic in detail.
- When preparing a formal speech, follow the steps of pre-writing, writing, and revision.

Now Write   You have been asked to deliver a speech at your high school commencement ceremony. Choose a topic. Narrow it. Gather information. Organize this information. Write an introduction, body, and conclusion. Revise and proofread this draft.

You're a Natural!

Practicing and Presenting a Speech

Here's the Idea   To practice a speech, first decide how much of the speech you want to memorize. You can memorize the entire speech. You can also memorize just the introduction and conclusion. If you choose the second approach, use notes or an outline for the body of the speech. Practice with your notes and outline. During the speech, however, avoid looking at your notes or outline too often.

The following method can be used when memorizing all or part of a speech:

1. Read one sentence.
2. Recite the sentence several times without looking at it.
3. Read the next sentence.
4. Recite both sentences without looking.
5. Go through all the material in this manner.

Practice by saying your speech aloud several times. If you can, perform the speech in front of a mirror. This will allow you to check your posture, facial expressions, and gestures. Also try to make a tape recording of the speech. By listening to a recording, you can check your pace, pitch, tone. You can also listen for variety in each of these things. Ask friends or relatives to listen to your speech. They may be able to make suggestions.

When you deliver your speech, keep in mind the guidelines for speaking given in Part 1, **So To Speak.** Use a strong, clear voice. Be relaxed and confident. Look at your audience. Use natural gestures and expressions to communicate your feelings.

Check It Out   Read the following notes made by a student while practicing a speech.

began too slowly—pick up pace

pause before last sentence in intro. to emphasize main idea of speech

voice sounds bored throughout—use more emotion

keep shoulders back (don't slouch)

"theater" pronounced "thē-*uh*-ter," not "thē-*ay*-ter."

voice should get gradually louder and faster during story as action described becomes more intense

- Which of these notes could have been made based on hearing a tape?
- Which could have been made based upon performing in front of a mirror?

Try Your Skill   Choose one of the informal talks that you wrote for Part 3, **To Say the Least.** Practice giving this talk. As you practice, list any problems that you notice in your delivery.

Keep This in Mind

- You may memorize your entire talk. You may also memorize the introduction and conclusion and use notes or an outline for the body.
- Practice your talk until it seems natural. Use a tape recorder and a mirror to identify problems.
- Ask your friends and relatives to listen to your talk.
- When you deliver your talk, follow the guidelines given in Part 1, **So To Speak.**

Now Speak   Practice the commencement speech that you wrote for Part 4, **According to Form.** Practice the speech several times, both by yourself and in front of others. Make a list of any improvements that you make as you practice.

Group Work

Organizing a Group Discussion

Here's the Idea   As a student you have participated in many group discussions. You therefore know that discussions can be very useful. In a discussion, people can explore ideas or exchange information. They can also plan actions or solve problems. However, if a discussion is not well organized, its usefulness can be lost. This is why you should learn how to organize discussions effectively.

All group discussions should have a leader, or **chairperson.** The chairperson guides the discussion and keeps order. In addition to the chairperson, a group may have a secretary. The **secretary** takes notes on what is said during the discussion. The other members of a discussion group act as participants. The **participants** are the people who discuss the topic under the guidance of the chairperson.

A discussion should follow an orderly plan. First, the chairperson should state the topic and purpose. Then, the participants should define any key terms that will be used in the discussion. By defining these terms, the participants can make sure that they are talking about the same things. The participants may also wish to narrow their discussion topic to save time. Once the topic is narrowed and defined, the discussion itself begins. Members of the group should ask to be recognized by the chairperson before speaking.

When the discussion is finished, the chairperson or the secretary should summarize what the participants have said. This summary should include all the important points that were made. It should also include any agreements or decisions made by the members of the group.

Check It Out   Read the following description of a discussion.

The student council met after school to discuss the senior prom. The president of the council was absent. Therefore, no one guided the discussion. A great deal of time was spent talking about school parking regulations and pass/fail classes. At the end of an hour, the bell rang. Everyone left as one council member was making a suggestion.

- What went wrong in this discussion?
- How could the discussion have been improved?

Try Your Skill   Suppose that your class is going to hold a discussion on "Careers in the Future." Write two possible purposes, or reasons, for holding such a discussion. Then, find the key terms in the discussion topic. Write definitions for these key terms.

Keep This in Mind

- A member of a discussion group may act as a chairperson, a secretary, or a participant.
- Discussions should include these steps: introduction of topic, definition of key terms, discussion, and summary.

Now Write   People hold discussions all the time in their personal lives. These discussions are usually less organized than a discussion for a class or meeting. However, informal discussions can be very valuable.

Recall a useful discussion that you have had with your friends. Write a paragraph describing it. What was the discussion topic? Did anyone direct the discussion in any way? What conclusions, agreements, or decisions were reached?

Let's Talk

Participating in a Discussion

Here's the Idea   Two important roles in a discussion are those of the chairperson and the participants. Each of these roles involves its own special duties. These duties must be carried out well for the discussion to be a success.

Chairperson
1. Prepare for the discussion. Gather facts about the topic.
2. Introduce the topic. Explain the purpose of the discussion.
3. Plan carefully to allow time for an introduction, a discussion, and a summary.
4. Allow members of the group to speak only after they have been recognized. Allow only one person to speak at a time.
5. Encourage everyone to participate in the discussion.
6. Keep the discussion on the topic.
7. Ask interesting questions to make the ideas clearer.
8. Take notes. Be ready to summarize the discussion.

Participants
1. Do not speak until you have been recognized.
2. Take part in the discussion.
3. Use facts to support your opinions.
4. Listen courteously. (See Part 2, **Are You Listening?**)
5. Be courteous to other group members. When disagreeing, do so politely. Use expressions such as "From one point of view, you're absolutely right. However . . ."
6. Try to see things the way other group members do. Be open-minded. If you do not understand another member's point, ask questions.

Check It Out   Read the following selection from a discussion.

• Is the chairperson doing his or her job? Why or why not?

Chairperson:	Today we are going to discuss the plans for this year's senior trip. This trip is a tradition at . . .
Lenny:	(Interrupting) Wait a minute. I don't think there's anything to discuss. Let's just pick some places and have the seniors vote on . . .
Chairperson:	Just a moment, Len. Please wait until I have recognized you. Also, please let me introduce today's topic first. This trip is a tradition at Central High School. However, this year there is very little money with which to finance it.
Amy:	(Interrupting) Speaking of money, I think the refreshments sold at the games cost way too much. We should complain to the principal.

Try Your Skill Imagine that you are going to lead a discussion on a famous person from American history. Choose your subject. Write a list of five questions that you could ask.

Keep This in Mind

- A chairperson should introduce the topic and purpose, keep order, and encourage participation. The chairperson should also ask questions and keep the discussion from wandering from the topic.
- A participant should discuss the topic, listen to other group members, and be polite.

Now Speak If your teacher directs you to do so, join a small discussion group. Choose one of the following topics.

Should high schools put more emphasis on job skills?
What are the responsibilities of a pet owner?

Then, elect a chairperson and a secretary. Hold a discussion. Have the secretary report your group's decisions or conclusions to the rest of the class.

Handbook

A detailed Table of Contents for the Handbook appears in the front of this book.

The Sentence and Its Parts

Sentences are structures. They are made up of various parts. These parts can be put together to create good, clear sentences. The arrangement of the parts of a sentence is important, just as the choice of words is.

In this section you will study the different parts of sentences. You will learn how to put these parts together to build clear, effective sentences.

Part 1 The Sentence

In conversation, you might use only parts of sentences. For example, you sometimes reply to questions with a word or two.

    See you later.   Not Again!   Right.

However, in writing, complete sentences are important. With them, your ideas are clear and understandable.

A sentence is a group of words that expresses a complete thought. A sentence makes sense because it is a whole idea, not just part of one.

Look at these sentences:

    Diana opened a checking account.
    Air controllers use radar.
    During the crisis, people panicked.

If part of an idea is missing from a sentence, a fragment results. A **sentence fragment** is a group of words that does not express a complete thought. These are sentence fragments:

    Opened a checking account. (Who opened an account?)
    Air controllers. (What about air controllers?)
    During the crisis. (What happened?)

Exercise A For each group of words that is a sentence, write *S* on your paper. For each sentence fragment, write *F*.

1. Craig lounged in front of the TV.
2. Palm trees line the avenue.
3. A seat on the bus.
4. Accepts only exact fare.
5. Artists painted a mural on the walls.
6. Six flights of stairs.
7. On the dashboard of the Toyota.
8. Has green and orange stripes.
9. Randy works at a beauty salon.
10. An axle and the two rear tires.

Exercise B Follow the directions for Exercise A.

1. Snowplows cleared the major highways.
2. Low-interest loans from the bank.
3. At the nearest grocery store.
4. This practice is not fair to the consumer.
5. This store advertised for clerks.
6. Keith returned Carlotta's letter.
7. Finally got a driver's license.
8. Four lanes of traffic.
9. Checked the oil and the water.
10. This practice is not fair to the consumer.

Part 2 The Subject and the Predicate

All sentences have two basic parts: the subject and the predicate. The **subject** tells *who* or *what* the sentence is about. The predicate tells something about the subject.

Subject (Who or What)	Predicate (What is said about the subject)
The defendant	pleaded with the judge.
The race-car drivers	awaited their signals.
A jazz band	played outside.

Each sentence above expresses a complete thought.

Remember the parts of a sentence in this way. Think of the sentence as telling who did something or what happened. The subject tells *who or what*. The predicate tells *did* or *happened*.

Who or What	Did or Happened
A group of reporters	interviewed the mayor.
The huge trailer	barely cleared the bridge.
That hot-air balloon	dropped sharply.

The subject of the sentence tells *who* or *what* did something, or what the sentence is about.

The predicate of the sentence tells what is done or what happens.

Exercise A Head two columns *Subject* and *Predicate.* Write the words from each sentence in the correct columns.

1. All the scenery was made by the cast.
2. Hundreds of people gathered in the town square.
3. Evan quickly gulped down the soup and sandwiches.
4. The Garcia family lives down the hall.
5. The west side street fair attracted large crowds.
6. Jerry's brother works the night shift at the factory.
7. Many athletic records will be broken at Los Angeles.
8. This restaurant's service is very fast.
9. Police cars sped to the scene of the break-in.
10. Many employees receive a bonus each December.

Exercise B Follow the directions for Exercise A.

1. The value of gold rose sharply last week.
2. All the clerks added up their receipts for the day.
3. That dingy old hotel was once a glamorous resort.
4. Cam Stevens caught a seventy-yard pass.
5. Christy waited nervously by the phone.
6. The primary elections show voters' preferences.
7. The Sunday newspaper weighs ten pounds.
8. A letter without postage is returned to the sender.
9. Trisha was a bridesmaid in her sister's wedding.
10. A misty waterfall tumbled down the mountainside.

Part 3 The Verb and the Simple Subject

There are a few words in every sentence that are more important than the rest. These essential words form the basic framework of the sentence. Look at these examples.

Subject	Predicate
The **defendant**	**pleaded** with the jury.
The race-car **drivers**	**awaited** their signal.
A jazzy **band**	**played** outside.

All the words in the subject part of the sentence are called the **complete subject.** Within the complete subject is a key word, the **simple subject.** In the last example above, *a small band* is the complete subject. *Band* is the simple subject.

The **complete predicate** is all the words that tell what is done by, or what happens to, the subject. The key word within the complete predicate is the **simple predicate** or **verb.**

In the sentence about the band, the complete predicate is *played outside.* The key word is *played.*

The key word in the subject of a sentence is called the simple subject. We will refer to it as the *subject.*

The key word in the predicate is the simple predicate. The simple predicate is the **verb.** Hereafter, we will refer to the simple predicate as the *verb.*

Finding the Verb and the Subject

The verb and the subject are the essential words in any sentence. Other words only tell more about these key words. Locate these key words in any sentence by first finding the verb. It shows action or a state of being. Then ask *who* or *what* before the verb. That answer will give you the subject of the verb.

Ralph Nader responded in a TV editorial.
   Verb: responded
   Who responded? Ralph Nader
   The subject is *Ralph Nader.*

The automobile in the museum display ran on steam.
   Verb: ran
   What ran? automobile
   The subject is *automobile.*

Diagraming Subjects and Verbs

Any sentence can be diagramed to show its parts. A sentence diagram shows how the parts fit together.

A sentence diagram shows the importance of the subject and the verb. These key parts are placed on a horizontal main line. They are separated by a vertical line that crosses the main line. The subject appears before the verb. Later you will learn how every other word in the sentence has its own place in the diagram, too.

Within the diagram, only words capitalized in the sentence are capitalized. No punctuation is used.

These two diagrams show subjects and verbs.

Amy stubbornly insisted.

Amy	insisted

The operator helped us.

operator	helped

Exercise A Label two columns *Verb* and *Subject.* Number your paper from 1 to 10. For each sentence, write the verb and its subject.

1. Unfortunately, Tom lost his temper.
2. This year a biologist won the Nobel Prize.
3. That mitt in the closet is Danielle's.
4. Many stations program soft-rock music.
5. Two fire trucks pulled out of the station.
6. This garage holds eight hundred cars.
7. Jeff routinely compares prices at different stores.
8. During the avalanche, huge rocks rolled downhill.

9. The shortstop relayed the ball for a double play.
10. The corner bookstore sells only paperbacks.

Exercise B Follow the directions for Exercise A.

1. Luckily, Maureen saved her ticket stub.
2. Josh rarely sleeps late on Saturdays.
3. Finally, the paramedics arrived.
4. A team of doctors operated for four hours.
5. Many small cars get good gas mileage.
6. In speeches today, the candidates discussed the issues.
7. Proudly, Jenny displayed her trophy.
8. Just before dawn, the blizzard struck.
9. Twenty people came to Rick's party.
10. Kyle fiercely defended the goal.

Part 4   The Parts of a Verb

While many verbs consist of one word, others consist of several words. A verb is often composed of a **main verb** and one or more **helping verbs.**

Helping Verbs + Main Verb = Verb

has	sent	has sent
will	leave	will leave
must	see	must see
could have	heard	could have heard

In naming the verb in any sentence, you must name all the words that make up the verb.

The following words are frequently used as helping verbs.

am	are	have	will	may
is	be	do	would	might
was	has	does	can	shall
were	had	did	could	should

Separated Parts of a Verb

In some sentences, you will find words inserted between the parts of the verb. These words are not part of the verb. Look at the following sentences. The parts of the verb are in bold print.

> Darrel **has** never **seen** a Mel Brooks movie.
> The warehouse **was** recently **converted** into stores.
> That amendment **has** not **been passed.**

Some verbs are joined with other words to make contractions. To name a verb that appears in a contraction, pick out only the verb. The word *not* and its contraction *n't* are never verb parts.

> Bob **could**n't **swallow** the oyster. (*Could swallow* is the verb.)
> The singer **did**n't **know** the lyrics. (*Did know* is the verb.)

Exercise A   List the verbs in the following sentences.

1. Production of electric cars may soon begin.
2. Those cars are illegally parked.
3. Susan couldn't find a pay phone.
4. You shouldn't have brought gifts.
5. Some apes are being taught sign language.
6. Most people would never camp during the winter.
7. Old silent movies are sometimes shown on TV.
8. The plastic lenses in your glasses won't break easily.
9. Three players were recently elected to the Baseball Hall of Fame.
10. The author will probably appear on talk shows.

Exercise B   Follow the directions for Exercise A.

1. Income tax forms must be mailed by April 15.
2. The police can't explain the strange footprints.
3. The basketball tournament will surely be cancelled.
4. Because of an injury, Bailey couldn't play.
5. Alice would surely have noticed any rust on the car.

6. An earthquake had suddenly struck San Francisco.
7. Your backpack will never hold all that food.
8. Jeremy didn't have enough money for tolls.
9. Carrie has recently enlisted in the navy.
10. Linda has already seen this double feature.

Part 5 Sentences in Unusual Order

In most sentences, the subject comes before the verb. Sometimes, though, part or all of the verb comes before the subject of a sentence.

To find the subject of a sentence, first find the verb. Then ask *who* or *what* before it. That answer will be the subject.

Sentences Beginning with *There*

The verb often comes before the subject in sentences beginning with *there.*

There may be used in two different ways. It may be used to explain the verb and tell where something is.

> There are your photos. (*Photos* is the subject; *are* is the verb. *There* tells where your photos are.)
>
> There is the entrance. (*Entrance* is the subject; *is* is the verb. *There* tells where the entrance is.)

Sometimes *there* is used simply as an introductory word to help get the sentence started.

> There is no cure for a cold. (*Cure* is the subject; *is* is the verb.)
>
> There are four candidates. (*Candidates* is the subject; *are* is the verb.)

To diagram a sentence starting with *there,* you must know if *there* tells *where* or is an introductory word. If *there* tells *where,* it belongs on a slanted line below the verb. If *there* is an introductory word, it is placed above the subject on a parallel line.

There is the control panel.

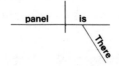

There has been a big response.

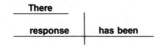

Exercise A   Write the subject and the verb in each sentence. Tell whether *there* is used to tell *where* or is an introductory word.

1. There is a chance of rain tomorrow.
2. There is the entrance for employees.
3. There were only five of us.
4. There went your last chance.
5. There are several kinds of billiards.
6. There is the cap for the radiator.
7. There is the editorial page.
8. There goes the last runner.
9. There is the owner's manual.
10. There are too many ruts in this road.

Exercise B   Follow the directions for Exercise A.

1. There will be a discount on certain items.
2. There goes a Yamaha cycle.
3. There must be a restaurant in this town.
4. There are programmers for each station.
5. There are 100 centimeters in a meter.
6. There goes my whole paycheck!
7. There is the last tangerine.

8. There is the boundary line.
9. There will be a rematch.
10. There are many types of health foods.

Other Sentences with Unusual Word Order

Besides sentences beginning with *there*, there are other kinds of sentences with unusual word order. The following examples show some of them.

1. Sentences beginning with *here*

Here come the paramedics. (*Paramedics* is the subject. *Come* is the verb.)

Here is the leak in the tire. (*Leak* is the subject. *Is* is the verb.)

The word *here*, unlike *there*, always tells *where* about the verb.

2. Questions

Do you use the metric system? (*You* is the subject; *do use* is the verb.)

Can Wendy keep her deadline? (*Wendy* is the subject; *can keep* is the verb.)

3. Sentences starting with phrases or other descriptions

Inside the drawer were our candles. (*Candles* is the subject; *were* is the verb.)

Steadily came the signal. (*Signal* is the subject; *came* is the verb.)

To find the subject in a sentence with unusual word order, first find the verb. Then ask *who* or *what*.

Here is a shortcut.
Verb: is
Who or what is? shortcut
Subject: shortcut

To diagram a sentence with unusual word order, use the usual format. The verb and the subject still belong on the horizontal main line with the subject written before the verb.

From the bleachers came hisses.

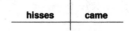

| hisses | came |

Sentences Giving Commands

Most sentences that give commands do not state the subject. Because commands are always given to the person spoken to, the subject is *you.* Although *you* is not stated, we say that it is *understood.*

Check the sports page. (*You* is the subject of *check.*)
Play your favorite albums. (*You* is the subject of *play.*)

The sentence diagram for a command shows the subject *you* in parentheses.

Watch for landmarks.

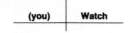

| (you) | Watch |

When you diagram, remember to keep capitalization as it appears in the original sentence.

Exercise A Label two columns *Subject* and *Verb*. Number your paper from 1 to 10. Write the subject and verb for each sentence.

1. Across the lake whisked the sailboat.
2. Can you swim?
3. Out of the debate came a proposal.
4. Have you recorded the concert?
5. Does the bus stop here?
6. Count your change.
7. Here is the teller's window.

8. Guess again.
9. Park closer to the curb.
10. Here is the briefcase.

Exercise B Follow the directions for Exercise A.

1. Over the dunes bounced a jeep.
2. Here is the fan belt.
3. Send a telegram.
4. Does your brother work at the hospital?
5. Tell me your idea.
6. Here is a calendar for 1956.
7. Inside the van was a studio.
8. Did Gail laugh into the microphone?
9. Was the film shown in slow motion?
10. Ask for the manager.

Part 6   The Objects of Verbs

In many sentences, the verb does not need another word to complete its meaning. The action the verb describes is complete.

> Paul Williams *performed.*   These jeans *have shrunk.*
> Chris *was pitching.*   The jet *will land.*

However, other verbs do not express complete meanings by themselves. Additional words must complete their meaning in the sentence.

> A trailer carried _____. (Carried what?)
> The mayor signed _____. (Signed what?)

The Direct Object

> A trailer carried two *horses.*
> The mayor signed the *bill.*

As shown above, one kind of word that completes the action of a verb is called the **direct object.** The direct object receives the action of a verb. In the sentences above, *horses* receives the action of *carried. Bill* receives the action of *signed.*

At times, the direct object may tell the *result* of an action.

> Marco makes great *tacos.*
> Nicole finished her *report.*

To find the direct object, first find the subject and verb. Then ask *whom* or *what* after the verb.

> The agency hired Barbara.
> *Verb:* hired
> *Hired whom?* Barbara
> *Direct object:* Barbara

> This machine makes snow.
> *Verb:* makes
> *Makes what?* snow
> *Direct object:* snow

When a verb has a direct object, it is called a **transitive verb.** When a verb does not have a direct object, it is called an **intransitive verb.** Look at how these verbs differ.

> The raft *disappeared.* (*Disappeared* is intransitive. It has no direct object.)

> This center *recycles* newspapers. (*Recycles* is transitive. It has a direct object, *newspapers.*)

The same verb may be transitive in one sentence and intransitive in another.

> Intransitive: Rick cooked.
> Transitive: Rick cooked spaghetti.

Transitive or Intransitive?

Are the verbs in the following sentences transitive or intransitive?

Leona *watched* closely.
Leona *watched* from the back row.
Leona *watched* the play-offs.

In the first two examples, the verb *watched* has no direct object. *Watched* is intransitive in those sentences. In the third sentence, however, if you ask *whom* or *what* after the verb, you find that *play-offs* is the direct object. *Watched* is a transitive verb in that sentence.

Leona watched the play-offs.
   Verb: watched
   Watched what? play-offs
   Direct object: play-offs

Exercise A   Write the direct object of each verb.

1. The ballplayers have signed their contracts.
2. Derek dealt the cards.
3. Ellen has found a part-time job.
4. Three prisoners plotted their escape.
5. Has Congress considered the new bill?
6. Quickly, the lawyers selected a jury.
7. Don't the Steelers have a good record?
8. My friends attended a rally.
9. We need more wood for the fire.
10. Lynn will exchange her sweater.

Exercise B   Decide whether the verb in each sentence is *Transitive* or *Intransitive.*

1. The bank increased its interest rate.
2. Ben's dad opened a new restaurant here.
3. Gas prices have risen recently.
4. Dad's ideas have certainly changed.
5. Top officials will meet tomorrow.
6. Shawn left the package in the hall.

7. Cindy has changed the tire.
8. Last weekend the new arcade opened.
9. Sandy left early.
10. You will meet lobbyists outside.

The Indirect Object

Along with direct objects, some sentences also have indirect objects of the verb. Sometimes indirect objects tell *to whom* or *to what* about the verb. At other times they tell *for whom* or *for what* about a verb.

> The bank gave **Aaron** a *loan*. (gave *to* Aaron)
> David left the **waiter** a *tip*. (left *for* the waiter)
> The director gave the television **crew** a *break*. (gave *to* the crew)

The words in bold type in the sentences above are the indirect objects. The words in italics are the direct objects.

Only sentences with direct objects can have indirect objects. Indirect objects appear between the verb and direct object. The words *to* and *for* are not used with an indirect object.

> Sarah handed her *sister* the phone. (*Sister* is the indirect object of *handed*.)
>
> Sarah handed the phone to her *sister*. (*Sister* is not an indirect object.)

To diagram a direct object, place it on the main line after the verb. The vertical line between the verb and object does not go below the main line.

Emily made a sweater.

| Emily | made | sweater |

An indirect object belongs on a horizontal line attached below the verb.

Emily made her friend a sweater.

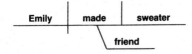

Exercise A Label three columns *Verb, Indirect Object,* and *Direct Object.* For each sentence below, write those parts. Not all sentences will have all three parts.

Example: The clerk gave Kelly her receipt.

Verb	Indirect Object	Direct Object
gave	Kelly	receipt

1. The candidate showed the audience some charts.
2. Adam gave Marla a striped shirt.
3. Carlos lifts weights every day.
4. The salesperson showed Tim a stereo.
5. Melissa Manchester gave Daniel her autograph.
6. The prisoner was serving a light sentence.
7. The director gave Deena a part in the film.
8. Coupons can save consumers money.
9. Our public TV station has no commercials.
10. Mr. Gage gave the employees their assignments.

Exercise B Follow the directions for Exercise A.

1. Kate ate lunch in the park.
2. Both parties held conventions in Miami.
3. Ms. Rogers left her secretary a message.
4. Johnson fumbled the ball.
5. Police must read suspects their rights.
6. Bill's car needs new brakes.
7. Rachel gave the machine a kick.
8. Jon tossed Ricardo the ball.
9. Todd always wears dark clothes.
10. The officer handed Jamie a ticket.

Part 7 Linking Verbs with Predicate Words

Instead of expressing action, some verbs tell of a state of being. Such verbs link the subject of a sentence with a word or group of words in the predicate. Since they link the subject with some other word or words, they are often called **linking verbs.**

Bo *is* the lead-off hitter. The road *must be* slick.
The meeting *was* secret. The winners *were* the Knicks.

The most frequently used linking verb is *to be. To be* can have many forms. The list below will help you to become familiar with them.

be	been	is	was
being	am	are	were

Helping verbs are sometimes used with the verbs *be, being,* and *been.* Here are examples:

might be	are being	has been
can be	were being	should have been
will be	is being	may have been

The words linked to the subject by linking verbs like *to be* are called **predicate words.** The three kinds of predicate words are **predicate nouns, predicate pronouns,** and **predicate adjectives.** They always tell something about the subject.

The main dish is *veal.* (predicate noun)

This is *she.* (predicate pronoun)

Laws are *necessary.* (predicate adjective)

The linking verbs *is* and *are* join the subjects and predicate words in the above sentences.

Here are some other common linking verbs:

appear	seem	sound	grow
feel	look	taste	become

The above linking verbs, like *be*, have various forms. (*sounded, became, seems*) They can be used with helping verbs, as in *had tasted, would seem,* and *might have looked.*

John *looks* pale.

The judge *seemed* fair.

This record *has become* a hit.

For a sentence diagram, place a predicate word after the verb on the main line. A slanted line above the main line separates the verb from the predicate word. That line, like the predicate word, points back toward the subject.

Art Buchwald is a columnist.

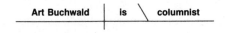

| Art Buchwald | is \ columnist |

These pretzels seem stale.

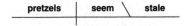

| pretzels | seem \ stale |

Direct Object or Predicate Word?

Two kinds of words can complete verbs. A verb may have a direct object, or it may have a predicate word. How can you tell the difference between a predicate word and a direct object?

The verb is the clue. Determine if the verb is an action verb. If so, the word following it that tells *whom* or *what* is a direct object.

> A barge blocked the *river.* (*Blocked* is an action verb. *River* is its direct object.)
> This machine shreds *paper.* (*Shreds* is an action verb. *Paper* is its direct object.)

In contrast, the verb may be a linking verb. If so, the word following it that tells about the subject is a predicate word.

Megan is an identical *twin*. (*Is* is a linking verb. *Twin* is a predicate word.)

Those wax figures look *real*. (*Look* is a linking verb. *Real* is a predicate word.)

Look at the following sentences.

Nathan is a blood *donor*.
Nathan needs a blood *donor*.

The first sentence has a linking verb, *is*. The word *donor* follows the linking verb and tells about the subject. It is a predicate word. The second sentence has an action verb, *needs*. In this sentence, *donor* tells *whom* about the action verb. It is a direct object.

Exercise A Label three columns *Subject, Linking Verb,* and *Predicate Word*. Find these parts in the sentences below, and place them in the proper columns.

1. Jesse Owens was an Olympic athlete.
2. The eye chart looks blurry.
3. Susan seems uncomfortable.
4. Christina's native language is Swedish.
5. The governor has become seriously ill.
6. Kurt Vonnegut is the author.
7. Wendy is good at ice hockey.
8. Some diets have become fads.
9. Moon boots look very warm.
10. Ruth Streeter was the first female major in the Marines.

Exercise B Make four columns on your paper. Head the columns *Subject, Verb, Direct Object,* and *Predicate Word*. Find these parts in the sentences below, and place them in the correct columns.

1. Brad won a prize in the lottery.
2. Nuclear power has become a controversial issue.
3. Inflation has become a problem for everyone.

4. Sunspots are dark regions on the sun.
5. With a long vacation ahead of him, Tim grew lazy.
6. Pam devoured the cheese sandwich.
7. The ice cream became a liquid.
8. The Illini cut the Buckeyes' lead.
9. Rivera hit a grounder to left field.
10. Donna rents a small apartment downtown.

Part 8   Compound Sentence Parts

Sentence parts can be *compound,* which means "having two or more parts."

All of the sentence parts described so far in this section can be compound—subjects, verbs, direct objects, indirect objects, and predicate words.

A conjunction (*and, or, but*) joins the two parts in a compound form. In a compound form of three or more parts, the conjunction usually comes between the last two parts.

Diagraming Compound Subjects

To diagram compound subjects, split the subject line. The conjunction belongs on a dotted line connecting the subjects.

Clowns, mimes, and dancers performed at the street fair.

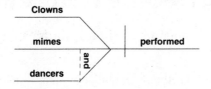

Diagraming Compound Verbs

To diagram compound verbs, split the verb line in the same way that you split the subject line.

The leaders met and signed the treaty.

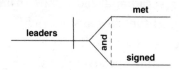

Diagraming Compound Objects

To diagram compound direct objects or indirect objects, split the object line.

> The Mets have six wins and four losses. (compound direct object)

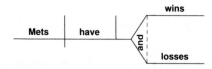

> Ed told Amy and Debbie a joke. (compound indirect object)

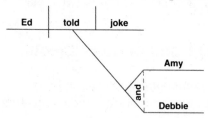

Diagraming Compound Predicate Words

To diagram compound predicate words, split the predicate word line.

> The main ingredients in chili are meat, tomatoes, and beans.

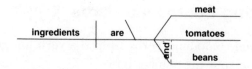

Exercise A As your teacher directs, show the compound parts in the following sentences. Tell whether they are compound subjects, verbs, objects, or predicate words.

1. Dan's Great Dane looks huge but friendly.
2. The fire sputtered and finally died out.
3. Paco added mushrooms and cheese to the salad.
4. Both TV and radio broadcast the President's speech.
5. Traditional holiday foods are ham, duck, and turkey.
6. Ramon and Laura got the best work schedules.
7. The car skidded and then slid around.
8. Was the stoplight red or yellow?
9. Randy served tacos, tostadas,and enchiladas.
10. The team practiced free throws and layups.

Exercise B: Writing For each of the following sentences, make the part noted in parentheses compound. Write the new sentences.

1. The pitcher warmed up. (*subject*)
2. Does the car have radial tires? (*direct object*)
3. Kim can fix the projector. (*direct object*)
4. Becky gave her collie a bath. (*indirect object*)
5. The parachutist floated to earth. (*verb*)
6. The Cardinals are in the National League. (*subject*)
7. That steep driveway looks slippery. (*predicate word*)
8. Carefully, we washed the fragile glasses. (*verb*)

Part 9 The Four Kinds of Sentences

You use different kinds of sentences for different reasons. You may want to state something, or you may want to ask a question. Sometimes you may want to give a command. At other times, you may want to express strong feeling. For each of these times, you use a different kind of sentence.

A **declarative sentence** is used to make a statement. It ends with a period (.).

> Wings gave a benefit performance.
> Critics praised that director.

An **interrogative sentence** asks a question. It ends with a question mark (?).

> Do you like classical music?   Is the snake loose?

An **imperative sentence** gives a command. It usually ends with a period.

> Enjoy yourselves.   Change the channel, please.

An **exclamatory sentence** shows strong emotion. It ends with an exclamation point (!).

> What an upset that was!   It's so dark in here!

Exercise A   For each of these sentences, write *Declarative, Interrogative, Imperative,* or *Exclamatory* on your paper to show what kind each is. Add the proper punctuation mark.

1. Soon the cameras were pointing at me
2. Last year the company went bankrupt
3. Carrie waded through flooded streets
4. Do you have an ID card
5. Compare these two brands
6. What a dull match that was
7. Are the car windows rolled up
8. Who scored the field goal
9. Don't forget your hat and gloves
10. How thoughtful you are

Exercise B   Follow the directions for Exercise A.

1. Which jockey is riding Silver Streak
2. I'm so scared

3. How did you make those braids
4. Keep your comments to yourself
5. Are you influenced by ads
6. Last night Pete called a hotline
7. Hold the line, please
8. At the end of the film, everyone was crying
9. What terrific pastry Lutz's Bakery has
10. We must reserve seats in advance

Part 10   Sentence Patterns

The various sentence parts can be shaped into sentences in an endless number of ways. Most sentences, however, follow certain basic **sentence patterns.** The five patterns that follow are the most common ones.

Pattern One

Pattern One is the most basic type of sentence. It has a subject and a verb. The subject is usually a noun or pronoun. In this chart, N stands for the noun (or pronoun) in the complete subject. V stands for the verb in the complete predicate.

N	V
The amendment	passed.
The union	is striking.

Pattern Two

Pattern Two sentences have a noun (or pronoun) following the verb. This noun is a direct object.

N	V	N
The referee	made	a bad call.
Mariya	has	an unusual name.

Pattern Three

In this pattern, two nouns follow the verb. The first noun (or pronoun) is an *indirect object*. The second is a *direct object*.

N	V	N	N
The woman	handed	me	my ticket.
Jennifer	showed	the guard	her badge.
The singer	gave	the old song	a new twist.

Pattern Four

In a Pattern Four sentence, the verb is a *linking verb* (LV). Following the linking verb is a *predicate noun* (or pronoun).

N	LV	N
My brother	became	plant supervisor.
Gonzalez	is	an outfielder.
Those shoes	are	hers.

Pattern Five

A linking verb is followed by a *predicate adjective* (Adj) in this pattern.

N	LV	Adj
The last lap	will seem	easy.
That shirt	is	too expensive.
Foxboro Stadium	must be	full.

Exercise A Tell which sentence pattern is used in each sentence.

1. The coach showed films of the last game.
2. The American family has changed.
3. Those stories are rumors.
4. The octane level is too low.
5. This gas tank holds twenty gallons.

6. The bookcase toppled over.
7. Leslie is wearing her roommate's jacket.
8. Mark gave the Datsun a tune-up.
9. The scouts are watching Darnell.
10. The pecan pie is delicious.

Exercise B   Follow the directions for Exercise A.

1. The musical was a flop.
2. Mr. Ridolfi gave me a job application.
3. Tony seems restless.
4. Jamie saw a bullfight in Mexico.
5. The matador was a young boy.
6. The horses are rounding the final bend.
7. Tomahawk is lagging behind.
8. Gena taught the understudy her lines.
9. That explosion sounds close.
10. All the trains are running late.

Exercise C: Writing   Write original sentences using the following sentence patterns.

1. Four sentences in the N V pattern
2. Four sentences in the N V N pattern
3. Two sentences in the N V N N pattern
4. Two sentences in the N LV N pattern
5. Two sentences in the N LV Adj pattern

ADDITIONAL EXERCISES

The Sentence and Its Parts

A. Sentences and Sentence Fragments Number your paper from 1 to 10. For each group of words that is a sentence, write *S*. For each sentence fragment, write *F*. In class, be ready to add words to change the fragments into sentences.

1. Stuck the note under the windshield wiper
2. Johnny set up the volleyball net
3. The sky looks closer in winter
4. The hardware store down the street
5. Felt a bit dizzy
6. Cleaned the cleats on her shoes
7. Ruth sat on the bottom step
8. Moss grew on the stones in the creek
9. Eugene has no middle name
10. Everybody dreams

B. Subjects and Predicates Number your paper from 1 to 10. Label two columns *Subject* and *Predicate*. Write the proper words in each column.

1. One of the skaters has injured his knee.
2. The officer completed her inspection.
3. Television sets conduct lightning.
4. Barbi's tooth needs a cap.
5. We went to the concert in the park.
6. Sabrina bought a picture frame for her blue ribbon.
7. Drivers should stop for pedestrians using white canes.
8. Joaquin watched the lunar eclipse last night.
9. The mail carrier finished her route early.
10. The collision damaged the van's muffler.

C. Verbs and Simple Subjects
Number your paper from 1 to 10. Write the simple subject and the verb in each sentence.

1. Birds fly in formation for a good reason.
2. At midnight the clock chimed.
3. Holly carried the flag in the parade.
4. The neighbors always have a barbecue on Labor Day.
5. Mr. Chesley is in the hospital again.
6. Finally she remembered us.
7. Noisy crowds scare Pinky.
8. Josie rented a canoe for the day.
9. The clerk at the front counter weighs the fruit and vegetables.
10. A long yellow convertible blocked the exit.

D. Main Verbs and Helping Verbs
Write the helping verb and main verb for each sentence. Label them *HV* (helping verb) and *MV* (main verb).

1. Underground homes can save energy.
2. The heavy rain had flattened the sunflowers.
3. Ed was looking through the catalog again.
4. I could use some help.
5. The dog would have barked at a stranger.
6. You might have some trouble with the transmission.
7. The library will be closing in five minutes.
8. Jeannie is listening to the game on the radio.
9. Somebody should have warned us.
10. The shoe repair shop can put a new heel on the boot.

E. Separated Parts of a Verb
Write the verb and its simple subject from each sentence. Underline the subject once and the verb twice.

1. The new security system hasn't been installed yet.
2. The fish were not biting.

3. You have not really been listening to me.
4. Dennis had finally found the keys.
5. The field will probably be too muddy for the game.
6. I would certainly have told you.
7. Connie had accurately measured the plywood.
8. The wind had almost blown the car off the road.
9. Eric was carefully taking notes.
10. Bonita had never before noticed the sign.

F. Verbs and Subjects in Unusual Order Number your paper from 1 to 10. Label two columns *Subject* and *Verb*. Write the subject and verb for each sentence.

1. There is the clinic.
2. How does a videotape recorder work?
3. Then came the applause.
4. Inside the machine is a tiny computer.
5. On most radio stations, does the disc jockey choose the songs?
6. Here comes a northbound bus.
7. Have the Oscars been awarded yet this year?
8. There are many single parents.
9. Have a seat.
10. Is there enough room?

G. Sentence Parts Number your paper from 1 to 10. Label three columns *Verb, Indirect Object,* and *Direct Object.* For each sentence below, fill in those parts that you find. After each verb write *T* (*Transitive*) or *I* (*Intransitive*).

1. Mary Ann has shown Len the error in his checkbook.
2. The factory pays its workers a good wage.
3. Alison poured chlorine into the pool.
4. Just for fun, I requested some brochures.
5. The flowers floated on the water.

6. Wasn't he in your history class?
7. Haven't you mailed that letter yet?
8. That store will not sell anything on the layaway plan.
9. Even her worst jokes were funny.
10. Joyce described the program to Tony.

H. Predicate Words, Linking Verbs, and Direct Objects

Number your paper from 1 to 10. Label four columns *Subject, Verb, Direct Object,* and *Predicate Word.* Fill in the parts that you find for each sentence. You will find either a direct object or a predicate word in each sentence.

1. Five good films are the nominees for the award.
2. That is my favorite station.
3. Quentin tasted the new cereal.
4. The ride was very bumpy.
5. Janet has memorized her notes.
6. Craig wrapped the package in orange burlap.
7. These green apples are ripe.
8. The Bells installed a stove in their van.
9. The weather forecast might be wrong.
10. The supervisor must be the woman at the desk.

I. Compound Sentence Parts

As your teacher directs, show the compound parts in the following sentences. Tell whether they are compound subjects, verbs, direct objects, or predicate words.

1. The doors and windows have bars.
2. The twins' names are Brent and Brian.
3. Most guests attended the wedding and the reception.
4. That beach forbids goggles, flippers, and snorkels.
5. You could have asked Celia or Ed for an explanation.
6. Daisies and buttercups grow in that meadow.
7. Ms. Alonso gave Valerie and Faye two of the kittens.
8. This dress pattern is difficult but attractive.

9. Ross told Jim and Billy the new game plan.
10. The leftovers and warm lemonade tasted fine to the hungry hikers.

J. Kinds of Sentences
Number your paper from 1 to 10. For each of the following sentences, write *Declarative, Interrogative, Imperative,* or *Exclamatory* to show what kind it is. Add the correct punctuation mark at the end of each sentence.

1. Each jet must follow a flight pattern
2. Did Bart nick his thumb with the vegetable peeler
3. Make a copy of this memo, please
4. Has Consumers' Union rated motorcycles
5. How dismal this weather is
6. How did you manage that
7. What a shocker that movie was
8. What kind of bait did you use
9. Use less salt
10. There is no amusement park in the city

K. Sentence Patterns
Write the pattern for each of the following sentences. Each sentence follows one of these patterns: N V, N V N, N V N N, N LV N, N LV Adj.

1. The lyrics were predictable.
2. Somebody sneezed violently.
3. Volunteers searched for the lost child.
4. Dwayne became a marine biologist.
5. Shirley held both reins in one hand.
6. The microphone whined during the speech.
7. Nina prefers computer games to board games.
8. Sandy studied electronics for two years.
9. The vendor sold Carson a tamale.
10. Insurance is often quite expensive.

MIXED REVIEW

The Sentence and Its Parts

A. Finding subjects and predicates and identifying fragments Decide whether the following groups of words are sentences or fragments. Copy each sentence and draw a vertical line between the subject and predicate. Then write *Declarative, Interrogative, Imperative,* or *Exclamatory* to show what kind of sentence it is. If a group of words is not a sentence, write *Fragment.*

1. What is that gadget
2. What a surprise that was
3. Every car on the lot and in the showroom
4. Every game was an upset
5. Forgot the telephone number of his last employer
6. Try the next size
7. Right through the hole in the coat's pocket
8. Wakes up full of energy every morning
9. Somebody wakes Casey up every morning
10. Wake Casey up

B. Finding helping verbs, main verbs, and simple subjects Number your paper from 1 to 10. Label three columns *Helping Verbs, Main Verbs,* and *Simple Subjects.* For each sentence, write the parts in the proper columns. If a sentence does not have a helping verb, write *none* in that column.

1. Do you work in the mailroom?
2. Here is the mistake.
3. Haven't you adjusted the rearview mirror?
4. Juanita would never borrow anything from anyone.
5. Never pry the toast out with a knife.
6. Into the pins slammed the ball.
7. There have certainly been harder times.

8. I can just barely shut the suitcase now.
9. For many years the restaurant has been serving free meals on Thanksgiving.
10. Under the bed were hidden the presents.

C. Finding sentence parts

Number your paper from 1 to 10. Label five columns on your paper *Subject, Verb, Predicate Word, Indirect Object,* and *Direct Object.* Fill in the parts that you find in each sentence. No sentence will have every part.

1. He plays basketball.
2. He plays for the Blazers.
3. He was their most valuable player.
4. He was quicker last year.
5. Jackie is buying a yearbook.
6. The smog is very thick today.
7. The movie gave my nephew a nightmare.
8. Shana gave the leftovers to the dog.
9. Did you hear me?
10. During the drought Ms. Kovac watered the trees.

D. Finding compound sentence parts

Number your paper from 1 to 10. Write the compound parts for the following sentences. Write the kind of compound part each is.

1. Truman scrubbed and peeled the potatoes.
2. The island in the river was small and rocky.
3. The Demon, the Cycle, and the Octopus are popular rides at the amusement park.
4. Are the dance and the party on the same night?
5. Are those children playing or fighting?
6. She sent Carmen and Terri the same gifts last year.
7. I remembered but then forgot again.
8. Is Sheila your sister or your cousin?
9. Fred and another hitter shattered their bats.
10. Some people put ice or cold water on bee stings.

E. Finding sentence patterns Write the pattern for each of the following sentences.

1. The movie is starting.
2. Her sign is Leo.
3. Kevin had already skimmed the chapter.
4. Aunt Pauline slipped Dee some extra money.
5. A seadog is a rainbow in the fog.
6. Moths ate holes in the wool jacket.
7. The moose is the largest animal in the deer family.
8. Michael Jackson has been popular for years.
9. During lunch Becky scribbled Lamont a note.
10. The club decorated a flatbed truck for their parade float.

F. Using sentence patterns Write two original sentences with each of the following sentence patterns.

1. NV
2. NVN
3. NVNN
4. N LV N
5. N LV Adj

USING GRAMMAR IN WRITING
The Sentence and Its Parts

A. Many newspapers and magazines publish columns of helpful hints from their readers. Tips on how to open tight jar lids might appear in the home section of a daily newspaper. Ideas for making a program run faster might appear in a computing magazine. Think about helpful hints, shortcuts, or good ideas that you could pass on to someone else. Choose one and explain it in a paragraph. You might write directions telling how to handle and care for records. You might tell how to keep a paintbrush from becoming hard and brittle.

Use at least one example of each sentence type in your paragraph.

B. Linking verbs and predicate nouns or adjectives are especially useful in descriptions. They enable a writer to create a vivid picture of the subject. Suppose that you are a reporter for a radio news program. You are present at a news conference where a new robot has been unveiled. Imagine what the robot is like. Write a paragraph of at least five sentences to describe the robot for your listeners. Use a linking verb and a predicate noun or predicate adjective in each sentence. You may want to use the following verbs.

looks   is   seems   sounds   appears

C. Imagine that you and a group of your friends have competed as a team in an athletic event or another kind of contest. Choose any contest you like. It might be a game of volleyball, a scavenger hunt, or a trivia contest. Write a paragraph of at least five sentences telling how you and your friends did in the event. Use a compound subject, verb, direct object, indirect object, or predicate word in each sentence.

Using Complete Sentences

You use sentences to communicate ideas and feelings. If a sentence is well written, it will express your ideas clearly and completely.

Occasionally, though, people put words together carelessly. Then the message is confusing.

One cause of confusion is leaving out part of a sentence. The remaining group of words is a **sentence fragment.** Another problem is created when two or more sentences are written as one. This group of words is called a **run-on sentence.**

Both of these writing errors weaken communication. In this section you will learn how to avoid them.

Part 1 Recognizing Sentence Fragments

If a group of words is only part of a sentence, it is called a **sentence fragment**. A sentence fragment does not express a complete thought.

Since something is missing from the sentence, a fragment is quite confusing. Frequently, the subject is left out. If so, the reader wonders *who* or *what* the sentence is about. Otherwise, the verb may be left out. Then the reader wonders *what happened?* or *what about it?*

Fragment:	Opened the box slowly. (Who or what opened? The subject is missing.)
Sentence:	I opened the box slowly.
Fragment:	The producer at the control panel. (What happened? The verb is missing.)
Sentence:	The producer fell asleep at the control panel.

Fragments Due to Incomplete Thoughts

Fragments can occur when a writer is in a hurry. He or she jots down only bits of ideas. These ideas are incomplete. The writer's pen doesn't keep up with his or her flow of thoughts.

These pieces of ideas might make sense to the writer. To a reader, however, they will probably seem unclear.

Here is an example of a series of fragments.

New TV shows. Introduced in the fall each year.
Never finish the season. Cancelled due to low ratings.
Or get different time slots.

These complete sentences show what the writer meant:

Many new TV shows are introduced in the fall each year. Many of them, however, never finish the season. Due to low ratings, they are cancelled by the networks. Other new shows with poor ratings get different time slots.

Fragments Due to Incorrect Punctuation

Every sentence ends with a punctuation mark. That mark may be a period, a question mark, or an exclamation point. Sometimes a writer uses one of these punctuation marks too soon. The idea is incomplete. A sentence fragment results.

Fragments: The gossip columnist. Made many enemies.
Sentence: The gossip columnist made many enemies.

Fragments: Because of the rain. The picnic was cancelled.
Sentence: Because of the rain, the picnic was cancelled.

Fragments: The President named Clark. To a cabinet post.
Sentence: The President named Clark to a cabinet post.

Exercise A For each group of words that is a sentence, write *S* on your paper. For each sentence fragment, write *F*. Add words to change the fragments into sentences.

1. Works as a social service aide
2. Late in the third quarter
3. Many new cars have front-wheel drive
4. Had a strange nickname
5. About the First Amendment
6. Brad takes vitamins
7. At a local health-food store
8. A victory for the Celtics
9. That truck is carrying an overweight load
10. Denim jeans usually fade

Exercise B Follow the directions for Exercise A.

1. Bargain-hunters head for auctions
2. A ferry boat on the river
3. The most outstanding player on the court
4. Raced on their motorcycles
5. Warm coffeecake every morning

6. The Black Hawks won in a powerplay
7. Eric ate nothing but eggs
8. Organized a garage sale
9. Adult evening classes are offered
10. Plunged into the icy waters

Part 2 Recognizing Run-on Sentences

A **run-on sentence** is two or more sentences written incorrectly as one.

A run-on is confusing. The reader keeps going without knowing where the first idea ends and the second one begins. To recognize the end of each complete thought, the reader needs a period or other punctuation mark. These are some examples:

Run-on: Scott works at a photo studio he develops film.

Correct: Scott works at a photo studio. He develops film.

Run-on: Voting age was once 21 now it is 18.

Correct: Voting age was once 21. Now it is 18.

A common error is using a comma instead of a period. Again, the result is a run-on.

Run-on: This year, we will get to see the Olympic Games, we will watch them on TV.

Correct: This year, we will get to see the Olympic Games. We will watch them on TV.

Run-on: Some cars use leaded gas, others need unleaded.

Correct: Some cars use leaded gas. Others need unleaded.

Exercise A Correct the following run-on sentences.

1. A film board rates movies, the ratings are G, PG, PG 13, R, and X.
2. Shana keeps a diary she writes in it daily.

3. Last year, our town had a record snowfall it exceeded fifty inches.
4. This grocery store has generic brands, they are economical.
5. Jordan is a candidate for the state legislature her platform is lower taxes.
6. Households are becoming smaller, one-child families are fairly common.
7. There are many kinds of RV's, vans, campers, and trailers are three.
8. A ground crew checked the plane, then the plane took off.
9. Emily gave up she couldn't win the argument.
10. Do you play a team sport which one do you like best?

Exercise B   Follow the directions for Exercise A.

1. Foster Beach is closed the waves are too high.
2. The population of the city is rising people are moving back to the city.
3. Gregory blushed he was embarrassed.
4. Cable TV has many types of programs, it requires a monthly fee.
5. There are three major commercial networks they are ABC, NBC, and CBS.
6. The temperature was 20 degrees the wind made it seem even colder.
7. A plane crashed into the lake, firefighters rescued the four passengers.
8. Cora charged the car's battery, she used jumper cables.
9. Voter turnout was low, Stanley won easily.
10. The wilderness school offers backpacking trips, students spend time alone in the wilderness.

ADDITIONAL EXERCISES

Using Complete Sentences

A. Fragments   Number your paper from 1 to 10. Write *Fragment* or *Sentence* for each of the following groups of words.

1. Were formerly called the Oilers
2. Do people dream in color
3. Records are still more popular than tapes
4. Anita and Ron, together with their families
5. On fourth down with twenty yards to go
6. An outdoor job rather than a desk job
7. A third-floor apartment with many windows
8. Likes ice cream with root beer
9. Has gone on a camping trip
10. Wore an old baseball hat backwards

B. Run-on Sentences   Number your paper from 1 to 10. Write *Sentence* or *Run-on* for each of the following groups of words. If a group is a run-on, rewrite it correctly.

1. The President appoints Supreme Court justices
2. Many people wear glasses, others wear contact lenses
3. Rescue workers used a helicopter they dropped rafts
4. The Cubs beat the Pirates, the Braves edged out the Dodgers
5. TV news gives brief reports newspapers give more details
6. Radio announcers must have pleasant voices
7. George reads lips he is deaf
8. The train takes a scenic route it runs along the Grand Canyon
9. First aid for burns is ice water and ointment
10. Jerome sat on the rocks by the lake and played his harmonica

MIXED REVIEW

Using Complete Sentences

A. Identifying sentences, fragments, and run-ons Write *Fragment, Sentence,* or *Run-on* for each of the following groups of words. Add words to make the fragments complete sentences. Correct run-ons by using the correct capitalization and punctuation.

1. Raked the leaves into piles and then bagged them
2. Vince dodged
3. In summer we played ball, in winter we sledded
4. Kim used the yellow pages to find the address
5. Not enough gas in the tank for a ride in the country
6. Milly took off her shoes she waded across the creek
7. The city needs new traffic lights it cannot afford them
8. Passport, credit cards, driver's license, and checkbook
9. A tidy student and a messy one
10. Thieves broke into the van, they stole the radio

B. Correcting fragments and run-ons Rewrite the following paragraph, correcting the fragments and run-ons.

One of the meanest "con artists" in the sea. Is the saber-tooth blenny. This coral fish closely resembles the cleaner wrasse fish, both the blenny and the cleaner wrasse are narrow. With black, horizontal stripes. Along their bright-blue and silver bodies. Both fish wiggle. However, there is an important difference between them other fish welcome the cleaner wrasse. It eats their troublesome parasites. These fish are easily fooled by the wrasse's look-alike, they do not flee from the blenny. The blenny, though, approaches them with a different purpose in mind. It does not gently nibble away parasites. Instead, the saber-tooth blenny takes a big bite. Out of the fish itself.

USING GRAMMAR IN WRITING
Using Complete Sentences

A. Imagine that you have seen a fire break out somewhere near your home or school. You dash to the nearest telephone and dial the emergency number. Tense and nervous, you report the fire to the fire department. Of course, you are speaking rapidly on the telephone. Here is a transcript of your call.

> I want to report a fire. Corner of Harris Street and Green Street. Lena's Pizza. Not much smoke yet, but I was walking past I saw flames in the kitchen at Lena's Pizza so I ran to the pay phone on the corner of State street. I called right away that's where I am now. Want me to wait here? Or go to Harris Street?

Notice the run-on sentences and sentence fragments that show your tension and your nervousness. Rewrite the paragraph. Correct the run-on sentences and fragments.

B. Imagine that you have just finished driving in a five-hundred-mile stock car race. You missed winning the race by inches when a flat tire slowed you on the final lap. When you leap out of your car, reporters want a statement from you. You are tired and disappointed. Here is the statement that you make.

> It was close, but close isn't good enough. Thought we had a chance. The car was running well, the pit crew was great. Really worked hard to get here. It's hard to miss winning by such a narrow margin that's part of racing, I guess you have to say that you did as well as you could. I'll be back, I hope some of the breaks go my way next time.

Notice the run-on sentences and fragments that reflect your tiredness and exasperation. Rewrite the paragraph. Correct the sentence fragments and run-on sentences. Add details about the race and the reason for your not winning.

Using
Nouns

Clear, effective sentences result from knowing how words work.

The words used in sentences fall into certain groups or classes. You can talk and write without knowing these labels. Skilled speakers and writers, however, understand the different classes of words.

In this section you will learn about one important group of words: nouns.

Part 1   What Is a Noun?

You use words to name people, places, and things around you. Whenever you name something, you are using a noun.

A noun is a word used to name a person, place, or thing.

Nouns name things that can be seen, such as foods, clothes, machines, and animals. In addition, they name things you cannot see, like thoughts, emotions, and beliefs.

Persons: librarian, Martina Navratilova, singer, pilot
Places: valley, Detroit, hallway, beach
Things: book, honesty, ribbon, love

Exercise   Make three columns on a sheet of paper. Label them *Names of Persons, Names of Places,* and *Names of Things.* Find the nouns in the following paragraph. List each one in the proper column.

In the middle of the nineteenth century, gold was discovered in California. Soon afterward, the Gold Rush began. Many people picked up pans and headed for the West. These miners were seeking instant wealth. As a result, many people settled in California.

Proper Nouns and Common Nouns

In the following sentence, notice how the two italicized nouns differ.

One *driver, Peter Holmes,* lost control.

Driver, the first noun, is a general word. It refers to many people. It is a **common noun.** A common noun is a general name.

The second noun, *Peter Holmes,* refers to only one person. It is a proper noun. A **proper noun** is a specific name.

A common noun is the name of a whole class of persons, places, or things. It is the name that is common to the class.

A proper noun is the name of a particular person, place, or thing. Proper nouns are capitalized.

Look at the following examples of common nouns and proper nouns. As you can see, some nouns are made up of more than one word.

Common Nouns	Proper Nouns
island	Jamaica
restaurant	Villa Rosa
athlete	Joan Benoit
cereal	Total
congresswoman	Elizabeth Holtzman
street	Delaware Avenue
town	Savannah

Exercise A Make two columns on your paper. Label one column *Common Nouns* and the other *Proper Nouns*. Place each of the following nouns in the correct column. Capitalize all proper nouns.

1. stevie wonder, pianist, musician, herbie hancock, annie lennox
2. motorbike, harley-davidson, yamaha, motorcycle, scooter
3. river, lake huron, stream, ohio river
4. actress, jane fonda, james earl jones
5. month, time, july, thursday, september
6. department store, montgomery ward, macy's, nieman marcus
7. mount whitney, appalachian mountains, peak, hills, mount rainier
8. nurse, mercy hospital, emergency room, hospital
9. team, baseball, atlanta braves, dave kingman
10. japan, canada, greece, country, nation

Exercise B: Writing Write five sentences of your own, using at least one proper noun in each sentence.

Part 2 How a Noun Is Used

Using Nouns as Subjects

Frequently, a noun is used as the subject of a sentence. As you learned in **Section 1**, the subject tells *whom* or *what* is being talked about.

> This *job* provides many kinds of benefits. (The noun *job* is the subject of the verb *provides.*)
>
> *Damage* from the fire is covered by insurance. (The noun *damage* is the subject of the verb *is covered*. As you can see, the subject is not next to the verb.)

Two or more nouns may form a compound subject.

> Strange *lights* and eerie *noises* scared us. (Both the nouns *lights* and *noises* are the subject of the verb *scared.*)
>
> The *union* and *management* agreed. (The two nouns *union* and *management* are the subject of the verb *agreed.*)

Exercise A   Write the nouns used as subjects.

1. Death Valley has the lowest elevation in the country.
2. Molly went to the police academy.
3. Hundreds of people competed in a contest.
4. A hypnotist cured Amy of sleeplessness.
5. Alcohol from grain is used in gasohol.
6. Many species of animals are becoming extinct.
7. The hostages remained inside.
8. In the future, all foods will be dated for freshness.
9. Bus loads of fans arrived at the stadium.
10. After the dance, Phil and Marsha cleaned the gym.

Exercise B   Follow the directions for Exercise A.

1. The detective wore a bulletproof vest.
2. The city of Honolulu has clean air.

3. On most days, a seaplane takes off from this lake.
4. Gilda Radner and Bill Murray are comedians.
5. During the dry spell, water was scarce.
6. At the half, Wisconsin trailed by twelve points.
7. The University of Iowa has a famous writing program.
8. With a thud, the gymnast landed on the mat.
9. When will the race start?
10. John Travolta and ShaNaNa are on a TV special tomorrow.

Using Nouns as Direct Objects

Instead of being a subject, a noun may be a direct object. The direct object completes the action of a verb. It answers *whom* or *what* about the verb.

> Trade schools train *students* in carpentry. (The noun *students* tells *whom* about the verb *train*.)
>
> The trial drew heavy *publicity*. (The noun *publicity* tells *what* about the verb *drew*.)
>
> • A crew repaired the *boiler* and the leaky *pipes*. (Both the nouns *boiler* and *pipes* are direct objects. They tell *what* about the verb *repaired*.)

Exercise A Write the nouns used as direct objects.

1. On the train, we played Scrabble and Boggle.
2. In case of fire, ring this alarm.
3. Dori sold her car through a want ad.
4. This table will need two coats of paint.
5. Many TV shows have loyal fans.
6. Dennis pays his bills twice a month.
7. The laundromat has ten washers and four dryers.
8. The real estate agent made a large commission.
9. On that snowy day I got a sunburn.
10. The climber dug his ax into the mountainside.

1. Turn off your radio and headlights.
2. A mime uses only gestures and expression.
3. One reporter asked touchy questions.
4. This river has clear, clean water.
5. Marlene donated time and money to the campaign.
6. The *Farmer's Almanac* predicts a severe winter.
7. Different colors reflect different moods.
8. Does chicken soup cure colds?
9. Telephone repair crews must climb tall poles.
10. Lauren sanded the doors and woodwork.

Using Nouns as Indirect Objects

Sometimes a noun is used as an indirect object. An indirect object tells *to whom* or *for whom* or *to what* or *for what* about the verb.

> The Nineteenth Amendment gave *women* the vote. (*Women* is the indirect object. It tells *to whom* about the verb *gave*.)
>
> This tollway charges *cars* and *trucks* different tolls. (The nouns *cars* and *trucks* are the compound indirect object, telling *to what* about the verb *charges*.)

Only sentences with direct objects have indirect objects. The indirect object appears before the direct object.

Subject	Verb	Indirect Object	Direct Object
Dominic	sent	the bank	his application.
The rules	allow	each player	two guesses.

The word *to* or *for* is never used with an indirect object.

Exercise A Find the nouns used as indirect objects.

1. The secretary bought her boss lunch.
2. Karen tossed her brother the Frisbee.

3. The club served friends and family a vegetarian meal.
4. Jeff sent Linda a card.
5. The United States loans many countries money.
6. Ms. Scott gave each employee a raise.
7. I saved Bill a seat on the bus.
8. Some people tell therapists their problems.
9. Orlando sent the company a letter of complaint.
10. The clerk sold Carrie and Jenny a radio.

Exercise B Follow the directions for Exercise A.

1. The magician handed Tony the ace of spades.
2. Foster parents give children temporary homes.
3. The stars show sailors the way.
4. Lee found her brother and his wife an apartment.
5. The cashier gave Barry incorrect change.
6. The trucker wouldn't give Jack a ride.
7. This meeting has given Meg some good ideas.
8. The nurse handed Cody and Jessica magazines.
9. One good movie can bring an actor fame.
10. The man at the carnival gave Vicki a second chance at the ring toss.

Using Nouns as Predicate Words

At times, a noun in the predicate part of a sentence is linked to the subject. That noun is a predicate noun. It always follows a linking verb. The predicate noun and the subject mean the same thing.

Video games are costly *gifts.*

Two symptoms of the flu are *fever* and *aches.*

In the above sentences, the nouns *gifts, fever,* and *aches* are all predicate nouns.

Exercise A Find the nouns used as predicate nouns.

1. Bennie's Diner is a good place for a snack.
2. Martin Luther King, Jr. was a leader in civil rights.
3. During the winter, snow tires may be a necessity.
4. Alaska is the largest state in the United States.
5. Sherlock Holmes is a fictional character.
6. New Year's Eve is a time for celebration.
7. My favorite talk show hosts are Johnny Carson and Phil Donahue.
8. The second-largest urban area is Mexico City.
9. Bonnie's suggestion is a good idea.
10. Is Damascus the capital of Syria?

Exercise B Follow the directions for Exercise A.

1. Wimbledon is a tennis tournament.
2. The copperhead and the rattlesnake are poisonous snakes.
3. Kung fu is a form of self-defense.
4. Holistic medicine is an old concept in health care.
5. Ann Meyer is a fine basketball player.
6. Woody Allen once was a writer for TV shows.
7. Harry Reasoner is an interviewer on the program *60 Minutes.*
8. My favorite desserts are strudel and ice cream.
9. O'Hare is the world's busiest airport.
10. Short, spiky hair was a recent fashion.

Part 3 Making Nouns Plural

A noun that names one thing is singular. A noun that names more than one thing is plural.

The following rules will show you how to form the plurals of nouns.

1. **To form the plural of most nouns, just add -s.**

   bottles   rings   planes   baskets

2. **When the singular noun ends in s, *sh, ch, x,* or *z,* add -es.**

   glasses   flashes   ranches   foxes

3. **When the singular noun ends in o, add -s.**

   solos   radios   rodeos   pianos   altos

   For a few words ending in *o,* add *-es:*

   potatoes   heroes   echoes   cargoes   tomatoes

4. **If a singular noun ends in *y* with a consonant before it, change the *y* to *i* and add -es.**

   lady—ladies   family—families   hobby—hobbies

   When a vowel (*a, e, i, o, u*) comes before the *y,* do not change the *y* to *i.* Just add *-s:*

   way—ways   valley—valleys   boy—boys

5. **For some nouns ending in *f,* add -s to make the plural.**

   chiefs   griefs   roofs   proofs

   For many nouns ending in *f* or *fe,* change the *f* to *v* and add *-s* or *-es.* Since there is no rule to follow, you will have to memorize such words. Here are some examples:

   leaf—leaves   half—halves   life—lives
   wife—wives   elf—elves   self—selves

6. **The plural of some nouns is the same as the singular. These must be memorized.**

   deer   sheep   moose   salmon   trout

7. **Some nouns form their plurals in special ways. They, too, must be memorized.**

   tooth—teeth   ox—oxen   man—men
   mouse—mice   foot—feet   woman—women
   child—children   die—dice   goose—geese

Dictionaries show the plural of a word if it is formed in an unusual way. Here is a dictionary's entry for the noun *spy*. Its plural, *spies*, is shown.

spy (spī) *vt.* **spied, spy′ing** [< OFr. < OHG. *spehōn*, to examine < IE. base *spek-*, to watch closely, from which also comes L. *specere*, to see] to catch sight of; see [I *spied* her in the distance] —*vi.* **1.** to watch closely and secretly; act as a spy **2.** to look carefully —*n., pl.* **spies 1.** a person who keeps close and secret watch on another or others **2.** a person hired by a government to get secret information about the affairs, esp. military affairs, of another government, as of an enemy in wartime —**spy out** to discover or seek to discover by looking carefully

If you have a question about plurals, use a dictionary.

Exercise A Write the plural of each of these nouns. Then use your dictionary to see if you are right.

1. shelf	6. calf	11. belief	16. city
2. knife	7. horse	12. studio	17. envelope
3. ox	8. sheep	13. eyelash	18. library
4. church	9. scout	14. cavity	19. roof
5. tray	10. potato	15. tax	20. foot

Exercise B: Writing Write five sentences, using the plural form of any five of the words listed in Exercise A.

Exercise C Write each sentence. Correct the errors in plural nouns.

1. Workmans used knifes to prune branchs from the trees.
2. Each of the boxs contained twenty foots of rope.
3. The sheriffs and their deputys investigate robberys.
4. We bought radishs and tomatos at the roadside stand.
5. These companys reported losses last year.
6. Four womans and four mens trained as astronautes.
7. The codes use buzzs, rings, and beeps.
8. Those crews work for various Hollywood studioes.
9. Judith takes photoes at all the wrestling matchs.
10. On one of the bathroom shelfs are Grandpa's false tooths.

Part 4 Making Nouns Possessive

A noun can show possession or ownership.

> child's toy   Sally's car   horse's saddle

The possessive of a noun can show that something is part of a person.

> Jerry's knee   Jill's happiness   boy's smile

The above nouns show ownership with *'s*. Words like *child's, Sally's*, and *Jerry's* are possessive nouns.

While people and animals usually possess things, sometimes things are also used in the possessive. There is *a week's time, a restaurant's menu*, or *your life's work*, for example.

How To Form Possessives

Here are three rules for forming the possessive of nouns.

1. If the noun is singular, add an apostrophe (') and -s.

> Chris   Chris's glasses
> Florida   Florida's weather
> Ms. Healy   Ms. Healy's job

2. If the noun is plural but does not end in -s, add an apostrophe and -s.

> children—children's songs   men—men's clothes

3. If the noun is plural and ends in -s, add only the apostrophe.

> workers—workers' pay   Cohens—Cohens' driveway

Exercise A Write the possessive form of each of these nouns.

1. manager
2. city
3. Senate
4. Sandy
5. editor
6. Harris
7. year
8. David
9. Rick Fields
10. zoo
11. woman
12. July

457

13. skater   16. chairperson   19. hostess
14. player   17. committee   20. ranch
15. Katie   18. Les

Exercise B Follow the directions for Exercise A.

1. coaches   8. months   15. children
2. engineers   9. geese   16. divers
3. Bakers   10. drivers   17. cooks
4. people   11. tourists   18. Thompsons
5. dreamers   12. photographers   19. fish
6. Jets   13. cities   20. linemen
7. goalies   14. shoppers

ADDITIONAL EXERCISES

Using Nouns

A. Common and Proper Nouns Label two columns *Common Nouns* and *Proper Nouns*. Decide whether the following nouns are common or proper. Place each in the correct column. Capitalize the proper nouns.

1. land, place, republic, united states, mexico
2. central park, lincoln park, recreation, outdoors, rock creek park
3. government, bureau, internal revenue service, law, clerk
4. seaport, san juan, capital, island, puerto rico
5. vida blue, baseball, sports, national league, stadium
6. season, weather, christmas, holiday, hurricane david
7. west virginia, new york, indiana, state, ohio
8. ice skater, matador, olympics, track, kentucky derby
9. elizabeth, cashier, salesclerk, robert, bricklayer
10. vocalist, jazz, lena horne, billie holiday, blues

B. Nouns as Subjects Number your paper from 1 to 10. Write the nouns used as subjects in each of the following sentences.

1. From the center of the court, Williams sank a basket that tied the game.
2. The convention was held during April in Houston.
3. On the sixteenth day at sea, the skipper sighted the island of Oahu.
4. Mark Russell is a teacher at Whitney Young High School.
5. The bookseller searched for books about Mexico.
6. A soundproof booth overlooks the recording studio.

7. The counselors and the nurse ride in the camp bus.
8. Stevie Wonder and Paul McCartney sang "Ebony and Ivory."
9. Dusty, old magazines were piled in the basement.
10. Many victims of fire die of smoke inhalation.

C. Nouns as Direct Objects
Number your paper from 1 to 10. Write the nouns used as direct objects.

1. Customs agents inspect luggage.
2. Roberta tacked shingles onto the roof.
3. Did you make that sweater?
4. Shawn needs a narrower backpack.
5. We played softball in the vacant lot.
6. Yolanda directed the flashlight's beam to the crevice.
7. Mr. Herek first dampened the old wallpaper.
8. Bring hamburgers and pickles.
9. May I tape that record?
10. Nolan chopped celery and onions for the tuna salad.

D. Nouns Used as Indirect Objects
Indicate the indirect objects in the following sentences. Use diagrams or whatever method your teacher suggests.

1. Finally, Amanda told her friend the truth.
2. The beautician gave Dawn a free haircut.
3. Without a word, Nick handed Ginger the letter.
4. The church found the refugees homes and jobs.
5. The company sent Martin a rebate on the camera.
6. I mailed Delia and Jack separate invitations.
7. Aspirin gives some people stomachaches.
8. Jan fed the chickens some corn.
9. Ms. Stelzer asked Liz and Jo their sides of the story.
10. Did the Jacksons bring their friends souvenirs from Jamaica?

E. Predicate Nouns Number your paper from 1 to 10. List the predicate nouns in these sentences.

1. The only officer on board was an ensign.
2. Lee and Grant were not classmates at West Point.
3. When did Cambodia become Kampuchea?
4. Those sandals are a real bargain.
5. The alphabet is a code, of course.
6. Cynthia was the woman in the photograph.
7. All the basketball players are juniors and seniors.
8. Ms. Baptiste has been a lumberjack and a welder.
9. Her biggest concern now is her brother.
10. The bride and groom were Theresa and Michael.

F. Plurals of Nouns Write the plural of each of these nouns.

1. hero	6. grass	11. bath	16. Jones
2. splash	7. pulley	12. man	17. child
3. chef	8. loaf	13. proof	18. trout
4. deer	9. solo	14. tooth	19. bully
5. punch	10. ally	15. luxury	20. hoax

G. Possessives of Nouns Write the possessive form in the singular or plural as indicated.

1. Barry (singular) shaving kit
2. reader (plural) tastes
3. member (singular) discount
4. official (plural) identification badges
5. city (singular) skyline
6. nephew (singular) birthday
7. child (plural) games
8. Hollis (singular) mail
9. secretary (plural) duties
10. class (singular) yearbook

MIXED REVIEW

Using Nouns

A. Identifying nouns and their uses   Copy the nouns from these sentences. After each, write *Subject, Direct Object, Indirect Object,* or *Predicate Noun* to show how it is used.

1. The cafeteria serves hot meals.
2. Mr. Cortez served his guests lunch.
3. The manager fired the most recent employees.
4. Patricia McCormick was a bullfighter.
5. Gwen was studying the blueprints carefully.
6. That car is a Ford.
7. A severe drought hit the Midwest and the Southwest.
8. An asteroid could have made the crater.
9. Candlestick Park is a windy ballpark.
10. Aren't gold and silver soft metals?

B. Using plural and possessive forms correctly   Rewrite these sentences, correcting the errors in the plural and possessive forms of nouns. If a sentence is correct, write *Correct.*

1. A raccoon bit Joss's cat's paw during a fight.
2. A raccoons' tooths are quite sharp.
3. The pillowes are stuffed with feathers' from geeses.
4. The children can read these storys themselfs.
5. One citys alleys are paved with bricks.
6. The chieves of these tribes were not always old men.
7. Ladies' dresses are on the second and third floors.
8. Mr. Browns' pianos all have matching benchs.
9. Girls' and boys' often enjoy the same toys.
10. Both womens motorcycles have new tire's.

USING GRAMMAR IN WRITING
Using Nouns

A. You are in charge of arranging for a guest speaker for your English class or writing class. Fortunately for you, the first visitors from another galaxy will soon be coming to your area. Write a letter inviting the leader of the aliens to speak to your class. In the letter, suggest a landing place for the alien ship, which is as long as two football fields. Include a paragraph of directions telling how to get from the landing site to your school. Mention at least five specific landmarks along the way. The words that name these landmarks will, of course, be nouns. Underline all common nouns in your letter once and all proper nouns twice.

B. Sometimes the most common objects around a person's apartment, house, or room can reveal that person's character. Suppose that you are writing a story about a private investigator. The investigator is observing a suspect. The suspect seems to lead a dull life. However, the investigator is convinced that this person is an undercover agent. The investigator enters the suspect's apartment. Write a paragraph describing the contents of the suspect's refrigerator, a closet, or a drawer as the investigator examines them. List all the contents. Include things that are ordinary, and also include something that will give the agent away. Write at least ten sentences.

When you have finished your paragraph, list all the nouns that appear in it. The words that name the contents of the refrigerator, closet, or drawer will, of course, be nouns. Following each noun, write *S* for subject, *DO* for direct object, *IO* for indirect object, or *PN* for predicate noun to tell how the noun was used.

Using Pronouns

While nouns are valuable for naming people, places, and things, they can be overused. Sentences like this one show how awkward it is to use only nouns:

When Rita started Rita's job, Rita worked nights.

Instead, you can substitute pronouns for some of the nouns. Then you can say:

When Rita started *her* job, *she* worked nights.

You can see that the words *her* and *she* take the place of the noun *Rita*. These pronouns convey the same meaning clearly and concisely.

Part 1 Personal Pronouns

A pronoun is a word used in place of a noun. A pronoun is a useful word. It may be used in three situations.

1. It may refer to the person speaking.

   I went fishing.   *We* argued.

2. It may refer to the person spoken to.

   You like *your* co-workers, don't *you?*

3. It may refer to other people, places, or things.

   He stopped *them* in the doorway.   *She* left *her* post.

As you can tell from the examples above, a pronoun often refers to a person. Therefore, the most frequently used pronouns are called **personal pronouns.**

Personal pronouns have many variations. Just like the nouns they replace, personal pronouns may be singular or plural. Look at the following chart to see how personal pronouns change from singular to plural.

Singular:	I	me	my, mine
	you	you	your, yours
	he, she, it	him, her, it	his, her, hers, its
Plural:	we	us	our, ours
	you	you	your, yours
	they	them	their, theirs

The chart shows that most plural pronouns are totally different from their singular forms. Read the following examples.

Singular	Plural
I laughed.	*We* laughed.
Leave *it* alone.	Leave *them* alone.
She forgot.	*They* forgot.

Exercise A Write the pronouns used in place of nouns. After each pronoun, write the noun or nouns it stands for.

1. When Ken finally arrived, he apologized for being late once again.
2. You should not jump-start a frozen battery, Gene.
3. Claire said she had no insurance yet.
4. Leon filed his notes.
5. Mr. Walker, do you have an account here?
6. "I voted before work," said Pamela.
7. The fishermen wore their licenses on their jackets.
8. Beth chipped her front tooth.
9. Curtis sealed the envelope and stamped it.
10. The game has lost its appeal for Kim.

Exercise B Follow the directions for Exercise A.

1. Casey heard a noise, and it frightened her.
2. Ted had made up his mind, but then he changed it again.
3. "Is that your car?" the policewoman asked Lee.
4. The city condemned the building and had it torn down.
5. Rick told Nina, "I enjoy my job."
6. Ms. Corelli said to her students, "We have several problems to solve."
7. Bats rarely bite, but many people are afraid of them.
8. The deaf students watched their interpreter.
9. The workers felt cheated. They walked out.
10. Do some doctors joke while they operate?

Part 2 Forms of Pronouns

Pronouns can be used in all the ways that nouns are used. Like nouns, personal pronouns can be subjects, objects, predicate words, and possessives.

Exercise The following sentences use different forms of pronouns correctly. Read each sentence aloud.

1. The students filled out *their* schedules.
2. Is that *your* telephone?
3. *He* veered to the left.
4. The best lineman is *he*.
5. The tallest player is *she*.
6. Connie and *she* tied for first place.
7. The next apartment is *theirs*.
8. Red and gold are *their* colors.
9. The sugar doughnut is *mine*.
10. Is that bike *yours?*
11. Give *her* another chance.
12. Mack and *he* said the decision was *theirs*.

A personal pronoun changes form, however, as its use in a sentence changes.

> *He* swims every day. (*He* is the subject.)
> Nothing stops *him*. (*Him* is the direct object.)
> *His* strength has increased. (*His* is possessive.)

In the sentences above, all three pronouns refer to the same person. The forms, though, are different.

The three forms of personal pronouns are **subject form, object form,** and **possessive form.** This chart shows the forms for all the personal pronouns.

	Subject	Object	Possessive
Singular:	I	me	my, mine
	you	you	your, yours
	he, she, it	him, her, it	his, her, hers, its
Plural:	we	us	our, ours
	you	you	your, yours
	they	them	their, theirs

The Subject Form of Pronouns

Subject Pronouns

I	we
you	you
he, she, it	they

When a personal pronoun is the subject of a sentence, its subject form is used. Here are some examples.

> *We* jumped hurdles.   *He* ran a mile.
> *They* formed a carpool.   *She* has poison ivy.

You probably have little trouble using pronouns as subjects. Problems may occur, though, with the predicate pronoun. Predicate pronouns are pronouns that are linked to the subject. They follow linking verbs, just as predicate nouns do.

> That was *he* on the phone. (*He* is a predicate pronoun used after the linking verb *was.*)
>
> It must be *they*. (*They* is a predicate pronoun used after the linking verb *must be.*)

As you see, the subject forms of pronouns are used for predicate pronouns. Because that form may not sound natural at first, you may sometimes be confused about which form to use. In that case, try reversing the subject and the predicate pronoun. The sentence should still sound correct.

> The hero was *he*.
> *He* was the hero.

These sentences, too, correctly use the subject form for predicate pronouns.

> Is that *she?*
> It was *I* who called.
> Your best friend is *he*.

Remember to use the subject form for both subjects and predicate pronouns.

The Object Form of Pronouns

Object Pronouns

me	us
you	you
him, her, it	them

For an object, the object form of a personal pronoun is correct.

The three kinds of objects are direct objects, indirect objects, and objects of prepositions.

These sentences use the object form of the pronoun for direct objects.

> The assistant manager hired *her*.
> The noise awakened *them*.
>
> The Bears traded *him*.
> Dora warned *me*.

In these sentences, the object form is used for indirect objects.

> Dennis handed *me* a note.
> Jane gave *him* directions.
>
> I wished *them* success.
> Sue told *us* her predictions.

Besides direct and indirect objects, the other kind of object is the object of a preposition. A preposition is a short connecting word like *by, with,* or *from*. A pronoun that follows such a word is the object. For information about prepositions see **Handbook Section 7.**

The following sentences use the object form for objects of prepositions.

> Their patients depend on *them*.
> Come with *me* to the sneak preview.
> Connie sat next to *her* on the subway.

The Possessive Form of Pronouns

Possessive Pronouns

my, mine	our, ours
your, yours	your, yours
his, her, hers, its	their, theirs

A possessive pronoun shows belonging or ownership. Some possessive pronouns are used alone. Then the possessive pronoun is used like a noun. It is a subject, object, or predicate word. Here are some examples.

Yours is blue. (subject)
Doug borrowed *hers*. (direct object)
Roger gave *his* a shine. (indirect object)
Some campers left without *theirs*. (object of preposition)
This backpack is *mine*. (predicate pronoun)

At other times, possessive pronouns are not used by themselves. Rather, they are used to describe nouns. Notice how possessive pronouns tell about nouns.

The company opened *its* new branch office.
Jessica tallied *her* score on the pinball machine.
Brad put *his* last dime into the parking meter.
The girls ate *their* lunches in the park.

Exercise A Choose the correct pronoun from the two given in parentheses. Write it. Read the sentence to yourself.

1. Our first choice is (he, him).
2. Somebody followed (he, him) home.
3. That idea was (your, yours).
4. Cassie talked (I, me) into the job.
5. Maybe (she, her) has forgotten.
6. Of course (he, him) reads the fine print.
7. The lawyer is (she, her).
8. It was not (I, me).
9. The mail was all for (she, her).
10. The manager gave (they, them) a discount.

Exercise B Follow the directions for Exercise A.

1. The only volunteers were (they, them).
2. The man in charge of refreshments is (he, him).
3. Did (she, her) see you?

4. That career appeals to (she, her).
5. Wasn't the call for (I, me)?
6. The actual inventor of the gadget was (I, me).
7. Maybe the bus driver can tell (we, us).
8. Wasn't the Marine (he, him)?
9. Is this wallet (her, hers) or Pat's?
10. The paramedic gave (she, her) oxygen.

Exercise C The personal pronouns in the following sentences are in italics. Write each pronoun and label it *Subject Form*, *Object Form*, or *Possessive Form*.

1. *She* shook sand from the towel.
2. The jacket with the emblem is *mine*.
3. *My* interview is tomorrow.
4. Della parked *her* car in the alley.
5. James served *us* some chili.
6. The pollwatcher is *she*.
7. Finally *I* understood.
8. Does *he* need an interpreter?
9. Did *they* buy tickets?
10. Are *we* early?

Exercise D: Writing Write ten new sentences using the pronouns from Exercise C. Use each pronoun in the way it is used in the sentence in Exercise C.

Part 3 Using Pronouns in Compound Constructions

Compound sentence parts, or compound constructions in a sentence, have more than one part. The parts are joined by a word like *and, or,* or *nor,* as in *Carlo and I.* A pronoun may be one or both of these parts.

For compound constructions, you will have to decide which pronoun form to use. The following sentences use pronouns correctly as compound parts.

> *Yvonne* and *I* visited Denver. (*Yvonne* and *I* are both subjects. The subject form *I* is used.)
>
> Steve poured *her* and *me* some coffee. (*Her* and *me* are indirect objects. The object forms are used.)
>
> Just between *you* and *me*, I'm scared. (*You* and *me* are objects of the preposition *between*. The object forms are used.)

There is a way to avoid problems with compound parts. Just think of each part separately. For instance, in the first example above, omit the *Yvonne and*. Should the sentence read *I visited Denver* or *Me visited Denver?* The pronoun *I* is correct.

Here is another example.

> Lynn is helping Evan and (I, me).
> Lynn is helping *me*.

Exercise A Choose the right pronoun from the two given.

1. (We, Us) and our neighbors divided the expense.
2. The most careful workers are Carlos and (she, her).
3. The saddest faces belonged to Annie and (I, me).
4. Just between you and (I, me), I was late today.
5. My boss and (I, me) both wear a hearing aid.
6. Ms. Shore and (they, them) share the kitchen.
7. Teresa and (he, him) packed the cooler.
8. Karla frowned at Craig and (they, them).
9. Mick and (she, her) washed the lab utensils.
10. The candidate shook hands with Marta and (I, me).

Exercise B Follow the directions for Exercise A.

1. The coach can't decide between Ben and (he, him).
2. The band and (he, him) practiced daily.

3. That team has lost to both Phillips and (we, us).
4. The contenders are Clancy and (I, me).
5. (They, Them) and the Peace Corps do overseas work.
6. Somebody with a bad cold sat behind Trish and (I, me).
7. Chet and (they, them) rented a meeting hall.
8. Do you and (she, her) play tennis?
9. Magda and (I, me) took the auto maintenance course.
10. The other tenants and (we, us) are signing a petition.

Part 4 Antecedents of Pronouns

A pronoun is used in place of a noun. The noun it replaces is called the pronoun's **antecedent**. A pronoun refers to its antecedent.

Jeremy missed *his* friends. (His takes the place of the noun *Jeremy. Jeremy* is its antecedent.)

The stagehands waited for *their* cues. (*Their* refers to the noun *stagehands. Stagehands* is the antecedent.)

Usually, the antecedent appears before the pronoun. The antecedent may be either in the same sentence or in the preceding sentence, as in the following example.

The firefighters chopped a hole in the roof. *They* used axes. (*They* refers to *firefighters.*)

Pronouns may be the antecedents of other pronouns.

I choose *my* own hours. (*I* is the antecedent of *my.*)

In one important way, a pronoun must be like its antecedent. The pronoun must have the same number as its antecedent. If the antecedent is plural, then the pronoun must be plural.

A pronoun must agree with its antecedent in number.

The ranger grabbed *her* binoculars.
(*Ranger* is singular; *her* is singular.)

Drivers have *their* own pit crews.
(*Drivers* is plural; *their* is plural.)

Andrew Wyeth exhibited *his* paintings.
(*Andrew Wyeth* is singular; *his* is singular.)

Exercise A In these sentences the personal pronouns are italicized. Write each pronoun and its antecedent.

1. The waiter picked up the top and pocketed *it*.
2. Jeff, which books do *you* need?
3. The cashier in the express line closed *her* register before Lee got there.
4. All workers on duty must wear *their* badges.
5. Sloths hang upside down by *their* hook-like claws.
6. At first Ray wouldn't wear *his* glasses in public.
7. Some overactive children have high levels of lead in *their* blood.
8. "*I* lost *my* transfer," said Cindy.
9. "*We* left *our* hardest job until last," said Kit and Bill.
10. Glenn cut out the pieces of the pattern and pinned *them* together.

Exercise B Follow the directions for Exercise A.

1. Chip painted *his* car with a glass finish.
2. "*I* have never ridden in a sidecar," said Maggie.
3. Most students bring *their* own lunches.
4. The fans in the bleachers waved *their* hats.
5. Mark overheard the conversation and worried about *it*.
6. Suddenly Bev got *her* second wind.
7. Sue, train *your* foxhound not to chase rabbits.
8. Do *you* have to work overtime again this weekend, Jeremy?
9. "Pam and *I* have brought *our* enlistment papers," said Alice.
10. Gladys started the argument, and Angie ended *it*.

Part 5 Compound Personal Pronouns

A **compound personal pronoun** is a pronoun with *-self* or *-selves* added. These are the compound personal pronouns.

myself	ourselves
yourself	yourselves
himself, herself, itself	themselves

Compound personal pronouns are used for emphasis, as in the following examples.

The children planned the menu *themselves*.

Mr. Mendez *himself* apologized.

We chopped the firewood *ourselves*.

Exercise A Write a compound personal pronoun for each sentence. After it, write its antecedent.

1. Steve doesn't like to shop by (pronoun).
2. The lamp will turn (pronoun) off in ten minutes.
3. The diplomats (pronoun) were held hostage.
4. The dentist (pronoun) took the X-rays.
5. What do you want for (pronoun), Jenny?
6. The computer (pronoun) can correct the mistakes.
7. Mel treated (pronoun) to a pizza.
8. Tina blames (pronoun) for everything that goes wrong.
9. Some people expect too little of (pronoun).
10. We served (pronoun) at the reception.

Exercise B Follow the directions for Exercise A.

1. Gwen and I can do the work by (pronoun).
2. Have you students heard (pronoun) on tape?
3. That window couldn't have opened (pronoun).
4. The fans yelled (pronoun) hoarse.

5. Don't wear (pronoun) out, Georgia.
6. I (pronoun) took that message.
7. Even the chief (pronoun) pitched in.
8. Puzzled, the parakeet watched (pronoun) in the mirror for hours.
9. Harry weighs (pronoun) every morning.
10. The wrestlers prepared (pronoun) for the championship match.

Part 6 Demonstrative Pronouns

The pronouns *this, that, these,* and *those* point out people or things. They are called **demonstrative pronouns.**

This and *these* point to people or things that are close in space or time. The pronouns *that* and *those* point to people or things that are farther away.

> *This* is a drive-in.   *These* are the correct answers.
> *That* was her maiden   *Those* were my first words.
> name.

Exercise On your paper, write the correct demonstrative pronoun for each blank.

1. _____ is more expensive than these.
2. _____ are more expensive than those.
3. _____ is Ms. Prieto across the street.
4. _____ were exciting days.
5. _____ was my sister you saw.
6. _____ are my skates I'm carrying.
7. _____ was the hardest test I had ever taken.
8. _____ is Leon's birthday we're celebrating, not yours.
9. _____ was a close game last night.
10. _____ is my locker right here.

Part 7 Interrogative Pronouns

The pronouns *who, whom, whose, which,* and *what* are used to ask questions. They are called interrogative pronouns.

> *Who* rang the alarm? *Which* are the best seats?
> *Whom* did you meet? *What* is your advice?
> *Whose* is this?

Exercise Write all the pronouns in these sentences. After each pronoun, write *Demonstrative* or *Interrogative* to show what kind it is.

1. Whose are these keys?
2. To whom should Jim give these?
3. Those over there should be returned.
4. Is this the winning ticket?
5. To whom was the memo sent?
6. Who is the manager?
7. That was a good question.
8. Who checks air pollution levels?
9. Which is the best?
10. What are these for?

Part 8 Indefinite Pronouns

One type of pronoun does not refer to a definite person or thing. Such pronouns are called **indefinite pronouns.**
Here are some indefinite pronouns. All of them are singular.

another	each	everything	one
anybody	either	neither	somebody
anyone	everybody	nobody	someone
anything	everyone	no one	

Since they are singular, the pronouns above are used only with the singular possessive pronouns *his, her,* and *its.*

477

Everyone has *his* own interests.
Each of the delegates showed *his* pass.
Each of the delegates showed *his* or *her* pass.

In the last example, notice that the phrase *his or her* is used. That phrase points out that the indefinite pronoun may refer to either a male or a female. Many people prefer such a phrase.

Although most indefinite pronouns are singular, some are plural. They refer to more than one person or thing. The following indefinite pronouns are plural. They are used with the plural possessive *their*.

both   many   few   several

Both of my brothers brought *their* dates.
Few of the tenants have paid *their* rent.
Many of the patients leave *their* rooms.
Several of the oil companies have raised *their* prices.

Depending on their meaning in a sentence, a few indefinite pronouns can be either singular or plural. Look at these examples.

some   none   all   any   most

Most of the movie was better than *its* ending.
Most of the rebels hated *their* country's dictator.
All of this food has sugar in *it*.
All of the rock groups have *their* fans.

Exercise A Write each indefinite pronoun.

1. Everybody was watching the Super Bowl.
2. Have all of the raffle tickets been sold?
3. Neither of those cars has snow tires.
4. I'll try some of the potato salad.
5. Have you met any of her relatives?
6. Finally someone heard my shouts.
7. Few of the students are from Cuba.
8. We saw nobody we knew.

9. The reporter interviewed several of the Steelers before the game.
10. Ken got that watch from one of his aunts.

Exercise B   Choose the right pronoun from the two given.

1. One of the clinics has extended (its, their) hours.
2. Neither of the boxers was pulling (his, their) punches last night.
3. All of the schools must keep (its, their) costs down.
4. Everyone offered to share what little (he or she, they) had.
5. Everything was in (its, their) place.
6. Each of the sorters is good at (his or her, their) job.
7. Many of the drivers use (his or her, their) own cars in the race.
8. Some of them have changed (his or her, their) shifts.
9. Some of the food looked as if (it, they) had been out in the sun too long.
10. Nobody can do everything by (himself or herself, themselves).

Exercise C   For each sentence write the indefinite pronoun and the correct verb from the two given.

1. Some of the voters (is, are) undecided.
2. (Has, Have) anything happened?
3. Somebody always (times, time) the commercials.
4. Either of these albums (is, are) suitable.
5. Neither of the men (hears, hear) well.
6. One of your friends (is, are) here.
7. None of the work (is, are) dull.
8. Both of the taxis (looks, look) empty.
9. Everyone (remembers, remember) that wedding.
10. Each of these skirts (needs, need) to be dry cleaned.

Part 9   Special Problems with Pronouns

Contractions and Possessive Pronouns

Sometimes certain contractions are confused with possessive pronouns.

A contraction is created by joining two words. An apostrophe shows where one or more letters are left out when the words are joined.

> you're = you + are   it's = it + is
> they're = they + are   who's = who + is

The above contractions sound like the possessive pronouns *your, their, its,* and *whose.* Although the words are spelled differently, they may be confused.

> Incorrect: *Your* changing *you're* mind, aren't you?
> Correct: *You're* changing *your* mind, aren't you?

To decide which word is correct, replace the contraction with the words it stands for. If the sentence sounds right, then the contraction is correct.

> Incorrect: Call me when its time to leave.
> Correct: Call me when it's (it is) time to leave.

Exercise A Choose the right word from the two given.

1. (Your, You're) the referee.
2. (Whose, Who's) window overlooks the alley?
3. (Their, They're) playing a good defensive game.
4. (Whose, Who's) the jockey?
5. (Their, They're) looking for trouble.
6. The dancers were snapping (their, they're) fingers.
7. (Whose, Who's) your new neighbor?
8. (Their, They're) uncle will meet the children.

9. (Your, You're) sure about that, aren't you?
10. The welders are all wearing (their, they're) goggles.

Exercise B: Writing Write the words each contraction below stands for. Then write five new sentences using any of the contractions from this exercise.

1. We'd traveled by Greyhound before.
2. She's filed for unemployment compensation.
3. They're all getting a raise.
4. He'd never seen a play before.
5. They'll call me.
6. I'm busy right now.
7. You're next.
8. Who's in charge here?
9. Something's burning!
10. We've got our baggage claim checks.

Who and Whom

The pronouns *who* and *whom* cause problems for many people.

Who is used as the subject of a sentence. *Who* sounds natural in most questions.

Who moved the picture?   *Who* is on a diet?

Whom is harder to get used to. *Whom* is used as an object.

Whom did Ted Koppel interview?
  (direct object of the verb *did interview*)
For *whom* will you vote?
  (object of the preposition *for*)

Exercise A Choose the right pronoun from the two given.

1. With (who, whom) did you get a ride?
2. (Who, Whom) signed the check?

3. (Who, Whom) knows how to use an airbrush?
4. (Who, Whom) is carrying the ball?
5. To (who, whom) was that song dedicated?
6. (Who, Whom) won the first round?
7. (Who, Whom) was his stepmother?
8. (Who, Whom) did you ask?
9. (Who, Whom) did you speak with last time?
10. (Who, Whom) spoke with you last time?

Exercise B Follow the directions for Exercise A.

1. (Who, Whom) trained that dog?
2. About (who, whom) were you talking?
3. (Who, Whom) does she like?
4. (Who, Whom) did you see at the party?
5. (Who, Whom) will that Great Dane obey?
6. (Who, Whom) tackled Evans?
7. (Who, Whom) did Frank tackle?
8. (Who, Whom) would do a thing like that?
9. With (who, whom) does he feel comfortable?
10. Behind (who, whom) was she standing?

We and *Us* with Nouns

The pronouns *we* and *us* are often used with nouns, as in the phrases *we girls* and *us Americans.* Such phrases may sometimes cause problems.

To decide whether to use *we* or *us,* omit the noun. First say the sentence with *we,* and then with *us.* You will then probably be able to choose the correct pronoun.

Problem: (We, Us) players work out daily.
Correct: We work out daily.
Correct: We players work out daily.

Problem: There is a new theater for (we, us) young people.
Correct: There is a new theater for us.
Correct: There is a new theater for us young people.

Them and Those

Them and *those* are sometimes confused. To use the words correctly, remember that *them* is always a pronoun. It takes the place of a noun.

> Finally, someone noticed *them*. (In this sentence, *them* is used as the direct object.)

Them is never used to tell about a noun. *Those* should be used.

> Incorrect: Have you seen *them* stock cars?
> Correct: Have you seen *those* stock cars?

Exercise A Choose the correct pronoun from the two given.

1. Loretta was accepted by one of (them, those) training programs.
2. (Them, Those) elephant seals often weigh as much as two tons.
3. Of course, (we, us) trainees get paid.
4. Is that one of (them, those) water filters?
5. (We, Us) recruits cannot live off base.
6. Slide rules have been replaced by (them, those) calculators.
7. Barbados is one of (them, those) new nations.
8. Do you like (them, those) mushroom and pepperoni pizzas?
9. The orientation session is for (we, us) new students.
10. (We, Us) Puerto Rican students will translate that article for you.

Exercise B Follow the directions for Exercise A.

1. Listen to (them, those) sirens.
2. (We, Us) sheet metal workers serve a long apprenticeship.

3. Sitting this close to (them, those) poison ivy plants is unwise.
4. (Them, Those) X-ray technicians wear lead aprons to protect themselves.
5. Ms. Sobecki congratulated (we, us) finalists.
6. What is delaying (them, those) ambulances?
7. (We, Us) volunteers are proud of ourselves.
8. Recently I went to one of (them, those) appliance shows.
9. (We, Us) pedestrians aren't using any energy but our own.
10. (Them, Those) crash helmets have saved some lives.

Exercise C: Writing Write ten original sentences using each of the pronouns that you did not use in the sentences in Exercise B.

ADDITIONAL EXERCISES

Using Pronouns

A. Pronouns Number your paper from 1 to 10. Write the pronouns you find in each of the following sentences. After each pronoun, write the noun or nouns it stands for.

1. The officers wore their dress uniforms.
2. Marcy laced her ice skates tightly.
3. Ross, can you get the car started?
4. "My zip code has been changed," said Maureen.
5. "Your game has improved, Walt," said Carl.
6. The ranger set a trap and checked it daily.
7. Jim carried newspapers from the delivery truck and stacked them in the newsstand.
8. Judy said, "Cold weather doesn't bother me. In fact, I like it."
9. Ed did his exercises faithfully, and they did help him.
10. Joan told Jon and Bill why she was angry with them.

B. Correct Pronoun Usage Choose the correct pronoun from the two given in parentheses. Be ready to explain how it is used in the sentence.

1. (She, Her) checked the blueprints for errors.
2. Did (we, us) have any choice?
3. Could (he, him) have left already?
4. The news surprised (I, me).
5. The last contestant was (I, me).
6. Ask (you, your) doctor to sign this form.
7. The bowlers recorded (they, their) own scores.
8. I sold (he, him) the last ticket.
9. The host and hostess are (they, them).
10. Mrs. Bell found the knife and sharpened (it, its) blade.

C. Pronouns in Compound Sentence Parts Choose the correct pronoun from the two given in parentheses.

1. Norma and (I, me) took down the storm windows.
2. Between you and (I, me), I will vote for Thomas.
3. You or (she, her) can model the evening gown.
4. The finalists were Daisy and (she, her).
5. (They, Them) and the Grays vacation together.
6. Have you and (he, him) ever broken in a colt?
7. The supervisor and (he, him) checked our time cards.
8. Greg sent Anita and (I, me) the same birthday card.
9. Nobody could blame you or (they, them).
10. The only dancers still in the contest were Brenda, Gil, and (we, us).

D. Antecedents Write the antecedent of each italicized pronoun.

1. The teller looked at the check before cashing *it*.
2. The losers' disappointment showed in *their* faces.
3. Lonny patted Rover and Rattler and filled *their* bowls.
4. Ms. Haltom simply turned off *her* hearing aid.
5. The cat had a hairball in *its* stomach.
6. "Where did you put *my* jacket?" asked Mary.
7. Is that *you* in the photograph on the mantel, Joaquin?
8. Connie told Granddad that *she* would leave work early.
9. Ron didn't know the Hills, but *he* went to their party.
10. "*We* ran out of time," said Curt and his brother.

E. Compound Personal Pronouns Number your paper from 1 to 10. Beside each number write a correct compound personal pronoun for each of the following sentences. After it, write the noun or pronoun to which it refers.

1. The fugitives finally turned (pronoun) in.

2. You security guards must protect (pronoun), too.
3. Noah (pronoun) couldn't have built a better boat.
4. You need some time to (pronoun), Margaret.
5. The forms (pronoun) were not complicated.
6. Thunder (pronoun) is not dangerous.
7. I (pronoun) installed our telephone.
8. Ted bought (pronoun) the game.
9. Carolyn and June taught (pronoun) to drive.
10. We talked (pronoun) into it.

F. Different Kinds of Pronouns Number your paper from 1 to 10. Write all the pronouns in each sentence. After each pronoun, write *Indefinite, Demonstrative,* or *Interrogative* to show what kind it is.

1. That is the post office across the street.
2. These are sunflower seeds.
3. Either of those will be suitable.
4. Somebody might be able to use this.
5. Who is being evicted?
6. For whom does the bell toll?
7. Whose are the charcoal sketches?
8. Everyone asked if Mitchell needed anything.
9. That is not ripe yet; pick another.
10. Which of these is the dead battery?

G. Indefinite Pronouns Number your paper from 1 to 10. For each sentence write the indefinite pronoun. Write the possessive pronoun or phrase that agrees with it from those given in parentheses.

1. Everyone brought (his or her, their) own lunch.
2. One of the grocery stores closed (its, their) deli counter.
3. Each of the workers received (his, their) pay in cash.

487

4. All of the players had (his, their) own agents.

5. Most of the seniors plan (his or her, their) schedules
   themselves.

6. None of the forest had lost (its, their) enchanted look.

7. None of the programs had lost (its, their) funding.

8. Someone left (his or her, their) book.

9. Everything was still in (its, their) original container.

10. Few of the packages had lost (its, their) labels.

H. Special Pronoun Problems Choose the correct word
from the two given in parentheses.

1. (We, Us) waitresses can't wear (them, those) tight
   shoes.

2. (It's, Its) going to rain.

3. (Who, Whom) is the scout watching?

4. (Who, Whom) notices (we, us) busboys?

5. (We, Us) farmers buy a lot of food, too.

6. (Who's, Whose) shaking (those, them) castanets?

7. (You're, Your) getting in (you're, your) own way.

8. (Who, Whom) suspects (we, us) stock clerks?

9. (Who, Whom) should we send (you're, your) bill to?

10. (They're, Their) sure (they're, their) dog can find (it's,
    its) way home.

MIXED REVIEW

Using Pronouns

A. Using personal pronouns Write the correct pronoun for each of the following sentences. After each one write its antecedent.

1. The patient talks with the help of (him, his) computer.
2. The game today was (you, your, yours) best one ever, men.
3. Is the time sheet on the desk (you, your, yours), Loretta?
4. Chandra said, "Elizabeth has told (I, me) already, Judy."
5. "The operator on duty was (I, me), not George," said Mr. Vigoda.
6. Carl read the chapters and outlined the ideas in (it, them, they).
7. A cat can usually find (it, its, their) way home.
8. After several delays, Fran and Nat got (their, they) orders.
9. Amy pointed at Kay and asked, "Wasn't (her, she) on first base?"
10. On windy days, sand blows into the doors' locks. (Them, They, Their) become jammed.

B. Using compound pronouns and pronouns in compound parts correctly Some of the following sentences use pronouns incorrectly. Rewrite correctly any sentences that do. If a sentence is correct, write *Correct*.

1. Suzi and me moved the piano by ourselves.
2. Harry himself invited Leila and me to his party.
3. Weren't Rachel and him only joking?
4. Is something wrong between Mae and him?

5. Chrissy and she were standing by themself.
6. Did you and her find yourselves a ride?
7. The attendants and them checked the garage.
8. I myself gave Hendricks and they the directions.
9. Are the bridesmaids Joyce and she?
10. Us and the other tenants alerted Sheldon and them.

C. Using the correct form of pronouns   Write the correct pronoun from those given in parentheses.

1. (This, That, These, Those) are the class lists right here.
2. (This, That, These, Those) was yesterday.
3. (Who, Whose) is the blue nylon jacket?
4. (Who, Whose) is the owner of the blue nylon jacket?
5. All of the census takers carried (his or her, their) identification.
6. All of the lumber was on (its, their) way to the sawmill.
7. Neither of the referees had (his, their) eye on Jim.
8. Each of the students brought (his or her, their) schedule.
9. Both of the library books are missing (its, their) cards.
10. Nobody should put (her, their) purse down in a store.

D. Using pronouns correctly   Write the correct pronoun.

1. (Us, We) seniors had a separate assembly.
2. Maybe (your, you're) trying too hard.
3. (Who, Whom) brought the Lionel Richie album?
4. Put ointment on (them, those) mosquito bites.
5. (Their, They're) renting skates.
6. (Who's, Whose) lunch tray is that?
7. (Its, It's) very stuffy in the attic.
8. Kenny picked up the box and read (its, it's) label.
9. (Who, Whom) did Ms. Parks interview?
10. Can otters swim on (their, they're) backs?

USING GRAMMAR IN WRITING
Using Pronouns

A. Suppose that students from your school have performed in a variety show to raise funds for charity. The only scheduled performance of the show sold out. Since it was such a hit, the group has decided to give a second performance next month. Write a short article about the show that could be used as a press release to get publicity for the second performance. Write about the students who participated in the show. Include at least five pronouns in your article. When you have finished the article, list the pronouns and their antecedents.

B. Compound personal pronouns are especially useful when you want to emphasize that a person or group is doing something on its own. Imagine that you are part of a group of friends who have to divide a job among them. You might be deciding how to share chores at a camp or jobs at a fund-raising car wash. Write a conversation that you might have as you divide the chores among you. Use compound personal pronouns to emphasize what person or group will be doing each chore. Underline each compound personal pronoun.

C. Newspaper editorials are often addressed to the population as a whole or to the "average" person. Because that is so, indefinite pronouns play an important role in editorials. Write an editorial, for your school paper or for a local paper, about the responsibilities of drivers or pedestrians. Use at least five indefinite pronouns in your editorial. Underline each indefinite pronoun.

Using
Verbs

There is one kind of word that every sentence must have. It is the verb. The verb brings a sentence to life. Without a verb, a sentence would not exist.

In **Handbook Section 1** you found out how to recognize verbs. In this section you will discover more about verbs and how they are used.

Part 1 What Is a Verb?

A verb tells of an action or a state of being.

Action Verbs

Some verbs indicate action, even if the action is unseen.

Christy *listens*.   The Phillies *lost*.
A shark *surfaced*.   The crew *waited*.

An action verb tells that something is happening, has happened, or will happen.

Linking Verbs

Some verbs simply tell that something exists. Such verbs express a state of being rather than action.

My watch *is* wrong.   These footprints *are* a clue.
This room *seems* stuffy.   The chocolate *tastes* bitter.

These verbs are called **linking verbs.** They link the subject with some other word or words in the sentence.
The most common linking verbs are these:

be (am, are, is, was,	look	smell	seem
were, been, being)	appear	taste	sound
become	feel	grow	

Certain words can be used as linking verbs and can also be used as action verbs.

Linking Verb	**Action Verb**
The call *sounded* urgent.	Someone *sounded* the alarm.
My sister and I *look* alike.	Observers *look* through a telescope.

After you have found the verb in a sentence, see how it is used. Decide whether it expresses action or simply links the subject with a word in the predicate.

Transitive and Intransitive Verbs

In many sentences an action verb expresses an idea by itself. In other sentences a direct object completes the action of the verb. As you have learned, the direct object answers *whom* or *what* after the verb.

A verb that has a direct object is a **transitive verb.**

> The FBI agent *opened* the *letter.*
> (The direct object *letter* completes the meaning of the verb *opened.*)
> WNTH *broadcasts* humorous *plays.*
> (The direct object *plays* completes the meaning of the verb *broadcasts.*)

A verb that does not have a direct object is an **intransitive verb.**

> The cars *collided.*
> (The verb *collided* has no direct object.)
> My wallet *sank* into the mud.
> (The verb *sank* has no direct object.)

Some action verbs are always transitive or always intransitive. Other verbs can be either. A verb may be transitive in one sentence and intransitive in another. Compare these examples.

Transitive Verbs	Intransitive Verb
I *noticed* your haircut.	No one *noticed.*
The band *ended* its concert.	The movie *ended* happily.
The horse *kicked* its trainer.	The baby *kicked* furiously.

Exercise A   Write the verb in each sentence. After each verb, write *Action* or *Linking* to show what kind it is.

1. Megan removed the old paint.

2. A virus causes plantar warts.
3. The prairie dog village covered four acres.
4. Joan looked in the closet.
5. Harvey tasted the sauce.
6. The sauce tasted too salty.
7. The water looked deep.
8. Monday was my birthday.
9. He is sleepy.
10. The snow was melting.

Exercise B   Follow the directions for Exercise A.

1. The sky grew dark.
2. Darrell grew herbs on the windowsill.
3. We watched the pressure gauge.
4. Water is expensive in southern California.
5. The radiators feel cold.
6. The nurse felt Jan's swollen wrist.
7. Did you see that motorcycle?
8. Are you an officer?
9. Mitch sounded glum.
10. Debbie sounded the fire alarm.

Exercise C   Write the action verb in each sentence. After it write *Transitive* or *Intransitive* to show what kind it is.

1. Has the snow stopped?
2. The brakes squealed.
3. A beached whale's weight can crush its lungs.
4. Something glittered at the bottom of the pool.
5. We played electronic football.
6. Scrub the pan with steel wool.
7. Don't worry about anything.
8. The plane lost an engine.
9. Did anyone help you?
10. Ted bought an ant farm for his niece.

Part 2　Parts of a Verb

Verbs often have more than one part. They may be made up of a **main verb** plus one or more **helping verbs.**

The most common helping verbs are forms of *be, have,* and *do.* They may also be used as main verbs. Notice their forms.

> be—am, is, are, was, were, been, be
> have—has, have, had
> do—does, do, did

Used as Main Verb	Used as Helping Verb
Sue *is* sorry.	Sue *is* talking on the phone.
Bill *has* many friends.	Bill *has* worked as a stuntman.
You *did* me a favor.	You *did* win the election.

These are other frequently used helping verbs.

can	will	shall	may	must
could	would	should	might	

Helping verbs combine with the main verb to become parts of the verb.

Helping Verb(s) + Main Verb = Verb

must	allow	must allow
should have	known	should have known
had	skated	had skated
will be	arriving	will be arriving

At times the parts of the verb are separated. The words that come between them are not part of the verb. For example:

> *Do* you *want* more syrup on your pancakes?
> Eric *has* just recently *begun* junior college.
> They *are* not *sitting* beside me.

As you can see from the last example, negatives such as *not,* or *never,* are not part of the verb. Neither is a negative contraction.

> They *couldn*'t *find* their way home.

Exercise A Make two columns. Label them *Helping Verb* and *Main Verb*. Write the parts of the verbs in the proper columns.

1. That class has been cancelled.
2. Can you help me?
3. Nan will draw a map.
4. I might make some vegetable soup.
5. Somebody should have told the shop steward.
6. Nobody could run that fast.
7. Caesar had not been listening to the radio.
8. The fish were biting.
9. The ice had melted.
10. May I see that newspaper?

Exercise B Follow the directions for Exercise A.

1. Wilma might have noticed something.
2. Martin has been telling us about his car.
3. I am teaching myself.
4. You should have used transistor batteries.
5. Marilyn was whistling a happy tune.
6. Did all the doctors agree?
7. Their overalls were spattered with paint.
8. Has the pork been cooked long enough?
9. When was the phone disconnected?
10. Would anyone else have agreed to such a ridiculous plan?

Part 3 Tenses of a Verb

Verbs indicate time. They tell when an action or state of being occurs. By changing form, verbs can show past time, present time, or future time.

Changes in the form of verbs to show time are called **tenses.** Forms usually change in one of two ways:

1. Different spellings

   cry—cried   spin—spun   pull—pulled

2. Use of helping verbs

   will work   has worked   had worked

This list shows examples of the six main tenses for the verbs *dance* and *stop*.

Present Tense	I dance.	She stops.
Past Tense	I danced.	She stopped.
Future Tense	I will dance.	She will stop.
Present Perfect Tense	I have danced.	She has stopped.
Past Perfect Tense	I had danced.	She had stopped.
Future Perfect Tense	I will have danced.	She will have stopped.

Simple Tenses

The **present tense** shows time in the present. The form of the present tense is usually the same as the name of the verb. With singular subjects, other than *I* and *you*, add -*s* to the verb.

I *swim*.   You *swim*.   Leslie *swims*.   My brother *swims*.

The **past tense** shows past time. To form the past tense of most verbs, add -*d* or -*ed*.

She *worked*.   Bob *agreed*.   They *acted*.

A number of verbs form the past tense in unusual ways.

Kevin *drove*.   The choir *sang*.   The room *shook*.

The **future tense** indicates time in the future. To form this tense, use *shall* or *will* with the verb.

The players *will rest*.   Don *will know*.
I *shall demand* an answer.

The three tenses described above are called the **simple tenses**.

Perfect Tenses

You use **perfect tenses** when you refer to two different times, one earlier than the other. The helping verbs *has, have,* and *had* are used to form the perfect tenses.

The **present perfect tense** tells of something ocurring in some indefinite time before the present. The helping verb *has* or *have* is used in present perfect tense.

> Kim and Ann *have met.*   Bo *has placed* in the finals.
> The judge *has decided.*   We *have baked* muffins.

The **past perfect tense** tells of a time that occurred before another time in the past. The helping verb *had* is used.

> Megan *had guessed* our names even before she *met* us.
> Rod *had brought* the albums that Neil *played.*

The **future perfect tense** tells of some time in the future occurring *before* a different time in the future.

> By the time Sally is twenty, she *will have finished* nurse's training.
> The waves *will have worn* away this land before the sea wall can be built.

Exercise A   Find the verbs. Tell the tense of each.

1. She had accepted the nomination by the end of the discussion.
2. Dave had a good suggestion.
3. We buy our groceries there.
4. Every day there are thousands more people on earth.
5. Terry pitched the ball.
6. By then we will have graduated.
7. Lisa will adjust the stereo.
8. The band had already left.
9. Ruth was the captain.
10. Steve plays hockey.

Exercise B: Writing Write a sentence for each of these verbs.

1. gulp (past)
2. stroll (present)
3. salute (past)
4. watch (future)
5. close (past perfect)

6. dance (present perfect)
7. sing (present)
8. delay (future)
9. finish (future perfect)
10. talk (past perfect)

Part 4   Principal Parts of a Verb

The **principal parts** of a verb are its three basic forms. By combining these forms with various helping verbs, you can make all tenses. The principal parts of a verb are the **present tense,** the **past tense,** and the **past participle.** You will usually find them listed in that order.

The past tense and past participle of most verbs are formed by adding -*d* or -*ed* to the present form. These verbs are called **regular verbs.** They form their past tense and past participle in regular ways.

Present	Past	Past Participle
walk	walked	(have) walked
play	played	(have) played
move	moved	(have) moved

Certain regular verbs change their spelling when the -*d* or -*ed* is added. The following verbs are examples.

Present	Past	Past Participle
pay	paid	(have) paid
rip	ripped	(have) ripped
carry	carried	(have) carried
flip	flipped	(have) flipped

The past participle is used for perfect tenses. It must always be used with a helping verb.

The mourners *had cried.*   Dale *has lost* weight.
My jeans *have faded.*   The Cubs *have rallied.*

Exercise Label three columns *Present, Past,* and *Past Participle.*
List the principal parts of these verbs in the proper columns.

1. save
2. march
3. crash
4. start
5. dress
6. type
7. hurry
8. play
9. greet
10. stamp
11. whisper
12. name
13. hope
14. invite
15. groan

Part 5 Irregular Verbs

You have learned the principal parts for regular verbs. However, many verbs do not follow the regular pattern of adding *-d* or *-ed* to form the past tense and past participle. Such verbs are called **irregular verbs**. Here are some examples.

Present	Past	Past Participle
fall	fell	(have) fallen
make	made	(have) made
buy	bought	(have) bought
read	read	(have) read
go	went	(have) gone

As you see, irregular verbs have one or more different forms.
Use a dictionary if you need to know the principal parts of a verb. If the dictionary doesn't list parts, then the verb is regular. For irregular verbs, the dictionary will list the irregular forms. It will give two forms if both the past and past participle are the same, as in *meet, met,* for instance. If all principal parts are different, it will give three forms, as with *take, took, taken.*

Using Irregular Verbs

You can be sure of the forms of an irregular verb in one of two ways. You can check the parts of a verb in the dictionary. Otherwise, you will have to learn the principal parts of commonly used irregular verbs.

Once you know the principal parts, use them correctly. Use the past participle with *have* and *be* helping verbs. The past participle is used for the present perfect and past perfect tenses. The past form is not used with helping verbs.

Although irregular verbs may seem confusing, they may seem simpler when you study the following patterns.

Group 1 Certain irregular verbs keep the same form for all three principal parts. Verbs like this are easy to remember.

Present	Past	Past Participle
burst	burst	(have) burst
cost	cost	(have) cost
cut	cut	(have) cut
let	let	(have) let
put	put	(have) put
set	set	(have) set

These sentences use irregular verbs from this group.

> Every morning, we *let* the dog out. (present)
> That new coat *cost* Gary half of his paycheck. (past)
> The hypnotist *has put* Olivia to sleep. (past participle)

Group 2 Some irregular verbs change form only once. Both the past form and the past participle are the same.

Present	Past	Past Participle
bring	brought	(have) brought
catch	caught	(have) caught
lead	led	(have) led
lend	lent	(have) lent
lose	lost	(have) lost
say	said	(have) said
sit	sat	(have) sat

Here are some sentences using irregular verbs from Group 2.

> The tests *say* the suspect is lying. (present)
> On that play, Oakland *lost* control of the ball. (past)
> An octopus *was caught* in the fishing nets. (past participle)

Exercise A Choose the correct form of the verb.

1. The bride's family (sat, sitted) in the front pew.
2. We have not (losed, lost) the game yet.
3. Gene has (sayed, said) enough.
4. The dog (leaded, led) the blind woman across the street.
5. I have (putted, put) my winter coat away.
6. The water main had (bursted, burst).
7. No charges have been (brought, brung).
8. She (letted, let) down the hem of the skirt.
9. Ms. Natti (lent, lended) us her tape recorder.
10. The fines will have (cost, costed) more than the book.

Exercise B Follow the directions for Exercise A.

1. The boss (letted, let) Sam leave early.
2. A pair of footprints (leaded, led) to the window.
3. The warm air (bringed, brought) rain.
4. Jack (caught, catched) the express bus.
5. Karen (sayed, said) nothing.
6. We (sitted, sat) on the floor.
7. The driver had (lost, losted) her way in the fog.
8. Gwen jumped and (catched, caught) the ball.
9. A few items (costed, cost) more in the 1950's.
10. Harry (lended, lent) me his dictionary.

Group 3 Verbs in this group add *-n* or *-en* to the past tense to form the past participle.

Present	Past	Past Participle
break	broke	(have) broken
choose	chose	(have) chosen
freeze	froze	(have) frozen
speak	spoke	(have) spoken
steal	stole	(have) stolen
wear	wore	(have) worn

These three sentences have Group 3 verbs.

Many construction workers *wear* hard hats. (present)
Berger *stole* third base. (past)
Cass's fishing line *has broken*. (past participle)

Exercise A Choose the correct form of the verb from the two forms given.

1. Tara has (chose, chosen) to stay home.
2. The ushers (wore, worn) bow ties.
3. The burglar (stole, stolen) the television.
4. The skater didn't realize he had (broke, broken) his ankle.
5. Someone had (stole, stolen) the equipment.
6. Walter Payton (spoke, spoken) to the students.
7. Pete has (wore, worn) his favorite shirt today.
8. The ice cream has not yet (froze, frozen).
9. The caseworker had never (spoke, spoken) with her before.
10. The dancer had (wore, worn) out another pair of shoes.

Exercise B Follow the directions for Exercise A.

1. The stranger (stole, stolen) quietly away.
2. The smaller army should have (chose, chosen) to retreat.
3. The windows were (froze, frozen) shut.
4. The springs have (wore, worn) out.
5. Elliot (spoke, spoken) without looking up.
6. Someone had (stole, stolen) their savings.
7. The splinter had (broke, broken) as she was prying it out.
8. I have (spoke, spoken) my last words on the subject.
9. Frank (froze, frozen) some of the spaghetti sauce.
10. One of the trappers (chose, chosen) to continue west.

Group 4 In this group, the verbs change their final vowels. The vowel changes from *i* in the present tense, to *a* in the past tense, and *u* in the past participle.

Present	Past	Past Participle
begin	began	(have) begun
drink	drank	(have) drunk
ring	rang	(have) rung
sing	sang	(have) sung

Here are examples of irregular verbs from Group 4.

> I *drink* coffee with breakfast. (present)
> Bette Midler *sang* her new hit. (past)
> The Passover service *has begun*. (past participle)

Exercise A   Choose the correct verb form.

1. I (drank, drunk) fresh orange juice in Florida.
2. Linda Ronstadt (sang, sung) an old song.
3. I have just (began, begun) to cook the chicken.
4. The meter reader (rang, rung) the doorbell.
5. Gary (began, begun) to think about his future.
6. Ms. Ramirez has (swam, swum) in Sand Lake.
7. Summer has finally (began, begun).
8. The telephone has not (rang, rung) once all day.
9. The group has (sang, sung) in that club before.
10. Natalie (swam, swum) across the pool underwater.

Exercise B   Follow the directions for Exercise A.

1. A shark (swam, swum) close to the boat.
2. Who (sang, sung) "Nine to Five"?
3. The patient (began, begun) coughing.
4. The woods (rang, rung) with birds' songs.
5. Maria has (rang, rung) up another victory.
6. The dog (drank, drunk) the rainwater.
7. Ernestine has (began, begun) basic training.

8. This medicine can be (drank, drunk) in juice.
9. The basketball game had (began, begun) at eight o'clock.
10. We have not (swam, swum) in the Potomac for years.

Group 5 Irregular verbs in this group form the past participle from the present tense. The past participle looks more like the present tense than the past tense.

Present	Past	Past Participle
come	came	(have) come
do	did	(have) done
eat	ate	(have) eaten
fall	fell	(have) fallen
give	gave	(have) given
go	went	(have) gone
grow	grew	(have) grown
know	knew	(have) known
ride	rode	(have) ridden
run	ran	(have) run
see	saw	(have) seen
take	took	(have) taken
throw	threw	(have) thrown
write	wrote	(have) written

These examples use Group 5 verbs.

The Coopers *run* a laundry. (present)
Darnell *grew* a full beard. (past)
The coach *has taken* Robin out of the game. (past participle)

Exercise A Choose the correct verb form from the two given.

1. Have you ever (ate, eaten) homemade ravioli?
2. He had (grew, grown) tired of waiting.
3. The rescue party had almost (gave, given) up hope.
4. Ten inches of snow had (fell, fallen) overnight.
5. We (ran, run) for shelter.
6. Wendy (rode, ridden) part of the way.

7. Jay (wrote, written) the message on the telephone book.
8. We (ate, eaten) lunch standing up.
9. Eileen has (rode, ridden) the world's largest roller coaster.
10. Claire (knew, known) she was right.

Exercise B Follow the directions for Exercise A.

1. Chrissy (saw, seen) that Jason was upset.
2. Dion (did, done) his homework before work.
3. The truck had (went, gone).
4. I have already (took, taken) that course.
5. The news had not (came, come) as a surprise.
6. The temperature had (fell, fallen) quickly.
7. Jody (threw, thrown) salt on the icy sidewalk.
8. The typists (gone, went) back to work.
9. The carpenter had (wrote, written) down the measurements.
10. The horse had never (ran, run) on a muddy track.

Part 6 Active and Passive Verbs

You have seen how the tenses of verbs indicate time. There is another way that verbs help you say exactly what you mean.

Let's look at an example. Suppose there is a fire, and you know who controlled it. You can say:

Forest rangers controlled the fire.

However, you might not know who controlled the fire. Then you would probably say:

The fire was controlled.

The subject of the first sentence tells who performed the action. When a subject performs the action of the verb, the verb is said to be active.

In contrast, the subject of the second sentence tells what received the action. When the subject is the receiver or the result of the action, the verb is said to be passive. The word *passive* means "acted upon."

Forming the Passive

The passive form of a verb is made with the past participle. A form of *be* is the helping verb.

Active	Passive
Dr. Chang *put* Lee's arm in a cast.	Lee's arm *was put* in a cast by Dr. Chang.
Mike's boss *has promoted* him to assistant manager.	Mike *has been promoted* to assistant manager by his boss.
Terry and Margaret *have saved* all receipts.	All receipts *have been saved* by Terry and Margaret.

Notice what happens to the direct objects in the sentences in the *Active* column above. Those direct objects become the subjects of the sentences in the *Passive* column. Only verbs that have objects (transitive verbs) can be changed from active to passive.

A verb is active when its subject performs the action stated by the verb.

A verb is passive when its subject names the receiver or result of the action stated by the verb.

Exercise A Write the verb in each sentence. After each, write *Active* or *Passive* to tell what kind it is.

1. The privates saluted the officer.
2. War was declared by Congress.
3. Jamal added pepper sauce to the stew.
4. The petition was signed by seventy people.

5. Scuba divers use a form of sign language.
6. The referee started the count.
7. Gina made a storage shed under the porch.
8. A silver trophy was presented to Tracey.
9. The decision was upheld by a higher court.
10. Take the flag down at sunset.

Exercise B: Writing   Change the verbs in the following sentences from passive to active. Rewrite the sentences.

1. The stock car was driven by Neal.
2. Some posters will be done by Anita.
3. The school's new name was chosen by the students.
4. The horn was played by Angela.
5. The explorers were led by Father Marquette.
6. The fat was trimmed off by the butcher.
7. All shop projects must be approved by Mr. Morales.
8. A tree was planted by the block club.
9. The telephone had been taken off the hook by someone.
10. Electrical power had been cut off by the storm.

ADDITIONAL EXERCISES

Using Verbs

A. Verbs Label three columns *Transitive, Intransitive,* and *Linking.* Number your paper from 1 to 10. Find the verb in each of the following sentences. Write the verb in the proper column.

1. The shadow of the picket fence fell across the broken sidewalk.
2. Simon is afraid of heights.
3. A computer prepares the bills.
4. Dan sent her some roses for her birthday.
5. Horror movies are artistic sometimes.
6. Your car definitely needs oil.
7. The motorcycle skidded dangerously.
8. She carried the basket of laundry on her head.
9. The new moon looked delicate.
10. Spencer looked at the firefly in his hand.

B. Helping Verbs and Main Verbs Label two columns *Helping Verbs* and *Main Verbs.* Find all the parts of the verb. Write them in the proper columns.

1. Mary will be the driver.
2. Have you ever wired a lamp?
3. The miner could barely stand in the tunnel.
4. Willie may have already left for school.
5. Something must be bothering Maureen.
6. Val has been watching the clock all day.
7. Did Caroline buy a car?
8. Where have you worked before?
9. How does Hector find time for guitar lessons and piano lessons?
10. Her arm had been badly injured.

C. Verb Tenses Write each verb and its tense.

1. The nurse pulled the bandage off quickly.
2. I had turned the pockets inside out beforehand.
3. By then, the party will have ended.
4. She remembers all her grandchildren's birthdays.
5. You will get a ticket for that U-turn.
6. Spies sometimes have false identities.
7. The snow has stopped.
8. Spices will lose some of their flavor in a few months.
9. By his tenth birthday, David had lived in four countries.
10. Stacey had no credit cards.

D. Principal Parts of the Verb Make three columns on your paper. Label them *Present, Past,* and *Past Participle.* List the principal parts of these verbs in the proper columns.

1. zip	6. glitter	11. kick
2. hike	7. mention	12. fry
3. spill	8. wash	13. grin
4. giggle	9. work	14. wonder
5. wince	10. tighten	15. add

E. Irregular Verbs: Group 1 and Group 2 Choose the correct verb from those in parentheses.

1. Linda (sitted, sat) on the radiator.
2. The reporter (catched, caught) the politician at a bad time.
3. The car's upkeep has (costed, cost) Ann a lot.
4. Michael (letted, let) his sideburns grow.
5. The Warrens have (broughted, brung, brought) their grill to the park.
6. The new guide (leaded, led) us right into a swamp.
7. Her balloon had (bursted, burst).
8. Which barber (cutted, cut) your hair?

9. Sam (sayed, said, saided) that he had (setted, set) the table.
10. She (losed, lost) the umbrella that I had (lended, lent) her.

'F. Irregular Verbs: Group 3 Choose the correct verb from those in parentheses.

1. The slush had (froze, frozen) on the sidewalks.
2. Maybe Hank (spoke, spoken) too soon.
3. The family had (spoke, spoken) only Spanish at home.
4. The knees of the jeans (wore, worn) out first.
5. The rock had (broke, broken) the windshield.
6. Amy has (choose, chosen) challenging courses.
7. The thief had (stole, stolen) the watchdog.
8. A nail had (wore, worn) through the sole of the shoe.
9. Sammie almost (froze, frozen, freezed) waiting for the bus.
10. The boiler (breaked, broke, broked); it couldn't have (choosed, chose, chosen) a worse time.

G. Irregular Verbs: Group 4 Choose the correct verb from those in parentheses.

1. The graduation parties (began, begun) in May.
2. He (rang, rung) the little silver dinner bell.
3. Have you ever (drank, drunk) fresh coconut milk?
4. The congregation (sang, sung) the minister's favorite hymn.
5. For once, the school play had (began, begun) on time.
6. Shelia had (swam, swum) into a thicket of water reeds.
7. The sergeant (sang, sung) out the orders.
8. The door-to-door saleswoman had (rang, rung) her last doorbell of the day.
9. The cat (drank, drunk) from the goldfish bowl.
10. Has Keith ever (sang, sung) without accompaniment?

H. Irregular Verbs: Group 5 Choose the correct verb from those in parentheses.

1. Al has (wrote, written) new lyrics.
2. The hurricane (did, done) a lot of damage.
3. Herman might have (ran, run) into some problems.
4. Mice had (ate, eaten) through the wrapper.
5. His sister has (gave, given) him good advice.
6. Geraldine (threw, thrown) baking soda onto the grease fire.
7. He (knew, knowed) that he should say something.
8. The car (went, gone) right through the store window.
9. Shirley (saw, seen) an empty seat in the front row.
10. Have you ever (took, taken) a ride in a sailboat?

I. Active and Passive Verbs Change the verbs in the following sentences from passive to active. Rewrite the sentences.

1. The coleslaw was made by Simon.
2. The tractor was driven by Jessica.
3. After the heavy snow, streets were plowed by garbage trucks.
4. The denim skirt was bought by Eileen.
5. *You Can't Keep a Good Woman Down* was written by Alice Walker.
6. The diner was converted from an old railway car by the owner.
7. A neighborhood patrol was started by Ms. Hayes and Mr. Link.
8. Artis Gilmore was traded by the Bulls to San Antonio in 1982.
9. The mail was delivered by a substitute carrier today.
10. My check was cashed by the currency exchange on the corner.

MIXED REVIEW

Using Verbs

A. Finding action verbs and linking verbs Write the verbs from each sentence. Next, write whether they are *Action Verbs* or *Linking Verbs*. If a verb is an action verb, write whether it is *Transitive* or *Intransitive*.

1. The spotlights are too dim.
2. The glossary at the back of the book will define that word.
3. Connie attached a graph to her report.
4. Maria whistled sharply for her dog.
5. The wind blew throughout the night.
6. Is your sister still a news editor?
7. The audience grew restless during the delay.
8. Is Barney a basketball player?
9. Does Tanya play volleyball?
10. Is the top of the convertible stuck again?

B. Helping verbs and main verbs Label two columns on your paper *Helping Verbs* and *Main Verbs*. Fill in the proper parts from each of the following sentences.

1. Something is bothering Antoine.
2. The voters were waiting at the polls.
3. The team will eventually recover from this slump.
4. The code has probably been cracked.
5. Judy has always been a football fan.
6. Many accidents could be avoided.
7. Does the apartment have a separate entrance?
8. Wouldn't you have done the same thing?
9. Maybe Stephanie was not listening.
10. Can anybody ever really understand another person?

C. Using verb forms correctly

Write each of the following sentences, using the verb and the verb form given in parentheses.

> EXAMPLE: The potatoes in the cellar (*freeze*, past).
> The potatoes in the cellar froze.

1. The bus (*come*, present) on time.
2. Nervously, Adam (*begin*, past).
3. A pattern (*form*, past) on the screen.
4. Mollie (*see*, past perfect) the Statue of Liberty.
5. The firefighters (*break*, present perfect) down the steel door.
6. By then, the library fines (*cost*, future perfect) more than the book.
7. Somebody (*steal*, past) the ornament from the car's hood.
8. Andre Crouch (*sing*, past) at the services.
9. A passenger (*lose*, past perfect) his ticket.
10. The others (*go*, present perfect) without us.

D. Recognizing active and passive verbs

Write down the verb in each sentence. Then write *Active* or *Passive* to tell what kind it is. Finally rewrite each sentence. Change each active verb to a passive verb and each passive verb to an active verb.

1. The icicles were melted by the sun.
2. Surprise caught Amy.
3. Emotion choked John's voice.
4. This station is listened to by most students.
5. Diesel fuel is used by this engine.
6. A club scrapbook was kept by Gina.
7. General Electric brought you this special.
8. The ball was passed by Bill.
9. The police questioned the suspect.
10. Lynn's wallet was found by an honest man.

USING GRAMMAR IN WRITING
Using Verbs

A. Think about an athlete whose abilities you especially admire. Either picture the athlete in your mind or actually watch the athlete in action. Take notes on his or her actions. Write a paragraph that shows how good this athlete is. You might concentrate on a key play in a game that shows his or her abilities. Or you might use many examples from several games or matches. Verbs will be very important to your description. Use vivid verbs that capture the speed, grace, or power of the athlete's actions.

B. You are writing an article for a popular magazine. Your topic will be popular music. Write your article in three parts.

First, write a paragraph about one specific aspect of popular music in the past. You might write about one performer, one popular song, or one type of song. If you can, do some research for this part of the essay. Use past tenses for the verbs in this paragraph.

Next, write a paragraph about one specific aspect of popular music today. Use present tenses for the verbs in this paragraph.

Finally, write a paragraph predicting what one specific aspect of popular music will be like in the future. Use future tenses for the verbs in this paragraph.

Using Modifiers

Imagine trying to tell about your home or your job by using only nouns, pronouns, and verbs. Nouns and pronouns name. Verbs show action or state of being.

> We live in an apartment.   I am a typist.

You can see, however, that these words are not enough to express much information. You need to use other words that describe these names and actions.

> We have *always* lived in *this small, cozy* apartment.
> *Fortunately*, I am a *full-time* typist with a *flexible* schedule.

The differences in these two sets of examples result from the use of modifiers. Modifiers are words that modify, or change, other words.

Besides describing, modifiers can also help you to explain and express feeling.

> I accept your invitation.

> I *gratefully* accept your *thoughtful* invitation.

If you didn't use modifiers, your writing would seem empty and dull. By using modifiers, you can express precise ideas. In this section you will learn to recognize and use the two kinds of modifiers.

Part 1 Using Adjectives

One kind of modifier is an **adjective.**

An adjective is a word that modifies a noun or pronoun.

Adjectives can tell three different kinds of things about nouns or pronouns.

Which one or ones?

this studio, *that* streetlight, *those* machines, *these* cars

What kind?

loud music, *soft* pillow, *sweet* drink, *cheerful* nurse

How many or how much?

four plants, *enough* food, *tremendous* joy, *few* fans

Proper Adjectives

One special kind of adjective is formed from a proper noun. It is a **proper adjective.**

Proper adjectives refer to specific persons, places, or things. They are always capitalized. For example:

Swiss cheese   the Jewish religion
A Republican governor   French pastry

Predicate Adjectives

A second kind of adjective is the predicate adjective.
Most adjectives come before the words they modify.

Sweet, soft tunes filled the studio.
(*Sweet* and *soft* modify *tunes*.)

The predicate adjective, though, comes after the noun or pronoun it modifies. A **predicate adjective** follows a linking verb and modifies the subject of the sentence.

Your T-shirt is *unusual*.
(*Unusual* modifies the subject, *T-shirt*.)

Everything looks *strange*.
(*Strange* modifies the subject, *everything*.)

Unusual and *strange* are predicate adjectives. They follow linking verbs, *is* and *looks*. Each one modifies the subject of the sentence.

Articles

Three special adjectives, *a*, *an*, and *the*, are called **articles.** *The* is called the **definite article.** It refers to a specific person, place, or thing.

The penalty went to *the* Vikings. (a particular penalty, a particular team)

A and *an* are called **indefinite articles.**

Please find *a* chair. (any chair)
Pam wants *an* ice cube. (any ice cube)

Notice that *a* is used before a consonant sound (*a cart, a field, a smile*). *An* is used before a vowel sound (*an oval, an area, an edge*). The sound, not the spelling, is important. We say *a hurry* but *an honest bid*, for instance.

Diagraming Adjectives

In a sentence diagram, an adjective appears below the word it modifies. It is placed on a slanted line.

All new members have special cards.

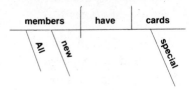

Predicate adjectives are diagramed in a different way. Like predicate nouns and pronouns, they are placed on the main line. Between the verb and the predicate adjective is a slanted line.

This melody sounds familiar.

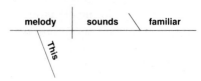

A compound predicate adjective is on a split line.

The chicken is tender and crispy.

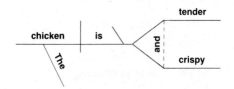

Exercise A Write each adjective. After each adjective, write the word it modifies. Ignore articles.

1. The Jaguar is a British car.
2. A former professional actress is coaching us.
3. Fresh corn, ripe tomatoes, and shiny cucumbers filled the basket.
4. Jeff rubbed some ointment on the sprain.
5. The new towel left green lint on everything.
6. The large goldfish was chasing the small one.
7. Most people think of cornbread as a Southern food.

8. Is there an American style of cooking?
9. There are many definitions of modern art.
10. He had wide cheekbones and a square chin.

Exercise B   Write the predicate adjectives in these sentences.

1. White canaries are rare.
2. Almond shells are soft.
3. Marsha seems forgetful today.
4. His excuse sounded sincere to me.
5. That pronunciation of *New Orleans* sounds French.
6. Most of the refugees were hungry and sick.
7. Are you nervous?
8. Does the engine sound good to you?
9. The first half of the game was slow and dull.
10. Quite suddenly the sky became golden.

Part 2   Adjectives in Comparisons

Frequently, you learn about new things through comparisons. You compare something new with what you already know. You might describe a car as "*smaller* that most compacts." Or you might refer to the new mayor as *more powerful* than the former mayor. Adjectives help you to make such comparisons.

The Comparative

Adjectives have special forms for expressing comparisons. If you are comparing one person or thing with another, use the **comparative** form of an adjective. Here are some examples.

This van is *smaller* than that one.
Which is the *better* job?
Recently, fuel has become much *more expensive*.

The comparative is made in two ways:

1. Add *-er* to short adjectives like *tall* and *sweet*.

> heavy + er = heavier   wise + er = wiser
> hot + er = hotter   tight + er = tighter

Notice that the spelling of some adjectives changes in the comparative form.

2. Use *more* for longer adjectives like *comfortable*.

> more reasonable   more sensible

The comparative of most adjectives ending in *-ful* or *-ous* is formed with *more*.

> more graceful   more ridiculous

The Superlative

If you are comparing a person or thing with all others in its class, use the **superlative** form of the adjective. Also, use the superlative for comparing a person or thing with two or more others. Here are some examples.

> The cheetah is the *fastest* animal of all.
> Of the three desserts, this pie is *highest* in calories.

Superlative forms of adjectives are made by adding either *-est* or by using *most*. Adjectives that add *-er* for the comparative add *-est* for the superlative. Adjectives that use *more* for the comparative use *most* for the superlative.

Adjective	Comparative	Superlative
bitter	more bitter	most bitter
new	newer	newest
hopeful	more hopeful	most hopeful
realistic	more realistic	most realistic

Keep the following three points in mind when you use comparison.

1. To compare two people or things, use the comparative. To compare more than two, use the superlative.

> The defense is *stronger* than the offense.
> Naomi told the *funniest* joke I've ever heard.

2. Use the word *other* when you compare something with everything else of its kind.

> Incorrect: Adams is harsher than any judge.
> (This sentence says that Adams is not a judge.)
> Correct: Adams is harsher than any *other* judge.

> Incorrect: This commercial is more clever than any on TV.
> Correct: This commercial is more clever than any *other* one on TV.

3. Do not use *-er* with *more*, or *-est* with *most*.

> Incorrect: This is the most dullest game of the season.
> Correct: This is the *dullest* game of the season.

Irregular Comparisons

Certain comparatives and superlatives are formed in unusual ways.

Adjective	Comparative	Superlative
bad	worse	worst
well	better	best
good	better	best
little	less or lesser	least
much	more	most
many	more	most
far	farther	farthest

Exercise A If a sentence is correct, write *Correct*. If it is incorrect, write it correctly.

1. Althea is the more ambitious of the three students.

2. This winter is worse than last winter was.

3. That was the baddest disaster in aviation history.

4. He can jump farrer than much taller contestants.

5. Rosa's argument is more reasonabler than Elizabeth's.

6. I bought the most warmest boots in the store.

7. Norma plays a gooder game than any other guard.

8. Cliff made more home runs than any person on the team.

9. Dan seems more efficienter than any other orderly.

10. Ms. Sydris is the better educated of the two candidates.

Exercise B   Follow the directions for Exercise A.

1. Your cold seems worser today.

2. Ted was more accurater than any other typist.

3. Solar energy costs littler than most other kinds.

4. That plaid is more cheerfuller than the other.

5. Bottled water is much more expensiver than tap water.

6. Copperheads are more dangerouser than black snakes.

7. That job offers more benefits but a smaller salary than the other.

8. The toboggan run is the bestest in New England.

9. The Bengal tiger had eight cubs, the most largest number ever born in captivity.

10. Chess is harder for me than any other game.

Part 3   Using Adverbs

Another kind of modifier is the adverb. With adverbs, you can express yourself clearly and vividly. Adverbs tell *how, when, where,* or *to what extent* about something.

Adverbs are words that modify verbs, adjectives, or other adverbs.

Using Adverbs with Verbs

Adverbs often modify verbs. Then they tell *how, when, where,* or *to what extent* something happened.

Adverbs tell *how* about verbs.

Sharon *confidently* faced the audience.

Al teetered *dangerously* on the rooftop.

Adverbs can tell *when* about verbs.

Dolores *finally* collapsed at the finish line.

Many employees have been fired *lately.*

Adverbs also tell *where* about verbs.

A rock concert will be held *here* next week.

Two birds flew *inside.*

Finally, adverbs can tell *to what extent.*

The blaze *almost* destroyed the nursing home.

Jeff could *barely* speak.

Study the following list of adverbs.

How?	When?	Where?	To What Extent?
terribly	soon	behind	barely
gloomily	then	there	not
heroically	afterward	around	nearly
slowly	recently	close	partly

Using Adverbs with Adjectives and Other Adverbs

In addition to modifying verbs, adverbs also modify adjectives and other adverbs. Look at the following sentences.

Business is *quite* brisk on weekends.
(*Quite* tells to what extent. It is an adverb modifying the adjective *brisk*.)

The trainer treated the animals *very* harshly.
(*Very* tells to what extent. It is an adverb modifying the adverb *harshly*.)

Certain adverbs often modify adjectives or other adverbs. Here are some examples.

too	rather	truly
extremely	so	more
fairly	most	just
nearly	really	somewhat

All these adverbs tell *to what extent* something is true.

Forming Adverbs

One way to form adverbs is to add *-ly* to adjectives.

serious + ly = seriously   usual + ly = usually
public + ly = publicly   direct + ly = directly

This addition of *-ly* sometimes results in a spelling change for the adjective.

simple + ly = simply   greedy + ly = greedily
full + ly = fully   angry + ly = angrily

A few adverbs are not formed from adjectives. Some examples are *just, too, so,* and *quite.*

That blues singer is *quite* good.
Matt put *too* much sauce on his sundae.

Some adverbs are also used as adjectives. Two examples of such words are *fast* and *low*.

The pit crews for the race cars moved *fast*.
(*Fast* is an adverb modifying the verb *moved*.)

David bought himself a *fast* car.
(*Fast* is an adjective modifying the noun *car*.)

During her spin, the skater crouched *low* on the ice.
(*Low* is an adverb modifying the verb *crouched*.)

Sara cleared the *low* hurdles easily.
(*Low* is an adjective modifying the noun *hurdle*.)

Diagraming Adverbs

Like an adjective, an adverb is placed on a slanted line. That line is attached to the word the adverb modifies. This diagram shows an adverb that modifies a verb.

The health department routinely inspects restaurants.

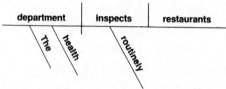

When adverbs modify adjectives or other adverbs, they are diagramed in this way:

Quite often Don wears very flashy clothes.

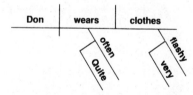

Exercise A Write the adverbs in these sentences. After each adverb write the word it modifies.

1. Suddenly the muffler fell off.
2. He works rather slowly.
3. She speaks clearly now.
4. Donna climbed down carefully.
5. The bus arrived very late.

6. The weather seems unusually cold today.
7. Hal smiled gently at his brother.
8. Finally the clerk looked up.
9. Strangers can be very kind sometimes.
10. The pressure rose too quickly.

Exercise B Follow the directions for Exercise A.

1. Sheldon always moves into the lead early.
2. Somewhere an alarm was whining shrilly.
3. Later Dwayne skated less cautiously.
4. Rarely has she insisted so firmly.
5. The engine started rather slowly this morning.
6. These bills have not been paid yet.
7. The soldiers cheered happily.
8. Janet soon became more serious.
9. I do not know a less tactful person than Pat.
10. Recently the city balanced its budget.

Exercise C: Writing Choose any five adverbs from Exercise B. Write new sentences, using these adverbs.

Part 4 Adverbs in Comparisons

Adverbs help you to compare actions. You might say, for instance, "I wake up early, but Abby wakes up *earlier*." Or you might say, "Of all the horses, this one runs *fastest*." With comparisons like these, you can express ideas clearly. Adverbs, like adjectives, have special forms for making comparisons.

The Comparative

For comparing one action with another, use the **comparative** form of an adverb.

This car rides *more smoothly* than that one.

Form the comparative in one of two ways.

1. Add -er to short adverbs like *hard* and *soon*.

   WBBM has been broadcasting *longer* than WLAK.

2. Use *more* with most adverbs ending in *-ly*.

   Gil does business *more honestly* than some other builders.

The Superlative

The **superlative** form of an adverb compares one action with two or more others. Here are some examples.

Of the three contenders, that boxer hits *most powerfully*.
The last dart came *closest* to the bull's-eye.

The superlative is formed either by adding -est or *most*. Adverbs that add -er for the comparative add -est for the superlative. Adverbs that use *more* for the comparative use *most* for the superlative.

Adverb	Comparative	Superlative
high	higher	highest
carefully	more carefully	most carefully
early	earlier	earliest

Remember the following points about adverbs in comparisons.

1. To compare two actions, use the comparative. To compare more than two actions, use the superlative.

Computers solve problems *more quickly* than people do.
Of all the snacks, the popcorn disappeared *most quickly*.

2. Use the word *other* when you compare with every other action of the same kind.

Incorrect: "Mean Max" plays more roughly than any football player.

Correct: "Mean Max" plays more roughly than any *other* football player.

3. Do not use -er with more, or -est with most.

Incorrect:	With a sledge hammer, you could hit more harder.
Correct:	With a sledge hammer, you could hit harder.

Irregular Comparisons

From the comparative to the superlative form, some adverbs change completely. Here are a few examples.

Adverb	Comparative	Superlative
little	less	least
much	more	most
well	better	best
far	farther	farthest

The old Camaro runs *well*.
The new Firebird runs *better*.
The Celica runs *best* on the open road.

Exercise A Write the comparative and superlative forms.

1. wildly	4. frequently	7. bravely	9. briefly
2. late	5. near	8. sharply	10. low
3. often	6. gladly		

Exercise B If a sentence is correct, write *Correct*. If there is an error in the comparison of adverbs, write the sentence correctly.

1. Handle the thermometer more carefullier.
2. A hammer works more simply than almost any tool.
3. Computerized laser beams cut fabric efficientlier than machines do.
4. The red kite soared more farther than the green one.
5. Sal will play her part less awkwardly after a few rehearsals.
6. Jackson draws the most skillfully of the two cartoonists.
7. Of the three drummers, Lynn plays best.

8. That turntable works the bestest of the four.
9. Few machines run more smoothlier than this one.
10. Maybe the crew will work more better after lunch.

Exercise C: Writing   Write new sentences using four of the comparative forms from Exercise A. Then write new sentences using four different superlatives, also from Exercise A.

Part 5   Adjective or Adverb?

When you read these sentences, which one sounds right?

> The outlaws fought *desperate.*
> The outlaws fought *desperately.*

You are correct if you said the second sentence. To modify the verb *fought,* an adverb (*desperately*) is needed.

At times you may be confused about whether to use an adjective or an adverb. To decide, ask yourself:

1. What kind of word does the modifier tell about?
   If your answer is an action verb, adjective, or adverb, use the adverb. If your answer is a noun or pronoun, use the adjective.
2. What does the modifier say about the word it goes with?
   If it tells *how, when, where,* or *to what extent,* use the adverb. If it tells *which one, what kind,* or *how many,* use the adjective.

An adjective tells	An adverb tells
Which one	How
What kind	When
How many	Where
	To what extent
About a noun or pronoun	About a verb, adjective, or adverb

Exercise A   List each adjective and adverb, together with the word each modifies. Do not list articles.

1. One acrobat leapt effortlessly into the air.
2. Many guests had dressed formally.
3. That bread is more nutritious than these rolls.
4. Several pushy starlings drove the hungry sparrow away.
5. Clumsy bulldozers lumbered past.
6. She shoveled the soft snow easily.
7. Finally the long, dreary play ended.
8. Suddenly the red light went on.
9. Tonight my best friend will get here.
10. The immediate future seems somewhat unpredictable.

Exercise B   Choose the correct modifier from the two in parentheses. Tell whether it is an adjective or an adverb.

1. The omelet tasted (awful, awfully).
2. Katie finished the work (quick, quickly).
3. Mel stirred the gravy (careful, carefully).
4. His reply was (tactful, tactfully).
5. I am (dreadful, dreadfully) sorry.
6. Regina acted (real, really) glad to see us.
7. The day had begun (peaceful, peacefully).
8. Matt can be (awful, awfully) sensitive.
9. The fans went (wild, wildly) when the score became tied.
10. The patient seems (alert, alertly).

Adverb or Predicate Adjective?

As you have learned, a predicate adjective is used with a linking verb, and it modifies the subject. Besides forms of *be*, other linking verbs are *become, seem, appear, look, sound, feel, taste, smell,* and *grow.*

The rescue *looked* easy.

That rumor *sounds* unbelievable.

Jamie *feels* sick.

The verbs used above, *looked, sounds*, and *feels*, can also be action verbs. So can *grow, appear, smell*, and *taste*. As action verbs, these verbs are used with adverbs instead of predicate adjectives. Adverbs tell *how, when, where*, or *to what extent* about action verbs.

The following sentences use the same words both as linking verbs and as action verbs.

Linking Verbs with Adjectives	**Action Verbs with Adverbs**
I *appeared* confident.	He *appeared* suddenly.
The night *grew* cold.	My plants *grew* fast.
The granola *tasted* sweet.	Donna quickly *tasted* the pudding.

To determine whether to use an adverb or an adjective in a certain sentence, ask these questions:

1. Can you substitute *is* or *was* for the verb? If so, the modifier is probably an adjective.
2. Does the modifier tell *how, when, where*, or *to what extent*? If so, the modifier is probably an adverb.

Exercise Choose the right modifier for the following.

1. The rug felt (soft, softly) and thick.
2. Weeds can grow very (quick, quickly).
3. Harriet looked (suspicious, suspiciously) to us.
4. Dracula laughed (soft, softly).
5. Water dripped (slow, slowly) from the ceiling.
6. Harriet looked (suspicious, suspiciously) at us.

7. The defendant grew (nervous, nervously) during the delay.
8. Tina felt (careful, carefully) around the floor for her needle.
9. Rita appears careful and (competent, competently).
10. Patches of fog (sudden, suddenly) appeared.

Part 6 Troublesome Modifiers

The modifiers that follow are often confused or used incorrectly.

Them and Those

Those can be used correctly as an adjective.

Did the FBI trace *those* fingerprints?

Them is never an adjective. It cannot substitute for *those*.

Incorrect: Put putty in them cracks.
Correct: Put putty in *those* cracks.
Correct: Put putty in *them*.

Here and There

You may hear incorrect phrases like "this here room" or "that there part." "This here" and "that there" repeat ideas unnecessarily. The meaning of *this* includes the idea of *here*. The meaning of *that* includes the idea of *there*. Avoid "this here" and "that there."

Kind and Sort

Kind and *sort* are singular. *Kinds* and *sorts* are plural. No matter what words follow, use *this* or *that* with *kind* and *sort*.

Use *these* and *those* with *kinds* and *sorts*.

This kind of truck has four axles. (singular)
Those sorts of batteries don't last long. (plural)

Good and Well

Good and *well* have similar meanings, but the words are not the same. Look at the differences in the following sentences.

This is a good magazine. (The adjective *good* modifies the noun *magazine*.)

Jesse types well. (The adverb *well* modifies the verb *types*.)

Good is always an adjective. It describes people, places, and things. It never tells about actions.

Well can be either an adjective or an adverb. In the sentence above, *well* is used as an adverb modifying an action verb. *Well* can also be used after a linking verb to mean "in good health."

Since Monday, my brother hasn't been well.
(*Well* is a predicate adjective modifying *brother*.)

That tape deck works well.
(*Well* is an adverb modifying the action verb *works*.)

To tell about an action, use *well*.

The Double Negative

Two negative words used together when only one is necessary is called a double negative. Avoid using double negatives.

Incorrect: Lopez didn't make no free throws.
Correct: Lopez did*n't* make *any* free throws.

Incorrect: Shawn never throws nothing away.
Correct: Shawn *never* throws *anything* away.

Incorrect: I don't like none of those pictures.
Correct: I do*n't* like *any* of those pictures.

535

Not is a negative word. Its shortened form (*n't*) is part of contractions like *hasn't* and *didn't*. Do not use other negative words after such contractions.

Common negative words include *no, none, not, nothing,* and *never.* Instead of such words, use *any, anything,* or *ever* after a negative contraction.

> Gail has*n't ever* outscored that center.
> The summit meeting did*n't* resolve *anything.*
> Some storekeepers wo*n't* extend *any* credit.

Other negative words are *scarcely, barely,* and *hardly.* Avoid using them with negative contractions.

> Incorrect: I couldn't barely stay awake for the late show.
> Correct: I could *barely* stay awake for the late show.

> Incorrect: The new laws aren't scarcely enforced.
> Correct: The new laws are *scarcely* enforced.

Exercise A Choose the correct word from the two given.

1. (This, These) kind of paperback does not fall apart.
2. You may use (that, that there) phone.
3. The candidate felt (good, well) about her chances.
4. The movie was one of (them, those) documentaries.
5. (This, This here) perfume is made from gardenias.
6. (Them, Those) vitamins cost more than food.
7. Cheese and mustard taste (good, well) together.
8. Diane checked the engine (good, well).
9. The job was going (good, well).
10. Turkey reheats (good, well).

Exercise B Correct the double negatives in the following sentences. If a sentence contains no double negative, write *Correct.*

1. I didn't hardly recognize anybody at first.
2. The pawnbroker gives nothing to nobody.

3. Carol wouldn't ever tell anybody a lie.
4. I hadn't barely touched the accelerator.
5. Nobody hasn't seen Aaron lately.
6. That drill press didn't never work properly.
7. The tornado siren hadn't scarcely started wailing.
8. The band didn't know no old songs.
9. Please don't serve me none of that pie.
10. The supervisor hasn't said nothing about overtime.

Exercise C: Writing Use each of the following words in a sentence according to the directions in parentheses.

1. good (Use as a predicate adjective.)
2. well (Use as an adverb.)
3. kinds (Use with *these* or *those*.)
4. sort (Use with *this* or *that*.)
5. hardly (Use as a negative.)

ADDITIONAL EXERCISES

Using Modifiers

A. Adjectives   Number your paper from 1 to 10. Write the adjectives you find in each sentence. After each adjective, write the word it modifies. Ignore any articles.

1. She made the necklace from bright wooden beads.
2. I listened to the Spanish station.
3. Several local stores sell Chinese vegetables.
4. Those three old men sit on that bench everyday.
5. Have you seen a small calico cat, by any chance?
6. He almost tripped on the torn linoleum.
7. Perry always wears a black beret.
8. The new tenants work odd hours.
9. Solar eclipses are not at all mysterious.
10. Original ideas are always welcome here.

B. Comparisons of Adjectives   Number your paper from 1 to 10. Two of the comparisons in the following sentences are correct, but the others are wrong. If a sentence is correct, write *Correct*. If there is an error, write the sentence correctly.

1. You must be more careful with natural fabrics than with artificial ones.
2. Real vanilla suddenly became more expensiver.
3. Lately Ron has been less talkative than he was before.
4. Hal is often more wittier than any other student.
5. This summer is more hot than last summer was.
6. Of my four interviews, the one at Sears went better.
7. The flu is worst than a cold.
8. Clyde is the valuablest player.
9. A picture can be powerfuller than a speech.
10. Dr. Hill was kinder than any doctor.

C. Adverbs Number your paper from 1 to 10. Write the adverbs in the following sentences. After each adverb, write the word it modifies.

1. Can anybody drive too cautiously?
2. The power often goes out.
3. Two of the guests left very early.
4. Mattie is not an aide.
5. Somewhere nearby there is a McDonald's.
6. Big white snowflakes floated lazily down.
7. Sometimes he behaves strangely.
8. No situation comedy is ever too dull for him.
9. Nat never saw them again.
10. The day was unusually warm for April.

D. Comparisons of Adverbs One of the following sentences is correct. The others contain errors in the comparative form. Number your paper from 1 to 10. If the sentence is correct, write *Correct*. If there is an error, write the sentence correctly.

1. Move more close to the front of the room.
2. The rebels fought fiercelier than the invaders.
3. Harry sings even worst than Fred.
4. He plays worst of all the rookies.
5. Janet uses her calculator more oftener than Bo does.
6. Norris lays bricks more faster than any other bricklayer.
7. The major fought more bravely than any officer.
8. Of the four runners, Michelle tires least easily.
9. Of my two aunts, Pam writes to me most often.
10. Of the three insects, the bee travels the most farthest.

E. The Correct Use of Modifiers Choose the correct modifier for these sentences.

1. Eileen read the contract (careful, carefully).
2. He didn't look (attractive, attractively) in any style.

3. Some of the passengers grew (hysterical, hysterically).
4. The water was (real, really) cold.
5. I am (certain, certainly) sure of my answer.
6. I am (certain, certainly) of my answer.
7. Oliver (respectful, respectfully) requested more information.
8. The audience became (impatient, impatiently) with the projectionist.
9. Most trees grow (slow, slowly).
10. Linda feels (terrible, terribly) about spilling the paint.

F. Special Problems with Modifiers Number your paper from 1 to 10. If the sentence is correct, write *Correct*. If there is an error, write the sentence correctly.

1. Everybody was playing good by the end of the game.
2. The coffee tasted well.
3. These kind of cartridge works well.
4. Sterling had never before seen none of them.
5. Pull up them dandelions over there.
6. That there video game is more challenging than this kind.
7. The suspect knew her rights well and wouldn't say nothing.
8. Those sorts of running shoes offer hardly any support.
9. The patient looked well but couldn't hardly speak.
10. Don't them new Buicks look good?

MIXED REVIEW

Using Modifiers

A. Finding adjectives and adverbs Copy the following sentences. Underline each adjective once and each adverb twice. Then draw an arrow from each modifier to the word it modifies. Do not include articles.

1. Unfortunately, woolen sweaters are often itchy.
2. Curtis hung the Navaho rug on the wall.
3. The huge rats were fearless and very dangerous.
4. Sadly, Joachim returned to the bench.
5. Anna's slight Polish accent sounds quite exotic.
6. I've looked everywhere for that magazine.
7. The school is offering a course in Spanish literature this year.
8. Have you ever seen a red Mercedes?
9. One new worker almost quit today.
10. Most students had taken similar tests before.

B. Using modifiers correctly All of these sentences contain errors in the use of modifiers. Rewrite each sentence correctly.

1. Have you ever seen a more bigger pumpkin?
2. Jimmy Cliff is the more popular of the four singers.
3. An apple tastes better to me than any food.
4. Isn't ice hockey violenter than football?
5. He is certainly the bestest rookie of the season.
6. Of the two woods, oak burns the slowest.
7. Most oftenest, Brenda arrives earlier than Janine.
8. She had the worstest style but hit the ball farthest.
9. Terry earns the mostest money and has the least expenses.
10. Does the moray eel bite worst than a shark?

C. Choosing the correct modifier Write the correct word from the words in parentheses.

1. Danny dresses (stylish, stylishly).
2. Almost everybody looks (slender, slenderly) in that mirror.
3. The jeweler looked (careful, carefully) at the new shipment of diamonds.
4. Did you see (that, that there) Camaro?
5. He never said (anything, nothing) at all in class discussions.
6. The small scissors don't cut very (good, well).
7. Mr. T. can be good in (that, those) kind of role.
8. Tara (could, couldn't) hardly see through the icy windshield.
9. Brendan was on the phone for a (real, really) long time this morning.
10. Let's tie the hammock to (them, those) trees.

USING GRAMMAR IN WRITING
Using Modifiers

A. Suppose that you work for a consumer testing group. Your group has examined three kinds of personal portable radios with headphones. Write a report comparing the three radios. Adjectives will be useful in your report. They will help you describe the radios. The comparative and superlative forms will help you show ways in which one radio is better than the others.

B. Imagine that you are writing an adventure novel. The main characters are in a small boat, heading for an island off the rocky coast of Maine. They run out of gas. A storm is approaching. Write a description of the onset of the storm. Describe the sky and clouds, the wind and rain, the movement of the waves and the boat, and the reactions of the people. Use vivid adjectives and adverbs to set a frightening mood. Underline each adjective once and each adverb twice.

C. Imagery is the technique of using words that appeal to the senses. By using imagery, you often suggest a comparison between the two things. For example, in the following sentence, *stormy* brings a vivid image to the reader's mind.

Stan had a *stormy* look in his eyes.

Try using imagery in a description. Choose a situation that would be likely to make a person angry. Imagine a character in that situation. Try to build on the "storm" image presented in the example. You may want to use the following words and phrases or ones similar to them:

stormed into the room	gusty gestures
thundered	a torrent of complaints
squalled	a roaring tempest of fury

Using Prepositions and Conjunctions

Short sentences like these can sometimes express what you mean.

> Tim called.
> The spy escaped.

Frequently, though, you will want to provide more information. Modifiers are useful for that purpose.

> Tim called early.
> The foreign spy escaped.

There are other ways to add information. Maybe you want to say when Tim called. Maybe you want to add that the spy was never seen again. You will need different kinds of words to connect these ideas to your sentences.

> Tim called early *in* the morning.
> The foreign spy escaped *and* was never seen again.

Relationships dealing with people, actions, and things are expressed by words that connect other words. In this section you will learn about the two kinds of connecting words: **prepositions** and **conjunctions**.

Part 1 What Are Prepositions?

To join words or word groups, **connectives** are used. One important kind of connective is the **preposition**. Prepositions show relationships. Notice the different relationships in the following sentences.

> The road runs *over the mountain.*
> The road runs *through the mountain.*
> The road runs *around the mountain.*

The prepositions *over, through,* and *around* show the relationship between the noun *mountain* and the verb *runs. Mountain* is the object of the preposition in all of the above sentences. Like all prepositions, *over, through,* and *around* connect their objects to another part of the sentence.

However, prepositions do not show relationships all by themselves. Each preposition begins a *phrase,* a group of words without a subject or verb. As a whole, the **prepositional phrase** makes the relationship clear. The prepositional phrases in the above sentences are *over the mountain, through the mountain,* and *around the mountain.* The following sentences, too, have prepositional phrases.

> The crowds were entertained *by a band.*
> Nick poured two cups *of coffee.*
> The driver hopped *into the rig.*

A preposition is a word used with a noun or pronoun, called its *object,* to show the relationship between the noun or pronoun and some other word in the sentence.

A prepositional phrase consists of a preposition, its object, and any modifiers of the object.

There may be more than one prepositional phrase in a sentence. For example:

The books *on this shelf* are *from the library.*

Words in the list below are often used as prepositions. Quite a few, like *toward, below, near,* and *at,* help to show location. Others like *during, since,* and *before,* show a relationship of time. Some show other types of relationships. Study these prepositions and consider the relationship each one suggests.

Words Often Used as Prepositions

about	behind	during	off	to
above	below	except	on	toward
across	beneath	for	onto	under
after	beside	from	out	until
against	between	in	outside	up
along	beyond	inside	over	upon
among	but (*except*)	into	past	with
around	by	like	since	within
at	concerning	near	through	without
before	down	of	throughout	

Exercise A Find the prepositional phrases in these sentences.

1. After the movie we looked for a restaurant.
2. Ryan is, without a doubt, the best choice for captain.
3. Something was under the rug.
4. The Olympic Games were held in Los Angeles.
5. The neighbors had a meeting concerning the vandalism.
6. The smell of garlic spread throughout the house.
7. Several squad cars raced to the scene.
8. I propped a chair against the door.
9. Under attack from the press, the city manager resigned.
10. A group of volunteers organized the telethon.

Exercise B Follow the directions for Exercise A.

1. I felt nothing but sympathy for them.
2. Keith drives a truck for Meyer's Bakery.
3. Over the bleachers and into the street soared the ball.
4. By the way, Jeff is outside the door.
5. Nothing like that had ever happened in the city.
6. The tar stuck to the soles of my shoes.
7. On Monday, Meg goes to her first job interview.
8. During the trial, cameras were barred from the court.
9. On the way to the station, we had a flat tire.
10. The quarterback walked toward the bench without a word.

Preposition or Adverb?

Many words used as prepositions may also be used as adverbs. How can you tell when a word is an adverb and when it is a preposition?

A preposition is never used alone. It is always followed by a noun or pronoun as part of a phrase. Therefore, if the word is in a phrase, it is probably a preposition. However, if the word has no object, it is probably an adverb.

> Camilla's little sister always tags *along*. (adverb)
> The circus performer walked *along the ledge*. (preposition)
>
> A group of reporters waited *outside*. (adverb)
> A limousine stopped *outside my door*. (preposition)

Exercise A Write *Adverb* or *Preposition* for each sentence to indicate how the italicized word is used.

1. Who left the book *outside* in the rain?
2. Watch *out* for the potholes.
3. The puck slipped *past* the goalie into the net.
4. Rick shook the beach bag *out*.
5. The ball was clearly *outside* the line.

6. The ball was *out*.
7. Keep the dog *outside*.
8. The burglar climbed *up* this pole.
9. Put the bleach *up* out of reach.
10. Anita pressed a button *inside* the drawer.

Exercise B   Follow the directions for Exercise A.

1. His foot went right *through* the floor.
2. Goldie was *through* with the job.
3. Push the tile back *into* place.
4. The match was *over*, and she had won.
5. Guards patrol *along* the border.
6. Lena sent a card at Christmas but hasn't written *since*.
7. Chris was *in* a happy mood.
8. On Friday the dentist will not be *in*.
9. A tow truck drove *by*, but it didn't stop.
10. Can you back *up*?

Part 2   Prepositional Phrases as Modifiers

Modifiers are frequently single words. Groups of words, however, may also be modifiers. Prepositional phrases modify various sentence parts. These phrases modify words the same way that adjectives or adverbs do.

An adjective phrase is a prepositional phrase that modifies a noun or pronoun.

Hollywood is the home *of many stars*.
　　(*Of many stars* is an adjective phrase, modifying the noun *home*. It tells *what kind* of home.)

The coach is the woman *on the sidelines*.
　　(*On the sidelines* is an adjective phrase, modifying the noun *woman*. It tells *which one*.)

Many *of the parachutists* do free falls.

(*Of the parachutists* is an adjective phrase, modifying the pronoun *many*. It tells *what kind*.)

The above sentences show that adjective phrases tell *which one* or *what kind* just as adjectives do.

Adverbs tell *how, when, where,* and *to what extent* about verbs. Adverb phrases modify verbs in the same way.

Adverb phrases are prepositional phrases that modify verbs.

The Winter Olympics were held *in Sarajevo*.

(*In Sarajevo* is an adverb phrase that tells *where*. It modifies the verb *were held*.)

During the summer the factory closes.

(*During the summer* is an adverb phrase that tells *when*. It modifies the verb *closes*.)

The ice dancers moved *with graceful polish*.

(*With graceful polish* is an adverb phrase. It tells *how* about the verb *moved*.)

At times, one prepositional phrase may follow another. The second phrase is often an adjective phrase that modifies the object in the first phrase.

Kenneth sat *on a stack of newspapers*.

(*On a stack* is an adverb phrase. It tells *where* about the verb *sat. Of newspapers* is an adjective phrase modifying the noun *stack*.)

Half *of the people in America* watch the Super Bowl.

(The adjective phrase *of the people* tells *what kind* about the noun *half. In America* is an adjective phrase describing the noun *people*.)

Diagraming Prepositional Phrases

To diagram a prepositional phrase, place it under the word it modifies.

Wild horses run free in the canyon.

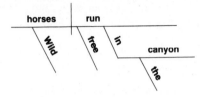

A preposition with two or more nouns or pronouns as objects in the prepositional phrase is diagramed in the following way.

At the zoo, we sketched pictures of the lions and the leopards.

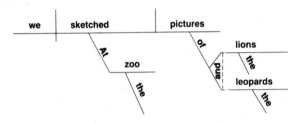

Exercise A Copy these sentences. Circle each prepositional phrase. Draw an arrow from the phrase to the word it modifies. Tell whether the phrase is an adjective or an adverb phrase.

1. In summer we eat dinner on the porch.
2. The bank served coffee to the customers in line.
3. The Mardi Gras parade goes along Canal Street.
4. Ms. Reyes solved the problem about our claim.
5. The tape pulled a patch of paint from the wall.
6. Many of the viewers responded to the poll.
7. The information in the ad was incorrect.
8. Walt scored fourteen points in twenty minutes.
9. The carpenter slipped off the ladder.
10. The paper with no title belongs to me.

Exercise B Follow the directions for Exercise A.

1. Few of the landlords live on the premises.
2. The watchdog slept under the counter.

3. People in street shoes are not allowed in the gym.
4. Two of the presidential candidates withdrew after the first primary.
5. During the cross-country bus ride I talked with my seatmate often.
6. The dime slipped into the crack in the sidewalk.
7. Gold and silver jewelry rose sharply in price.
8. At the party Ed danced only with Dawn.
9. The tomb of Tutankhamen was discovered by Howard Carter.
10. Nobody but Sue could think of a plan like that.

Part 3 What Are Conjunctions?

A second kind of word that shows relationships is the conjunction. A conjunction is a word that connects words or groups of words.

Notice how conjunctions are used in the following sentences.

The transmission *or* the brakes need repair.
(connects nouns)

The FDA tests drugs *and* cosmetics.
(connects nouns)

The clown winked *and* smiled at us.
(connects verbs)

Proudly *and* happily, Sally looked at her family.
(connects adverbs)

We bike in summer *and* during the fall.
(connects prepositional phrases)

Conjunctions, like prepositions, show a relationship between the words they connect. However, in contrast to prepositions, conjunctions link similar kinds of words. These might be two nouns or two phrases, for example. Another difference is that conjunctions do not have objects.

Coordinating Conjunctions

A **coordinating conjunction** joins single words or groups of words of the same kind. The most common coordinating conjunctions are *and, but,* and *or.*

Words joined by coordinating conjunctions are called compound constructions. Examples of compound constructions include compound subjects and compound verbs.

William *and* Lena work on an assembly line.
(*And* links *William* and *Lena,* making them a compound subject of the verb *work.*)

The glasses fell *and* shattered.
(*And* connects *fell* and *shattered,* forming a compound verb.)

San Francisco is hilly *and* scenic.
(*And* connects two predicate adjectives.)

The couple argued quietly *but* openly.
(*But* connects two adverbs.)

A hurricane hit Cuba, Florida, *and* the East Coast.
(*And* connects the three parts of the compound direct object.)

Congress gave the FBI *and* CIA new powers.
(*And* connects the compound indirect object.)

Carolyn greets everyone with a joke *or* a kind word.
(*Or* connects compound objects of a preposition.)

Correlative Conjunctions

Conjunctions that are used in pairs are called **correlative conjunctions.** For example:

both . . . and   not only . . . but (also)
either . . . or   whether . . . or
neither . . . nor

Ella sings *both* blues *and* jazz.
Good discipline is *not only* firm *but also* fair.
Neither money *nor* power insures happiness.

Exercise A Find the conjunctions in the following sentences. Tell what words or word groups are connected by the conjunctions.

1. Ms. Doyle bought and installed a new sink.
2. Snow and colder weather are predicted.
3. The photograph was too old and fuzzy to use.
4. I asked whether Nick or Betsy had called.
5. Either a check or a credit card will do.
6. Jason spoke shyly but clearly to the recruiter.
7. Both the soup and the crackers are homemade.
8. That gossip is not only untrue but also unkind.
9. He neither knew nor cared.
10. Julie finally arrived but stayed only a few minutes.

Exercise B Write the kind of compound construction in each sentence. Write the construction with its conjunction.

1. Either Ms. Glass or Mr. Santo will interview applicants for the job.
2. The boots are neither warm nor waterproof.
3. Is the holiday "President's Day" or "Presidents' Day?"
4. Karen teaches both judo and karate.
5. The headlights and the radio are working.
6. He has raced not only at Daytona but also at Indianapolis.
7. There are naval bases at both San Diego and Waukegan.
8. Did Amy or Mandy win?
9. He is underweight but healthy.
10. She pivoted and tossed the ball.

Exercise C: Writing Using the following conjunctions, write five new sentences.

but	both . . . and	or
either . . . or	not only . . . but (also)	

ADDITIONAL EXERCISES

Using Prepositions and Conjunctions

A. Prepositions Number your paper from 1 to 10. Write the prepositions in the following sentences. Write the object of each preposition.

1. Everyone but Jerry rode the Ferris wheel.
2. The old path was slippery with moss.
3. Needles from the tree showed up for months after Christmas.
4. Remove the stuffing from the turkey immediately.
5. The lake looked like glass under the fierce sun.
6. Fred sat and dozed all night in the bus station.
7. Without a worry in the world, she set off for California.
8. Isaac drove out beyond the city limits.
9. Most of the pitchers and catchers have started spring training.
10. For six months he dieted and exercised.

B. Adverbs and Prepositions Decide whether the italicized words in these sentences are adverbs or prepositions. Write *Adverb* or *Preposition* for each sentence.

1. When should I turn the pancakes *over?*
2. *Over* the table hung a chandelier.
3. Wasps hovered *around* the picnic area.
4. The dial spun *around* and shuddered to a stop.
5. Ty's beard grew *down* to his chest.
6. The crowd shouted the speaker *down*.
7. This elevator is going *up*, Sir.
8. Don't put grease *down* the drain.
9. Sandra poked the broom *up* the chimney.
10. Eugenia went *outside* for some fresh air.

C. Prepositional Phrases as Modifiers Copy these sentences. Circle each prepositional phrase. Draw an arrow from the phrase to the word it modifies. Label each phrase *Adjective* or *Adverb* to tell how it is used.

1. The alley was littered with garbage after the thaw.
2. I have a message for you from Yvonne.
3. She fastened the belt of her raincoat.
4. During the game Willie became ill.
5. The alarm went off at seven o'clock.
6. We pushed through the defense without much difficulty.
7. Efren will be stationed at Fort Bragg for two more months.
8. The car with the hood ornament belongs to me.
9. The drugstore on the corner is open until nine.
10. The woman at the window is from Chile.

D. Conjunctions Find the conjunctions in the following sentences. Tell which words are connected by the conjunctions.

1. Her eyeshadow was a blend of green and blue.
2. The sea snake is not only fast but also deadly.
3. The rainbow faded but reappeared.
4. That number reaches both the police and the fire department.
5. You can use either oil or butter.
6. He neither fouled nor scored during the game.
7. Wayne scrubbed not only the burners but also the oven.
8. We will send a basket of flowers or fruit.
9. Mosquitoes and sand flies made the beach unpleasant.
10. Joyce will take the shuttle bus or a taxi.

MIXED REVIEW

Using Prepositions and Conjunctions

A. Recognizing prepositional phrases Copy these sentences. Circle the prepositional phrases. Draw arrows from each prepositional phrase to the word it modifies.

1. A fire in a coal mine is a major disaster.
2. After all, it can't rain forever.
3. Marcella works on Saturdays until noon.
4. Every continent but Antarctica has a permanent human population.
5. From time to time, Joan telephones.
6. The electrical socket is behind the couch.
7. We pulled off the road during the blizzard.
8. Sometimes he acts exactly like his brother.
9. I was saving that chicken for dinner.
10. The scuba diver's endurance seemed beyond belief.

B. Recognizing adverbs, prepositions, and conjunctions Write the italicized words in the following sentences. After each, write *Adverb, Preposition,* or *Conjunction* to show how it is used in the sentence.

1. Your time is *up*.
2. Harris whizzed *down* the water slide.
3. Canals connect the Great Lakes *and* the Atlantic.
4. Don't put the dog *outside* in this weather.
5. Everything was dark *beyond* the campfire.
6. Annette laughed *but* said nothing.
7. Everybody *but* Eddie was wearing a hard hat.
8. The helicopter whirred *past* and frightened the gulls.
9. The union is worried *about* safety conditions.
10. Puerto Rico has *not only* rich soil *but also* mineral deposits.

USING GRAMMAR IN WRITING
Using Prepositions and Conjunctions

A. Imagine that you are part of a group that is exploring beneath the sea. The group is testing a new underwater research vessel. This vessel travels far beneath the surface of the sea. The vessel is a giant ball, made almost entirely of glass. From inside the ball, you and the other members of the group will be able to see in all directions. Your job is to keep the log describing what you see each day. Write a paragraph describing some of the things that you see on the first trip beneath the sea. Prepositional phrases will be useful in your description. They will help you describe the creatures you see, and they will be essential in describing where you see these creatures.

B. You have been selected as the first high school student to ride the space shuttle. A national magazine is eager to have you write about your experience. Write a paragraph describing the launch of the shuttle. Use your imagination to decide how the launch would feel to someone inside the shuttle. Use prepositional phrases as modifiers. Adjective phrases will be useful in describing the inside of the shuttle. Adverb phrases will be useful in describing *when, where,* and *how* events happen.

C. You are writing predictions for the yearbook. You will find conjunctions useful for writing your predictions. For example, you might write:

You will make a great deal of money, but you will spend it on a scheme for shipping icebergs to tropical countries.

Write predictions for ten of your classmates. Be sure your predictions include conjunctions.

Review of Parts of Speech

Part 1 The Parts of Speech

You have studied nouns, pronouns, verbs, adjectives, adverbs, prepositions, and conjunctions. All of these classes of words are called **parts of speech.** A word may be a particular part of speech because of the way it is used in a sentence.

Altogether, there are eight parts of speech. In addition to the seven groups listed above, there is another part of speech. It is called the **interjection.**

What Is an Interjection?

An interjection is a word or group of words used to express strong feeling.

An interjection may be either a phrase or a single word that shows strong feeling. That feeling, for example, might be fear, horror, happiness, sorrow, or surprise. Interjections are followed by exclamation points.

Look at the following interjections.

> *Ouch!* That hurts.
> *Aha!* I've found the solution.
> *Oh, no!* We lost the ball.

You have now studied all eight parts of speech.

The Parts of Speech			
nouns	verbs	adverbs	conjunctions
pronouns	adjectives	prepositions	interjections

Exercise A   Write what part of speech each italicized word is.

1. The television is still not working *well.*
2. The truck was stuck *under* a viaduct.
3. *Terrific!* There's an empty seat.
4. The conductor *checked* the doors.
5. Donna stretched the canvas *herself.*
6. The *noise* came from upstairs.
7. Mack certainly *needs* a vacation.
8. Lamar keeps a first-aid kit *and* a lantern in the car.
9. You made a *wrong* move.
10. *Several* of the apartments are vacant.

Exercise B   Follow the directions for Exercise A.

1. Who *wishes* upon stars?
2. Simon looks *good* in that hat.
3. The country of Thailand was once called *Siam.*
4. Priscilla bought a *Japanese* motorcycle.
5. *You* are carrying the pizza box upside down.
6. *Uh, oh!* This ice-cream bar is melting.

7. The drain is backing up *again*.

8. I have *never* been to a parade.

9. He always stretches his legs out *into* the aisle.

10. I will replace *or* pay for the damaged album.

Part 2 Using Words as Different Parts of Speech

One word can often be used as more than one part of speech. For example, the same word might be a verb in one sentence and a noun in another.

There is only one way to tell what part of speech any word is. You must know how that word is used in a sentence.

These sentences show examples of one word used as two different parts of speech.

The director *cast* Redford in the starring role. (*Cast* is used as a verb.)

Amid applause, the *cast* bowed. (*Cast* is used as a noun, the subject of the verb *bowed*.)

Susan and Lars *work* as zookeepers. (*Work* is used as a verb.)

Soon the *work* week may shrink to four days. (*Work* is used as an adjective, modifying *week*.)

The old woman travels *alone*. (*Alone* is used as an adverb, modifying the verb *travels*.)

For days, Bert was *alone* in the cave. (*Alone* is used as a predicate adjective.)

Park in the lot, please. (*Park* is used as a verb.)

A horse-drawn carriage circled the *park*. (*Park* is used as a noun, the direct object of the verb, *circled*.)

Every day we eat lunch on the *park* bench. (*Park* is used as an adjective, modifying the noun, *bench*.)

Greg turned *around* and went home. (*Around* is used as an adverb, modifying the verb *turned*.)

Put the ribbon *around* the package. (*Around* is used as a preposition.)

Great! I was hoping for this. (*Great* is used as an interjection.)

Einstein was a *great* scientist. (*Great* is used as an adjective modifying the noun *scientist.*)

Exercise A Write what part of speech each italicized word is.

1. Pat applied a light *finish* to the wood.
2. I did not have the exact *change.*
3. *Skid* marks can be used as evidence.
4. Light bikes *skid* easily.
5. *No!* Don't throw the instructions away.
6. *No* information was available.
7. Janet lunged toward the *finish* line.
8. *Finish* your story.
9. We pay several kinds of *taxes.*
10. Sweden *taxes* its citizens heavily.

Exercise B Follow the directions for Exercise A.

1. Maria checked the car for *rust* spots.
2. This metal *rusts* easily.
3. From his window he watches the world go *past.*
4. As we rode along, I watched the scenery slip *past* us.
5. The *past* week has been very busy.
6. Randy lives in the *past.*
7. Many people *shop* on Saturdays.
8. The Beckers own a shoe-repair *shop.*
9. *That* joke was not funny.
10. Did she really say *that?*

ADDITIONAL EXERCISES

Review of Parts of Speech

Parts of Speech   Number your paper from 1 to 25. Read each sentence. Then copy the italicized word. Write what part of speech the word is in that sentence.

1. *Certainly!* Help yourself.
2. Morrison is *my* favorite novelist.
3. *That* color is called magenta.
4. The *morning* stars glittered above the treetops.
5. Mothballs hung among the *wool* clothes.
6. Gerry *bags* groceries on weekends.
7. *Leave* your boots in the hall.
8. *Overnight,* the leaves turned gold.
9. Oil *spills* kill sea creatures.
10. Gene's clock has no *alarm.*
11. The laundromat is a *very* sociable place.
12. Dreams are *different* from daydreams.
13. Several countries have red, white, *and* blue flags.
14. Penny arrived *early* for practice.
15. Suddenly, the shade flew *up.*
16. A deep wrinkle appeared *between* her eyes.
17. *Neither* of these sweaters is in style.
18. Do *not* throw water on a grease fire.
19. I had never seen anything *like* it.
20. *This* is a good time for a break.
21. Can you fix *this* electronic game?
22. The soup *smells* good.
23. Delicious *smells* drifted from the bakery.
24. This is Nelson's *last* season.
25. Some styles *last* for a long time.

MIXED REVIEW

Review of Parts of Speech

Recognizing the Parts of Speech   Number your paper from 1 to 25. Copy the italicized words from these sentences. Write what part of speech each is used as.

1. *My!* You were certainly hungry.
2. A *fast* car is usually wasted in the city.
3. An elephant can run quite *fast*.
4. Members of some religions *fast* on certain holy days.
5. An occasional *fast* from food is part of many religions.
6. Bear cubs *climb* trees.
7. The hikers began their *climb* at dawn.
8. Did Jackie paint *those* portraits?
9. *Those* are catfish.
10. The display window caved *in* during the storm.
11. We sat *in* the shade and watched the game.
12. Wendy *or* David mops the kitchen floor every evening.
13. Should I use *oil* or margarine?
14. *Sleep* is controlled by the brain.
15. *Sleep* on a firmer mattress.
16. He never got to *California*.
17. The store sells *African* fabrics.
18. You should *slice* a grapefruit this way.
19. She spoke sharply *but* then apologized.
20. I remembered everything *but* the plates.
21. Which Presidents were *not* college graduates?
22. The homeless man made *himself* a shelter out of boxes.
23. They drove *south* along the backroads.
24. Sandra jogged *by* and waved.
25. The viceroy butterfly looks *like* the monarch butterfly.

USING GRAMMAR IN WRITING
Review of Parts of Speech

A. You are riding in a crowded subway car. Suddenly the lights in the car go out. Slowly, the car coasts to a halt. What happens next? Do the people on the car panic or stay calm? Do the lights come back on? Does the car start moving again, or does the power remain off? Do the people have to leave the car? Write about the events that follow the discovery. You may want to include some dialogue. Use all eight parts of speech. Label each one the first time you use it. Be sure to use strong verbs, vivid modifiers, and prepositional phrases to make your story lively.

B. Each word below can be used as at least two different parts of speech. Write two or three sentences for each word, using that word as a different part of speech in each sentence. Try writing a story using at least two different meanings for each of the words.

Example: coil
The rope was wound in a neat coil. (noun)
This car uses coil springs on all four wheels. (adjective)
Coil the extension cord so that it doesn't snarl. (verb)

1. double
2. exhaust
3. grasp
4. knock
5. place
6. trace

CUMULATIVE REVIEW

The Parts of Speech

A. Identifying parts of speech Decide how each underlined word is used. Number your paper from 1 to 20. Write *Noun*, *Verb*, *Pronoun*, *Adjective*, *Adverb*, *Preposition*, or *Conjunction* for each word.

Soccer is the world's most popular sport. One of the reasons for its popularity is that the game is simple. The object of the game is to score goals by putting the soccer ball past the opposing team's goalie into the net. Because it is so simple to play, there are even pre-school soccer teams. A second reason for soccer's popularity is that the game is inexpensive. The only equipment that you really need is a ball. In addition, the game can be played outdoors or indoors. A fourth reason for soccer's popularity is that it is a relatively safe sport. Soccer players sustain fewer and less severe injuries than participants in most other sports. Moreover running after the ball keeps the players in tip-top shape.

B. Recognizing how words are used Decide how the italicized words are used. Number your paper from 1 to 5. Write *Subject*, *Verb*, *Direct Object*, *Indirect Object*, *Object of the Preposition*, *Predicate Noun*, or *Predicate Adjective* to show what each word is.

1. Grant *deposited* his paycheck in the bank.
2. The usher gave *us* programs for the play.
3. Has the *water* begun to boil yet?
4. The baby's hands were *sticky*.
5. Mike wears a *brace* on his left leg.

Using Verbals

In previous sections you have learned about the eight parts of speech.

nouns	verbs	adverbs	conjunctions
pronouns	adjectives	prepositions	interjections

In addition to the parts of speech, our language also contains three other kinds of words. They are **gerunds, participles,** and **infinitives.** All three look like verbs. Therefore, they are called **verbals.** A verbal is a word that is formed from a verb but is never used as a verb. In this section you will become familiar with the three kinds of verbals.

Part 1   Using Gerunds

A gerund is a verb form that is used as a noun. Gerunds end in *-ing*. They may be used in all the ways that nouns are used. Like a noun, a gerund may be used as a subject.

> *Smoking* is hazardous to your health.
> (*Smoking* is a gerund, the subject of the verb *is*.)

Like a noun, a gerund may be used as a direct object.

> Some states allow *gambling*.
> (*Gambling* is a gerund, the object of the verb *allow*.)

Like a noun, a gerund may be used as an object of a preposition.

> Noah lost twenty pounds by *exercising*.
> (*Exercising* is a gerund, the object of the preposition *by*.)

Gerund Phrases

In many sentences, the gerund is not used alone. Often a gerund has a modifier or an object or both. Together, they form a **gerund phrase.** The whole gerund phrase is used like a noun.
Because a gerund is formed from a verb, it can have an object.

> *Winning Olympic medals* was Heiden's goal.
> (*Winning* is a gerund; *medals* is the object of *winning*. The phrase *winning Olympic medals* is the subject of the verb *was*.)

Because a gerund is formed from a verb, it can be modified by adverbs.

> The troops began *turning back*.
> (*Turning* is a gerund; *back* is an adverb modifying *turning*. The phrase *turning back* is the object of the verb *began*.)

Because a gerund is used as a noun, it can be modified by adjectives.

That comedian has *good timing*.

(*Timing* is a gerund; *good* is an adjective modifying *timing*. The phrase *good timing* is the direct object of the verb *has*.)

Gerunds can also be modified by prepositional phrases.

Telescopes are used for *looking at the stars*.

(*Looking* is a gerund; *at the stars* is a prepositional phrase modifying *looking*. The entire gerund phrase is the object of the preposition *for*.)

All of the above examples show that gerunds are used as nouns, even though they look like verbs. *Smoking, gambling, exercising, winning, turning, timing,* and *looking* all resemble verbs. However, because they are used as nouns, they are gerunds. Modifiers and objects that are used with them form gerund phrases.

Diagraming Gerunds

To diagram a gerund or gerund phrase used as a subject or direct object, place it on a line above the main line. The line for the gerund is drawn as a step. The gerund's modifiers are placed on slanted lines below it. Its object appears on the horizontal line following the gerund.

Starting a business is very risky.

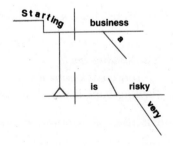

Marshall heard soft singing in the hallway.

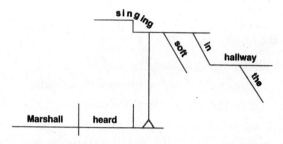

When a gerund or gerund phrase is used as the object of a preposition, it is diagramed below the main line. The preposition belongs on a slanted line going down from the word it modifies.

Once again, the gerund appears on a line drawn as a step.

The detective began by searching the room.

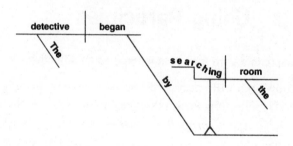

Exercise A   Find the gerunds or gerund phrases in these sentences.

1. Begin by budgeting your time.
2. Scheduling the events was tricky.
3. Monty tried gluing the cup back together.
4. Swimming is a very healthy sport.
5. She makes a good living.
6. A misunderstanding caused the argument.
7. Shopping can be hard work.
8. Braking on ice is difficult.

9. I used that towel for drying the dog.
10. Who enjoys defrosting a refrigerator?

Exercise B Follow the directions for Exercise A.

1. The chef began stuffing the turkey.
2. Rhonda stopped dancing around the room.
3. Parking in the alley is prohibited.
4. Skipping lunch won't hurt Lee.
5. The politician began by discussing the economy.
6. He can't tell a joke without laughing.
7. He does push-ups without bending his knees.
8. She has a bad habit of interrupting.
9. The IRS encourages filing tax forms early.
10. Your mistake was thinning the paint.

Part 2   Using Participles

A participle is a verb form that is used as an adjective.

You know about the **past participle** as one of the principal parts of a verb. Usually, it is formed by adding *-d* or *-ed* to the present tense, as in *scrape—scraped* or *trust—trusted*. The past participles of irregular verbs are formed differently and must be learned separately: *ride—ridden, bring—brought*.

Besides the past participle, there is another kind of participle. It is called the **present participle.** Present participles are always formed by adding *-ing* to the present tense: *scrape—scraping, trust—trusting, ride—riding, bring—bringing.*

The following list shows more participles.

Verb	Past Participle	Present Participle
give	given	giving
fry	fried	frying
lose	lost	losing
attack	attacked	attacking

As verbals, participles are always used as adjectives. Participles modify nouns and pronouns.

> *Laughing,* Rita wiped the pie from her face.
> (*Laughing* is a present participle modifying the noun *Rita*.)
> *Panting,* he ran into the emergency room.
> (*Panting* is a present participle modifying the pronoun *he*.)
> Only *registered* voters were surveyed.
> (*Registered* is a past participle modifying the noun *voters*.)
> Tom made a *refreshing* dessert with pineapple juice.
> (*Refreshing* is a present participle modifying the noun *dessert*.)

Participial Phrases

A participle is not always used alone. Often a participle has a modifier or an object or both. Together, they form a **participial phrase.** The entire participial phrase is used as an adjective.

Because a participle is formed from a verb, it may have an object.

> The man *ringing our doorbell* looks angry.
> (*Ringing our doorbell* is a participial phrase modifying *man. Doorbell* is the object of the participle *ringing*.)

Because a participle is formed from a verb, it may be modified by adverbs.

> We walked along *brightly lighted* streets.
> (*Brightly* is an adverb modifying the participle *lighted*.)

A participle may also be modified by prepositional phrases.

> *Made by hand,* these rugs are works of art.
> (*Made by hand* is a prepositional phrase modifying *rugs. By hand* is a prepositional phrase modifying the participle *made*.)

All of the preceding examples show that participles are used as adjectives, even though they look like verbs. While *laughing, panting, registered, refreshing, ringing, lighted,* and *made* all look like verbs, they are not used as verbs. Since they are used as adjectives, they are called participles. Modifiers and objects used with them form participial phrases.

Diagraming Participles

To diagram a participle, place it below the noun or pronoun it modifies. Place the participle on an angled line. Place modifiers of the participle on lines slanted down from it. An object appears after the participle on a horizontal line.

Waving a flag, the man signalled oncoming traffic.

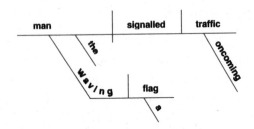

Exercise A Write the participles or participial phrases in these sentences. Show which word the participle or phrase modifies.

1. The gusting wind ripped the loose shingles off.
2. Loosening his tie, James breathed deeply.
3. Remembering the main switch, she raced to the basement.
4. Complaining loudly, the customer demanded a refund.
5. A boiled egg has fewer calories than a hamburger.
6. The coach restored the team's badly shattered morale.
7. The crowd on the platform looked anxiously at the train roaring past.
8. We watched the laughing children.
9. The yearbook brought back nearly forgotten memories.
10. He wore a wrinkled shirt and a baggy suit.

Exercise B Follow the directions for Exercise A.

1. Pulling on her gloves, the surgeon rushed inside.
2. Marcie told us an amazing story.
3. The captain read the list of soldiers missing in action.
4. The smoldering chair suddenly burst into flames.
5. The hair stylist groaned at Bess's tangled hair.
6. He likes sliced carrots with his cheese.
7. Grant wrote the terms of surrender with ink borrowed from Lee's aide.
8. Luckily, there was only one broken ornament.
9. Closing his eyes, the child recited the speech.
10. Using a calculator, he balanced his checkbook.

Gerund or Participle?

Gerunds and participles, the two kinds of verbals you have studied, may look exactly the same. Both gerunds and present participles are formed by adding -*ing* to verbs. If they look alike, how can you tell them apart?

To tell whether a word is a gerund or a present participle, look at how it is used. If it is used as a modifier, it is a participle. If it is used as a noun, it is a gerund.

Compare these two sentences.

> *Returning to school* will prepare me for a better job.
> (The gerund phrase *returning to school* is the subject of the verb *will prepare*.)

> *Returning to work*, Gail noticed new faces.
> (The participial phrase *returning to work* modifies the noun *Gail*.)

Exercise For each sentence, write the gerund or participle and say which each is. Be prepared to explain your answer.

1. What is a tuning fork?
2. Steaming the wrinkles might work.

3. Pam is the player dribbling the ball.
4. Pinching his finger in the drawer, he yelped.
5. Complaining will not help.
6. Fixing a hem with a safety pin is an emergency repair.
7. The man leaning against the post is Mr. Bobek.
8. Taping the pieces, Rob made a mistake.
9. Just watching the waves from the shore makes her seasick.
10. During the movie Steve had a bad coughing fit.

Part 3   Using Infinitives

Finally, the third kind of verbal is the **infinitive. An infinitive is a verbal form that usually begins with the word *to*.** *To* is called the **sign of the infinitive.** Here are some infinitives.

to call	to wish	to draw	to wrestle
to buy	to see	to plan	to plan

Note: As you have learned, the word *to* can be a preposition. *To* is a preposition when it is followed by its object, a noun or a pronoun. When *to* is followed by a verb, though, it is the sign of the infinitive. Look at these examples.

Prepositional Phrases	**Infinitives**
The boys went to the game.	The situation started to improve.
Everything is back to normal.	Our plane stopped to re-fuel.

Infinitive Phrases

Infinitives, just like gerunds and participles, are not always used alone. Many infinitives are used with modifiers and objects. An infinitive, together with its modifiers and objects, forms an **infinitive phrase.**

Because an infinitive comes from a verb, it is like a verb in certain ways. Like a verb, an infinitive may have an object.

> *To make new friends,* Jenny joined some clubs.
> (*Friends* is the direct object of the infinitive *to make.*)
>
> The manager has agreed *to give us longer breaks.*
> (*Us* is the indirect object and *breaks* is the direct object of the infinitive *to give.*)

Because an infinitive is formed from a verb, it may be modified by adverbs.

> I plan *to repay the loan immediately.*
> (*Immediately* is an adverb modifying the infinitive *to repay.*)
>
> Yolanda promised *to come back soon.*
> (*Back* and *soon* are adverbs modifying the infinitive *to come.*)

An infinitive may also be modified by prepositional phrases.

> Astronauts are trained *to live in outer space.*
> (*In outer space* is a prepositional phrase modifying the infinitive *to live.*)
>
> This vacuum cleaner is guaranteed *to work for five years.*
> (*For five years* is a prepositional phrase modifying the infinitive *to work.*)

Uses of the Infinitive Phrase

Unlike gerunds and participles, infinitives can be used as more than one part of speech. Infinitives and infinitive phrases can function as the following: nouns, adjectives, or adverbs.

Infinitives and infinitive phrases can be used in ways that nouns are used. Specifically, they may be subjects or direct objects, as well as predicate nouns.

> Subject: *To sign a petition* is a citizen's right.
> (*To sign a petition* is the subject.)

Direct Object: Janet wanted *to refinish the bookcase.*
(*To refinish the bookcase* is the direct object.)

Infinitives and infinitive phrases can also be used as adjectives or adverbs. If an infinitive or infinitive phrase modifies a noun or pronoun, it is functioning as an adjective. If it modifies a verb, adjective, or adverb, it is functioning as an adverb.

Adjective: In case of fire, this is the switch *to pull.*
(*To pull* modifies the noun *switch.*)

Adjective: Do you have anyone *to counsel you?*
(*To counsel you* modifies the pronoun *any one.*)

Adverb: Bonnie was hired *to process insurance claims.*
(*To process insurance claims* modifies the verb *was hired.*)

Adverb: The field was too muddy *to play on.*
(*To play on* modifies the adjective *muddy.*)

Adverb: Ron didn't run enough *to get into shape.*
(*To get into shape* modifies the adverb *enough.*)

All of these examples show that while infinitives look like verbs, they are not used as verbs. Instead, infinitives and their phrases are used as nouns, adjectives, and adverbs.

Split Infinitives

At times you may see a modifier between the word *to* and the verb of an infinitive. A modifier in that place is said to split the infinitive. In general, a split infinitive sounds awkward and should be avoided.

Awkward: Kate plans to *carefully* study.
Better: Kate plans to study *carefully.*

Diagraming Infinitives

To diagram an infinitive or infinitive phrase used as a noun, place it on a bridge above the main line. *To,* the sign of the infinitive, is shown on an angled line. The infinitive belongs on a horizontal line. Modifiers appear on lines slanted down from the infinitive. An object is shown on a horizontal line following the infinitive.

The actor tried to remember his lines.

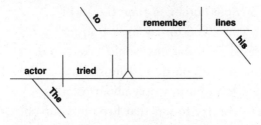

To diagram an infinitive or infinitive phrase used as a modifier, place it under the word it modifies. Modifiers and objects of the infinitive appear as explained above.

Ms. Minsky is the person to see about repairs.

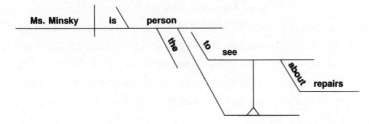

Exercise A Write each infinitive or infinitive phrase.

1. How was he supposed to know that?
2. Glenn likes to walk in the rain.
3. Visitors are not allowed to feed the animals.
4. To give up snacks was their goal.
5. Grace attempted to find a foothold.
6. I used a carton to prop the table up.
7. Rochelle did not mean to bump into you.
8. To get to the library is my project for today.
9. The patient was encouraged to walk to the lounge.
10. To win by default is unsatisfying.

Exercise B Follow the directions for Exercise A.

1. Jess has no time to waste.
2. Did you remember to ask for a receipt?
3. Use ammonia and water to clean the ring.
4. Did anyone bother to time the race?
5. Were you asked to pay for a transfer?
6. To travel there by bus would take two days.
7. To get to work on time, I must leave at 6:00 A.M.
8. Gina is too thin to worry about calories.
9. Don't even try to put that fire out yourself.
10. Juanita promised to send the negative to us.

Part 4   A Review of Verbals

Verbals, as you have learned, are verb forms. However, they are never used as verbs. They are used as other parts of speech.

The three kinds of verbals are gerunds, participles, and infinitives. All three may be used alone or in phrases. These phrases are called gerund phrases, participial phrases, and infinitive phrases. In phrases, all three kinds of verbals may have objects or modifiers or both.

Gerunds are the verb forms used as nouns. Gerunds, which end in *-ing*, may be used in all the ways nouns are used.

> Steve enjoys *shopping*. (direct object)
> *Shopping for bargains* sometimes pays off. (subject)
> Adam goes to Franco's Market for *his weekly grocery shopping*. (object of preposition)
> By *shopping wisely*, we save money. (object of preposition)

Participles are verb forms used as adjectives. Participles modify nouns and pronouns just as adjectives do. Present participles end in *-ing*. Past participles of regular verbs end in *-d* or *-ed*.

> *Writing carefully*, Greg signed the contract.
> Pam sat at a special *writing* table.

Writing on a blackboard, the coach reviewed strategy.
We watch the reporter *writing his story.*

Infinitives are verb forms that start with the word *to.* Infinitives may be used as nouns, adjectives, or adverbs.

To win the race was my goal. (noun, subject)
The photographer wants *to take her picture.* (noun, object)
Peterson Avenue is the best route *to take.* (adjective)
Marcy left *to take Jeremy home.* (adverb)
The battery is easy *to take out.* (adverb)

Exercise A   Write the verbal or verbal phrase in each sentence. Tell whether the verbal is a gerund, a participle, or an infinitive.

1. The starched collar felt too stiff to Vince.
2. Would you wear a silk shirt with faded jeans?
3. Dominick asked to speak with the manager.
4. Within minutes he had mended the badly torn shirt.
5. Carol began by explaining her experiment.
6. Joking happily, Tony left for work.
7. The soldiers passed the time by joking together.
8. Anita wants to wear a costume to the party.
9. I carried the buttered popcorn back to our seats.
10. Carefully observing the current, she steered the boat.

Exercise B   Follow the directions for Exercise A.

1. With a puzzled look, Jeremy examined the engine.
2. The bank will send the cancelled checks to you.
3. Waking up Gregory is no easy job.
4. Waking up quickly, she ran to the window.
5. The lawyer questioned the badly shaken witness.
6. The prosecuting attorney objected to the questions.
7. Tiptoeing is normal for him.
8. Looking for an exit can waste valuable time.
9. I had hoped to drive you to the airport.
10. Do you want to rent a locker?

ADDITIONAL EXERCISES

Using Verbals

A. Gerunds and Gerund Phrases Find the gerunds and gerund phrases in these sentences.

1. The reporters were accused of spying.
2. The constant traveling tired the flight attendant.
3. Hosing the car down will wash the mud off.
4. I hate beginning the day without breakfast.
5. Don't buy anything there without bargaining first.
6. Have you considered renting an industrial vacuum cleaner?
7. Moving the victim should be the last resort.
8. Fingernail biting is one sign of tension.
9. Marty practiced kicking with his left foot.
10. Jumping bail got him into even more trouble.

B. Participles and Participial Phrases Find the participles and participial phrases in these sentences.

1. The housing market is bad right now.
2. Crops ruined by the flood included corn and beans.
3. Did you buy insulated wire?
4. Tammy has several very annoying habits.
5. Exhausted after the day's work, Lyle sat down to relax.
6. Many doctors and dentists have answering services.
7. Marshall's sunburned feet were swelling.
8. Saved by the bell, the boxer staggered to his corner.
9. Lynn, encouraged by her teacher, applied to several colleges.
10. Craig finally spotted the lost chameleon on the window screen.

C. Gerunds and Participles Write the gerund or participle from each sentence, and also write which it is.

1. Braiding Janine's hair took over an hour.
2. Finding the cause might help us with the cure.
3. That spotted horse is an appaloosa.
4. The lawn chairs, left out in the rain, were still wet.
5. The slashing wind held the searchers back.
6. My handwriting has changed in the last year.
7. Everybody on the team has her own bowling ball.
8. The main cause of yawning is too much carbon dioxide in the body.
9. Yawning loudly, Sara closed her eyes.
10. The baby wore tiny gold earrings in her pierced ears.

D. Infinitives and Infinitive Phrases Write the infinitives and infinitive phrases in these sentences.

1. Chip wanted to ask you but was too shy.
2. Leave yourself time to check your answers.
3. Ms. Martinez managed to locate the apartment.
4. Jacob will have to budget more carefully.
5. We had hoped to see more of the city today.
6. Emily seemed reluctant to introduce herself to Lee.
7. Ramona tried to carry two of the dogs.
8. To me it seems too late to start out.
9. To get all the soap out, add vinegar to the rinse water.
10. To see all the sights in one day would be impossible.

E. Verbals Write each verbal or verbal phrase. Label it *Gerund*, *Participle*, or *Infinitive*.

1. We often regret words spoken in anger.
2. Adjusting to the climate was difficult.
3. Carrying the goldfish bowl, he tripped and fell.
4. Sandy needs to find a steady job.
5. Pete offered to walk with them to the store.

MIXED REVIEW

Using Verbals

A. Recognizing verbals Write the verbals and verbal phrases. Write whether each is a gerund, participle, or infinitive. A sentence may contain more than one verbal.

1. Donna's bowling shoes are blue and red.
2. Marcus Allen broke the record for rushing.
3. She kept everything in her shopping bag.
4. Artis plans to take a course in woodworking.
5. The car has power steering and a good cruising speed.
6. The confused driver steered the car to the left.
7. Beginning athletes often want to gain weight.
8. The beginning of the movie confused me.
9. Glenn carried the smoking pan to the sink.
10. It will not be easy to get the ball away from Delisio.

B. Identifying verbals and their uses Write the verbals and verbal phrases. If a verbal is used as a noun, write whether it is a subject, an object, or a predicate word. If the verbal is used as a modifier, write whether it is an adjective or an adverb.

1. The water in the swimming pool felt cold to Tobias.
2. We hope to be on the road by dawn.
3. I need a folding music stand for the concert.
4. To work in a hospital is Wilson's current goal.
5. The sea turtle is an endangered species.
6. The union accused the management of endangering the workers.
7. Lisa found work in a refining plant.
8. Changing the subject, Denise asked about the dance.
9. Changing the subject seems like a good idea to me.
10. It's hard to study in a crowded room.

USING GRAMMAR IN WRITING
Using Verbals

A. "Seeing is believing." "A rolling stone gathers no moss." "To be or not to be: that is the question." Verbals play key roles in these and many other famous sayings. Write at least ten sayings—famous or original—that use verbals. You may want to use the following verbals:

saved and *earned*   *forgotten*   *to understand*
sleeping   *to live*   *winning*

B. Describe the key play in a sports event in a paragraph of at least five sentences. To describe the play, you will need a way to help your reader visualize the action and feel the excitement. Participles and participial phrases will be useful for this. If you were describing a double play in baseball you could use some of the following.

darting quickly to his right
tossing the ball to the second baseman
leaping over the sliding runner

C. Suppose that you were going to lead a group of foreign visitors on a walking tour of your favorite city or town. What would you want to show the visitors? What interesting facts would you want to tell them? Write a speech that you might use. Plan to include at least four or five interesting attractions. Include at least five infinitive phrases. Begin your paragraph with the sentence *To begin our tour, we will . . . .* You might want to include some of the following phrases.

to improve transportation   to understand our city's history
to celebrate the founding of the city

Making Subjects and Verbs Agree

Two people who accept the same idea are said to agree. Words, too, can agree. The subject and verb in a sentence agree when they are alike in certain ways. In this section you will find out how to make subjects and verbs agree.

Part 1 Making Subjects and Verbs Agree in Number

The **number** of a word refers to whether the word is singular or plural. A word is **singular** when it refers to one thing. A word is **plural** when it refers to more than one thing. When a subject and verb are the same in number, they agree.

A verb must agree in number with its subject. A singular subject belongs with a singular verb. A plural subject belongs with a plural verb.

Singular	Plural
He *guesses.*	They *guess.*
The balloon *rises.*	The balloons *rise.*
She *arrives.*	They *arrive.*
Food *spoils.*	Eggs *spoil.*

As you can tell from the examples, most singular verbs end in -*s*. The plural verbs do not end in -*s*. Verbs used with the first person pronoun, *I*, and the second person pronoun, *you*, also do not end in -*s*, although they are singular.

Usually, subject and verb agreement seems natural. You may have trouble, though, if you are not sure which word is the subject of the sentence. Remember that to find the subject, first find the verb. Then ask *who?* or *what?* before the verb.

> These posts in the ground support the fence.
> *Verb:* support
> *What supports?* posts
> The subject is *posts.*

The subject of the verb is never in a prepositional phrase. A prepositional phrase often appears between the subject and the verb of a sentence. Ignore phrases when you are trying to make subjects and verbs agree.

> *Water* from the streams *runs* into the river.
> *One* of the factories *has* a job opening.
> The *people* on our block *were* helpful.

Phrases beginning with words like *with, together with, including, as well as,* and *in addition to* are also not part of a subject.

The *glue*, as well as the paper, *is stuck* to my hand.
My jacket, together with my vest, *is* at the cleaner's.
Cereal with milk *makes* a good breakfast.

Exercise A   Choose the verb that agrees with the subject.

1. The peaches in the bowl (is, are) ripe.
2. Those men in the picture (looks, look) familiar.
3. The woman in the big sunglasses (is, are) the coach.
4. The waters of the Nile (overflows, overflow) annually.
5. The director of the projects (has, have) resigned.
6. The opponents in the election (is, are) friends.
7. The visit from his friends (has, have) cheered him up.
8. Some beetles, as well as the chameleon, (changes, change) colors.
9. The workers, together with the boss, (demands, demand) a safety check.
10. All of the musicians, including Celia, (gets, get) paid promptly.

Exercise B   Follow the directions for Exercise A.

1. A car with no plates (is, are) usually stopped.
2. The dancer in red suspenders (is, are) out of step.
3. Boxes on this conveyor (requires, require) special handling.
4. Her denial of the rumors (was, were) published.
5. The handles on that suitcase (is, are) loose.
6. Hank's nerves of steel (seems, seem) to be melting.
7. The mind as well as the muscles (needs, need) exercise.
8. Complaints about city services (goes, go) to the mayor.
9. The vision in both her eyes (seems, seem) to be better.
10. Mae's sketches, together with her photos, (shows, show) talent.

Part 2 Compound Subjects

A compound subject joined by *and* is plural. Therefore, it requires a plural verb.

> Flannel *shirts* and wool *socks* **keep** me warm.
> *Seals* and *Crofts* **have performed** here before.

If the parts of a compound subject are joined by *or* or *nor*, the verb should agree with the subject nearer to the verb.

> Neither Adam nor his *cousins were* at the reunion.
> The bank or the grocery *store cashes* my paychecks.

Exercise A   Choose the verb that agrees with the subject.

1. Kay and Ben (attends, attend) night classes.
2. Doughnuts and coffee (was, were) served.
3. Stripes and plaid (looks, look) wrong together.
4. The cuffs and the collar (is, are) too tight.
5. Batfish and viperfish really (exists, exist).
6. Warmth and light (was, were) provided by the fire.
7. Neither the salad nor the dessert (is, are) included.
8. Neither pears nor apples (requires, require) peeling.
9. Either the computer or programmers (is, are) wrong.
10. Either the needle or the tubes (needs, need) to be replaced.

Exercise B   Follow the directions for Exercise A.

1. Either Claire or her sisters (feeds, feed) the stock.
2. Either her sisters or Claire (feeds, feed) the stock.
3. Both Claire and her sisters (feeds, feed) the stock.
4. Neither pancakes nor waffles (is, are) high in protein.
5. The trains and the buses (is, are) running late.
6. Her coordination and speed (improves, improve) daily.
7. Hamburgers and chocolate (is, are) both high in calories.
8. Neither the paper nor the string (is, are) secure.

9. Either rats or squirrels (has, have) chewed this rope.
10. The fare and the cost of a transfer (has, have) increased.

Part 3　Indefinite Pronouns

To make a verb agree with an indefinite pronoun used as its subject, you must know if the pronoun is singular or plural. As you have learned, some indefinite pronouns are singular while others are plural. Still others may be either singular or plural. The following indefinite pronouns are **singular.**

another	each	anything	one	neither
anybody	either	everything	somebody	nobody
anyone	everybody	everyone	someone	no one

Everyone needs leisure time.
Somebody in this room *is* the winner.
Each of the girls *is* in a car pool.

The following indefinite pronouns are **plural.**

both　few　many　several

Many of my friends *work* overtime.
Both of the elevators *are broken.*

The following indefinite pronouns are **singular** when they refer to one thing. They are **plural** when they refer to several things.

all　any　most　none　some

All of this paper *is* for decorations.
All of the reporters *have* deadlines.
Most of this money *is* counterfeit.
Most of the Senators *travel* to foreign countries.
Some of my work *is* difficult.
Some of the vineyards *are* open to visitors.

Exercise A　Choose the verb that agrees with the subject.

1. All of the fat (was, were) trimmed off.
2. All of the bikers (wears, wear) helmets.

3. Most of the students (works, work).
4. Everybody in the building (wants, want) to move because of the high rent.
5. Few of the vents (is, are) open.
6. None of the cheese (is, are) moldy.
7. Most of the players (is, are) under contract.
8. Nobody even (suspects, suspect) the surprise.
9. Something in the oven (smells, smell) good.
10. Another of those big jets (has, have) flown by.

Exercise B Follow the directions for Exercise A.

1. Few of the musicians still (takes, take) lessons.
2. Neither of the solutions (seems, seem) correct.
3. Everything in the islands (has, have) changed.
4. Some of the wood (looks, look) rotten.
5. Each of these games (needs, need) batteries.
6. Both of the ties (goes, go) with the suit.
7. Most of the park (is, are) closed after dark.
8. Some of the instructions (makes, make) no sense.
9. Nothing from the stores (fits, fit) him well.
10. Either of the ties (goes, go) with the suit.

Part 4   Other Problems of Agreement

Doesn't and Don't

The verb *doesn't* is always singular. *Doesn't* is used with the subjects *she, he,* and *it*. *Don't* is used with all other personal pronouns.

It *doesn't* seem right.   We *don't* argue.
She *doesn't* care.   I *don't* drive.
He *doesn't* live here.   They *don't* understand.

Sentences Beginning with *There*

In sentences beginning with *there, here,* or *where,* the subject comes after the verb. Look ahead to find the subject of the sentence. Use the verb that agrees with that subject.

> There *are* some *letters* here for you.
> Here *is* a *piece* of sugarless gum.
> Where *are* the application *forms?*

Exercise A Choose the verb that agrees with the subject.

1. The coach (doesn't, don't) look pleased.
2. Where (is, are) the rubber bands?
3. The stapler (doesn't, don't) have any staples in it.
4. There (was, were) two errors on the bill.
5. (Isn't, Aren't) there any parking places?
6. Here (is, are) my keys.
7. (Doesn't, Don't) the subway stop at Clark Street?
8. (Doesn't, Don't) the lights look lovely?
9. Shauna (doesn't, don't) ever seem hungry.
10. This glue (doesn't, don't) stick to vinyl.

Exercise B Follow the directions for Exercise A.

1. Here (is, are) the latest scores.
2. (Doesn't, Don't) graham crackers contain wheat?
3. There (is, are) no cures for some diseases.
4. The situation (doesn't, don't) look good.
5. Those movers certainly (doesn't, don't) move fast.
6. Where (is, are) the loudspeakers?
7. Here (is, are) a good spot.
8. (Doesn't, Don't) everybody like some kind of music?
9. Where (is, are) my yellow sandals?
10. There (is, are) some ice cubes in the freezer.

ADDITIONAL EXERCISES

Making Subjects and Verbs Agree

A. Agreement in Number Choose the verb that agrees with the subject in number.

1. Only the dents in the fender (is, are) rusty.
2. The coat with leather buttons (belongs, belong) to me.
3. Other clerks in addition to Phil (is, are) bonded.
4. Floods in India (kills, kill) many people.
5. Smoke as well as flames (means, mean) danger.
6. (Is, Are) two slices of bacon enough?
7. The cause of the explosions (has, have) been found.
8. The vendors, including Mattie, (has, have) licenses.
9. Terence, together with his brothers, (plans, plan) to cut a demonstration record.
10. Homes without running water (violates, violate) the housing code here.

B. Compound Subjects Choose the verb that agrees with the compound subject.

1. That truck and the van (gets, get) poor gas mileage.
2. Allergies and asthma sometimes (disappears, disappear).
3. Neither the lobby nor the stairs (is, are) well lit.
4. Either the downspouts or the gutter (is, are) clogged.
5. Bees, birds, and bats, as well as the wind, (carry, carries) pollen.
6. Neither the slides nor the microscope (was, were) in the cabinet.
7. The cats and the dog (has, have) had their rabies shots.
8. The manager or the ushers (cleans, clean) up the aisles.
9. The writers and the star (is, are) leaving that TV series.
10. Butter and margarine sometimes (contains, contain) salt.

C. Indefinite Pronouns   Choose the verb that agrees with the subject.

1. Several of the windows (does, do) not open.
2. One of the space heaters (is, are) very old.
3. Most of the painting (has, have) been done.
4. Few of the tellers (works, work) on Saturday.
5. Some of the milk (has, have) spoiled.
6. All of the students (takes, take) math.
7. Most of the verbs (was, were) irregular.
8. All of the money (was, were) counterfeit.
9. (Is, Are) everybody happy?
10. (Was, Were) everything counted in the inventory?

D. Other Problems of Agreement   Choose the verb that agrees with the subject.

1. There (is, are) hot peppers in that sauce.
2. Where (is, are) the brakes?
3. Annette probably (doesn't, don't) remember me.
4. Here (is, are) your X-rays.
5. There (is, are) some people here to see you.
7. (Doesn't, Don't) Fred live there anymore?
8. Where (does, do) these drainpipes empty?
9. There (is, are) no one answer to that question.
10. (Doesn't, Don't) the birds sound peaceful?

MIXED REVIEW

Making Subjects and Verbs Agree

A. Choosing the correct verb In each of the following sentences, write the verb in parentheses that agrees with the subject.

1. The owl only (seems, seem) wise.
2. The owls in the barn (seems, seem) almost tame.
3. A cat without claws (is, are) at a disadvantage.
4. Several cards from this deck (is, are) missing.
5. Neither the stairs nor the elevator (is, are) safe.
6. The stairs and the elevator (is, are) being repaired.
7. Her license as well as her keys (was, were) gone.
8. After the game, reporters and a photographer (was, were) pushing into the locker room.
9. Either a sled or two bicycles (had, have) gone down the snowy hill.
10. Several pieces of the pattern, along with the instructions, (was, were) spread on the table.

B. Using the correct verb Some of the following sentences contain errors in subject-verb agreement. If a sentence contains an error, rewrite it correctly. If a sentence is correct, write *Correct*.

1. A brass band don't sound as good indoors.
2. There was nobody in the defensive zone.
3. There is four levels of difficulty in this game.
4. Both of the holidays fall on Monday this year.
5. Each of the holidays falls on a weekend.
6. Don't anybody want this onion roll?
7. Here is the computer printouts.
8. Most of the story is true.
9. Everything in the story are true.
10. Where's the vending machines?

USING GRAMMAR IN WRITING
Making Subjects and Verbs Agree

A. Suppose that you are corresponding with a student in another country. The student has asked you to tell what hobbies and other leisure-time interests students in the United States have. What would you want to say? You would certainly want to tell about your own interests. You would probably also want to tell about things that interest others but do not interest you. Make a list of ways that people use their leisure time, and then write a letter to the foreign student. Begin at least one sentence with *there*. Also use at least six of the following indefinite pronouns in your letter. Be certain that all verbs agree with their subjects.

each	many	several	all	none	some
anyone	everyone	nobody	someone	something	

B. You have won a contest sponsored by a local newspaper. The prize is an all-expenses-paid trip with an expedition that is searching for the lost continent of Atlantis. However, there is a catch. You must act as a reporter and write an article for the paper about the expedition. Imagine that you have just returned from the first voyage. Write a paragraph about your observations. Use the following as subjects for your sentences. Be certain that the verbs you use agree with their subjects.

many of the researchers
all of their hard work
all of the other reporters
most of my time
most of our discoveries
some of the creatures that we saw far beneath the sea

Using Compound and Complex Sentences

In preceding sections, you have studied sentence parts and how they work together. Now you are ready to examine four different kinds of sentences. In this section, you will learn about simple sentences, compound sentences, complex sentences, and compound-complex sentences.

Part 1 A Review of the Sentence

Any sentence has two basic parts. These basic parts are the subject and the predicate.

Subject	Predicate
The bus	left.
The last bus from the city	left at midnight.

The **subject** of a sentence names the person or thing about which something is said. The **predicate** tells what happens.

The **simple predicate** is the verb. The **simple subject** is the subject of the verb. Within the subject of the sentence are the simple subject and its modifiers. Within the predicate, are the verb, objects, and predicate words, and their modifiers.

Compound Parts in a Sentence

Any of the parts within a sentence may be **compound.** In other words, each one may have more than one part.

Compound subject:	*Cats, dogs,* and other stray *animals* are taken to the city pound.
Compound verb:	Sheila *turned* and *walked* away.
Compound predicate:	Pat *glazed the clay pot* and then *baked it in the kiln.*
Compound object:	The 76ers' lineup includes *Erving, Collins,* and *Jones.*
Compound object of the preposition:	Fashion models in *magazines* and *newspapers* look perfect.
Compound predicate word:	That injury is neither *severe* nor *painful.*

The Simple Sentence

While the preceding sentences have compound parts, each still expresses only one main idea. Such sentences, like all of those you have been studying, are called **simple sentences.**

A simple sentence is a sentence with only one subject and one predicate. However, the subject, the predicate, and any of their parts may be compound.

You are now prepared to tell simple sentences from other types of sentences.

Exercise A Copy each of the following simple sentences. Then draw a line between the subject and the predicate.

1. Editorials and news stories have different purposes.
2. Humans and other primates walk upright.
3. The waitress looked up and hurried over.
4. Political cartoons can be funny or serious.
5. Marshall and Ed set out for the stadium.
6. Bert sorted and filed the letters.
7. Sue loaded the wheelbarrow and pushed it away.
8. The clinic opens at seven and closes at five.
9. The manager hired typists, machinists, and keypunch operators.
10. The saguaro cactus can grow fifty feet high and weigh six tons.

Exercise B Write the compound subjects, verbs, and objects you find in these simple sentences.

1. Arsonists destroy both life and property.
2. Are the stores and banks closed today?
3. Both heating costs and cooling costs have gone up.
4. Frank danced and sang in the variety show.
5. That reporter investigates consumer fraud and other swindles.
6. He won the Cy Young Award and a big contract.
7. Dancers and athletes must practice daily.
8. Dave tasted and then carefully seasoned the chili.
9. The spy hid the notes under the rugs and in books.
10. Mel, Ann, and Nat got a permit and went into business.

Part 2   The Compound Sentence

When two simple sentences express related ideas, they are sometimes joined to form one sentence. The sentence that results has more than one subject, each with its own predicate. It is called a **compound sentence.**

A compound sentence consists of two or more simple sentences joined together. The parts of the compound sentence may be joined by a coordinating conjunction (*and, or, but*) or by a semicolon(;). Look at the following examples.

> Many horror films are truly scary, **but** others are simply silly.
> The quintuplets were born last month, **and** they are still in the hospital.
> Does Todd work at the bakery, **or** does he work for the city?
> Some comic strips are syndicated; they are purchased by various newspapers across the country.

Why are compound sentences used? Why don't writers use only simple sentences? This passage will help you to see why.

> Barry works for the city. He drives a snowplow. Most of the time he has regular hours. During snowstorms, Barry is on call.

Repeating simple sentences one after another becomes dull and tiresome. Notice how much better the same paragraph sounds with compound sentences.

> Barry works for the city, and he drives a snowplow. Most of the time he has regular hours, but during snowstorms, Barry is on call.

Diagraming Compound Sentences

Once you know how to diagram simple sentences, you can diagram compound ones. A diagram simply shows that a compound sentence is two or more simple sentences joined together. The simple sentences are diagramed one below the other. Then the two sentences are connected with a dotted line. The coordinating conjunction is placed on a "step" in the dotted line.

Lennie dashed for the bus, but he missed it.

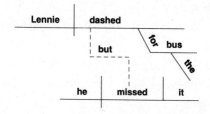

Exercise A Label three columns *Subject/Verb, Conjunction,* and *Subject/Verb.* For each sentence, fill in the columns.

Example: Ray types and takes shorthand, but he wants outdoor work.

Subject/Verb	Conjunction	Subject/Verb
Ray/types, takes	but	he/wants

1. Maine has lovely beaches, but the water is cold.
2. Wild elephants eat a variety of foods, but elephants in zoos eat hay, apples, and carrots.
3. The bus is very late, or maybe we have missed it.
4. The plan seemed silly, but it worked.
5. Emma opened a checking account, and she deposited her check.
6. Lydia makes the calls, and Jan visits the customers.
7. Nobody seemed interested, and I canceled the reservations.
8. Shall we give her a graduation party, or would she prefer a gift?
9. Have Dee and Ken found jobs yet, or are they still looking?
10. Rummage sales and thrift shops offer bargains, but they have few selections.

Exercise B   Follow the directions for Exercise A.

1. The weather was cold and damp, but the baseball fans did not mind.
2. Not every player had signed a contract; some were still negotiating.
3. You can tell the truth, or you can take the consequences.
4. The lipstick and polish match, but they are too light.
5. Ms. Wright wants to buy the house, but she cannot get a mortgage.
6. The wrecked cars are shredded, and the pieces are melted down.
7. Hank baked some oatmeal cookies, and he served them to his friends.
8. The car went into a skid, but Kelly pulled it out.
9. Are you allergic to something, or do you have a cold?
10. Nan has no checking account, but she does have cash.

Compound Sentence or Compound Predicate?

Can you tell the difference between a compound sentence and a simple sentence that has a compound predicate? Both have two verbs. Furthermore, a coordinating conjunction is used within both compound predicates and compound sentences.

> Keane *was ahead in the polls* but *lost the election.*
> (This compound predicate is joined by *but.*)
> *Keane was* ahead in the polls, but *he lost* the election.
> (This is a compound sentence joined by , *but.*)

There is one clear-cut way to tell if a sentence is compound or if it has a compound predicate. If each verb has its own subject, then the sentence is compound. If the verbs share the same subject, then only the predicate is compound.

     s.   **v.**   **v.**

Smugglers buried gold under the sea and *recovered* it later.
(This simple sentence has a compound predicate. Both
verbs, *buried* and *recovered*, have the same subject,
smugglers.)

     s.   **v.**   **s.**   **v.**

Smugglers buried gold under the seas, and *divers recovered*
it later.
(This is a compound sentence. The verb *buried* has its own
subject, *smugglers.* The verb *recovered* has its own subject, *divers.*)

     s.   **v.**   **v.**

Rachel walked into the day-care center and *smiled* warmly.
(The conjunction *and* joins the compound predicate of this
simple sentence. Both verbs, *walked* and *smiled*, have the
same subject, *Rachel.*)

     s.   **v.**   **s.**

Rachel walked into the day-care center, and the *children*
v.
smiled warmly.
(This compound sentence is actually two simple sentences
joined by the conjunction *and.*)

Exercise A Decide whether the following sentences are compound sentences or simple sentences with compound predicates.
Write *Compound Sentence* or *Compound Predicate* on your paper.

1. Jeff raises parakeets and sells them from his home.
2. Laurie discovered the error but did not correct it.
3. Norm yells and Lisa mumbles.
4. Will you stay on the job, or will you quit?
5. The magician performed amazing tricks and entertained
   us all evening.
6. He turned off the gas and padlocked the valve.
7. She does not look like her father, but she acts like him.
8. Did you see or hear anything suspicious?
9. Have you eaten, or can I make you a snack?
10. Curiosity is admirable, but nosiness isn't.

Exercise B Follow the directions for Exercise A.

1. I have an idea, but I don't know for sure.
2. The hospital ran out of funds and had to close.
3. Antibiotics cure many diseases but do not help colds.
4. The tools were old, and they needed repair.
5. The doctors went on strike, but they treated emergencies.
6. Nobody but Ginny could think of such a scheme and carry it out.
7. He must have been delayed, or maybe he has forgotten.
8. The linoleum was worn and torn but shone with wax.
9. Did Kay make the basket, or did Linda make it?
10. The National Guard was put on alert but was not called.

Exercise C: Writing Below are three groups of words. Write three sentences, using each of these groups as the subject of a simple sentence with a compound predicate. Then write a compound sentence, using two of the subjects below.

Marsha and her dog   The trucker   My brother

Punctuating Compound Sentences

One of two punctuation marks is used in a compound sentence. Either a **comma** before a coordinating conjunction or a **semicolon** is needed to separate the two parts of a compound sentence. A punctuation mark shows the division between the two parts. It also shows where to pause in reading the sentence.

When a comma is used in a compound sentence, it belongs before the coordinating conjunction. Notice how the comma is used in these compound sentences.

First Cary nailed the wallboard in place, **and** then Laura taped it.

                    s.   v.   s.   v.
    Some people hide their feelings, **but** others display them
    openly.

    Instead of a comma and a conjunction, a semicolon may be
used in a compound sentence.

                    s.   v.   s.   v.
    Samantha is superstitious; she avoids black cats.

                    s.   v.   s.   v.
    Melissa met Phil on a bus; they were married two years
    later.

    Often a semicolon is used with a **conjunctive adverb.** Conjunc-
tive adverbs are adverbs like *however, nevertheless, therefore,
otherwise, furthermore,* and *consequently.* They help to join the
two parts of a compound sentence. In addition, they show the
relationship between the parts.

                    s.   v.   v.   s.   v.
    Roberto does not swim; *consequently,* he stays away from
    boats.

                    s.   v.   s.   v.
    Elaine was ahead in the polls; *however,* she lost the election.

As you can see, a conjunctive adverb is placed after a semicolon,
and it is followed by a comma.
    Either a comma or a semicolon separates the parts of a com-
pound sentence. However, no punctuation is used between the
parts of a compound predicate. Look at these simple sentences
with compound predicates.

                    s.   v.   v.
    A witness went to the police and told his story.

                    s.   v.   v.
    Linda gets less pay now but enjoys her work more.

    Finally, no commas are necessary in very short compound
sentences.

    The Rangers won and everyone cheered.

Exercise A Commas and semicolons have been omitted between the parts of the following compound sentences. For each sentence, write the two words between which punctuation belongs. Put in the comma or semicolon. If a sentence needs no punctuation, write *correct*.

1. Jackie Wilson hasn't sung for years but many fans remember him.
2. Tyrone lost a quarter in the machine and wrote to the manufacturer.
3. Central City, Colorado, was once a busy mining town but most of the mines are closed now.
4. We wrote to our Congresswoman she answered promptly.
5. I get no sick leave otherwise, I would have stayed home.
6. Did Cora fill out the census form or did you?
7. The new filling fell out and Dawn complained to the dentist.
8. The apartment is on the corner and gets lots of sunlight.
9. Eileen is good at her work moreover, she enjoys it.
10. Neal belongs to a union however, he crossed the picket line.

Exercise B Follow the directions for Exercise A.

1. Jenny found the water meter and copied down the reading.
2. Clayton has an answering machine therefore, he misses no calls.
3. The snake was coiled it was about to strike.
4. Mac is happy with his job and his parents are proud of his success.
5. Squeeze toothpaste from the bottom the tube will last longer.

6. Many great civilizations have fallen and others have taken their places.
7. Rose and Don helped us but would take no pay.
8. Should I straighten the picture on that wall or does it look all right?
9. Terry jumped from the plane and her parachute opened.
10. The bag tore groceries spilled everywhere.

Part 3 The Complex Sentence

You have learned about simple sentences and compound sentences. Another kind of sentence, the **complex sentence,** can also help you to express your ideas. In order to understand the structure of a complex sentence, you must first know what a **clause** is.

A clause is a group of words containing a verb and its subject.

According to this definition, a simple sentence is a clause. It has a verb and a subject.

    s.   **v.**
James retired from baseball.

    s.   **v.**
The trip ended too soon.

However, the structure of sentences will be easier to understand if you think of a clause as *a part of a sentence.* Think of a clause as *a group of words within a sentence.*

Compound sentences contain clauses. Compound sentences have two or more groups of words, each having a subject and verb. Look at the following examples.

    s.   **v.**   **s.**   **v.**
We applied too much paste, and the wallpaper slid off the wall.

$$\overset{\text{s.}}{\text{The twins}} \overset{\text{v.}}{\text{look}} \text{ alike, but their } \overset{\text{s.}}{\text{personalities}} \overset{\text{v.}}{\text{are}} \text{ very}$$

different.

Clause or Phrase?

Keep in mind that clauses differ from phrases. Both clauses and phrases are sentence parts. However, a clause has a subject and a verb. A phrase does not.

Phrases: since Wednesday
before the class

Clauses: since the $\overset{\text{s.}}{\text{campaign}} \overset{\text{v.}}{\text{began}}$

before $\overset{\text{s.}}{\text{I}} \overset{\text{v.}}{\text{went}}$ to the dentist

Subordinate Clauses

The clauses of a compound sentence are actually separate sentences. Each one can stand on its own. Each is a **main clause.** A main clause, also called an **independent clause,** is a clause that can stand alone as a sentence.

Subordinate clauses, or **dependent clauses,** are clauses that cannot stand alone. A subordinate clause is not a complete sentence. Study these examples.

Because the $\overset{\text{s.}}{\text{window}} \overset{\text{v.}}{\text{broke}}$

When the $\overset{\text{s.}}{\text{strike}} \overset{\text{v.}}{\text{was}}$ over

Both of the subordinate clauses above contain subjects and verbs. However, neither of them expresses a complete thought. Neither of them can stand alone. Both leave you wondering *then what?*

A word that begins a subordinate clause has an important function. Without *because* and *when*, the clauses above would

be sentences. Words like *because* and *when* are called **subordinating conjunctions.** They *subordinate*, or make *dependent*, the
words they introduce. Most, but not all, subordinate clauses
begin with subordinating conjunctions.

Words Often Used as Subordinating Conjunctions

after	because	so that	when
although	before	than	whenever
as	if	though	where
as if	in order that	till	wherever
as long as	provided	unless	while
as though	since	until	

Note: Most of the words above can be used in different ways.
They are subordinating conjunctions only when they begin
clauses.

Morever, subordinate clauses do not always begin with subordinating conjunctions. Clauses may begin with words like these:

that	who, whom, whose	why	which
what, whatever	whoever, whomever	how	

Exercise: Writing Using *if, because, when, after,* and *since,*
make subordinate clauses out of these sentences. Then turn the
clauses into sentences by adding a new main clause to each.

1. Lightning struck the shed.
2. Delia used live bait.
3. The orchard is open to the public.
4. The heavy rains caused mudslides.
5. The steps have been repaired.
6. I have no more change.
7. The lamp was unplugged.
8. Paul dislikes seafood.

9. A wire is loose.
10. Kit stole third base.

Definition of the Complex Sentence

Now that you know the difference between main clauses and subordinate clauses, you can understand the complex sentence.

A complex sentence is a sentence that contains one main clause and one or more subordinate clauses.

Main Clause	Subordinate Clause
The tape recorder will start	when you press this button.
The Mayor wouldn't decide	until he asked his advisers.
Frankenstein is a character	that Mary Shelley created.

Exercise A   Copy each subordinate clause in these complex sentences. Underline the subject once and the verb twice.

1. Did you see the Grand Canyon while you were there?
2. Does Carson realize that he needs a ticket?
3. Although his nickname is Lucky, he isn't.
4. Mike knows that we trust him.
5. Margie asked where the pliers were.
6. This is the last time that we will play in this gym.
7. For as long as I can remember, we have shopped at that grocery store.
8. It looks as though the secret is out.
9. Sam works on the car whenever he has a chance.
10. Whenever Carl eats anything, he records the calories.

Exercise B   Follow the directions for Exercise A.

1. Gene always talks as if he has a sore throat.
2. Whenever Rae is in town, we have a family reunion.
3. Ask Allison if she remembers the tune.
4. Weeds grow wherever there are gardens.

5. Donna painted the gutters black so that they would retain heat.
6. Don't sign anything before you have read it.
7. We will not begin until they all arrive.
8. Erin wondered why the dogs were barking.
9. If she cannot sell the van, she will refinance it.
10. You will lose your seat unless you hurry back.

Part 4 Adverb Clauses

By definition, a complex sentence contains a subordinate clause. The subordinate clause may be one of three kinds. One kind is the **adverb clause.** An adverb clause has the same function as an adverb.

An **adverb** modifies a verb, an adjective, or another adverb. It tells *how, when, where,* or *to what extent.*

Adverb: Doug fishes *here.*

An **adverb phrase** is a prepositional phrase used as an adverb.

Adverb phrase: Doug fishes *from this pier.*

An adverb clause is a subordinate clause used as an adverb.

Adverb clause: Doug fishes *whenever he can.*

Adverb clauses, like adverbs and adverb phrases, tell *how, when, where,* or *to what extent.* They modify verbs, adjectives, and adverbs. Don't forget that a clause, unlike a phrase, has a subject and a verb.

Diagraming Adverb Clauses

To diagram an adverb clause, place it on a separate horizontal line below the main line. With a dotted line, connect the adverb clause to the word it modifies in the main clause. Place the subordinating conjunction on the dotted line.

The town has grown since a factory opened here.

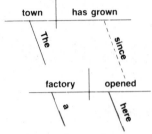

Exercise A   Copy the adverb clause from each sentence.

1. Turn the television off if no one is watching it.
2. Nothing is a bargain unless you need it.
3. While Jay listened, his mind was on his own problems.
4. Because we arrived first, we could sit in the front.
5. Cleo met nice people wherever she traveled.
6. Although slang is lively, it quickly becomes outdated.
7. Dr. Sanchez answers questions more carefully than the other doctors do.
8. When a bus is crowded, Rita waits for the next one.
9. John stays inside whenever the smog is thick.
10. Even the judge was surprised when the defendant pleaded guilty.

Exercise B   Follow the directions for Exercise A.

1. Betsy takes her camera wherever she goes.
2. Although he definitely heard the reporter's question, he ignored her.
3. Treatment cannot be started until the lab report is in.
4. Since the house became vacant, it has been a trouble spot.
5. Lonnie must quit unless his hours are changed.
6. After Tasha passed the test, she celebrated.

7. When the sun sets, the windows look goldplated.
8. Tim lost control of the car as he rounded the curve.
9. As long as you are up, please let the dog in.
10. Because the funds were cut, the day-care center closed.

Part 5 Adjective Clauses

A second kind of subordinate clause is the **adjective clause.** An adjective clause has the same function as an adjective.

An **adjective** modifies either a noun or pronoun.

Adjective: Leslie found *three silver* coins.

An **adjective phrase** is a prepositional phrase that modifies a noun or pronoun.

Adjective phrase: Wendy needs a pair *of crutches.*

An adjective clause is a subordinate clause used as an adjective to modify a noun or pronoun.

Adjective clause: The truck *that was towing my car* broke down.

Adjective clauses, like adjectives and adjective phrases, tell *what kind* or *which one.* They usually appear directly after the noun or pronoun they modify. Adjective clauses, unlike adjective phrases, have subjects and verbs.

There are several words that can introduce adjective clauses. *Where* and *when* are two of them.

Damen is the street *where the accident occurred.*

This is the time *when the tide goes out.*

Relative Pronouns

Besides *when* and *where,* the words *who, whom,* and *whose* are also used to begin adjective clauses. *Who, whom,* and *whose* are called **relative pronouns.** They relate a clause, called a **relative clause,** to a noun or pronoun in the sentence. Sometimes *that* and *which* are relative pronouns.

These words are used as relative pronouns.

who   whom   whose   that   which

The relative pronoun in a complex sentence is special because it has three functions.

1. It introduces an adjective clause.
2. It links the clause to a word in the main clause.
3. It serves a function within the clause. Its role may be subject, object, or predicate pronoun of the verb within the adjective clause. Otherwise, it may be the object of a preposition in the clause. The relative pronoun *whose* is used as an adjective.

Lynn was one of the runners *who finished the marathon.*
(*Who* is the subject of *finished.*)
The pen name *that Samuel Clemens used* was Mark Twain.
(*That* is the direct object of *used.*)
We saw the galley, *which is the kitchen of a ship.*
(*Which is* the subject of *is.*)
The people *with whom I work* bought me a birthday cake.
(*Whom* is the object of the preposition *with.*)
People *whose taxes are late* may be fined.
(*Whose* modifies *taxes,* the subject of the clause.)

Sometimes you may be confused about whether *who* or *whom* is the correct relative pronoun. To decide, see how the pronoun is used within the clause. Remember to use *who* as the subject form and *whom* as the object form.

Diagraming Adjective Clauses

To diagram an adjective clause, place it on a separate line under the main line. A dotted line connects the relative pronoun to the word in the main clause that the adjective modifies.

Do you know anyone who repairs motorcycles?

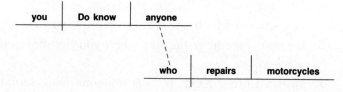

The clerk with whom Val spoke gave her incorrect information.

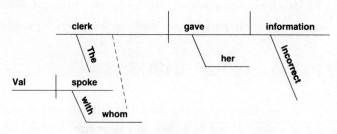

Exercise A   Copy each adjective clause. Write the word it modifies.

1. Smoke filled the only hallway that was open.
2. The room where Mary practices is soundproof.
3. Many of the people to whom we sent questionnaires replied.
4. Sojourner Truth was one of the abolitionists who supported women's rights.
5. The fish that has the worst reputation is the piranha.
6. She is the reporter who uncovered the scandal.
7. Tell her about the time when the accelerator stuck.
8. Did you read the notice that was posted in the hall?
9. That was the last time that I saw Bernie.
10. Houdini was a magician who was known for escapes.

Exercise B   Follow the directions for Exercise A.

1. The wind was the only sound that we heard.
2. Workers who put in overtime received a bonus.

3. The town where he was born no longer exists.
4. The bag in which she put the books was torn.
5. The base to which she was assigned was in Hawaii.
6. Do you remember the day when you first entered school?
7. Martin Luther King, Jr. was someone who combined philosophy and action.
8. Horror movies were the kind that Ms. Zima liked least.
9. Bowlers whose scores are high can enter the contest.
10. Lee Street, which runs east, is the quickest route.

Part 6   Noun Clauses

The noun clause is the third kind of subordinate clause. **A noun clause is a clause used as a noun in a sentence.** A noun clause can be used any way that a noun can be used. It can be a subject, an object of the verb, a predicate word, or an object of a preposition. Unlike adverb and adjective clauses, noun clauses do not modify.

Uses of Noun Clauses

Subject:	*What he expects* is perfection.
Direct object:	Can you explain *how you solved the problem?*
Object of preposition:	The mayor agreed with *whatever the neighborhood group said.* (The clause is the object of the preposition *with*.)
Predicate noun:	Joe's objection was *that the law was out of date.*

These examples show that many noun clauses begin with the words *that* and *what*. The words *whatever, who, whom, whoever,* and *whomever* can also introduce noun clauses. *Where, when, how,* and *why* are used, too.

Diagraming Noun Clauses

To diagram a noun clause, use a bridge extended from the point where the clause is used in the sentence. Place a word that introduces a clause on a line above the clause.

1. Noun clause used as subject

What propels this plane is a jet engine.

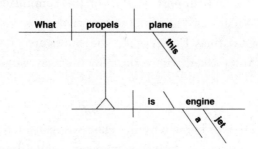

2. Noun clause used as object of the verb

Mark said that he lives on a houseboat.

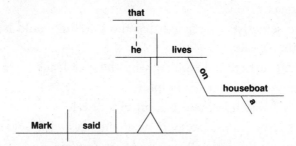

3. Noun clause used as object of a preposition

We talked about how we had become friends.

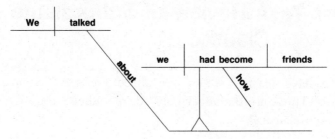

1. Nobody knows how long the strike will continue.
2. Ms. Varner will hire whoever is best qualified.
3. I forgot what I should do next.
4. Travers said that he would be gone for a long time.
5. Why Bobbi said that worries me.
6. Set the dial at whatever number is recommended.
7. We will support whomever the committee chooses.
8. What Clark needs is more privacy.
9. Christmas Eve is when the stores are most crowded.
10. Anita asked where the new highway would go.

Exercise B   Follow the directions for Exercise A.

1. Do you know why the class was canceled?
2. Give these clothes to whoever wants them.
3. Lou complained that the referee had ignored the foul.
4. Newspapers speculated about how the mayor would react.
5. The scientists calculated that the satellite would land in the ocean.
6. Don't just sit and wonder why the roof leaks.
7. Whatever he does is helpful.
8. Why bears hibernate is a bit of a puzzle.
9. The lawyer must support what she says with evidence.
10. Jim muttered that the decision was unfair.

Part 7   A Review of Subordinate Clauses

You have learned about the three kinds of subordinate clauses. These are the adverb clause, the adjective clause, and the noun clause.

The only way to identify the kind of clause is to look at its use in the sentence. A clause used as a noun is a noun clause. A clause used as a modifier is an adverb or adjective clause, depending on the word modified.

Exercise A   Write the subordinate clause in each sentence. If the clause is used as a noun clause, tell how it is used in the sentence. If the clause is used as an adjective or adverb clause, tell what it modifies.

1. Ted asked how old the bike was.
2. Keep going until you reach an intersection.
3. That was the book that made Baldwin's reputation.
4. I suspect that the trouble is in the engine.
5. Who would have believed that this could happen?
6. Ted asked because he is taking a poll.
7. Bev is the only member of the choir who sings solos.
8. How Gillespie discovered his unique sound is a good story.
9. Lena traveled alone when she was in Mexico.
10. Twilight is the time when some people feel lonely.

Exercise B   Follow the directions for Exercise A.

1. I put the message where Sara would be sure to see it.
2. After all, Terry works because she has to.
3. Chuck exercises while he washes the dishes.
4. Sunday, which is the pastor's busiest day, passed quickly.
5. Dr. Weiss, who chaired the conference, teaches here.
6. The writer who is quoted most often is Shakespeare.
7. There is a shuttle helicopter that carries passengers from the city to the airports.
8. China is the country that has the largest population.
9. That explains why the smoke detector went off.
10. Who asked who is in charge here?

Part 8 Clauses as Sentence Fragments

Earlier, you learned about sentence fragments. The kind of fragments you studied did not have subjects and verbs.

a successful business   jogged along the road

There is another kind of fragment that does have a subject and verb. It is a subordinate clause. Because a clause does not express a complete thought, it is a sentence fragment. It is only part of a sentence. It is not meant to stand alone.

Look at how these word groups differ.

Jennifer smiled   when Jennifer smiled

The first word group is a sentence. Because the second word group uses the subordinating conjunction *when*, it is a sentence fragment. Subordinate clauses should be used only within sentences.

A subordinate clause must not be written as a complete sentence. It must always be joined to a main clause.

Fragment: Because he lost his keys
Sentence: Because he lost his keys, Eric was locked out of his apartment.
Fragment: What the code meant
Sentence: The agent explained what the code meant.

Exercise A Number your paper from 1 to 10. Decide whether the groups of words below are sentences or fragments. Write *S* for *Sentence* and *F* for *Fragment*. Add words to make each fragment a complete sentence. Punctuate and capitalize where necessary.

1. The cook who made the tacos
2. June asked who had made the team
3. When the Ice Age was over
4. Before a game Millie skips dinner

5. Before I saw that movie
6. Why is there no hot water
7. What a gyroscope is
8. When is Easter this year
9. Because fish are sensitive to vibrations
10. Until the storm is over

Exercise B   Follow the directions for Exercise A.

1. Remember when we saw the falling star
2. The panda which is not really a bear
3. Just before the game was over
4. What did Marla say to you
5. What the fight was about
6. How do you get to school
7. The night when the water main burst
8. Sal left
9. Because Sal had already left
10. Since breakfast I have had nothing to eat

Part 9   The Compound-Complex Sentence

You can recognize simple, compound, and complex sentences. The last kind of sentence is the **compound-complex sentence.**

A compound-complex sentence consists of two or more main clauses and one or more subordinate clauses.

In other words, think of a compound-complex sentence as a compound sentence plus a subordinate clause. Within a compound-complex sentence, two sentences are joined. At least one of them has a subordinate clause, which may be an adjective, adverb, or noun clause. Between the main clauses is either a coordinating conjunction or a semicolon.

Main Clause   **Main Clause**   **Subordinate Clause**

Carol felt dizzy, and we noticed that she looked pale.

Subordinate Clause   **Main Clause**

When a shark was sighted, the beach was closed, and

Main Clause

everyone went home.

Exercise Identify the two main clauses and the subordinate clause in these compound-complex sentences.

1. She realized that I was listening, and she whispered.
2. I played in the band before I took a job, but now I don't have time.
3. Ike knew that the machine would not fit through the doorway, and he called his boss.
4. Watch where you're going, or you will slip.
5. Don't ask why you were invited; just accept.
6. Watch the machine, and you'll see how it works.
7. Usually the goalie is the player who is most important; this game was unusual.
8. Al plays bass, but he also sings if you ask.
9. Egypt hated its Persian conquerors; it was glad when Alexander the Great defeated them.
10. Native Americans had cures that impressed European doctors; however, most of the cures are now lost.

Part 10 A Review of Sentences

There are four basic kinds of sentences.

A **simple sentence** contains one subject and one predicate. Parts of the simple sentence, however, may be compound. A simple sentence tells one idea.

      s.   v.   v.

Lou was born in Ohio but grew up in Oregon.

A **compound sentence** is made up of two simple sentences. These simple sentences are connected by a comma and coordinating conjunction or by a semicolon. Sometimes a conjunctive adverb follows the semicolon. A compound sentence expresses two related ideas.

> s.   v.   s.   v.
> Lou was born in Ohio; however, he grew up in Oregon.

A **complex sentence** contains one main clause and one or more subordinate clauses. The subordinate clauses may be used as adverbs, adjectives, or nouns. A complex sentence expresses one main idea and one or more dependent ideas.

> s.   v.   s.   v.
> *Although Lou was born in Ohio,* he grew up in Oregon.

A **compound-complex sentence** contains two main clauses and one or more subordinate clauses. The subordinate clauses may be adverb, adjective, or noun clauses. A compound-complex sentence expresses two main ideas, as well as one dependent idea.

> s.   v.   s.   v.
> *Although Lou was born in Ohio,* he grew up in Oregon; now
>
> s.   v.
> he lives in New Mexico.

Exercise A For each sentence, write *Simple, Compound, Complex,* or *Compound-Complex* to show what kind it is.

1. Mike said that he would be late.
2. Kenny and his friends went to a movie at the Uptown Theater.
3. Are these keys yours, or do they belong to Troy?
4. Kathy wrote a letter to the editor, and the letter was published.
5. The salesclerk explained how the amplifier worked.
6. If you have any suggestions, write them down.

7. Did you buy the car because you liked its looks?
8. How pretty the room looks!
9. Carpet beetles eat rugs; however, the larvae can be easily killed.
10. Nobody but Jim stayed and helped after the party.

Exercise B   Follow the directions for Exercise A.

1. The Watsons bought postcards, but they forgot to send them.
2. Tony put the pizza in the oven and set the timer.
3. Before you leave, look at these pictures.
4. Doesn't Ed realize that he is being immature, or doesn't he care?
5. A van pulled up, and the band piled in.
6. How many people live in that apartment building?
7. The album that Christina bought was warped.
8. Until Ann moved, she walked or biked to work.
9. She stopped singing when the audience began cheering.
10. Lower the thermostat if you want to save energy.

Exercise C: Writing   Using the sentence *Janet likes cats* as a base, write one simple sentence with a compound predicate, one compound sentence, one complex sentence, and one compound-complex sentence.

ADDITIONAL EXERCISES

Using Compound and Complex Sentences

A. Simple Sentences Label four columns *Subject, Verb, Object*, and *Predicate Word*. For each sentence fill in the appropriate columns. Some sentences may have compound parts.

> Example: The plumber and the electrician worked for the
> same contractor.

Subject	Verb	Object	Predicate Word
plumber	worked		
electrician			

1. The school has a gym and an auditorium.
2. Snakes, lizards, and mealworms shed their skin.
3. The hollow tree is still alive.
4. The coach benched Charley and Clayton.
5. The jeans faded and shrank in the hot water.
6. Bobbi and Kate shared the job.
7. Long ago the Walkers and the Drews quarreled and
   never spoke to each other agan.
8. The moon and stars looked bright and distinct.
9. The streets in the town were wide, quiet, and
   tree-lined.
10. The stew bubbled and steamed on the stove.

B. Compound Sentences Number your paper from 1 to 10. Label three columns *Subject/Verb, Conjunction,* and *Subject/Verb.* For each sentence, fill in the columns. If a sentence does not have a conjunction, write *semicolon* in the conjunction column.

1. Priscilla bought a newspaper, but she left it on the bus.
2. A rolling stone gathers no moss, but nobody wants to
   be mossy.

3. Few dentists still use novocain; they now use lidocaine.
4. First Shelly swept the room, and then she vacuumed it.
5. Valenzuela played for nine innings, and then Howe relieved him.
6. The candle had dropped onto the tablecloth, and Eric scraped off the wax.
7. Should I serve these leftovers, or are you saving them?
8. Luke and Tom argued often, and finally the boss gave Tom a different counter.
9. The snow stopped, but the wind picked up.
10. Cara and Bert went to the public pool; Kit and Red are at the beach.

C. Compound Predicates and Compound Sentences

Number your paper from 1 to 10. Decide whether these sentences are compound sentences or simple sentences with compound predicates. Write *Compound Sentence* or *Compound Predicate*.

1. The days were short, and the nights were long.
2. The canoe drifted, hit a floating log, and capsized.
3. Yellow curtains framed the window and went well with the blue sky outside.
4. The old man started across the street but stopped in the middle.
5. The driver signalled a left turn, but then he went straight.
6. Cass fell, but Alice helped her up.
7. Fran pickled the cucumbers, canned the peaches, and froze the broccoli.
8. Roosters crowed and doves cooed.
9. Olivia ordered a hamburger, and Bennie ordered a salad.
10. Nina swims at the Y or jogs several blocks every day.

D. Compound Constructions Copy each sentence. Add punctuation if it is needed. If it is not needed, write *Correct* after the sentence.

1. Sid's aim was off consequently the ball veered.
2. The grapefruit looked ripe but it tasted sour.
3. Nora and Marie checked the basement but they found nothing.
4. He held his nose and jumped into the water.
5. Hal draws the blueprints and Kay or Chip gives the estimates.
6. Suzy cut the cartoon out and tacked it to the office bulletin board.
7. Today is a holiday no mail is delivered.
8. Neal must make the payment otherwise he will lose the car.
9. He sat and waited but she had forgotten all about him.
10. The outdoor stage was shallow and uneven thus the dancers did not want to perform on it.

E. Adverb Clauses Copy each adverb clause. Underline its subject once and its verb twice. Draw a circle around the subordinating conjunction.

1. Don't spread the frosting until the cake has cooled.
2. When Cornwallis surrendered to George Washington, the English band played "The World Turned Upside Down."
3. Joanne can't wash the dishes because she is allergic to that soap.
4. Unemployment rose as financial aid declined.
5. While we were in Florida, we rode in a glass-bottomed boat.
6. Dan becomes breathless when he's nervous.
7. Borrow my bike if you must.

8. The casserole tasted better than it looked.

9. Carl lived with his grandmother until he could afford an apartment.

10. After being repainted, the radiator worked better than it had before.

F. Adjective Clauses Copy the adjective clause from each sentence. Underline the subject once and the verb twice. Before the clause, write the word it modifies.

1. Ms. Baptiste is the woman who runs the program.
2. The passenger whose luggage was lost was reimbursed.
3. The compartment in which she stowed away was unheated.
4. Which is the hotel where the movie was filmed?
5. The hair stylist whom you requested is on vacation.
6. Three-D glasses, which you need for the movie, are in the lobby.
7. That was the night when the power went off.
8. Boots that cost the most aren't always the best.
9. There were days when Melissa would have cheerfully junked the temperamental old truck.
10. Is that the best that you can do?

G. Noun Clauses Copy the noun clause in each sentence. Tell how the clause is used.

1. I didn't know that you worked at Head Start.
2. We could not tell where the noise was coming from.
3. Give the circular to whoever opens the door.
4. Travis worried about why his dogs were barking.
5. Why did you ask where the train schedule is?
6. Why this equation works is not fully understood.
7. How would I know when the movie ends?
8. Exactly how the video game operated intrigued Vicky.

9. Suzanne explained that she had a flexible work schedule.
10. That kind of pessimism is not what we need right now.

H. Subordinate Clauses
Write the subordinate clause in each sentence. Tell whether it is an *Adjective, Adverb,* or *Noun* clause. If it is a noun clause, tell how it is used in the sentence. If the clause is used as an adjective or adverb clause, tell what it modifies.

1. Jonas has an uncle who sells used cars.
2. I wonder who taught Jill how to play the piano.
3. Who knows how the story ends?
4. If it's nine o'clock here, then it's ten o'clock on the East Coast.
5. Take the medicine before you feel seasick.
6. Before long, Vivian realized that the valve was open.
7. The package that you delivered belongs next door.
8. That was the summer when Charlie was working on a road crew.
9. Do crickets chirp faster when it's hot or cold?
10. Where is the hill that has the toboggan run?

I. Sentence Fragments
Number your paper from 1 to 10. Decide whether the groups of words below are sentences or fragments. Write *S* for *Sentence* and *F* for *Fragment.* Add words to make each fragment a complete sentence. Punctuate and capitalize where necessary.

1. The athletes that will be participating
2. That is a shark's fin
3. Why the walls feel damp
4. Why did the circuit breaker malfunction
5. After that we bought a portable fan
6. After the audience had seen the sneak preview
7. Where the waterfalls are
8. Where are the waterfalls

9. Because the crowd at night games is noisy
10. Until then take care

J. Compound-Complex Sentences
Number your paper from 1 to 10. Skip two lines between the numbers. Write the first main clause of each sentence, and label it *Main Clause*. Do the same with the second main clause. Then write the subordinate clause. Label it *Subordinate Clause*.

1. A child was lost at the beach, and the lifeguard asked that we make a human chain in the water.
2. I know what the surprise is, but I certainly won't tell you.
3. Everyone thought that the war in Vietnam would not last long; however, it went on for years.
4. Rochelle stopped and sipped some water, and then she resumed the speech where she had left off.
5. When did the agent realize that the message was in code, and how did she break the code?
6. Gordon tried to weed the garden, but he had to stop because he couldn't tell a weed from a seedling.
7. Have you forgotten where you left the umbrella, or can you go back and get it?
8. If Frank is at home, we will get a warm welcome; Andy, however, will probably not invite us in.
9. Although it was sleeting, Agnes hiked to the river, and there she met Stephanie.
10. After the graduation ceremony, we returned our caps and gowns, which were rented, to the gym; our relatives and friends met us outside.

MIXED REVIEW

Using Compound and Complex Sentences

A. Identifying sentences and fragments Decide whether the following groups of words are sentences or fragments. If a group is a sentence, write *S.* If a group is a fragment, write *F.* Then write whether the fragment is a *phrase* or a *clause.*

1. When the Dark Ages were
2. When were the Dark Ages
3. When we are in a dark room, the pupils of our eyes enlarge
4. When in doubt
5. Until about two thousand years ago
6. What he meant is quite clear
7. What the conductor is saying
8. Pakistan, which was once part of India
9. Leave if you want
10. Every year for ten years on the day before Thanksgiving

B. Identifying kinds of sentences For each sentence write *Simple, Compound, Complex,* or *Compound-Complex* to tell what kind it is.

1. Those dogs look very much like wolves.
2. Those dogs look as if they are wild.
3. After your birthday, you won't need a work permit.
4. He caught the ball in one hand and kicked it down the field.
5. Shirley talked, and Luther nodded.
6. Shirley talked while Luther nodded.
7. I know someone who repairs autos, but he won't work for pay.
8. Until Judy graduated, she had held part-time jobs.

9. Until the hurricane, cottages had lined the coast.
10. We can tell you what happened, or can you guess?

C. Recognizing subordinate clauses
Copy the subordinate clause from each of the following sentences. Underline its subject once and its verb twice. Then write *Adverb*, *Adjective*, or *Noun* to show what kind of clause it is.

1. Did Skip realize that he had erased the tape?
2. That is the Lombardi trophy that the coach is holding.
3. Some people moved to Texas because they had heard of jobs there.
4. Migrant workers move to where there is a harvest.
5. Like most of us, Daisy gets as much sleep as she can.
6. Ben always asks before he borrows anything.
7. Jenny asked why she could not see her personnel file.
8. In Japan there is a factory where robots make robots.
9. Let's sit where we'll be out of the wind.
10. Who knows where the time has gone, and who cares?

D. Using subordinate clauses correctly
Copy the subordinate clause from the following sentences. Write *Noun*, *Adjective*, or *Adverb* to show what kind it is. If it is a noun, write *Subject*, *Direct Object*, *Object of Preposition*, or *Predicate Noun*. If the clause is used as an adjective or adverb, write the word it modifies.

1. Most people who talk to plants are really quite sane.
2. I wonder who lives there now.
3. Mr. Valentino worried about what the doctor had said.
4. That is what she said.
5. Kitty found a gym where she could train.
6. Where did Fred go after he left the meeting?
7. Stay until the end if you like.
8. Ask whomever you like.
9. Before his diet, Al was much heavier than he is now.
10. One game that Maya plays better than Dee is chess.

USING GRAMMAR IN WRITING
Using Compound and Complex Sentences

A. A local travel agency has announced an exciting contest. You can win a trip to any place in the world. If you win, a friend will be able to go with you. All you have to do to win is write a paragraph about things that you and your friend would do on the trip. Compound sentences will be useful to you in writing this paragraph. Sentences joined by *and* will show that two things are similar. Sentences joined by *but* will show a contrast. Sentences with *or* will show a choice. At least one compound sentence should show that two of the things you'd like to do are similar. Another should show a contrast. A third should show a choice.

B. You are a writer for *Sports Illustrated.* Your assignment this week is to capture the color and excitement in the minutes before an important game. Write a paragraph or more about the feelings of the players or the spectators. Choose your favorite sport. You will find adverb clauses useful in this writing since they tell how, when, where, and why things happen. Adjective clauses will be useful because they help describe details. Write your report, using details from your experience or imagination. Use at least five adverb and adjective clauses. Underline each one.

CUMULATIVE REVIEW
The Sentence

A. Identifying kinds of sentences Copy the following sentences. Insert the correct punctuation. After each sentence, write *D* for declarative, *INT* for interrogative, *IMP* for imperative, or *E* for exclamatory. Underline each subject once and each verb twice.

1. Daffodils bloom in the spring
2. Is that an aluminum bicycle
3. Until 1866 most of the world's diamonds came from Brazil
4. Look out for that wire
5. Wash the dark laundry in cold water
6. Did Debbie Armstrong win a gold medal in the 1984 Winter Olympics
7. The book *Pumping Iron* is about bodybuilding
8. What a fascinating story that is
9. Put the titles in alphabetical order
10. Where is Cumberland Island

B. Understanding agreement in sentences Number your paper from 1 to 15. Write the correct word from the two given in parentheses.

1. The dresses on that rack (is, are) on sale.
2. There (was, were) a pack of wild dogs terrorizing the sheep.
3. Neither the teacher nor the students (was, were) aware of the commotion in the hall.
4. Each of the scientists (want, wants) to win that award.
5. Where (is, are) the garden hose?
6. A camera crew, as well as a crowd of reporters, (cover, covers) presidential news conferences.
7. That book of poems (is, are) humorous.

8. Everybody brought (his or her, their) own lunch.
9. Clare (doesn't, don't) enjoy watching baseball on TV.
10. Here (is, are) a pen and some stationery.
11. Where (do, does) the eagles make their nests?
12. One of the contestants (was, were) disqualified.
13. Most of the students (seem, seems) prepared for the quiz.
14. Some of this paint (is, are) oil base paint.
15. Either your class notes or the textbook (contain, contains) the answer to that question.

C. Correcting fragments and run-on sentences Rewrite the following paragraph. Use capitalization and punctuation to correct fragments and run-ons. Do not add or change any words.

The roadrunner, a member of the cuckoo family. Is found in the desert states of the American Southwest. The roadrunner is only about nine inches tall. And less than two feet long. Although it is small. It can run almost twenty miles an hour. Nestling roadrunners eat reptiles the diet of a full-grown roadrunner is more varied. It includes plants and insects. As well as other birds, snails, mice, bats, scorpions, tarantulas, and black widow spiders. A roadrunner is indeed fearless it will even attack a rattlesnake. In Mexico, the bird is called *paisano*. Which means "countryman." Some folk healers believe that a roadrunner stew can cure diseases. From tuberculosis and backaches. To itches, boils, and leprosy. The roadrunner is also a good luck omen. If it crosses your path. You will have a safe trip.

D. Writing good sentences Rewrite each of the following sentences. Follow the directions in parentheses.

1. Marla wrapped the birthday gift in the comic papers. (Add the prepositional phrase *for her brother*.)

2. Jake washed the outside of the car. He vacuumed the interior. (Combine these two sentences into one with a compound predicate.)

3. Rhonda wrote an article for the school newspaper. Elsa wrote one, too. (Combine these two sentences into one with a compound subject.)

4. Sean set his alarm for six o'clock. He still missed the bus. (Combine these two simple sentences into one compound sentence using ,*but*.)

5. Bonnie painted the trim. Alex wallpapered the walls. (Combine these two simple sentences into one compound sentence using ,*and*.)

6. It rained. The field trip to the arboretum was cancelled. (Combine these two simple sentences into one complex sentence using *because*.)

7. The Eli Bridge Company designed a portable Ferris wheel. The company is located in Jacksonville, Illinois. (Combine these two simple sentences into one complex sentence using *which*.)

8. Strawberries taste delicious. They are not fattening. (Combine these two simple sentences into one complex sentence using *although*.)

9. Craig ordered from the dinner menu. (Change this NV sentence to one with a NVN pattern.)

10. Miriam is an athletic person. (Change this N LV N sentence into one with a N LV Adj pattern.)

The Right Word

In preceding sections you have examined the sentence and its parts. In this section you will examine some general ideas about the English language and some specific words that cause confusion.

Part 1 Standard and Nonstandard English

The language that is presented in this textbook would be appropriate at all times and in all places. It is **standard English.** Standard English is the language used by educated people. It is the language that is correct in any situation.

If you do not use standard English in certain situations, people may think of you as less careful or less intelligent. Language

guage that is not considered correct or acceptable by all people in all situations is called **nonstandard English.**

Compare these examples of standard and nonstandard English.

Standard	**Nonstandard**
Lou and I have gone on that road before.	Me and Lou has went on that there road before.
There aren't any people anywhere.	There ain't no people anywheres.
They were hurt badly.	They was hurt bad.

Part 2 Formal and Informal English

Even if you always use standard English, you will use different levels of language at different times. For instance, you wouldn't use the same words in a letter requesting a job interview as you would on the phone to a friend. Some situations are simply more formal than others. Likewise, the appropriate language is either formal or informal. Compare the following examples.

Formal: Formed by the skeletons of marine organisms, a coral reef acts as a barrier against powerful ocean waves. Within the lagoon enclosed by a reef, fish and plant life flourish.

Informal: Isn't this coral reef fantastic? I can see lots of colorful fish and plants under the water. With scuba equipment, we could see more.

In general, formal English is marked by a more precise and factual presentation of information. It is marked also by longer sentences with longer words and fewer contractions. Formal English is appropriate for writing some papers, articles, and books. On the other hand, informal English is appropriate for speaking and for more casual writing situations.

Part 3   Other Types of Language

There are other uses of language that you may encounter in everyday situations. **Slang,** for example, is unusual, continually changing language. "Rap," "totally awesome," and "power trip" are examples of slang. Slang expressions are acceptable only in the most informal speaking situations. Such expressions are not acceptable in your writing.

Sometimes when you read, you may find language you do not understand because it is no longer used. Outdated language is called **archaic** or **obsolete,** and it is usually labeled so in a dictionary.

In addition, certain language related to sports, music, science, law, and the military often has special meanings. Consequently, a word may have different meanings under different circumstances. On board a ship, for example, the word *up* is used to mean "windward." However, on a baseball field *up* is used to mean "at bat."

All of these uses of language are appropriate at certain times. However, using certain language in the wrong situation is inappropriate and confusing. For example, using slang in a business report or formal English in a shopping list is not a suitable or sensible use of language. As you become more skillful with standard English, you will be better able to use language appropriate to a particular time and place.

Part 4   Words Often Confused

Certain words are often confused because they look alike or sound alike or because they have similar meanings. However, the words grouped in the following list are not alike. One word cannot substitute for another. Study this list of words often confused. Practice using the right word at the right time.

adapt means "to adjust."
adopt means "to take up and use as one's own."

Can you *adapt* this engine for a smaller bike?
The club recently *adopted* a new motto.

advice means "an opinion."
advise is "to suggest or give advice to."

Anita needed help and asked for *advice*.
The campaign manager *advised* the candidate.

des′ ert means "a dry, barren region."
de sert′ means "to leave or abandon."
des sert′ (note the difference in spelling) is a usually sweet
food served at the end of a meal.

There is an oasis in the *desert*.
Did the man *desert* his family?
We will have coffee with *dessert*.

hear means "to listen to or to receive sound by the ear."
here refers to this place.

Did you *hear* the newscaster's comments?
New townhouses will be built *here*.

its is a possessive, meaning belonging to *it*.
it's is a contraction for *it is* or *it has*.

The show is in *its* third season.
It's curtain time!

lead (lēd) means "to guide or head." Its past tense is *led*.
lead (led) is a soft metal.

Please *lead* us home. Ryan *led* us the wrong way.
Strips of *lead* hold the pieces of stained glass together.

loose means either "not tight" or "free and untied."
lose means "to be unable to find or keep." It is also the
opposite of *win*.

Since I lost weight, my clothes are *loose*.
Did you *lose* your job?
Usually I *lose* at games.

principal means "leading, chief, or highest in importance." It also means "the head of a school."

principle refers to a basic truth, rule, or law.

> The *principal* water supply comes from underground.
> Our *principal* is not as strict as she looks.
> One *principle* of a democracy is rule by the people.

stationary means "not moving, fixed."

stationery refers to materials for writing, especially paper and envelopes.

> The *stationary* ship is a floating museum.
> Nicole's *stationery* has her initials on it.

their shows possession by *them*.

there means "in that place."

they're is the contraction for *they are*.

> *Their* plates were loaded with food.
> The doughnut shop is *there* on the corner.
> *They're* listening to their new albums.

to means "toward or as far as."

too means "also or extremely."

two is the number between one and three.

> This rickety old staircase leads *to* the attic.
> Dwayne plays the trumpet and the trombone, *too*.
> I am the younger of *two* sisters.

weather refers to the condition of the atmosphere, including its heat or cold, wetness or dryness.

whether indicates a choice between two things.

> The *weather* was unusually calm.
> Stacy couldn't decide *whether* to go out or to stay home.

who's is the contraction for *who is* or *who has*.

whose is the possessive form of *who*.

> *Who's* the drummer for the Police?
> *Whose* bike did you borrow?

your shows possession by *you.*

you're is the contraction for *you are* or *you were.*

> I'd recognize *your* voice anywhere.
> *You're* leaving now, aren't you?

Exercise Choose the right word from the words given.

1. (Weather, Whether) is affected by air pressure.
2. The sheriff (adviced, advised) us to avoid Interstate 80.
3. (Their, There, They're) is the snow shovel.
4. Do you know (who's, whose) in command?
5. We'll be taking inventory next week, (to, too).
6. (Your, You're) name is in the newspaper!
7. David gave me some good (advice, advise).
8. Those gymnasts never (loose, lose) their balance.
9. For (desert, dessert) the choices are sherbert, torte, or fresh fruit.
10. His parents (adapted, adopted) two homeless children.
11. The dancers rehearsed (their, there, they're) numbers for the talent show.
12. Camels are used for crossing the (desert, dessert).
13. The play was (adapted, adopted) slightly for TV.
14. Shale is a (principal, principle) source of oil.
15. When you mumble, I can't (hear, here) you.

Part 5   Troublesome Verbs

The following pairs of verbs are often confused. Examine the differences between them.

Bring and Take

Bring refers to movement toward the person speaking. Example: Trucks *bring* goods here to the loading dock.

Take refers to motion away from the speaker. Example: Did you *take* the chipped plate back to the store?

Here are the principal parts of the verbs.

bring, brought, brought

Present:	*Bring* home some bread, please.
Past:	The doctor *brought* an assistant with her.
Past Participle:	You *have brought* me good luck.

take, took, taken

Present:	*Take* some coffee out to the workers.
Past:	Carruthers *took* the ball out of bounds.
Past Participle:	Somebody *has taken* my jacket.

Learn and Teach

Learn means "to gain knowledge or skill." Example: Did you *learn* what the code means?

Teach means "to help someone learn." Example: Will you *teach* me how to lift weights?

Here are the principal parts of these verbs.

learn, learned, learned

Present:	*Learn* your lines before Monday.
Past:	Beth *learned* how to place-kick.
Past Participle:	We *have learned* a lot about tropical fish.

teach, taught, taught

Present:	Julia Child *teaches* viewers about cooking.
Past:	The foreman *taught* us to use the drill press.
Past Participle:	Derek *has taught* his dog simple commands.

Let and Leave

Let means "to allow or permit." Example: *Let* us in.

Leave means "to go away from" or "to allow something to remain." Example: *Leave* the boxes here.

Here are the principal parts of the verbs.

let, let, let

Present:	The rangers *let* people into the park.
Past:	Jane *let* the dog in.
Past Participle:	The supervisor *has let* us work overtime.

leave, left, left

Present:	*Leave* the door open, please.
Past:	Barrett *left* his business card on the table.
Past Participle:	The photographer *has left* with her camera.

Lie and Lay

Lie means "to rest in a flat position" or "to be in a certain place." Example: *Lie* on your back.

Lay means "to place." Example: *Lay* your cards down. These are the principal parts of these verbs.

lie, lay, lain

Present:	*Lie* down on the examining table.
Past:	The keys *lay* on the seat.
Past Participle:	All day Brian *has lain* under a palm tree.

lay, laid, laid

Present:	*Lay* the logs on the fire.
Past:	The plumber *laid* out his tools on the floor.
Past Participle:	The workers *have laid* the tile.

May and Can

The helping verb *may* refers to permission. *May* also indicates that something is possible. *Might* is another form.

May I *continue?*   Nancy *might forget.*

The helping verb *can* refers to ability. *Can* means being able, physically or mentally, to do something. Another form is *could*.

How far *can* you *run?*   Nobody *could see.*

May and *might* and *can* and *could* have no principal parts.

Rise and Raise

Rise means "to go upward." Example: Warm air *rises*.

Raise means "to lift or make something go up." Example: *Raise* your left hand.

Here are the principal parts of the verbs.

rise, rose, risen

Present: Gliders *rise* with the wind.

Past: The symphony members *rose* and bowed.

Past Participle: Because of heavy rains, the river waters *have risen*.

raise, raised, raised

Present: Every year the owner *raises* our rent.

Past: The mechanic *raised* the car on a lift.

Past Participle: The judge *has raised* the fine.

Sit and Set

Sit means "to occupy a seat." Example: *Sit* next to me.

Set means "to put." Example: *Set* the tea here.

These are their principal parts.

sit, sat, sat

Present: *Sit* in the penalty box for five minutes.

Past: Lauren and I *sat* in the balcony.

Past Participle: All season Roberts *has sat* on the bench.

set, set, set

Present: *Set* your packages on the table.

Past: Ann *set* the message next to the phone.

Past Participle: They *have set* their luggage on the conveyor belt.

Exercise   Choose the right verb from those given.

1. Don't (sit, set) that paintbrush on my jacket.
2. (May, Can) I please borrow your saw?

3. (Bring, Take) those keys over here, please.
4. The instructor (learned, taught) us how to spot faulty wiring.
5. The driver (let, left) me operate the forklift.
6. Exhausted, Meredith (lay, laid) on the couch all day.
7. The nurse (rose, raised) Diana's hospital bed.
8. (Let, Leave) the dough (rise, raise) for two hours.
9. A pile of bills (lay, laid) on the desk.
10. The passengers (sat, set) in small lifeboats.
11. Kim has (brought, taken) us some egg rolls from her mother's restaurant.
12. The mail carrier (let, left) our package outside in the rain.
13. We must (bring, take) these cans out to the recycling center.
14. Lee (rose, raised) the hood of the car.
15. (Lie, Lay) the packing slip on the top of the crate.

Part 6 Usage Problems

The following words are often used incorrectly. To avoid problems, study these examples of standard usage.

accept means "to agree to something or to receive something willingly."

except means "to leave out." *Except* also means "not including."

> The Raiders *accepted* the fifteen-yard penalty.
> No one is *excepted* from the terms of the contract.
> We have all the ingredients *except* corn syrup.

all right is the correct spelling. *Alright* is nonstandard and should be avoided.

> *All right,* I'll stop by later.   Do I look *all right?*

among refers to more than two people or things.
between refers to only two people or things.

> There was a fake stone *among* the jewels.
> We split the granola bar *between* the two of us.

amount refers to a certain quantity that cannot be counted. It is used with singular nouns.
number refers to items that can be counted. It is used with plural nouns.

> Frieda poured a small *amount* of milk into a cup.
> A large *number* of travelers visit the Grand Canyon.

bad is an adjective. Besides modifying nouns and pronouns, *bad* is also used with linking verbs like *feel*.
badly is an adverb. It is used only with action verbs.

> Ramon feels *bad* about the mix-up.
> Chris had a *bad* day yesterday.
> Gustafson pitches *badly*.

beside means "at the side of." It points out location.
besides means "in addition to."

> We sat *beside* the wood-burning stove.
> *Besides* tacos, I also like tamales and enchiladas.

borrow means "to receive something on loan." Don't confuse it with *lend*, meaning "to give out temporarily."

> Nonstandard: Will you borrow me your fishing pole?
> Standard: Will you *lend* me your fishing pole?
> Standard: May I *borrow* your fishing pole?

fewer refers to numbers or things that can be counted.
less refers to a certain amount or quantity.

> There are *fewer* people here today.
> This recipe calls for *less* flour.

Exercise Rewrite those sentences with nonstandard usage. Use the right words. If a sentence is correct, write *Correct*.

1. Besides papers, the newsstand also sells magazines.
2. Only a small amount of tickets are unsold.
3. Eliza works fewer hours on weekends.
4. When he makes a mistake, Ken feels badly.
5. All right, I'll use less onions.
6. We shared the supplies between the four of us.
7. Everyone accept Judith went home early.
8. The personnel department accepts applications for summer jobs.
9. Lisa's parents will borrow her some furniture for her apartment.
10. The patient seems alright today.
11. A large amount of old buildings have been renovated.
12. Many people are trying to use less fuel.
13. There is a picnic table besides the stream.
14. Both quarterbacks played bad in last night's game.
15. Between the four of us, we should be able to think of a solution.

had of and **off of** are nonstandard. In both cases, *of* is unnecessary and should be omitted.

Nonstandard: If you had of helped, I'd be done by now.
Standard: If you *had* helped, I'd be done by now.
Nonstandard: The clasp came off of Gina's necklace.
Standard: The clasp came *off* Gina's necklace.

himself and **themselves** are standard usage. *Hisself, theirselves,* and *themself* are nonstandard.

Nonstandard: The mayor hisself led the parade.
Standard: The mayor *himself* led the parade.
Nonstandard: The campers found theirselves in a dark cave.
Standard: The campers found *themselves* in a dark cave.

in means "inside something."
into tells of motion from the outside to the inside of something.

Nonstandard:	The tightrope walker fell in the net.
Standard:	The tightrope walker fell *into* the net.
Nonstandard:	Drop your ballot in this box.
Standard:	Drop your ballot *into* this box.

kind of and **sort of** are not acceptable as modifiers. To be correct, use *rather, fairly, slightly,* or *somewhat* instead.

Nonstandard:	Danny is sort of shy.
Standard:	Danny is *rather* shy.
Nonstandard:	I have been kind of lonely lately.
Standard:	I have been *somewhat* lonely lately.

like is a preposition. Using *like* as a conjunction before a clause is not fully accepted. Especially in writing, *as* or *as if* is better.

Nonstandard:	Jay looks like he's pleased.
Standard:	Jay looks *as if* he's pleased.
Nonstandard:	Just like I thought, the tank was empty.
Standard:	Just *as* I thought, the tank was empty.

of is used incorrectly in phrases like *would of, must of,* or *couldn't of.* The proper word to use is the verb *have* or its contractions: *would have, must have, couldn't have, might have, shouldn't have.*

Nonstandard:	Alex shouldn't of run away.
Standard:	Alex shouldn't *have* run away.

percent is correct only when it follows a number.
percentage is used when there is no number.

The supermarket's profit is 3 *percent.*
A large *percentage* of the votes went to O'Neal.

says is present tense. It is not standard usage to indicate past action. Use *said* instead. *Goes* is also mistakenly used for *said.* Avoid this incorrect usage.

Nonstandard:	Jan saw Les and says, "Where were you?"
Standard:	Jan saw Les and *said,* "Where were you?"
Nonstandard:	Then he goes, "I've been waiting for you."
Standard:	Then he *said,* "I've been waiting for you."

that, which, and **who** are all relative pronouns. *That* may refer to people, animals, or things. However, *which* is used only for animals and things. *Who* refers only to people.

> The bookcase *that* Tom built is in the hallway.
> Yvonne is one friend *that* can be trusted.
> Yom Kippur, *which* is a Jewish holiday, is a time of prayer.
> The athletes *who* came to these games have trained for years.

Exercise A Number your paper from 1 to 15. Look for sentences with nonstandard usage. Rewrite those sentences, using the right words. If a sentence is correct, write *Correct* after that number.

1. Dick came up to me, and he says, "I'm sorry."
2. Randy tossed an important letter in the wastebasket.
3. Viewers could hear the coach, which was wearing a microphone.
4. The salesperson gets a percentage of each sale.
5. If Mike had of been in a better mood, he wouldn't of been so quiet.
6. The strangers made theirselves comfortable.
7. Karen looks like she's having a good time.
8. Betty thought, as I did, that the house was sort of shaky.
9. That is the woman which drives the lead car.
10. A stunt man dove in a tiny pool.
11. Ted stood by hisself in the corner.
12. One glass fell off of the table.
13. Did you sand the wood just as I told you?
14. "You should of seen the scary part," Mandy said.
15. Late at night the trucker became kind of tired.

Exercise B: Writing Choose three pairs of words from the list on pages 644-647. Write sentences which show that you understand how to use these words.

ADDITIONAL EXERCISES

The Right Word

A. Words Often Confused Choose the correct word from those in parentheses.

1. (Your, You're) taking a course in wilderness survival, aren't you?
2. Do you know (who's, whose) books these are?
3. (Its, It's) hard to study (here, hear).
4. The realtor's (advice, advise) was to sell the property.
5. Michelle's brother (lead, led) the search party.
6. The spy changed his name and (adapted, adopted) a new identity.
7. The bakery sells fancy (deserts, desserts).
8. The muffler on your car is (loose, lose); you are about to (loose, lose) it.
9. Many of us have never thought about the (principals, principles) that we use to make a decision.
10. (They're, Their, There) holding the wedding outside even though the (weather, whether) seems (too, to) cold (too, to) me.

B. Problems with Verbs Choose the correct verb from those in parentheses.

1. (Bring, Take) your tickets to me at the box office.
2. The Suzuki method (learns, teaches) young children to play musical instruments.
3. Brandon (let, left) a big walleye get away.
4. "The Amazing Renaldo" (lay, laid) on a bed of nails.
5. (May, Can) I finish the pie, please?
6. The elevator (rose, raised) to the top floor.
7. We'll (sit, set) outside and listen to the music.

8. People (sat, set) their tickets on the counter.
9. Justine (lay, laid) the campfire.
10. Vic soaked his work clothes in a plastic tub before (bringing, taking) them to the laundromat.

C. Standard and Nonstandard English
Number your paper from 1 to 10. Look for sentences with nonstandard usage. Rewrite those sentences, using the right words. If a sentence is correct, write *Correct* after that number.

1. Alright, I'll make several copies.
2. I'll divide this small amount of lemonade between the three of us.
3. Michael goes, "I could of told you that."
4. Adam replaced the muffler hisself.
5. The singers which made this record are kind of well known.
6. There are less clouds now, but the sky still looks like rain.
7. A small percentage of the students have found theirselves jobs.
8. Gladys looks like she feels bad.
9. The man looked at us and says, "Get off of my lawn."
10. All of the passengers except Jody kept their luggage beside them.

MIXED REVIEW

The Right Word

A. Using standard English Look for incorrect word use and nonstandard usage in these sentences. Rewrite them and correct the errors. If a sentence is correct, write *Correct.*

1. Most trees adopt to cold weather sort of quickly.
2. You should not of desserted your car in the traffic jam.
3. The clerk goes, "Its too bad that you don't like your engraved stationery."
4. My principal advice is to accept your duty like an adult.
5. The new biker boots feel like they're made of lead.
6. Jerome pulled the lose bandage off of his knee, which was hurting bad.
7. My sister, which found a large number of errors in my essay, is lending me her dictionary.
8. It's alright to throw the bad apples in the bin beside the door.
9. Even the foreman hisself has worked here less years than Sy.
10. Whose willing to divide the money among the six of us?

B. Using troublesome verbs correctly The verbs in some of these sentences are used incorrectly. Rewrite the sentences and correct the errors. If a sentence is correct, write *Correct.*

1. Bring your receipt to the office across the hall from mine.
2. A watchdog sets in the back of the delivery truck.
3. The director learned the actor how to leave the stage gracefully.
4. Can the actors learn the new lines by tomorrow?
5. Can I please leave these packages under the counter?

USING GRAMMAR IN WRITING
The Right Word

A. You have just started work at a newspaper. You have the job of correcting errors in letters to the editor. Of course, you may not change any of the ideas in a letter. However, you may correct errors of grammar and usage. Following is one of the letters that you must correct. Read the letter to learn what the writer's ideas are. Then rewrite the letter, using standard English.

I have seen the plans for the lake in the dessert near hear. We will have to adopt the plans to make them work. Their too complicated now. At last week's meeting, I asked the builder, "How long will it take?" He says to me, "Its hard to say." Well, I can tell you. If they have a large amount of trucks, they might be able to dig the lake in six months. Then they will have to let the lake settle for two years. That's alright with me. Let's get started.

B. Rewrite the following passage in standard English.

The work on the hospital is finished accept for the roof. Some parts of the roof still leak bad. Beside that, we can't get enough workers. We have less than six people on the job now. If we could of got more, we could of finished by now. The whether hasn't helped, neither. All these problems have effected our work. Even so, it looks like we'll finish in two weeks.

CUMULATIVE REVIEW
Usage

A. Choosing the correct word   Write the correct word.

1. The team feels (bad, badly) about losing (its, it's) game.
2. (May, Can) we (sit, set) in the balcony?
3. Laverne (may, can) play the violin (good, well).
4. Don't you have (any, no) (good, well) recipes?
5. (Lie, Lay) the mail on the tray in (their, they're) hall.
6. Mitchell can (teach, learn) me to drive on any afternoon (accept, except) Saturday.
7. We (raise, rise) (this, those) kind of orchid.
8. The keys are (lying, laying) by (your, you're) purse.
9. (Who, Whom) did Officer Katz question?
10. Jake (doesn't, don't) want to split the money.

B. Using words correctly   Ten of the following underlined words contain errors in the use of verbs, nouns, pronouns, adverbs, and adjectives. Rewrite the paragraph, correcting the errors.

"Look at them clowns," said Scott. Two red-haired, baggy-pants clowns on tall unicycles raced towards us. Each of them was juggling their own pins. The nearest one started swaying back and forth until we thought he was sure going to fall on us. However, he surprised everybody and grabbed onto the tightrope wire. You won't never believe what he did then! He got up on the wire and began walking slow across it. Well, his side-kick decided to join he. And he brought along five pin to juggle! The two clowns juggled the pins among themselves while they walked the wire until the crowd began clapping wildly. Then the two partners swung graceful to the ground and took their bows.

Capitalization

The use of capital letters makes your writing easier to read. Capital letters call attention to certain special words, as well as to words that begin sentences.

There are specific rules for capitalizing words. This section will present those rules. If you have questions about capitalization, refer to this section.

Proper Nouns and Adjectives

Capitalize proper nouns and proper adjectives.

Common nouns are the names of whole groups of people, places, or things. **Proper nouns** are the names of particular persons, places, or things. **Proper adjectives** are adjectives formed from proper nouns.

Common Noun	Proper Noun	Proper Adjective
mountains	Alps	Alpine
country	Spain	Spanish
state	Texas	Texan

The following rules will help you to determine if a noun is a proper noun.

Names and Titles

Capitalize people's names. Also capitalize the initials or abbreviations that stand for names.

A. E. Housman	Alfred Edward Housman
John W. Coltrane	John William Coltrane

Capitalize the titles used with people's names. Also capitalize the initials or abbreviations that stand for those titles. Always capitalize *Ms., Miss, Mrs.,* and *Mr.*

Rev. Adam Moses	Professor Helmer
Mr. Eugene O'Malley	Dr. Lucille Ortez
Gen. J. G. Fine	Mayor Young

Do not capitalize a title that is used without a name. It is a common noun.

Sarah Kimpel was made a vice-president of her company.

Capitalize titles of very high importance, even when they are used without names.

the President of the United States
the Secretary of State
the Queen of England
the Secretary-General of the UN
the Pope

Family Relationships

Capitalize such family words as *mother, father, grandma,* and *uncle* when they are used as names. If the noun is preceded by a possessive word or by *a* or *the,* it is not capitalized.

We planned an anniversary party for Mom and Dad.
My mother left Japan when she was ten.
Last year Grandma started ice-skating.
The aunt I have never met is Aunt Bobbie.

The Pronoun *I*

Capitalize the pronoun *I*.

I meant what I said.   Yes, I'll go.

The Supreme Being and Sacred Writings

Capitalize all words referring to God, to the Holy Family, and to religious scriptures.

the Son of God	the Almighty	the Bible
the Lord	the Old Testament	the Talmud
the Blessed Virgin	Allah	the Holy Gospel

Capitalize personal pronouns referring to God.

They prayed to the Lord and gave Him thanks.

Exercise A   Copy these sentences. Change small letters to capital letters wherever necessary.

1. My brother and i like danish pastries.
2. Is indira gandhi still the prime minister of india?
3. The manager is ms. suzy kraske.
4. Sometimes president johnson was called l.b.j.
5. Mayor martinez has a large mexican-american con-
   stituency.
6. The british author g. k. chesterton wrote about a priest,
   father brown, in his detective stories.
7. According to mom, pizza is not an italian food.
8. The children recited bible verses for rev. parks.
9. Did senator baker sponsor the bill?
10. Has sgt. jones reported to the captain yet?

Exercise B   Follow the directions for Exercise A.

1. Do lt. graves and her husband live on the base?

2. Was president hoover related to j. edgar hoover?
3. When my grandmother is sick, dad takes care of her.
4. None of the doctors but dr. cane make house calls.
5. Many troops are stationed near the chinese border.
6. Recently uncle bob reread the new testament.
7. None of my other aunts are like aunt dorothy.
8. My sister lynn and i helped at the telethon.
9. She lit a candle to st. jude.
10. The new dean of the college is dr. rachel shapiro.

Geographical Names

In a geographical name, capitalize the first letter of each word except articles and prepositions.

The article *the* used before a place name is not part of the name. Therefore it is not capitalized.

Continents:	South America, Australia, Asia, Africa
Bodies of Water:	the Red River, Lake Superior, the Pacific Ocean, the Bering Sea, Chesapeake Bay, Salt Creek
Landforms:	the Mohave Desert, the Channel Islands, Cape Horn, Mt. Rainier, Grand Canyon, the Great Plains, Shenandoah Valley
Political Units:	Michigan, Houston, Scotland, Republic of Korea, Province of Alberta, Sixth Congressional District, the Middle East
Public Areas:	Washington Memorial, Rocky Mountain National Park, Peabody Museum, Disneyland, Indiana Dunes
Roads and Highways:	Peachtree Avenue, Route 6, Interstate 101, Indiana Tollway, Central Street, Governor's Highway

Directions and Sections

Capitalize names of sections of the country.

The East is more urban than the West.
Hillary wants to move to the Southwest.

Capitalize proper adjectives that come from names of sections of the country.

Southern fried chicken   a Northern state
a Midwestern farmhouse   a West Coast resort

Do not capitalize directions of the compass.

Brookfield is west of Chicago.
Go east to the second stoplight.

Do not capitalize adjectives that come from words showing direction.

The White Mountains are in northern Vermont.
The tornado is moving in a southerly direction.

Exercise A Find the words in these sentences that should be capitalized. Write the words using the necessary capital letters.

1. I live in the fourth congressional district.
2. The new england settlers made the most of their natural resources.
3. The dead sea is an inland sea.
4. Is greenland an island, and is it warmer than iceland?
5. Go east on main street to reach the lake.
6. Is north america larger than south america?
7. Much of our shellfish comes from chesapeake bay.
8. Leaves turn later in the south than in the north.
9. Dale grew up in dayton, ohio, and has a midwestern accent.
10. We drove south through the great smoky mountains.

1. The indian ocean is west of australia.
2. The northeast is heavily industrialized.
3. He is buried in arlington national cemetery.
4. Is nevada rich in minerals?
5. Sid's cousin lives in east moline, a city in illinois.
6. Does interstate 74 run through champaign county?
7. The statue of liberty is located on liberty island.
8. Many counties in colorado have indian names.
9. The longest river in africa is the nile river.
10. The beaches on the east coast are very popular.

Names of Organizations and Institutions

Capitalize the names of organizations and institutions, including political parties, governmental bodies or agencies, schools, colleges, churches, hospitals, clubs, businesses, and abbreviations of these names.

Democratic Party	Glenbrook Hospital
Federal Aviation Administration	Chicago Motor Club
Wright Junior College	Pacific Stereo
Trinity Lutheran Church	FBI

Do not capitalize words like *hospital, school,* and *company* when they are not used as part of names.

Two companies bid for the contract to build a new school.

Names of Events, Documents, and Periods of Time

Capitalize the names of historical events, documents, and periods of time.

Battle of Bunker Hill	Bill of Rights	the Crusades
World War II	the Elizabethan Age	Magna Carta

Months, Days, and Holidays

Capitalize names of months, days, and holidays, but not the names of seasons.

Memorial Day	November	winter
Monday	Fourth of July	spring

Races, Languages, Nationalities, and Religions

Capitalize the names of races, languages, nationalities, and religions. Also capitalize any adjectives that come from these names.

Japanese	Italian	Latin	Moslem
Indian	English	Judaism	Catholic

School Subjects

Do not capitalize the names of school subjects, except specific course titles followed by a number.

math	World History 300
art	Consumer Problems I

Remember that the names of languages are always capitalized.

Spanish	English	Russian	German

Ships, Trains, Airplanes, and Automobiles

Capitalize the names of ships, trains, airplanes, and automobiles.

U.S.S. *Lexington*   *San Francisco Zephyr*   Pontiac Firebird

B.C., A.D.

Capitalize the abbreviations *B.C.* and *A.D.*

Augustus ruled Rome from 27 B.C. to A.D. 14.

Exercise A Write the words that should be capitalized. Use the necessary capital letters.

1. The jewish holiday of hanukkah lasts eight days.
2. Ina translates chinese speeches at the united nations.
3. Shawn built a model of the *liberator,* a world war II bomber.
4. Many famous writers, like hemingway and orwell, fought in the spanish civil war.
5. The *orient express* was a unique train that traveled between france and romania.
6. In june i begin my summer job at the wilson memorial hospital.
7. That hospital offers its employees english and other college courses.
8. Our business I test is on the monday after thanksgiving.
9. She teaches biology at oakland community college.
10. The day-care center is in mt. olivet baptist church.

Exercise B Follow the directions for Exercise A.

1. Dee has a degree in math and computer science and works for the irs.
2. The egyptians developed the first lunar calendar in about 4241 b.c.
3. Mr. elam teaches art at delgado junior college.
4. Lee got a mortgage guaranteed by the fha from the first national bank.
5. On saturday the pirates will play the cubs.
6. The world survived without aspirin until a.d. 1893.
7. The ford she drives is a company car.
8. My u.s. history teacher told us to memorize the bill of rights.
9. The a.m.a. is not a union.
10. Thornton worked for blue cross until last winter.

First Words

Sentences and Poetry

Capitalize the first word of every sentence and the first word of most lines of poetry.

> The plane passed the sound barrier. People in the area heard the boom.

> The woods are lovely, dark, and deep,
> But I have promises to keep . . .
>   —from "Stopping by Woods on a Snowy Evening," by Robert Frost

Sometimes in modern poetry, the lines of a poem do not begin with capital letters.

Quotations

Capitalize the first word of a direct quotation.

A **direct quotation** tells the exact words of a speaker or writer.

> William Shakespeare wrote, "The course of true love never did run smooth."

A **divided quotation** is a direct quotation broken into two parts by words such as *she said* or *he remarked*. The first word of the second part is not capitalized unless it starts a new sentence.

> "It is true," said Carrie, "that we can never please everyone."
> "It is true," said Carrie. "We can never please everyone."

Letter Parts

Capitalize the first word in the greeting of a letter. Also capitalize the name of the persons addressed, or words like *Sir* and *Madam* that stand for names.

Dear Ms. Oppenheim: Dear Sir or Madam:

In the complimentary close, capitalize only the first word.

Sincerely yours,   Very fondly,

Outlines

Capitalize the first word of each item in an outline. Also capitalize the letters before each line.

I. Film comedians
   A. Silent film comedians
      1. Individuals
      2. Groups
   B. Comedians of the 1930's

Titles

Capitalize the first word and all important words in the titles of chapters, magazine articles, short stories, essays, poems, radio programs, and songs or short pieces of music.

Chapter title:	Chapter 6, "The Astronauts"
Magazine article:	"Behind the Scenes with the Who"
Short story:	"Too Early Spring"
Essay:	"A World at Peace"
Poem:	"My Last Duchess"
Song:	"Happy Days Are Here Again"

Capitalize the first word and all important words in titles of books, newspapers, magazines, plays, movies, works of art, long musical compositions, and television programs.

Book title:	*Gnomes*
Newspaper:	*Boston Globe*
Magazine:	*Consumer Reports*
Play:	*No Place To Be Somebody*
Movie:	*Breaking Away*
Work of art:	*Winged Victory*
Long musical composition:	*Barber of Seville*
Television program:	*The Tonight Show*

Exercise A Capitalize the words that should be capitalized.

1. "why," asked Nina, "don't you think before you speak?"
2. "stop!" called Jake. "that's my suitcase."
3. the American anthem is "the star-spangled banner."
4. "did you have the winning number?" asked Rae.
5. i listen to "radio mystery theater."
6. "did Sal get a role in *romeo and juliet?*" asked Liz.
7. carrie's story "a prairie summer" appeared in *seventeen.*
8. dear mr. nolan:
     your subscription to *ms.* is about to expire. we have enclosed a renewal form so that you will not miss an issue.
                                         sincerely yours,
9. have you ever seen the movie *animal crackers?*
10. we discussed "notes of a native daughter" from *slouching towards bethlehem.*

Exercise B Follow the directions for Exercise A.

1. "when i was young," said Joe, "*sesame street* didn't exist."
2. marta didn't know the words to "silent night."
3. II. native american art
      A. practical arts
          1. wampum
          2. ceremonial bowls
4. the painting *government bureau* looks frightening.
5. the *sun-times* is a Chicago newspaper.
6. read Chapter 4, "defensive driving," in *let's drive right.*
7. i enjoyed the article "nicknames and social status" in *psychology today.*
8. "who," asked Lori, "took my copy of *time* magazine?"
9. matt recited the entire poem, "the skeleton in armor."
10. "would you like to hear Beethoven's *ninth symphony?*" asked Ann. "there's an extra ticket."

ADDITIONAL EXERCISES

Capitalization

A. Capital Letters Number your paper from 1 to 10. Find the words in the following sentences that should be capitalized. Write the words beside the proper numbers and capitalize them correctly.

1. Is dr. moore a surgeon?
2. One great Apache chief was cochise.
3. The story of adam and eve is in genesis.
4. Was senator long formerly a member of the Republican Party?
5. The man who played clubber lang in *Rocky III* was mr. t.
6. My mother said that i should visit dad on his birthday.
7. Louis gossett, jr. played sgt. foley, a drill sergeant.
8. Girl scouts promise to serve god and their country.
9. Is that a st. christopher medal, uncle luther?
10. My aunt is anne m. galleti; my sister is anne k. galleti.

B. Capital Letters Copy the following sentences, changing small letters to capital letters wherever necessary.

1. The southern pecan pie is the most popular item on the menu.
2. Drive north through canada to reach alaska.
3. The state of hawaii is composed of islands.
4. Immigrants from europe were questioned at ellis island.
5. Can you think of any network announcers with canadian accents?
6. Chuck visited mark twain state park in hannibal, missouri.
7. The blue mountains are west of baker county, aren't they?

8. Which western state has the most desert land?
9. Camel caravans crossed the sahara desert.
10. Continue north on route 81 until you come to elkhorn river.

C. Capital Letters
Number your paper from 1 to 10. After the proper number, copy the words from each sentence that should be capitalized. Use the necessary capital letters.

1. Is loyola university a catholic school?
2. The french fries at emory's diner are good.
3. We took lithuanian easter eggs to the children at mercy hospital.
4. The jewish prophet isaiah lived in the eighth century b.c.
5. Does modern dance I satisfy the physical education requirement?
6. Was the white house burned down in the war of 1812?
7. Certainly, chevrolets are manufactured by general motors.
8. Mary baker eddy founded the christian science religion.
9. The mormons settled salt lake city.
10. The first woman philosopher in recorded history was hypatia, who died in a.d. 415.

D. Capital Letters
Number your paper from 1 to 10. Find the words in the following sentences that should be capitalized. Write the words after the proper numbers, using the necessary capital letters.

1. read "the laughing man" in *nine stories* by j. d. salinger.
2. gus found a copy of *the new york times* on the park bench.
3. *the dollmaker*, a novel by harriet arnow, is about appalachia and detroit during world war II.

4. "wait!" said the clerk. "there's one copy of *news-week* left."

5. dear sir or madam:
     how often have you told yourself, "tomorrow, without fail, i will open a savings account"?

6. the assignment for monday is to read chapter 16, "open highway driving."

7. the movies *e.t.* and *the thing* showed very different views of creatures from outer space.

8. "battle cry of freedom" was a popular marching song among union troops during the civil war.

9. "last sunday," said pat, "the minister requested contributions for southeast asian refugees."

10. the list of articles included "blackwell's island" in *rolling stone*.

MIXED REVIEW

Capitalization

A. Using capitalization correctly Copy the following sentences. Use correct capitalization.

1. leontyne price sang at mount shiloh baptist church.
2. on winter mornings, only ms. page can start her car.
3. one prized american sports car is the '53 corvette.
4. last monday, modern literature II students read "one of these days" by gabriel garcia marquez.
5. she encouraged students to take math and science.
6. there is no literature from the stone age.
7. the dog rin tin tin was an honorary private in the cavalry.
8. a democrat, representative katie hall, sponsored the bill to make a new national holiday.
9. on which island is the hawaii volcanoes national park?
10. "for a while i drifted around the southwest," said joe.

B. Using capitalization correctly in proofreading Proofread this paragraph. Add the correct capitalization.

sometime after a. d. 1542, spanish missionaries traveled across the atlantic ocean to central america in order to convert the mayan indians. the catholic priests saw that christianity and the mayan religion already had features in common. baptism, confession, and pilgrimages were part of mayan worship. the indians, thought that the shape of a cross was holy. the cross was important to them, though, because it pointed north, south, east, and west like a compass. "perhaps," said the spaniards, "this country was visited by st. thomas hundreds of years ago." however, neither history nor the new testament gives any proof for their guess.

USING MECHANICS IN WRITING
Capitalization

A. Suppose that you have just written a book—a novel about international intrigue and adventure. The publisher of your book would like you to write a short autobiography for the dust jacket. Write a paragraph about yourself and your accomplishments. Be sure to include all the following information.

 a) your full name
 b) the city and state (or country) of your place of birth
 c) the names of places where you have traveled or would like to travel
 d) the names of clubs or other organizations to which you belong
 e) the names of schools that you have attended
 f) the titles of other books you have written
 g) the names of the four people you most admire

Check your work to be sure that the capitalization is correct. Underline each capital letter.

B. You are a person from another time who has been teleported into the present. The news media are making quite a fuss over you. One national magazine has offered a large sum of money for a few paragraphs of reminiscences. Write three paragraphs about life as you lived it during the time you came from. In your paragraphs, state your name, describe where you live, and tell about some of the famous people of your time. Provide dates for these events. Check your work to be sure that the capitalization is correct. Underline each capital letter.

Punctuation

Road signs guide you when you drive. Similarly, punctuation marks guide you when you read. Punctuation marks show readers where to stop, slow down, or change direction.

When you write, your punctuation signals your reader. It shows groups of words that belong together. It indicates how sentences should be read. Generally, punctuation helps your reader to understand your meaning.

End Marks

End marks are the punctuation marks that indicate the end of a sentence. The **period,** the **question mark,** and the **exclamation point** are the three kinds of end marks.

The Period

Use a period at the end of a declarative sentence.

A **declarative sentence** is a sentence that makes a statement. You use declarative sentences when you tell something.

> The rate of inflation is rising.

Use a period at the end of most imperative sentences.

An **imperative sentence** is a sentence that orders or requests someone to do something.

> Step to the rear of the elevator, please.

Imperative sentences sometimes express strong excitement or emotion. For these sentences, exclamation points, rather than periods, are used.

> Watch out!   Don't move!

Use a period at the end of an indirect question.

An **indirect question** tells that someone asked a question. However, it does not give the exact words of the question.

> Before take-off, the flight attendant asked if everyone was comfortable.

A **direct question** shows the exact words of the person asking the question. A direct question ends with a question mark. Notice how a direct question differs.

> Before take-off, the flight attendant asked, "Is everyone comfortable?"

Use a period at the end of an abbreviation or an initial. An **abbreviation** is a shortened form of a word. An **initial** is a first letter that stands for a word.

Col. B. Johnson, Jr.   10 ft., 2 in.   2:00 P.M.

Some abbreviations do not use periods. If you aren't sure whether or not to use a period with an abbreviation, check the abbreviation in your dictionary.

FM (*Frequency Modulation*)
NATO (*North Atlantic Treaty Organization*)
FBI (*Federal Bureau of Investigation*)

Use a period after each number or letter for an item in an outline or a list.

(An Outline)	(A List)
I. Records	1. names
A. Olympic	2. addresses
1. Winter Sports	3. phone numbers

Use a period between dollars and cents and before a decimal.

$42.50 $1.59   2.06   .667

The Question Mark

Use a question mark at the end of an interrogative sentence.

An **interrogative sentence** is a sentence that asks a question.

What are your strong points?

The Exclamation Point

Use an exclamation point at the end of an exclamatory sentence.

An **exclamatory sentence** expresses excitement or other strong emotion.

That's a mess!   How great you look!

Use an exclamation point after an interjection.

An **interjection** is one or more words that show strong feeling. Sometimes the interjection is a sound.

Hurray!   What luck!   Oh my gosh!   Pow!

Exercise A   Copy the following sentences, adding the necessary punctuation.

1. Well Look who's here
2. Doesn't he call the baby Sammy
3. The government agency that looks after working conditions is OSHA
4. Bill Mauldin became famous for his army cartoons
5. Does Mr. Nunez have an office in this building
6. Bill asked the conductor if she could change a twenty for the $125 fare
7. Rev J A Weaver is the chaplain at the hospital
8. Open the door for Col Kale, please
9. That FM station doesn't come on until 6:00 AM
10. Is Tracey an RN or an LPN

Exercise B   Follow the directions for Exercise A.

1. Does the FBI investigate airplane crashes
2. Carl asked whether Mt Fuji was in Japan
3. I Allergies
      A Reactions
         1 Sneezing
4. J. Edgar Hoover was the first director of the FBI
5. Is her address still 805 S Elm Street
6. Ow That hurts
7. Sixty percent of the students answered the questionnaire
8. Ann asked if we were from St Paul
9. Which states are part of the USSR
10. The turkey weighs 8 lbs 11 oz and costs $795

The Comma

A comma is used to separate words that do not go together. When you are speaking, you can pause for breaks in thought. When you are writing, however, you need commas for breaks. In this way, commas help you to communicate clearly.

Commas in a Series

Use a comma after every item in a series except the last one.

A series is three or more items of the same kind. You may use a series of words, phrases, or clauses.

Words: Flowers, candy, and other gifts crowded the hospital room.

Phrases: Vanessa hurried through the door, up the stairs, and into the president's office.

Clauses: The fire chief explained how the fire started, how it spread, and how much damage it caused.

Use commas after *first, second, third,* and so on, when these adverbs introduce a series.

The speaker told us how to succeed: first, believe in yourself; second, set goals; and third, work hard.

When there are two or more adjectives before a noun, use commas between them.

Tall, sleek, modern skyscrapers line Fifth Avenue.

Exercise A Copy these sentences. Add commas where necessary.

1. The tool is a clamp a wrench and a wire cutter all in one.
2. I wrote to the mayor the governor and the President.

3. Her thin lively face is almost never still.
4. He worked cheerfully carefully and quickly.
5. Old newspapers full ashtrays and dirty cups littered the room.
6. Dr. Wade Dr Yoshi and Dr. Bird were being paged a few minutes ago.
7. Decals posters and notices covered the window.
8. Paul hesitated shrugged and agreed.
9. Cleo gathered the firewood started the campfire and set up the tent.
10. First shampoo your hair; second apply the conditioner; third massage it into your hair; fourth rinse thoroughly.

Exercise B   Follow the directions for Exercise A.

1. First listen; second question; third form your opinion.
2. The tall unassuming man carried an umbrella a brief-case and a hat.
3. The pain of a heart attack can be felt in the chest arms and lower jaw.
4. The attendant wiped the dust grime and dead bugs from the windshield.
5. Roger has an evening class on Mondays Tuesdays and Fridays.
6. The workers packed crates in the hot dusty plant all morning long.
7. Mary looked through her notebook around her desk and then in her locker.
8. Check the lining the seams and the quality of the material.
9. Warmth rest and plenty of fluids can help colds and the flu.
10. Small pale lights shone dimly through the thick wet snow.

Commas with Introductory Words

Use a comma to separate an introductory word, a long phrase, or a clause from the rest of the sentence.

> Yes, I have plenty of time before I have to go out. (introductory word)

> After the last round of the match, Cosell interviewed the boxers. (prepositional phrase)

> Frowning slightly, Blake reached for a chess piece. (participial phrase)

> When you leave, remember to lock the door behind you. (adverb clause)

As you can see, commas are used after introductory words such as *yes* and *no*. They are also used after prepositional phrases, participial phrases, and adverb clauses that begin sentences.

Sometimes the comma may be left out. When there would be little pause in speaking, no comma is needed.

> At night we made a fire.

Commas with Interrupters

Use commas to set off one or more words that interrupt the flow of thought in a sentence.

> A doctor, therefore, needs malpractice insurance.

> The players were, I believe, unusually rough in the game last night.

> Linda Ronstadt, for example, requires no back-up singers.

The following words are additional examples of interrupters. Set them off with commas.

it appears	however	I suppose
by the way	in addition	furthermore
moreover	in fact	nevertheless

Exercise A Copy these sentences. Add commas correctly.

1. Moreover not all oil-producing countries belong to OPEC.
2. The United States for instance does not belong.
3. Ira however hasn't registered to vote.
4. Holding the baby in one arm he clutched the groceries with the other.
5. After her first week on the job Marilyn began to feel confident.
6. As most of us grow older we become less sensitive to pain.
7. When I opened the window I knocked over the plant.
8. No there's still time.
9. Ms. Barber I think is the expert.
10. Honey on the other hand does provide nutrition.

Exercise B Follow the directions for Exercise A.

1. Curt therefore declined the scout's invitation.
2. Briskly nodding to her nosy neighbor Celia strode by.
3. Laura has an original style to say the least.
4. Although she dances Tina can't skate at all.
5. In conclusion we must request a refund.
6. Furthermore tranquilizers can be deadly.
7. Your brother for instance is always very helpful.
8. Your Honda I am sorry to say is beyond repair.
9. If you try again however you might succeed.
10. Watching television in Herb's opinion is a waste of time.

Exercise C: Writing Write four original sentences, each using one of the following interrupters. Add commas wherever necessary.

by the way   furthermore
in addition   moreover

Commas with Nouns of Direct Address

Use commas to set off nouns of direct address.

When you speak or write to someone, you often use the person's name. The name of someone directly spoken to is a **noun of direct address.**

> Julie, listen to this song.
>
> The nearest gas station, Mark, is at least two miles away from here.
>
> Please, folks, stay in your seats.
>
> Are you ready yet, team?

As in the last example, nouns of direct address may sometimes be common nouns.

Commas with Appositives

Use commas to set off most appositives.

An **appositive** is one or more words that explain or identify another word. The appositive directly follows the word it explains.

> Most Chinese food is stir-fried in a wok, a rounded metal pan.
>
> The head nurse, Barbara Allen, instructs the aides.
>
> Langston Hughes, a poet and playwright from Missouri, wrote *Shakespeare in Harlem.*

As in the final example, an appositive may contain a prepositional phrase.

A noun used as an appositive is called a **noun in apposition.** If the noun in apposition is a single name, it is not usually set off by commas.

> My friend Brian plays the drums.

Commas with Quotations

Use commas to set off the explanatory words of a direct quotation.

Explanatory words are statements like *she said, Martin asked,* or *JoAnne noted.* Such words are not part of the quotation.

Explanatory words often come before the quotation. Use a comma after these explanatory words.

Debbie said, "I don't agree with that candidate."

Now look at this quotation:

"I don't agree with that candidate," Debbie said.

The explanatory words come after the quotation in the sentence above. Notice that the comma at the end of the quotation belongs inside the quotation marks.

At times, a quotation is divided into two parts. The explanatory words then separate the two parts. This is a *divided quotation:*

"I don't agree," Debbie said, "with that candidate."

In a divided quotation, use a comma within the quotation marks after the first part of the sentence. Use another comma after the explanatory words.

Remember that indirect quotations do not show the speaker's exact words. No commas are used.

Debbie said that she doesn't agree with that candidate.

Commas in Compound Sentences

Use a comma before the conjunction between the two main clauses of a compound sentence.

The taxi stopped, and five people hopped out.

When the main clauses are very short and are joined by *and,* the comma is not necessary.

I blinked and she disappeared.

Very short main clauses are sometimes joined by *but* or *or*. Since the words *but* and *or* mark a change in the flow of thought, a comma is used.

Lisa fell, but she wasn't hurt.

Remember that compound sentences differ from sentences with compound subjects or predicates. There is no comma before the *and* that joins a compound subject or predicate.

The test pilot flew a new jet and landed it safely.

Exercise A Copy these sentences. Add commas where they are needed.

1. Charles works and he works hard.
2. He laughed politely but he was not amused.
3. Millie have you seen Jerome?
4. India already an enormous country has a rapidly growing population.
5. The car an old Chevy seemed to be abandoned.
6. "Run ten laps" said the coach.
7. "Tom" said Maureen "here is my sister Nell."
8. Shovel the snow off the roof or it might collapse.
9. Jim Thorpe played in several sports but is best remembered for football.
10. Alice Walker a novelist and an editor appeared on *Today*.

Exercise B Follow the directions for Exercise A.

1. We stood still and listened but we didn't hear a sound.
2. Did she take your case or did she refer you elsewhere?
3. The Congo River in Africa curves widely and it empties into the Atlantic.
4. By the way Neal Ms. Mills called and wants you to call back.

5. Harry I would like you to meet Ms. Chen my math teacher.
6. "Did Elizabeth find that book yet Mel or is she still looking?" asked Carol.
7. Joan Baez is a singer but she also champions social causes.
8. Your taxi is here Gloria.
9. "Your jokes" muttered Gil "are not funny."
10. Have you seen my brother Joy?

Commas in Dates

In dates, remember to use a comma between the day of the month and the year.

> July 4, 1776   May 8, 1982

When a date is in the middle of a sentence, a comma follows the year.

> Ralph Nader was born on February 27, 1934, in Winsted, Connecticut.

Commas in Place Names

Use a comma between the name of a city or town and the name of its state or country.

> Nashville, Tennessee   Caracas, Venezuela
> Rome, Italy   Oakland, California
> Chicago, Illinois   Harare, Zimbabwe

If a sentence contains an address, use a comma after each item.

> Send your entry to Eastman Kodak Company, 343 State Street, Rochester, New York 14650

A comma is not used between the state and the ZIP code.

Commas in Letters

Use a comma after the salutation of a friendly letter. Use a comma after the closing of a friendly letter or a business letter.

Dear Erica,   Very truly yours,

Commas with Nonrestrictive Clauses

Use commas to set off nonrestrictive clauses.

A **nonrestrictive clause** is a clause that simply adds an idea to a sentence. The meaning of the sentence would be complete without it. The clause is not needed for the sense of the sentence.

A **restrictive clause** is a clause that is essential to the meaning of a sentence. For the sentence to make sense, the clause is needed. When a restrictive clause is dropped from a sentence, the meaning changes.

Nonrestrictive clause: The Black Hawks, *who lost today,* moved to third place.
The Black Hawks moved to third place. (The clause can be dropped from the sentence.)

Restrictive clause: The player *who made the winning goal* was Bob Santini.
The player was Bob Santini. (The meaning changes when the clause is dropped.)

To decide whether a clause is nonrestrictive, read the sentence without it. If the meaning doesn't change, the clause is nonrestrictive. It needs commas before and after it.

Restrictive clauses are often used to identify or to point out the person or thing they modify. Without such identification, the meaning of a sentence would not be clear. Nonrestrictive clauses, on the other hand, do not add any essential information to the sentence.

Restrictive clause:	The comedian who wears a white suit is Steve Martin. (The clause tells which one.)
Nonrestrictive clause:	Steve Martin, who wears a white suit, makes crazy faces.
	Steve Martin makes crazy faces.
	(The clause is not needed.)
Restrictive clause:	Carol Marin is the anchorperson who reports the news at 5 P.M. (The clause tells which one.)
Nonrestrictive clause:	Carol Marin, who reports the news at 5 P.M., explained the ruling.
	Carol Marin explained the ruling.
	(The clause is not needed.)

Commas To Avoid Confusion

Use a comma whenever the reader might otherwise be confused.
Although no rule may apply, some sentences might be misread
without commas.

For example, without commas, the following sentences could
be misunderstood.

> Whatever you sing you sing well.
> Outside the fairgrounds were crowded.

With commas, the sentences are clearer.

> Whatever you sing, you sing well.
> Outside, the fairgrounds were crowded.

Exercise A Copy the following sentences. Add commas where
necessary. Some sentences are correct.

1. The only antibiotic that the patient has had is penicillin.
2. Their family has moved to Wichita Kansas.
3. The address of the Northwest Campus is 3400 Broadway Street Gary Indiana 46408.

4. The first Ferris wheel which held more than a thousand passengers was built for the World's Fair in Chicago.
5. The Ferris wheel was designed by G. W. Gale Ferris of Galesburg Illinois.
6. Inside freshly baked bread awaited us.
7. Dear Ramona
   The roses that you sent were lovely. Thank you.
   Sincerely yours
8. Sissy Spacek whom I like played the lead.
9. The first workable light bulb was invented in Menlo Park New Jersey in October 1879.
10. We bought Alaska on March 30 1867 for $7,200,000.

Exercise B Follow the directions for Exercise A.

1. If Loretta walks over Jay drives her home.
2. Earl Campbell who plays in the NFL did the commercial.
3. The card was postmarked May 3 1985.
4. The people I like like me.
5. When Josh walks through the furniture shakes.
6. The electrician who wired this made a mistake.
7. The number that you called has been disconnected.
8. Carla who likes to travel is in Iowa.
9. The Jan Grey who won the trophy is not I.
10. Her address which she remembered to put on the letter is 522 Meade Avenue Chicago Illinois 60639.

The Semicolon

Use a semicolon to join the parts of a compound sentence if no coordinating conjunction is used.

The city has a phone number for emergencies; it is 911.

If the parts of a compound sentence contain several commas, separate the clauses with a semicolon.

The British flag is red, white, and blue; and the Irish flag is green, orange, and white.

When there are commas within parts of a series, use semicolons to separate the parts.

The members of the band are Ross Alonzo, drums; Marcy Donovan, guitar; Jeb O'Donnell, bass; and Katie Spencer, banjo.

Use a semicolon before a conjunctive adverb that joins the clauses of a compound sentence.

As you have learned, the parts of a compound sentence are often joined by words like *however, therefore, moreover, otherwise, so, then, yet, besides, consequently,* and *nevertheless.* Such words, called **conjunctive adverbs,** follow a semicolon.

Jonathan fell asleep on the subway; consequently, he missed his stop.

The Colon

Use a colon after the greeting of a business letter.

Dear Sir or Madam: Dear Mr. Williams:

Use a colon between numerals indicating hours and minutes.

10:27 A.M.   3:30 P.M.

Use a colon to introduce a list of items. The colon indicates a pause before the items that follow.

Air pollution comes from the following sources: cars, trucks, buses, factories, and smokers.

If there would be no pause in speaking, a colon is not used before a list.

The six largest American cities are New York, Los Angeles, Chicago, Philadelphia, Detroit, and Boston.

Exercise A Copy the word before and after each missing semi-colon or colon. Add the correct punctuation mark.

1. The class starts at 800, but Barb is there by 745.
2. Sunspots interfere with computers, radios, and civil defense sirens and these solar flares also affect the weather.
3. Ramsey was not fired furthermore, he was not asked to resign.
4. The train stops at these stations Grand, Western, and Belmont.
5. The park was filled with people the first day of spring had arrived.
6. These cities host nuclear power plants Crystal River, Florida Batavia, Illinois and Three Mile Island, Pennsylvania.
7. Beth had worked overtime she arrived home tired, cross, and hungry.
8. These books influenced public opinion greatly *Uncle Tom's Cabin, Oliver Twist, The Jungle,* and *Silent Spring.*
9. Dear Madam
   Please cancel my subscription to your newspaper.
10. Sandra enjoys fixing cars she wants to be a mechanic.

Exercise B Follow the directions for Exercise A.

1. We have abundant coal resources however, coal smoke is a pollutant.
2. The bus leaves at 215 you're just in time.
3. Dear Ms. Jackson
   Thank you for your generous contribution.
4. Brenda had an interview at 900 therefore, she set the alarm for 700.
5. Her collection includes records by Sonny Rollins, Nina Simone, and Bud Powell I was impressed.

6. Vote for me I'll get things done.
7. Gravy gets lumpy quickly therefore, stir it constantly.
8. Notify these departments immediately security, payroll, and personnel.
9. Ms. Kull is a dangerous imposter notify security, payroll, and personnel at once.
10. He turned in the air and caught the ball then he raced across the goal line.

The Dash

Dashes Used with Interrupters

As you have learned, commas set off words or short phrases, like *I believe* and *moreover*, that interrupt a sentence. When a long explanation interrupts the thought, however, use a **dash.**

> The "youth vote"—eighteen-year-olds got the vote in 1971—is sought by many politicians.
> Mother Nature's Restaurant—it specializes in health foods—opened in the old warehouse.

The Dash Before a Summary

Use a dash after a series if a summary statement follows.

> Louis Armstrong, Buddy Bolden, Bessie Smith, and Duke Ellington—they helped to develop jazz music.
> Chocolate chip, rocky road, peach, and peppermint—those are my favorite ice-cream flavors.

Exercise   Copy these sentences. Insert dashes as needed.

1. The brilliant colors yellow, red, lime caught the sun.
2. A school bus luckily it was empty blocked the alley.

3. A folding canteen, a wrist compass, a water purifier all could be found at the surplus store.
4. She keeps records of medical expenses, interest payments oh, everything that is tax deductible.
5. Scissors, tweezers, toothpick, blade they were all included in the Swiss army knife.
6. The recession a few had predicted it had arrived.
7. The Civil Service exam I plan to take it will be given next Tuesday.
8. Louis, Robinson, Ali he had seen them all.
9. "Turn the other cheek" that's what Brenda is saying.
10. Romeo and Juliet, Hamlet, Macbeth these are some of Shakespeare's most famous characters.

The Hyphen

Use a hyphen if part of a word must be carried over from one line to the next. Hyphens separate words only between syllables.

> I recognized an old, yellowed photo-
> graph of my grandfather.

Only words of two or more syllables can be broken by a hyphen. Never divide one-syllable words, like *shout* or *height*, at the end of a line. Use your dictionary to check syllables.

Never leave a single letter at the end of a line. This division of *isolate* for example, would be incorrect: *i-solate*. Do not begin a line with a single letter either. This divison of *imaginary* would be incorrect: *imaginar-y*.

Use a hyphen in compound numbers from twenty-one to ninety-nine.

> thirty-one days   seventy-nine clips

Use a hyphen in fractions.

> a three-fifths majority   one-half of the distance

Use a hyphen in certain compound nouns, such as *editor-in-chief, sister-in-law, spin-off,* and *great-uncle.*

The *stand-in* for the part is my *brother-in-law.*

Use a hyphen or hyphens between words that make up a compound adjective used before a noun.

Mohr Corporation has excellent *on-the-job* training.

but: workers are trained on the job.

When a compound adjective is used after a noun, as in the second example, it is not usually hyphenated.

Check a dictionary to find out if a word needs a hyphen. Here are some examples of compound adjectives.

eight-year-old girl	out-of-date fashions
run-down neighborhood	do-it-yourself project

Exercise Write the word or words that should be hyphenated. Add the necessary hyphens. Use a dictionary if you need to.

1. Self service stations have some drawbacks.
2. The half baked cake in the kitchen looked less than appetizing.
3. My great aunt bought me a warm up jacket.
4. A six year old child can usually pedal a bike.
5. The two wheeler is on sale for twenty five dollars.
6. Forty five minutes can pass quickly.
7. The Vice President visited the ex mayor.
8. The half awake janitor dragged herself upstairs.
9. The first two thirds of the outline is organized well.
10. The Commander in Chief had arrived.
11. The dark eyed man in the hand knit sweater had a worn out appearance.
12. With a short term loan, we were able to buy a car.
13. A sharp eyed cabbie noticed the smoke.
14. The medium rare steak was delicious.
15. My brother in law is twenty two.

The Apostrophe

One common function of the **apostrophe** is to form the possessive of nouns. To place the apostrophe correctly, you should know if a noun is singular or plural.

To form the possessive of a singular noun, add an apostrophe and an -s.

rider + 's = rider's	Barbara + 's = Barbara's
employee + 's = employee's	Gus + 's = Gus's

To form the possessive of a plural noun that does not end in s, add an apostrophe and an -s.

children + 's = children's   workmen + 's = workmen's

To form the possessive of a plural noun that ends in s, add only an apostrophe.

reporters + ' = reporters'	years + ' = years'
Simpsons + ' = Simpsons'	vistors + ' = visitors'

To form the possessive of indefinite pronouns, use an apostrophe and an -s.

nobody + 's = nobody's   anyone + 's = anyone's

Apostrophes are not used with personal pronouns to show possession.

hers   ours   yours   its   theirs

The stopwatch is *ours*.

Use an apostrophe in a contraction.

In contractions words are joined and letters are left out. An apostrophe replaces one or more letters that are left out.

they've = they have	couldn't = could not
I'm = I am	hadn't = had not
we'll = we will	won't = will not
it's = it is (or has)	you're = you are

Use an apostrophe to show the omission of numbers in a date.

the Class of '80 (*the Class of 1980*)

a '78 Toyota (*a 1978 Toyota*)

Use an apostrophe and *s* to form the plurals of letters, figures, and words used as words.

three *s*'s   two *6*'s   *good-bye*'s   *GI*'s

Exercise   Write the words that need apostrophes. Insert apostrophes where they are needed.

1. Was Supermans cape blue?
2. Mens suits are on the third floor, arent they?
3. Ive bought an 80 Nova.
4. The teachers union votes tonight.
5. Its brakes dont work well.
6. Thats Doloress book, not yours.
7. Youre the peoples choice.
8. Shes not crossing her *ts* or dotting her *is*.
9. They're using Nicks car, not theirs.
10. Nobodys future looks brighter than ours.
11. The nine Justices decision was unanimous.
12. The citys budget is already strained.
13. My dentists drill is operated by a pedal.
14. Jesss locker is next to hers.
15. Tanyas *for sures* are getting on my nerves.

Quotation Marks

Use quotation marks at the beginning and at the end of a direct quotation.

Quotation marks tell your reader that a speaker's exact words are being given. Here is an example.

Dennis said, "I have a headache."

An indirect quotation does not tell the speaker's exact words. Quotation marks are not used.

Dennis said that he has a headache.

Before a quotation, there are often explanatory words. Immediately after the words, insert a comma. Then begin the quotation with quotation marks. A period at the end of a sentence belongs *inside* the quotation marks.

Melissa said, "It's time for the news."

The explanatory words sometimes end the sentence. Then the quoted statement that begins the sentence is followed by a comma. The comma always belongs inside the quotation marks.

"It's time for the news," Melissa said.

Punctuating Divided Quotations

A quotation is sometimes divided into two parts by explanatory words. In that case, quotation marks enclose each part of the quotation.

"Sweet, sticky foods," he noted, "promote tooth decay."

If the divided quotation is a single sentence, the second part begins with a small letter. Notice the example above. However, the second part may begin a new sentence. Then the second part starts with a capital letter.

"The Knicks staged an upset," the sportscaster said. "They won in the last second of play."

In the middle of a divided quotation, the explanatory words are followed by either a period or a comma. If the first part completes a sentence, use a period. If the sentence continues after the explanatory words, use a comma.

"From a distance," Julie noted, "the area looks deserted."

"New Hampshire is a key state," said the campaign manager. "It has the first primary election."

Exercise: Writing Write each of the following sentences three ways as a direct quotation.

1. Yes, Ted, you may use my camera. (said Larry)
2. Maybe the Steelers will sign him up. (said Bonnie)
3. I know that pigeons don't migrate. (insisted Thomas)
4. After a few days, I adjusted to the noise. (Marie admitted)
5. I'm afraid that the pattern needs alteration. (Rob noted)

Using Punctuation with Quotation Marks

Place question marks and exclamation points inside the quotation marks only if they belong to the quotation itself.

Jane asked, "Are you on a diet?"

The man shrieked, "We need help!"

Place question marks and exclamation points outside the quotation marks if they do not belong to the quotation.

Did the doctor say, "Your X-rays are normal"?

How thrilled I was to hear her say, "You're hired"!

Remember that commas and periods, as you have seen, always appear within quotation marks.

Exercise A Copy the following sentences. Punctuate them correctly with quotation marks, end marks, and commas. (There are three indirect quotations that need only end punctuation.)

1. Who said that she wanted to leave early
2. Which team is Mark Aguirre on asked Joy
3. I like your coat Ron said Is it new
4. The mayor said Nobody leaves the room until we have reached an agreement
5. Nobody leaves the room the mayor said until we have reached an agreement

6. Look out screamed Dwight
7. Dawn said that she knew him
8. Marty asked where the pipes ran
9. How awful I felt when the boss said You're late
10. Did Ed really say I've forgotten her name

Exercise B Write each of the following sentences as a direct quotation. In some examples, put the quotation first. In others, put the quotation last. For variety, divide some quotations.

1. I said that I was sorry.
2. How many people live in this house?
3. Are gnomes the same as elves?
4. Have you ever played this game before?
5. I don't work in this department.
6. Did the drugstore go out of business?
7. Leave me alone!
8. Get out of the way!
9. Toast has as many calories as bread.
10. Do you have any insurance?

Using Long Quotations

When you are quoting two or more sentences by the same speaker, you may wonder how to use quotation marks. Study this example.

> "I work with primary colors," the artist said. "I think red, yellow, and blue are bold, clear, and forceful. They emphasize the lines of my painting."

Using Quotation Marks for Dialogue

Conversation between two or more people is called **dialogue**. Begin a new paragraph each time the speaker changes.

"What do you think you'll be doing ten years from now?" Darryl asked.

"That's a tough question," Al said. "Maybe I'll have a family of my own. At least I hope I will."

Carla said, "In ten years I think I'll have a good job. I think I'll travel out West, too."

"What about you, Darryl?" Al asked. "What will you be doing ten years from now?"

"I'll probably be sitting around," Darryl remarked, "wondering what I'll be doing ten years later."

Exercise: Writing Rewrite the following conversation. Make correct paragraph divisions, and use the right punctuation.

What makes you go to a doctor? asked Mary. I tend to go said Judy only when I'm very sick. I don't like to spend the money, and I don't like to spend the time. Angie said I make an appointment after I've exhausted my home remedies. Well said Jim I am distrustful. I go to the doctor if I already know what I have and what the cure is, but at no other time. You all sound ridiculous! said Lee. Don't you realize how important your health is?

Punctuating Titles

Use quotation marks to enclose the titles of magazine articles, chapters, short stories, essays, poems, songs, and short pieces of music.

Magazine article:	"The Best in Off-Road Vehicles"
Chapter title:	Chapter 3, "Africa Explored"
Short story:	"The Killers"
Essay:	"Nature"
Poem:	"Chicago"
Song:	"Too Much Heaven"

Underline the titles of books, newspapers, magazines, plays, movies, works of art, long musical compositions, and television programs.

In writing or typing, such titles are underlined like this: Newsweek. However, in print, these titles appear in italics.

Book title:	*Ordinary People*
Newspaper:	*Chicago Tribune*
Magazine:	*Rolling Stone*
Play:	*The Elephant Man*
Movie:	*The Natural*
Work of art:	*The Last Supper*
Long musical composition:	*American in Paris*
Television program:	*Nova*

Exercise A Copy the following sentences. Add quotation marks around titles or underline titles where necessary.

1. We discussed the article The Invisible Threat.
2. Please read Chapter 1, Let Justice Be Done.
3. Pollyanna is a novel about a girl who's always glad.
4. The choir sang The Battle Hymn of the Republic.
5. One business newspaper is the Wall Street Journal.
6. Are reruns of M.A.S.H. being shown on TV?
7. She's seen the movie Star Trek twice.
8. Who played in the movie Coal Miner's Daughter?
9. Is Picasso's Guernica in this museum?
10. The Outlandish Knight is a ballad.

Exercise B Follow the directions for Exercise A.

1. She has old issues of Scientific American.
2. The article appeared in Time magazine.
3. Blazing Saddles was a comic Western.
4. We listened to Beethoven's Pastoral Symphony.
5. At the funeral, Will the Circle Be Unbroken? was sung.
6. The choir sang Go Tell It on the Mountain.
7. We saw the musical The Evolution of the Blues.
8. The painting Winter hangs in the classroom.
9. The professor said that Peter Pan was a fine book.
10. The Drama Club presented The Miracle Worker.

ADDITIONAL EXERCISES

Punctuation

A. End Marks Copy these sentences, adding the necessary punctuation.

1. Is the USS *Nimitz* still the world's largest warship
2. What a miser he is
3. What did Dr Dempski say
4. Reba asked us to wake her at 5:00 AM
5. Ouch That tetanus shot hurt a lot
6. Bud earns $450 a hour; so he makes eighteen dollars a morning
7. Prof Hunt is an expert on the poetry of Edna St Vincent Millay
8. Do you have any albums by Oscar Browne, Jr
9. The National Institute of Mental Health, or NIMH, has regional offices throughout the country
10. The stories of O Henry usually have surprise endings

B. Commas Copy the following sentences. Add commas where necessary.

1. Jake and Fred eat too much sleep too much and exercise too little.
2. He has worked at fairs carnivals and amusement parks.
3. Huge seething waves swept across the beach over the boardwalk and even onto the highway.
4. The car has low mileage new tires and rubber bumpers.
5. First state your location; second state your destination; third state the time at which you wish to travel.
6. Colorful insignias and patches covered the faded old denim jacket.

7. His flat wide bare feet slapped against the pavement.
8. Maggie bought the stove Pauline contributed the refrigerator and Ruth paid for the table and chairs.
9. Actors and dancers work under hot glaring lights.
10. First check the animal shelter; second read the lost-and-found column in the classified ads; third run an ad yourself.

C. Commas Copy the following sentences, and add commas where necessary.

1. Squatting on his heels he drew a circle in the sand.
2. Dropping from the tree the mulberries stained the sidewalk.
3. Well I'm sure that there's an easier way.
4. St. Brendan it is said refused to listen to earthly music because he had once heard an archangel play.
5. The story I'm sure is fantasy.
6. Because Steve has not played all season he's out of practice.
7. The straw hats of course offer protection from the sun.
8. Amanda by the way has been learning judo.
9. After all Heather knows best I suppose.
10. Frogs for example do not cause warts contrary to a popular belief.

D. Commas Copy the following sentences. Use commas where they are needed.

1. *Sula* a novel by Toni Marrison is not available here.
2. The mood in the mayor's office was peaceful but the city outside was growing angry.
3. Luanne have you met Ms. Clay my music teacher?
4. Well sports' fans that's the game.
5. My sister Juanita moved to Iowa but she visits us at Christmas.

6. The plane a DC-10 made an emergency landing.

7. "Do a few warm-up exercises first Priscilla" said the instructor.

8. That patient an accident victim complained of a headache and was hospitalized for observation.

9. "This faucet" said the plumber "will be expensive to replace."

10. He had said that he couldn't dance and now I believe him.

E. Commas Number your paper from 1 to 10. Decide where commas should be used in the following sentences. Write the word before the comma, add the comma, and then write the word after the comma. If no comma is necessary, write *Correct*.

1. The address of the hospital where Roy works is 606 Clermont Road Batavia Ohio 45103.

2. Dear Fawn

    Here is the information that you need to chart my horoscope: I was born at 10:15 P.M. on July 17 1965 in Cabin John Maryland. Thank you!

    Yours truly

3. The crushed ice that Sheila is adding to the concrete will keep it from getting too warm and cracking when it hardens.

4. The first five digits of their telephone number which is unlisted are the same as their zip code.

5. The number that you requested is unlisted.

6. Tammy who works at the bank gets home before Cindy.

7. The woman who taught us Spanish was born in San Juan Puerto Rico.

8. A beaver lodge which can be entered only through underwater tunnels needs constant repair.

9. Whatever the paramedic did did Eric a lot of good.

10. Inside the flowers which had looked so bright outside wilted.

F. Semicolons and Colons   Add the correct punctuation.

1. Pet goldfish aren't much trouble they're not much fun, either.
2. If you think it's time to quit, check again it's only 415.
3. Dear Sir
   We have received your order for these items the vise, the cutting shears, and the portable gaslight.
4. We will send the first two items immediately however, we regret that the third item is out of stock.
5. Our most recent states are Alaska and Hawaii, which were admitted to the Union in 1959 Arizona and New Mexico, admitted in 1912 and Oklahoma, which was admitted on November 16, 1907.
6. Put the eggs in the water while it's cold otherwise, they are more likely to crack.
7. The flight departs at 149 P.M. it arrives at 450 P.M.
8. You can buy these decorations at the dime store crepe paper, balloons, and candles but you will have to go to the florist's for the roses, which are expensive.
9. Lizards, however, leap so do crickets.
10. Tara and Georgette were afraid that they would miss the train Molly, therefore, drove them to the station.

G. Dashes   Copy the following sentences. Add dashes where needed. If a sentence needs no dashes, write *Correct*.

1. The day it had been a long one was almost over.
2. Bermuda, Jamaica, Mexico he had brochures from all those beautiful places.
3. Haiti, which was once called Hispaniola, now shares the island Hispaniola with the Dominican Republic.
4. Her school, her job, her grandparents' pension they were affected by the budget cuts.
5. Take the signs of heat exhaustion among them are dizziness, faintness, and severe headache seriously.

6. I bought bread, milk, apples, and oh, no, I forgot the cheese.
7. Irv he's the one in the chef's hat barbecued the ribs.
8. Cooks, scrubs, irons, dusts that's what Ms. Yager does on holidays.
9. It's illegal you must know this for the catcher to block the plate if he doesn't have the ball.
10. Patience, politeness, and abundant pep are required of waitresses.

H. Hyphens Number your paper from 1 to 10. Copy these sentences. Add hyphens where they are needed. If a sentence needs no hyphen, write *Correct.*

1. The heavy duty flashlight is ten years old.
2. The Impala ran very well for a ten year old car.
3. The black eyed peas must be soaked for a long time before you cook them.
4. About three fourths of the fresh water on earth is in glaciers.
5. Send a self addressed, stamped envelope to this address.
6. Angie made a split second decision to hold the half drowned child upside down.
7. The editor in chief of the rock magazine is a sixty five year old grandmother.
8. Most colleges accept part time students.
9. Some ex football players have become movie actors.
10. Have you ever sold anything over the telephone?

I. Apostrophes Copy the following sentences. Add apostrophes where they are needed.

1. *Time* magazine was first published in the early 1920s.
2. Why do you make your 7s that way?
3. Those songs arent favorites of hers.

4. Its true, isnt it?

5. Josss picture is in todays newspaper.

6. Everybodys dues but theirs are in.

7. The womens exercise equipment doesnt belong in this closet.

8. Both doctors offices have copies of poems on the wall.

9. Teenagers styles of dress were different in the 50s.

10. Three employees paychecks contained serious errors: *O*s had been substituted for *1*s.

J. Quotation Marks Copy the following sentences. Add the necessary quotation marks and other punctuation marks.

1. Lu asked How do I set the time an hour ahead on a digital watch

2. It is possible said the doctor that there is no safe level of radiation

3. That's my bike yelled Ian Leave it alone

4. Marty explained that he needed to borrow the bike

5. Nobody the teacher said should ever ignore a fire alarm

6. This might be a drill she said We will not take that chance, though

7. Doesn't Hal's bumper sticker say I brake for whales

8. I know Don I said that I have missed a lot of meetings

9. I told him that I had been working overtime, and he understood.

10. How surprised Ike was when Ms. Ramirez said Here's your bonus

K. Quotation Marks and Underlining Copy the following sentences. Add quotation marks around titles or underline titles where necessary.

1. The national anthem of Canada is O, Canada.

2. Do you have any copies of yesterday's Daily News left?

3. Lynn tried to sing Nobody the way that Nina Simone did.

4. Please read the story Overdrawn at the Memory Bank in the book The Persistence of Vision.

5. I got Renaldo a birthday card with the poem If on it.

6. At the Metropolitan Museum, we saw Georgia O'Keeffe's painting Cow's Skull, Red, White, and Blue.

7. Beth Henley's play Crimes of the Heart is set in Mississippi.

8. My favorite Richard Pryor movie was Silver Streak until I saw Car Wash.

9. Jamaica Kincaid's stories have appeared in The New Yorker magazine, and her articles have been in The Village Voice.

10. Patricia xeroxed the photos in Chapter 2, No Substitute for Inches, of the book Classic American Automobiles.

MIXED REVIEW

Punctuation

A. Using punctuation marks correctly Copy these sentences, adding the correct punctuation.

1. What a long month January is sighed Ms. Jernigan
2. The tribe who sacked Rome in AD 455 was the Vandals
3. Terrel who had just arrived asked Fatima how she was
4. Oh I cant complain she said It wouldn't do any good
5. Stephen B Oates wrote Let the Trumpet Sound
6. Arent the suns rays used to light the Olympic torch
7. Justine asked When does the 800 AM train leave Sir
8. Johnny Cash Joan Baez Bob Dylan and Willie Nelson buy their guitars from C F Martin and Company
9. The early 80s brought some of St Louiss worst heat
10. On February 3 1959 Buddy Holly by the way the Beatles got the idea for their name from his Crickets died in a plane crash near Clear Lake Iowa.

B. Using punctuation in proofreading Proofread the following paragraph. Rewrite it, adding correct punctuation marks.

When Mr Moody was suddenly called back to work he had to find a babysitter for his daughter Dana right away He would be able to pay $250 an hour His next door neighbor offered to watch Dana but the neighbor had a huge dog who did not like children Mr Moody said Youre very kind but I cant accept Without any luck he called friends checked the ads and posted notices Wow Was finding a sitter going to be harder than finding a job He was ready to give up when he found this address 6501 Telegraph Avenue Oakland California 94609 It led him to a group that helped parents find care for their children With its aid Mr Moody quickly found someone who met Danas and his requirements

USING MECHANICS IN WRITING
Punctuation

A. You have a summer job with the chamber of commerce in Hargrove, a town somewhere near you. Your job consists of answering letters from people interested in visiting Hargrove. A form letter is stored on a floppy disk, and you use a word processor and printer to print a version of the letter for each person who writes. One day, something goes wrong. The word processor prints a number sign (#) in place of all punctuation marks. Here is a paragraph from the body of one of the letters. Copy the paragraph, inserting all necessary punctuation.

You will find that Hargrove offers #something for everyone## The whole family will enjoy camping at one of our modern campgrounds# Musgrave Swamp# Tepid Springs# or Muddy River# History buffs will enjoy a visit to the Hargrove Historical Society Museum# Sports fans will enjoy watching the Hargrove Stars softball team# which plays every Fri# and Sat# at 2#00 P# M## all summer long# Yes# Hargrove offers something for everyone#

B. Even in the most glamorous industries, there are jobs that young people can get with little training. Often, these are called "gopher" jobs, because the young person is asked to "go for coffee" or "go for some tape." You are applying for the gopher job of your dreams. What would that job be? Would you like to be a gopher on the road crew for your favorite musician's next tour? Would you like to be a gopher on a film set? Write a conversation that might take place between you and your possible boss when you were applying for the job. How would you convince the person to hire you? Use at least two divided quotations in your dialogue. Check all punctuation.

Spelling

One skill that will never lose its value is good spelling. It is a skill that is valuable in all writing, ranging from a school report, to letters, to a job or credit application. In many jobs, too, some writing is required. At all times good spelling is noticed and admired.

At first, learning to be a good speller may seem difficult. The spelling of many English words does not seem to make sense. Many words are not spelled the way they sound.

However, becoming a good speller is not impossible. There are patterns of spelling that many English words follow. There are general rules that make spelling easier. In addition, there are methods for attacking spelling problems. Using such tools, you can avoid many problems and improve your spelling. This section will show you some solutions.

How To Improve Your Spelling

1. Recognize and conquer your specific spelling problems. Do you make certain spelling errors over and over? Look over writing that you have done in the past. Make a list of the words you have misspelled. Try to master those words.

2. Pronounce words carefully. Are you misspelling words because you aren't pronouncing them right? For example, if you are writing *temperture* for *temperature* or *athelete* for *athlete,* you are probably mispronouncing the word. Work on pronouncing words more precisely.

3. Try to memorize the letters in new words. Do you look closely at the spelling of new or difficult words? That habit can help you to remember how new words are spelled. Practice spelling a new word by writing it several times.

4. Always proofread your writing. Do you misspell words out of carelessness? You may catch such errors if you examine what you write. Read over your work slowly, word by word.

5. Check difficult words in a dictionary. When you're unsure of a spelling, do you reach for the dictionary? Get into the habit of letting the dictionary help you to spell well.

6. Learn the few important spelling rules explained in this section.

How To Spell a Particular Word Correctly

1. Look at the word and say it to yourself. Be sure to pronounce it correctly. Say it twice, looking at the syllables as you say them.

2. Look at the letters and say each one. Sound out the word from its spelling. Divide the word into syllables and pronounce each syllable.

3. Without looking at your book or list, write the word.

4. Check to see if you spelled the word correctly. If you spelled the word correctly, repeat this process.

5. If you made an error, note what it was. Then repeat steps 3 and 4 until you have spelled the word correctly three times.

Rules for Spelling

Adding Prefixes

When a prefix is added to a word, the spelling of the word remains the same.

pre- + mature = premature   im- + mobile = immobile
mis- + inform = misinform   dis- + appear = disappear
re- + apply = reapply   un- + noticed = unnoticed

Suffixes and Silent *e*

When a suffix beginning with a vowel is added to a word ending in a silent *e*, the *e* is usually dropped.

hide + -ing = hiding   celebrate + -ion = celebration
sense + -ible = sensible   cube + -ic = cubic
believe + -able = believable   date + -ing = dating

When a suffix beginning with a consonant is added to a word ending in a silent *e*, the *e* is usually retained.

grate + -ful = grateful   life + -less = lifeless
safe + -ty = safety   strange + -ness = strangeness
move + -ment = movement   bare + -ly = barely

The following words are exceptions. Learn them.

ninth   wholly   truly   argument

Exercise A   Find the misspelled words. Spell them correctly.

1. The argument was completly unecessary.
2. The game was not wholely boreing.
3. The driver's car was weaveing strangely.
4. Peaceful cows were grazeing nearby.

5. Pat was disatisfied with the amount in her saveings account.
6. He practiced breakeing on ice.
7. Rita distrusted them completly.
8. The unlikely story was received impolitly.
9. The couragous deed was scarcly noticed.
10. He reentered school on the nineth of September.

Exercise B Add the prefixes and suffixes as shown. Write the new word.

1. dis- + abled
2. un- + needed
3. prepare + -ation
4. waste + -ful
5. mis- + matched
6. mis- + state
7. recite + -al
8. forsake + -ing
9. remarkable + -ly
10. strange + -ness
11. like + -able
12. like + -ly
13. re- + enforce
14. re- + instate
15. re + action
16. leisure + -ly
17. dis- + service
18. il- + legible
19. wave + -ing
20. smile + -ing

Suffixes and Final *y*

When a suffix is added to a word ending in *y* preceded by a consonant, the *y* is usually changed to *i*.

marry + -age = marriage
body + -ly = bodily
sorry + -est = sorriest
ready + -ness = readiness

pity + -ful = pitiful
twenty + -eth = twentieth
lazy + -er = lazier
mystery + -ous = mysterious

Note this exception. When *ing* is added, the *y* does not change.

carry + -ing = carrying
worry + -ing = worrying

fly + -ing = flying
copy + -ing = copying

When a suffix is added to a word ending in *y* preceded by a vowel, the *y* usually does not change.

$$stay + -ed = stayed \qquad convey + -or = conveyor$$
$$relay + -s = relays \qquad enjoy + -able = enjoyable$$

Adding the Suffixes *-ness* and *-ly*

When the suffix *-ly* is added to a word ending in *l*, both *l*'s are kept. When *-ness* is added to a word ending in *n*, both *n*'s are kept.

$$loyal + -ly = loyally \qquad open + -ness = openness$$
$$even + -ness = evenness \qquad final + -ly = finally$$

Doubling the Final Consonant

In words of one syllable that end in one consonant preceded by one vowel, double the final consonant before adding *-ing, -est, -ed,* or *-er.*

$$hop + -ing = hopping \qquad big + -est = biggest$$
$$sip + -ed = sipped \qquad nap + -ing = napping$$
$$plan + -er = planner \qquad win + -er = winner$$

In words of one syllable that end in one consonant preceded by two vowels, the final consonant is not doubled.

$$dear + -est = dearest \qquad need + -ing = needing$$
$$groan + -ed = groaned \qquad cool + -er = cooler$$

Exercise   Add the suffixes as shown. Write the new word.

1. foggy + -er
2. icy + -est
3. pretty + -est
4. twenty + -eth
5. hazy + -er
6. happy + -ly
7. scurry + -ed
8. employ + -ment
9. worry + -er
10. dreary + -est
11. fuzzy + -ness
12. replay + -ed
13. delay + -ing
14. mystery + -ous
15. joy + -ous
16. lazy + -ly

Words with the "Seed" Sound

Only one English word ends in -*sede: supersede*. Three words end in -*ceed: exceed, proceed, succeed*. All other words ending with the sound of seed are spelled *cede*.

secede   concede   recede   precede

Exercise A Find the misspelled words. Spell them correctly.

1. Margaret baged the groceries carefuly.
2. The child was poping the balloons out of meaness.
3. Jo dresses casualy.
4. The wind is realy roaring.
5. My vision is not usualy blured.
6. Lester went runing to find the nearrest phone.
7. His keeness made him a winer.
8. Finaly the clerks finished taging the garments.
9. After starring in the movie, he was mobed by fans.
10. Unmercifuly the agent draged the information out of the frightened spy.

Exercise B Add the suffixes as shown. Write the new word.

1. knit + -ed
2. mean + -ing
3. dot + -ed
4. stop + -er
5. pour + -ed
6. brazen + -ness
7. civil + -ly
8. bleak + -er
9. mop + -ing
10. hear + -ing
11. rip + -ed
12. soap + -ed
13. lawful + -ly
14. flip + -ing
15. zip + -er
16. read + -er
17. frail + -ly
18. hop + -ed
19. nip + -ing
20. thin + -ness

Words with *ie* or *ei*

For words with *ie* or *ei* pronounced as long *e* ($\bar{e}$), there is a general spelling rule. The correct spelling is *ie* except after a *c*.

I before E

siege	grieve	piece	chief	fierce
niece	shield	believe	relieve	retrieve
reprieve	pierce	shriek	grief	pier

Except after C

ceiling	receipt	perceive	deceit
receive	deceive	conceive	conceit

These words are exceptions to the rule. Study them.

either	leisure	weird
neither	species	seize

Exercise Find the misspelled words in these sentences. Spell them correctly.

1. I was releived to find the reciept.
2. Neither of the cheifs wore a headdress.
3. Mr. Blair beleived that he was the heir; he was de-ceived.
4. The plasterer conceeded that the cieling had been poorly done.
5. The dog, a retreiver, was barking feircely.
6. He succeded in persuading Maryland not to seceed.
7. Seizing the intruder by the hair, Ellie caught the theif.
8. Either his conciet or his beliefs will bring him greif.
9. This memo superceeds the one you recieved yesterday.
10. Lu percieved that she needed more liesure time.

ADDITIONAL EXERCISES

Spelling

A. Prefixes Find the misspelled words. Spell them correctly.

1. She reemphasized her belief that war is imoral.
2. That answer is unecessary.
3. That misstake was completely unnecessary.
4. The taxi driver's ilegal turn made us unneasy.
5. The doctor disapproved of keeping us unninformed.

B. Suffixes Add the suffixes as shown. Write the new word.

1. day + -ly
2. wheeze + -ing
3. aggravate + -ion
4. carry + -ed
5. deny + -al
6. glory + -ous
7. complete + -ly
8. greedy + -ness

C. Spelling Find the misspelled words. Spell them correctly.

1. Evidently he was not mortaly wounded.
2. The likeness was realy startling.
3. Nick gazed hopefuly at the pie.
4. Speediness is certainlly not his style.
5. Plainess of speech is usualy admirable.
6. I beleive you are exceding the speed limit.
7. Al's neice siezed the deed and tore it into pieces.
8. The concieted general led his troops into danger.
9. The theif's pretense of grief deceived niether of them.
10. Rhoda found the receipt for the cieling fixture.

D. The Final Consonant Add the suffixes shown.

1. jog + -ed
2. cut + -ing
3. spin + -ing
4. look + -ed
5. thin + -est
6. croon + -ing
7. slam + -ed
8. run + -er
9. suit + -ed

MIXED REVIEW

Spelling

A. Spelling words correctly Pick out the words that are spelled incorrectly in these sentences. Write them correctly.

1. Neither of these species is likly to survive.
2. Sherman was smileing and nodding his head.
3. The fish were flopping on the peir.
4. The preceeding memo caused the confuseion.
5. He is worryed that his hairline is receding.
6. Take your neice to the nearest hospital immediately.
7. Bakeing pastries on hot days is foolish.
8. You can succeed without using deciet.
9. With surprising suddeness, the chief resigned.
10. Originaly, I had planned on arriving earlyer.
11. A driping faucet can sound awfully noisey.
12. The spys had completly changed their identities.
13. Who could realy believe such nonnsense?
14. Not all misstakes are erasable.
15. We were truely disarmed by their frankness.

B. Using spelling in proofreading Proofread the following paragraph. Rewrite it, spelling all the words correctly.

Is your puppy biteing or hiding from you? Conversely, is it too friendly with strangers? Such behaveior is not wholely the puppy's fault. Frequently it comes from immproper handling. Puppys do need firmness, but they have no requirment for meanness. Are you constantly slaping your puppy or yelling at it? Try stopping. Insufficient handling, too, hurts all babys, includeing pups. Is your puppie recieving enough petting and brushing? Don't deceive yourself. Your puppy's missbehavior may simpley be an imitation of yours.

USING MECHANICS IN WRITING
Spelling

A.   You took a group of children to see a play performed by a local children's theater. The children seemed to have a wonderful time. The next day, you read a review of the play in your local newspaper. The reviewer thought the play was terrible. You disagree so strongly that you sit down and write a letter to the editor of the paper. Before mailing the letter, you check it for errors. You find that your strong emotions caused you to make quite a few spelling errors. The following paragraph is part of the letter. Read the paragraph, and correct the spelling errors within it.

Your writer was misstaken about the way children reacted to the play. When I saw the play, it was easy to percieve the happyness that the children felt. They were giggleing and claping for most of the play. I will conseed that a few of them groanned at the puns, but for most it was a joious evening. I'm gratful that I went. I am hopping that your reveiwer will see the play again.

B.   Read the following list of words. Write a story using as many of them as you can. Be sure to spell each word correctly.

anonymous, answer, appearance, believe, certain, curiosity, description, familiar, guard, immediately, noticeable, recognize, sergeant, thorough, undoubtedly, weird

The Correct Form for Writing

The people who read what you write notice the content. Your ideas are important. You may forget, however, that readers also notice the form of your papers. Your writing is judged not only by its content, but also by its form.

Good form is precise, neat, and consistent. Such form will impress any reader and present your ideas in their best light. Some schools set their own rules for the correct form for written work. In this section you will learn about the kind of form that is accepted by many schools.

Guidelines for Clear Writing

Neatness

Neat, legible papers can be read easily. Neatness also suggests that the writer cares about what he or she is writing. You can give your papers a neat appearance in several ways.

Legible Writing

Usually, typewritten papers are more legible than handwritten ones. If you do not have a typewriter, make your handwritten papers clear and legible. Write in ink, preferably blue or black. To make your handwriting easy to read, be sure that letters are distinct. Some letters look similar, like *a*'s and *o*'s, unless they are formed carefully. Other letters that can be confused are *e*'s and *i*'s.

The First Draft and the Final Copy

You cannot expect the first draft of a paper to be in perfect form. You write a first draft from your pre-writing notes or an outline. Then you need to correct or revise the first draft. At that time, you may need to change words, sentences, or whole sections.

After revising, you can make your final copy. Carefully proofread this new copy. You may find words left out or other errors. To insert a word, write it above the line. Use a caret (∧) to show where the word belongs. To change a word, draw a line through it, and write the correct word above it. If any page has more than about three corrections, you should recopy the page.

Acceptable Form

Using the correct form for writing involves more than simply making a paper neat. For a paper to have correct form, its various parts should be positioned correctly. Headings, titles, margins, and spacing should be in the correct form.

The Heading

The heading identifies your paper. It is usually placed in the upper right-hand corner of the first page. Place your name on the first line. Write the name of your class on the second line. Write the date on the third line. If a paper has a title page, the heading belongs in the upper right-hand corner of that page.

Except for page one, each page should be numbered. Beginning with page two, place the page number in the upper right-hand corner. You may want to put your name under the page number in order to identify all pages.

Some teachers require a different form for labeling your paper. Follow any special instructions you are given.

The Title

The title of a paper should appear near the top of the first page. In general, place the title two lines down from the last line of the heading. Two lines below the title, begin the first line of your paper.

The correct form for a title includes proper capitalization. Capitalize only the first letter of the first word and of all important words. Do not underline your title or place it in quotation marks.

Sometimes a title page is used when a paper is more than three pages long. The title page becomes the first page.

Margins and Spacing

To make a paper attractive, use correct margins and spacing. Margins of one inch at the top, bottom, and left side of the paper are suitable.

The right-hand margin should be fairly even. However, do not break too many words with hyphens in order to keep the margin straight. A safe rule is to avoid hyphens in more than two lines in a row.

Double-spacing makes typed papers look neat. Indent five spaces to begin each paragraph. Skip two spaces after the punctuation mark at the end of a sentence.

Writing Numbers

The form for writing numbers should be consistent. Numbers under 100 are usually spelled out. Larger numbers are written in figures.

> When Mark was *sixteen,* he moved *three* times.
> Union dues are *fifty* dollars a year.
> Anyone with an income of *$25,000* or more can afford to buy that house.

A number at the beginning of a sentence is always spelled out.

> *Five hundred* people were evacuated.
> *Nine million* automobiles were produced in this country last year.
> *Fifty-five* miles per hour is the speed limit.

Figures rather than words are used for the following: dates, street and room numbers, telephone numbers, temperatures, page numbers, decimals, and percentages.

> On July 13, 1977, a blackout hit New York.
> The branch office is at 21 East Huron Street.
> Jennifer is in room 72 at the hospital.
> Our phone number was changed to 555-4288.
> In Florida, winter temperatures are about 65 degrees.
> The letters to the editor are on page 15.
> The track is 2.8 miles long.
> The divorce rate increased 3 percent last year.

For expressions of large sums of money or large quantities, commas are used to separate the figures. However, commas are not used in dates, serial numbers, page numbers, addresses, or telephone numbers.

> Correct: The bills printed last year amounted to $58,714,890.
> Correct: That record sold 1,000,850 copies.
> Incorrect: In 1,953 Jonas Salk developed a polio vaccine.
> Correct: In 1953 Jonas Salk developed a polio vaccine.

Exercise   Correct any errors in the writing of numbers.

1. Please read pages one through forty by March third.
2. About twenty percent of the students work more than 20 hours a week.
3. The temperature drops below 40 degrees at least one hundred and eighty-two days a year here.
4. In the year seventeen hundred and ninety, the United States had a population of 3929214.
5. The planet Saturn takes twenty-nine point forty-six years to revolve around the sun.
6. The Atkins family moved to 11,502 Kedzie Street.
7. On November fourteenth, 1889, Nellie Bly set out to circle the globe. Her trip took seventy-two days.
8. 200 kilograms equal 440 pounds.
9. The patient's fever is one hundred and three degrees.
10. $75 is the cost of the rear wheel kit.

Using Abbreviations

Shortened forms of words are called abbreviations. Generally, in formal writing, abbreviations are not acceptable.

However, abbreviations are correct for most titles before and after names. Abbreviations may also be used for government agencies and for time.

Titles before proper names:	Dr., Rev., Mr., Mrs., Ms., Lt., Pvt., Cong., Gen.
Titles after proper names:	Jr., R.N., M.D., Ph.D., R.Ph.
Dates and times:	B.C., A.D., A.M., P.M.
Government agencies:	FCC, CIA, IRS, ICC

As you can see, periods are not used in the abbreviations of government agencies.

A title is abbreviated only when it is used with a person's name, as in *Cong. Don Jones*. For example, an abbreviation like this would not be acceptable: *The Cong. was not present.*

For certain titles, abbreviations are not correct. *Honorable* and *Reverend* are not abbreviated when preceded by *the: the Reverend C. D. Wolfe.* The titles of President and Vice-President of the United States are not abbreviated.

In general, abbreviations are not acceptable for the following: names of countries and states, months and days of the week, addresses, and company names.

Incorrect: Nev. got its name from a Sp. word meaning "snow-covered."

Correct: Nevada got its name from a Spanish word meaning "snow-covered."

Incorrect: The Jacksons' concert is Sat., Feb. 17.

Correct: The Jacksons' concert is Saturday, February 17.

Incorrect: Katy works at the Gibson Co. on Wayland Ave.

Correct: Katy works at the Gibson Company on Wayland Avenue.

In most writing, abbreviations are not acceptable for names of school courses and such words as *chapter*, *page*, and *Christmas*. Abbreviations for measurements, like *in.*, *mi.*, *ft.*, and *min.*, are also unacceptable.

Exercise Correct the errors in abbreviation in these sentences.

1. The dr. said that he would be well soon.
2. The phys. ed. teacher told us to exercise for ten mins.
3. In the last qtr. of the game, we scored fourteen pts.
4. Give the baby one oz. of formula for each lb. of body weight.
5. Nature Foods Co. has an advertisement on p. 4.
6. The Rev. E. B. Rice spoke about conditions in SE Asia.
7. The Hon. Neil Griffin is a Fed. judge.
8. We invited some sr. citizens for Xmas dinner.
9. Does the Pres. appoint the dir. of the F.B.I.?
10. Porter discussed the issues with the two sen. from Ill.

ADDITIONAL EXERCISES

The Correct Form for Writing

A. Writing Numbers   Correct any errors in the writing of numbers. If a sentence contains no error, write *Correct*.

1. The lifeguard test includes swimming 200 yards in less than three point five minutes.
2. $100,000 bills have President Wilson's portrait on them.
3. At the age of 10, he weighed 120 pounds.
4. Junior Achievement had 5000000 members in nineteen hundred and eighty-one.
5. California has eight state forests and one hundred and eighty state parks and beaches.
6. In Detroit ninety-eight percent of the households have television.
7. The temperature in Room Five was over eighty degrees on May 7.
8. The movie ads are on page 45.
9. In 1,982 the President's salary was $200,000, plus $50,000 for expenses and up to $100,000 for travel.
10. Two hundred friends sent Orlando cards when he became sixty-five.

B. Abbreviations   Copy these sentences, correcting errors in abbreviation. If a sentence contains no errors, write *Correct*.

1. Vice-Pres. Johnson became Pres. aboard *Air Force One*.
2. Ridge Rd. has been closed since last Aug. for repairs.
3. Judy Johnson, M.D., wrote the 1st chap. in the textbook.
4. Immediately after graduating from Howard Univ., Barbara got a job with HUD.
5. Rev. Tiggs helped Pfc. Fort get leave.

MIXED REVIEW

The Correct Form for Writing

Using the correct form for writing   The following composition contains errors in writing form and in the use of abbreviations and numbers. Copy the composition, correcting any errors.

STAR SHIP

1 of the most remarkable ships in U.S. history is the *U.S.F. Constellation*. This wooden sailing ship, now docked in Baltimore, Md., has given longer service in war and peace to the U.S.A. than any other warship. It has taken part in some of the most dramatic events in the hist. of the country.

The *Constellation* was first launched on Sept. 7, 1797. She was the 1st U. S. Naval ship to put to sea. Pres. George Washington had authorized a navy to defend American merchant ships, which were sailing the 7 seas unprotected. Pirates often attacked them & held the crews for ransom. By seventeen hundred and ninety-four, over one hundred captured Ams. had been jailed by the Barbary States in N. Africa. The French were also attacking Am. ships in the W. Indies.

The *Constellation's* first battle was with one of the best ships in the Fr. fleet. The *Constellation* defeated the ship in 1 hour. It was the new Navy's 1st big victory. The ship won the 2nd big victory, too, but this time it took her 5 hrs. to defeat a warship with 52 guns to her 38 guns. Captain Thomas Truxton commanded the *Constellation*. The capt.'s naval procedures are still used by the U. S.

During the War of 1812, the ship repelled an invasion force of seven hundred men. Then she resumed her protection of merchant ships.

In the 1840's, the *Constellation* sailed around the

world. On April Thirteenth, 1842, she became the first Am. ship to enter the inland waters of China, where her commander peacefully gained trading privileges for the United States. 15 months later, the ship protected the Sandwich Islands—later the Hawaiian Is.—from British annexation. (Over 100 years later, the *Constellation* helped welcome Hawaii as our fiftieth state.) She finished circling the globe on April 30, 1,844, having logged 58000 miles.

In 1859, the *Constellation* was the flagship of the African Squadron, formed to help stop the slave trade. She captured 3 slave ships. 1,000 slaves were freed. During the Civil War, she guarded Union ships.

Then she became a training ship at the Naval Academy. She left the acad. in 1880 to carry food to famine-stricken Ireland.

Although the *Constellation* was shown off sometimes, she had become a forgotten relic by 1,940. Then President Roosevelt, preparing the country for W. W. II, remembered the 1st U. S. warship. The Pres. made the 143-yr.-old wooden sailing ship the flagship of the Atlantic Fleet.

Now she is operated by the *U.S.F. Constellation* Foundation. The found. welcomes tourists aboard, where they can feel 100 % safe. Despite the weight of all the history she carries, the *Constellation* still rides high in the water of Balt. Harbor.

USING MECHANICS IN WRITING
The Correct form for Writing

Following is the beginning of a report about the interesting origins of some English words and phrases. The passage needs editing to put it in the correct form. Rewrite the passage, making all the necessary corrections.

by Ned Carle
Why Do We Say . . . ?
The Interesting Origins of Words and Phrases

there's a story behind most of the words we use every day. Some of our english words are very old; while others are so new that they aren't in last years dictionaries. Many interesting stories of word origins are contained in "Word Origins and their Romantic stories" by Wilfred Funk. This book was published by Crown Pubs. in N.Y., in 1,973.

CUMULATIVE REVIEW
Capitalization, Punctuation, and Spelling

A. Using capitalization, punctuation, and spelling correctly Copy the following sentences, correcting the errors in capitalization, punctuation, and spelling.

1. the situation comedy the jeffersons was a spin off of the show all in the family
2. havent you read trinity the novel about ireland asked mr cudahy
3. niether of these houses said ms levy the realtor has the openess of the house on sumac circle
4. the children who were realy frightened shreiked help us please
5. the brooklyn bridge in new york which spans the east river was openned on may 24 1883
6. elliots school is small there are only thirty six students
7. roadrunners birds found in the southwest usa will eat any of these things snakes insects mice bats scorpions or tarantulas
8. aunt mary took her neices and nephews to walt disney world in orlando florida
9. mrs. albertson tryed to find the reciept but she didn't succede
10. el greco a fameous 16th century greek artist lived and worked in toledo spain

B. Using proofreading skills Proofread the following paragraph. Copy it, correcting the errors in capitalization, punctuation, and spelling.

what is that prehistoric looking animal i cryed as we swerved around it on the texas highway. well i discovered that it was an armadillo. this strange animal has two large sheilds on it's body to protect its back and sides. these two plates of armor are conected by nine moveable bands. the armadillos head and tail are also armored but the stomach is not. although the armadillo looks feirce it realy isnt. they are not great hunters they usualy eat insects. in fact the armadillo belongs to the same family as the anteater. this homely animal can be found in mexico and all the states bordering the gulf of mexico. it has even migrated as far north as oklahoma arkansas missouri and georgia. this funny creature has also become very useful to medical researchers. national geographic magazine has reportted that the armadillo is helping scientists find a cure for leprosy. what a unique animal.

A

D

Dash, 687–688
Dates
  capitalization of, 660
  commas in, 681
Declarative sentences
  definition of, 425–426
  periods in, 426, 671
Definite articles, 519
Definition
  as context clue to word
    meaning, 2
  in dictionary, 30–32
  in compositions stating a
    definition, 239–247
  in paragraphs stating a
    definition, 165–173
Demonstrations, 390
Demonstrative pronouns, 476
Descriptions, 133–143
Descriptive compositions, 209–217
  ending, 214–215
  first draft of, 212–213
  planning, 210–211
  revising, 216–217
  using sensory details, 210–211
  spatial order in, 210–211
Descriptive paragraphs, 88–89,
  133–143
  definition of, 88–89
  first draft of, 140–141
  gathering sensory details for,
    134–135
  mood in, 138–139
  revising, 142–143
  using spatial order, 136–137
  using transitional words,
    140–141
desert/dessert, 638
Details
  descriptive, in paragraphs,
    86–87, 102–103

sensory, 18–21, 86–87,
  210–211
  in sentences, 52–53
Dewey Decimal System, 302–303
Diagraming
  adjectives, 519–520, 611–614
  adverbs, 527–528, 609–611
  commands, 411–412
  compound objects, 424
  compound predicate adjectives, 520
  compound predicate words, 424
  compound sentences, 598–599
  compound subjects, 423
  compound verbs, 423–424
  direct objects, 418
  gerunds, 568–569
  imperative sentences, 411–412
  indirect objects, 418–419
  infinitives, 577
  noun clauses, 615–616
  participles, 572
  predicate adjectives, 420, 421
  predicate nouns, 421
  predicate pronouns, 421
  prepositional phrases, 549–550
  sentences, 408–409
  subjects, 408–409
  subjects in unusual word order,
    411–412, 413–415
  verbs, 408–409
  you understood, 414
Dialects, 46–47
Dialogue, 186–187, 202–203,
  694–695
Dialogue tags, 202–203
Dictionary, 27–35
  abbreviations and symbols in,
    30–32
  abridged, 28
  accent marks in, 30
  alphabetical order in, 28
  antonyms in, 31

G

General-to-specific order, 104–105
Geographical names, capitalization of, 657
Gerunds, 567–570
good/well, 535
Graphic aids, 324–325
Greek word roots, 14–15
Group discussions, 396–397
Guide cards, 305–306
Guidelines for writing compositions, 190–191
Guide words
  in dictionary, 28–29
  in encyclopedia, 308–309

H

had of/off of, 646
have as helping verb, 502
Heading in letters, 336
Heading on papers, 717–718
hear/here, 638
Hearing words, 20
Helping verbs, 409–411, 496–497, 502
himself/themselves, 646
Hyphen, 688–689

I

I
  capitalization of, 656
  with first-person point of view, 126–127, 198–199, 250–251
ie/ei, 711–712
Imaginary narrative compositions (stories), 194–195
Imaginary subjects for paragraphs, 122–123
Imperative sentences
  definition of, 425–426
  period with, 426, 671

you as understood subject in, 414–415
Importance of reasons as method of organization, 104–105, 158–159, 232–233
in/into, 646
Incidents in paragraphs, 86–87
Indefinite article, 519
Indefinite pronouns, 477–478, 588–589
Indenting first line of paragraphs in letters, 336–337
Indirect objects, 418–419, 452–453
Indirect question, 671
Inference, as context clue, 4–5
Infinitive, 574–579
  phrase, 575–578
  split, 576
Informal English, 40–41, 636–637
Initials,
  capitalization of, 655
  periods with, 672
Inside address of business letters, 342–343
Interjections, 558–560
Internal conflict, 196–197
Interrogative pronouns, 477
Interrogative sentences
  definition of, 425–426
  period with, 671
  question mark with, 426
Interview, job, 373–377
Intransitive verbs, 416–417, 494–495
Introductions
  in compositions, 176–177, 196–197, 212–213, 224–225, 234–235, 242–243
  in speeches, 390–391
  in research papers, 261–263
Invitations. *See* Letters.

Irregular verbs, 500–507
  using a dictionary to find
    principal parts, 501
  and helping verbs, 501–502
  rules for, 502–507
Italics, underlining for, 695–696
its/it's, 638

J

Jargon, 44–45
Job applications, filling out,
  378–380
Job interviews, 373–377
Job opportunities, discovering,
  368–369
Journal keeping, 94–95
Judgment, 284–285

K

Kind/sort, 534–535, 647

L

Languages
  capitalization of, 660
  to express mood, 138–139
  loaded, 286–287
  for special fields, 24–25
Latin roots, 12–13
lay/lie, 642
lead, 638
learn/teach, 641–642
leave/let, 641–642
Legend. *See* Graphic Aids.
lend/borrow, 645
less/fewer, 645
let/leave, 641–642
Letters, 335–357
  business, 342–344
  capitalization in, 662–663
  commas in, 682

of complaint, 350–351
to the editor, 352–354
to an elected official, 355–357
of employment, 369–372
personal, 336–338
preparing for the mail,
  339–341
of request, 348–349
to schools, 381–382
social notes, 336–338
ZIP code in, 339–341
Library skills, developing,
  301–313
  author card, 305–306
  call numbers, 303
  card catalog, 305–307
  classification and arrangement of
    books in, 302–303
  cross-reference card, 305–306
  Dewey Decimal System,
    302–303
  encyclopedias, 308–309
  guide cards, 305–306
  reference works, 311–313
  subject card, 305–306
  title card, 305–306
lie/lay, 642
like, 647
Linking verbs, 420–423, 493–494
Listening skills, 388–389
Loaded language, 286–287
Logical order in composition. *See*
  Chronological order, General-to-
    specific order, Order of im-
    portance, Spatial order, *and*
    Step-by-step order.
Logical order in paragraphs. *See*
  Chronological order, General-to-
    specific order, Order of im-
    portance, Spatial order, *and*
    Step-by-step order.
lose/loose, 638

M

Magazines as sources, 312
Main clause, 606–607
Main idea
  in compositions, 176. *See also*
    Body.
  listening for, 388–389
  in paragraphs, 80–83
Main verbs, 409–411, 496–497
Matching tests, 328–329
may/can, 642
Mixed Review. *See* end of each
  lesson.
Modifiers. *See* Adjectives, Adverbs,
  and Prepositional phrases.
Mood, in descriptive paragraphs,
  138–139
More/most
  with adjectives, 521–524
  with adverbs, 528–531
Most familiar to least familiar
  method of organization, 104–105
Multiple-choice tests, 328–329

N

Narrative compositions, 193–207
  choosing point of view in,
    198–199
  chronological order in, 196–197
  conflict in, 194–195
  dialogue in, 202–203
  first draft of, 200–201
  planning a story, 194–195
  plotting a story, 196–197
  point of view in, 198–199
  revising, 206–207
  transitions in, 204–205
Narrative paragraphs, 88–89,
  121–131
  choosing point of view in,
    126–127

  chronological order in, 124–125
  definition of, 88–89
  developing, 122–123
  first draft of, 128–129
  revising, 130–131
  transitions, 128–129
Nationalities, capitalization of, 660
Negatives
  double, 535–537
  n't not part of verb, 410–411
Nonfiction books, 302–304
Nonrestrictive clause, 682–683
Nonstandard English, 37–39,
  636–637
Note cards, 253–255
Notes, social. *See* Letters.
Notetaking, 253–255
Nouns, 447–463
  in apposition, 678
  capitalization of, 448–449
  clauses, 614–616
  common, 448–449
  as compound objects, 424
  as compound subjects, 423
  definition of, 448
  as direct objects, 451–452
  as indirect objects, 452–453
  as objects of prepositions, 469,
    550
  plural forms of, 454–456
  possessive forms of, 455–456
  predicate, 420, 453–454
  proper, 448–449
  in sentence patterns, 427–428
  singular forms of, 454–456
  as subjects, 450–451
no words, *not* words. *See*
  Negatives.
Number of the verb, 585
Numbers in writing, 719–720
N LV Adj. sentence pattern, 428
N LV N sentence pattern, 428

739

order of importance in,
104–105, 158–159
organizing, 104–105, 114–115.
See also Order of writing.
point of view in, 126–127
presentation of ideas in,
110–111, 117
proofreading, 117–118
purpose of, 98–99, 114
revising, 92–93, 110–111,
116–117, 130–131, 142–143,
152–153, 162–163, 172–173
sensory details in, 18–21, 86–87
spatial order in, 104–105,
136–137
step-by-step order in, 148–149
style of, 110–111, 117
third-person point of view in, 126
topic for, narrowing, 96–97
topic sentence in, 84–85,
100–101
transitions in, 128–129,
140–141, 150–151, 160–161
unity in, 82–83
Parallel sentences, 60–61
Participial phrase, 571–572
Participle, 570–574
Parts of speech, 30, 558–565
definition of, 559
as shown in dictionary entries,
30
using words as different,
560–561
See also particular parts of
speech.
Passive verbs, 507–509
Past participle of verbs, 500–501
Past tense of verbs, 498
Past perfect tense, 499
percent/percentage, 647
Perfect tense of verbs, 499
Period, 671–672

Personal letters. *See* Letters,
personal.
Personal observation to obtain
information, 86–87
Personal point of view. *See* First-
person point of view.
Personal pronouns, 465–466
Phrases, transitional
in compositions, 180–181,
186–187, 204–205, 224–225
in paragraphs, 128–129,
140–141, 150–151, 160–161
Plagiarism, 254
Plot, 194–195
Plural forms
of nouns, 454–456, 584–594
of pronouns, 588, 589
as shown in dictionary, 30
of verbs, 584–594
Poetry line, capitalization of, 662
Point of view
first-person, 126–127, 198–199
omniscient, 198–199
third-person, 126–127, 198–199
third-person limited, 126–127,
198–199
third-person omniscient,
126–127, 198–199
Possessive nouns, 457–458, 690
Possessive pronouns, 469–470, 690
Predicate
complete, 407–408
compound, 596, 600–602
definition of, 406, 407
simple, 407–408
Predicate adjective, 420, 518–519
and adverb, 532–534
compound, 520
definition of, 519
diagraming, 520
Predicate noun, 420
compound, 524

Reading, 94–95, 322–323
Reading comprehension tests, 332–333
Real life narrative compositions, 194–195
Real life subjects for paragraphs, 122–123
Reference works, 94–95, 250–252
Regional words, 46–47
Regular verbs, 500. *See also* Verbs.
Relative clause, 611–614
Relative pronouns, 611–614
Religions, capitalization of, 660
Research, 250–252. *See also* Study and research skills *and* Research paper.
Research paper, 249–275
  bibliography in, 269–271
  bibliography card, 253–254
  body of, 264–266
  conclusion of, 264–266
  first-person point of view, 250–251
  footnotes, 269–271
  introduction, 261–263
  narrowing a topic, 250–251
  organizing, 256–257
  outline for, 253–254, 258–260
  revising, 267–268
  taking notes for, 253–255
  topic sentence in, 256–257
Restatement as clue to word meaning, 2
Restrictive clause, 682–683
Résumés, 365–367
Revision
  of compositions, 184–187, 206–207, 216–217, 226–227, 236–237, 246–247, 236–237
  definition of, 92–93
  of descriptive writing, 142–143, 216–217

of explanatory writing, 152–153, 162–163, 172–173, 216–217, 226–227, 236–237, 246–247
of narrative writing, 130–131, 206–207
of paragraphs, 92–93, 110–111, 130–131, 142–143, 152–153, 162–163, 172–173
as part of a process, 92–93, 116–118
of research papers, 267–268
rise/raise, 643
root, definition of, 12
Roots, Latin, 12–13
Run-on sentence, 442–443

S

s'/'s, 445–456
Salutation in letters, 336, 343
SAT test, 330–331
says/said, 647
Scanning, 322–323
Semicolon, 598, 684–685
Senses, as basis for gathering detail, 18–21
Sentence completion tests, 298–299
Sentence correction tests, 332–333
Sensory details, 18–21, 86–87, 210–211
Sentence fragments, 404, 440–442, 618–619
Sentence patterns
  N LV Adj., 428
  N LV N, 428
  N V, 427
  N V N, 427
  N V N N, 428
Sentences, 49–77, 403–446
  beginning with *here*, 413
  beginning with *there*, 411–412, 590

compound, 587–588
definition of, 406, 407
diagraming, 408–409
infinitive phrase as, 575–576
nouns as, 450–451
pronouns as, 467–468
simple, 407–408
understood (*you*), 414–415
in unusual positions, 411–415
of the verb, 407–409
Subordinate clause, 606–608,
616–617
Suffixes, 6–7, 10–11, 708–710
Superlatives
adjectives as, 522–524
adverbs as, 529–531
Syllables
as shown in dictionary, 30
dividing words into, 688–689
Synonyms, 16–17, 31, 294–295

T

take/bring, 640–641
Talks. *See* Speech.
Taste words, 21
teach/learn, 641–642
Tenses, verbs, 497–500
Test taking, 326–333
Thank-you notes. *See* Letters.
that, to combine sentences, 74–75,
648
their/there/they're, 639
theme, of compositions, 194–195
them/those, 483–484, 534
themselves/himself, 646
there/here, extra in sentence, 534
Third-person limited point of view,
126–127, 198–199
Third-person omniscient point of
view, 126–127, 198–199
Third-person point of view

in compositions, 198–199
in paragraphs, 126–127
those/them, 483–484, 534
Time sequence. *See* Chronological
order.
Title card, 305–306
Titles
abbreviations of, 720–721
capitalization of, 655, 663
of compositions, 188–189, 718
of persons, 655
of written works
quotation marks with,
695–696
underlining for italics,
695–696
to/too/two, 639
Topic, choosing, 94–95, 178–179
Topic, narrowing the
in compositions, 178–179
in paragraphs, 96–97
in research paper, 250–251
Topic sentence
in compositions, 180–181
in paragraphs, 84–85, 100–101
in research papers, 256–257
Touch words, 21
Transitions
showing chronological order,
128–129, 204–205
in compositions, 180–181,
186–187, 204–205, 224–225
showing order of importance,
104–105, 158–161, 232–233
in paragraphs, 128–129,
140–141, 150–151, 160–161
showing spatial order, 104–105,
136–137, 140–141, 210–211
showing step-by-step order,
150–151, 224–225
Transitive verbs, 416–417,
494–495